Century 21

Accounting

10e

Multicolumn Journal

Working Papers

Chapters 1-17

Claudia Bienias Gilbertson, CPA
Retired
North Hennepin Community College
Brooklyn Park, Minnesota

Mark W. Lehman, CPA, CFE
Associate Professor Emeritus
Richard C. Adkerson School of Accountancy
Mississippi State University
Starkville, Mississippi

Debra Harmon Gentene, NBCT
Business Teacher
Mason High School
Mason, Ohio

SOUTH-WESTERN
CENGAGE Learning

Australia • Brazil • Japan • Korea • Mexico • Singapore • Spain • United Kingdom • United States

SOUTH-WESTERN
CENGAGE Learning

ISBN-13: 978-1-111-57880-0
ISBN-10: 1-111-57880-X

South-Western
5191 Natorp Boulevard
Mason, OH 45040
USA

Cengage Learning is a leading provider of customized learning solutions with office locations around the globe, including Singapore, the United Kingdom, Australia, Mexico, Brazil, and Japan. Locate your local office at: **international.cengage.com/region**.

Cengage Learning products are represented in Canada by Nelson Education, Ltd.

For your course and learning solutions, visit **www.cengage.com/school**.

Visit our company website at **www.cengage.com**.

Printed in the United States of America
1 2 3 4 5 6 7 16 15 14 13 12

TO THE STUDENT

These *Working Papers* are to be used in the study of Chapters 1–17 of CENTURY 21 ACCOUNTING, 10E. Forms are provided for:

1. Study Guides
2. Work Together Exercises
3. On Your Own Exercises
4. Application Problems
5. Mastery Problems
6. Challenge Problems
7. Source Documents Problems
8. Reinforcement Activities 1 and 2

Printed on each page is the number of the problem in the textbook for which the form is to be used. Also shown is a specific instruction number for which the form is to be used.

You may not be required to use every form that is provided. Your teacher will tell you whether to retain or dispose of the unused pages.

The pages are perforated so they may be removed as the work required in each assignment is completed. The pages will be more easily detached if you crease the sheet along the line of perforations and then remove the sheet by pulling sideways rather than upward.

Study Guide 1

Name	Perfect Score	Your Score
Identifying Accounting Terms	27 Pts.	
Identifying Account Concepts and Practices	18 Pts.	
Analyzing How Transactions Change an Accounting Equation	10 Pts.	
Analyzing How Transactions Change Owner's Equity in an Accounting Equation	12 Pts.	
Total	65 Pts.	

Part One—Identifying Accounting Terms

Directions: Select the one term in Column I that best fits each definition in Column II. Print the letter identifying your choice in the Answers column.

Column I	*Column II*	*Answers*
A. account	1. The process of planning, recording, analyzing, and interpreting financial information. (p. 6)	1. ________
B. account balance	2. A planned process designed to compile financial data and summarize the results in accounting records and reports. (p. 6)	2. ________
C. account title	3. Financial reports that summarize the financial condition and operations of a business. (p. 6)	3. ________
D. accounting	4. A formal report that shows what an individual owns, what an individual owes, and the difference between the two. (p. 7)	4. ________
E. accounting equation	5. Anything of value that is owned. (p. 7)	5. ________
F. accounting system	6. An amount owed. (p. 7)	6. ________
G. asset	7. The difference between personal assets and personal liabilities. (p. 7)	7. ________
H. business ethics	8. The difference between assets and liabilities. (p. 7)	8. ________
I. business plan	9. The principles of right and wrong that guide an individual in making decisions. (p. 8)	9. ________
J. capital account	10. The use of ethics in making business decisions. (p. 8)	10. ________
K. creditor	11. A business that performs an activity for a fee. (p. 10)	11. ________
L. equities	12. A business owned by one person. (p. 10)	12. ________
M. equity	13. A formal written document that describes the nature of a business and how it will operate. (p. 10)	13. ________
N. ethics	14. Generally Accepted Accounting Principles. The standards and rules that accountants follow while recording and reporting financial activities. (p. 11)	14. ________
O. expense	15. Financial rights to the assets of a business. (p. 13)	15. ________
P. financial statements	16. The amount remaining after the value of all liabilities is subtracted from the value of all assets. (p. 13)	16. ________
Q. GAAP	17. The equation showing the relationship among assets, liabilities, and owner's equity. (p. 13)	17. ________
R. liability	18. Any business activity that changes assets, liabilities, or owner's equity. (p. 14)	18. ________
S. net worth statement	19. A record that summarizes all the transactions pertaining to a single item in the accounting equation. (p. 14)	19. ________
T. owner's equity	20. The name given to an account. (p. 14)	20. ________
U. personal net worth	21. The difference between the increases and decreases in an account. (p. 14)	21. ________

Column I	Column II	Answers
V. proprietorship	22. An account used to summarize the owner's equity in a business. (p. 14)	22. ________
W. revenue	23. A person or business to whom a liability is owed. (p. 16)	23. ________
X. sale on account	24. An increase in equity resulting from the sale of goods or services. (p. 18)	24. ________
Y. service business	25. A sale for which payment will be received at a later date. (p. 18)	25. ________
Z. transaction	26. The cost of goods or services used to operate a business. (p. 19)	26. ________
AA. withdrawals	27. Assets taken from the business for the owner's personal use (p. 20)	27. ________

Part Two—Identifying Account Concepts and Practices

Directions: Place a *T* for True or an *F* for False in the Answers column to show whether each of the following statements is true or false.

	Answers
1. Accounting is the language of business. (p. 6)	1. ______
2. A creditor would favor a positive net worth. (p. 7)	2. ______
3. The principles of right and wrong that guide an individual in making personal decisions is called business ethics. (p. 8)	3. ______
4. Keeping personal and business records separate is an application of the business entity concept. (p. 11)	4. ______
5. Generally Accepted Accounting Principles, GAAP, allows for flexibility in reporting. (p. 11)	5. ______
6. Recording business costs in terms of hours required to complete projects is an application of the unit of measurement concept. (p. 11)	6. ______
7. Assets such as cash and supplies have value because they can be used to acquire other assets or be used to operate a business. (p. 13)	7. ______
8. The relationship among assets, liabilities, and owner's equity can be written as an equation. (p. 13)	8. ______
9. The accounting equation does not have to be in balance to be correct. (p. 13)	9. ______
10. When a company pays insurance premiums in advance to an insurer, it records the payment as a liability because the insurer owes future coverage. (p. 15)	10. ______
11. When items are bought and paid for later, this is referred to as buying on account. (p. 16)	11. ______
12. When cash is paid on account, a liability is increased. (p. 16)	12. ______
13. When cash is received from a sale, the total amount of both assets and owner's equity is increased. (p. 18)	13. ______
14. The accounting concept Realization of Revenue is applied when revenue is recorded at the time goods or services are sold. (p. 18)	14. ______
15. When cash is paid for expenses, the business has more equity. (p. 19)	15. ______
16. If two amounts are recorded on the same side of the accounting equation, the equation will no longer be in balance. (p. 20)	16. ______
17. When a company receives cash from a customer for a prior sale, the transaction increases the cash account balance and increases the accounts receivable balance. (p. 20)	17. ______
18. A withdrawal decreases owner's equity. (p. 20)	18. ______

Name ______________________ Date ____________ Class ____________

Part Three—Analyzing How Transactions Change an Accounting Equation

Directions: For each of the following transactions, select the two accounts in the accounting equation that are changed. Decide if each account is increased or decreased. Place a "+" in the column if the account is increased. Place a "–" in the column if the account is decreased.

Transactions

1–2. Received cash from owner Nicole McGraw as an investment. (p. 14)

3–4. Paid cash for supplies. (p. 15)

5–6. Paid cash for insurance. (p. 15)

7–8. Bought supplies on account from Hyde Park Office Supplies. (p. 16)

9–10. Paid cash on account to Hyde Park Office Supplies. (p. 16)

Trans. No.	Assets			= Liabilities	+ Owner's Equity
	Cash	+ Supplies	+ Prepaid Insurance	= Accts. Pay.— Hyde Park Office supplies	+ Nicole McGraw, Capital
1–2					
3–4					
5–6					
7–8					
9–10					

Part Four—Analyzing How Transactions Change Owner's Equity in an Accounting Equation

Directions: For each of the following transactions, select the two accounts in the accounting equation that are changed. Decide if each account is increased or decreased. Place a "+" in the column if the account is increased. Place a "–" in the column if the account is decreased.

Transactions

1–2. Received cash from sales. (p. 18)

3–4. Sold services on account to New U Fitness. (p. 18)

5–6. Paid cash for rent. (p. 19)

7–8. Paid cash for telephone bill. (p. 19)

9–10. Received cash on account from New U Fitness. (p. 20)

11–12. Paid cash to owner A. Conrad for personal use. (p. 20)

Trans. No.	Assets				= Liabilities	+ Owner's Equity
	Cash +	Accts. Rec.— New U Fitness +	Supplies +	Prepaid Insurance =	Accts. Pay.— Hardcore Fitness Supplies +	A. Conrad, Capital
1–2						
3–4						
5–6						
7–8						
9–10						
11–12						

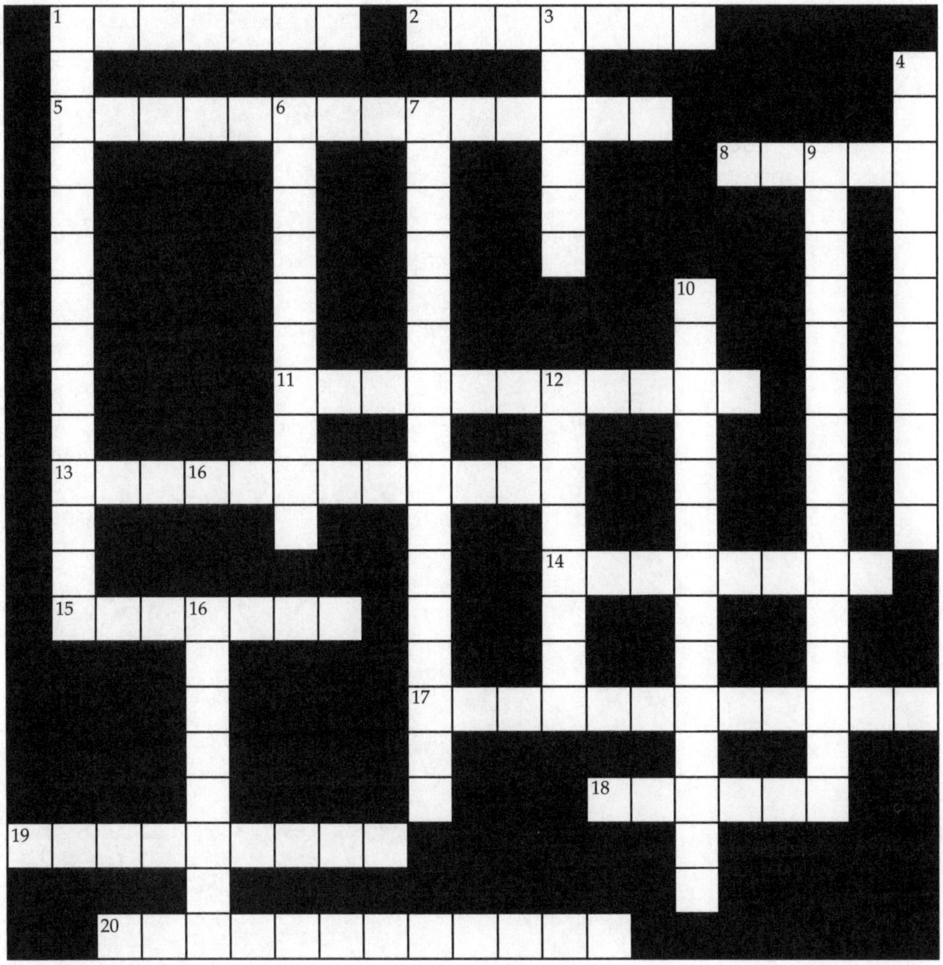

Across

1. A record that summarizes all the transactions pertaining to a single item in the accounting equation.
2. An increase in equity resulting from the sale of goods or services.
5. An account used to summarize the owner's equity in a business.
8. Anything of value that is owned.
11. Any business activity that changes assets, liabilities, or owner's equity.
13. The name given to an account.
14. An amount paid for the use of money for a period of time.
15. The cost of goods or services used to operate a business.
17. Someone who owns, operates, and takes the risk of a business venture.
18. The principles of right and wrong that guide an individual in making decisions.
19. An amount owed.
20. A formal written document that describes the nature of a business and how it will operate.

Down

1. The difference between the increases and decreases in an account.
3. The difference between assets and liabilities.
4. Assets taken from the business for the owner's personal use.
6. The process of planning, recording, analyzing, and interpreting financial information.
7. Interest paid on an original amount deposited in a bank plus any interest that has been paid.
9. A business that performs an activity for a fee.
10. A business owned by one person.
12. A person or business to whom a liability is owed.
16. Financial rights to the assets of a business.

Name ______________________ Date ____________ Class ____________

1-1 WORK TOGETHER, p. 9

Completing a net worth statement

1-1 ON YOUR OWN, p. 9

Completing a net worth statement

Name ______________________ Date ____________ Class ____________

1-2 WORK TOGETHER, p. 17

Determining how transactions change an accounting equation

Trans. No.	Assets	= Liabilities	+ Owner's Equity
1			
2			
3			
4			

1-2 ON YOUR OWN, p. 17

Determining how transactions change an accounting equation

Trans. No.	Assets =	Liabilities +	Owner's Equity
1			
2			
3			
4			
5			

Name ______________________ Date ____________ Class ____________

1-3 WORK TOGETHER, p. 22

Determining how transactions change an accounting equation

Trans. No.	Assets				= Liabilities	+ Owner's Equity
	Cash +	Accts. Rec.— Harmon Co. +	Supplies +	Prepaid Insurance =	Accts. Pay.— Corona Supplies +	Nathaniel Conrad, Capital
1						
2						
3						
4						
5						

1-3 ON YOUR OWN, p. 22

Determining how transactions change an accounting equation

Trans. No.	Assets				= Liabilities	+ Owner's Equity
	Cash	+ Accts. Rec.— Bethany Center	+ Supplies	+ Prepaid Insurance	= Accts. Pay.— McGrew Supplies	+ Bryan Arnett, Capital
1						
2						
3						
4						
5						

Name ______________________ Date __________ Class __________

1-1 APPLICATION PROBLEM (LO2), p. 25

Preparing a net worth statement

Lauren Juliana	
Net Worth Statement	
Assets	
Cash	
Jewelry	
Total Assets	
Liabilities	
Knapp College	
Ashley's Boutique	
Buzz Electronics	
Total Liabilities	
Owner's Equity (Net Worth)	
Assets − Liabilities = Net Worth	

1-2 APPLICATION PROBLEM (LO4), p. 25

Completing the accounting equation

Assets =	Liabilities +	Owner's Equity
15,650	11,475	
11,000		6,000
	2,000	3,300
12,000		7,000
125,000	69,000	
	1,875	15,750
35,000	13,000	
6,000		2,500
	139,000	4,650
17,000	2,800	
42,000		17,000
8,750	2,980	
	47,000	24,000
67,000		32,000
73,000	41,000	
	93,000	7,700
49,325		10,020
	21,250	2,800

Name ______________________ Date ____________ Class ____________

1-3 APPLICATION PROBLEM (LO4, 5), p. 26

Determining how transactions change an accounting equation

Trans. No.	Assets			=	Liabilities	+	Owner's Equity
	Cash +	Supplies +	Prepaid Insurance	=	Accts. Pay.—Knapp Co. +	Accts. Pay.—Hickman Mowing	+ Bethany Hartman, Capital
Beg. Bal. 1	0 +5,000	0	0		0	0	0 +5,000
New Bal. 2	5,000	0	0		0	0	5,000
New Bal. 3	-1800		1,800.00				
New Bal. 4		700				700	
New Bal. 5		200				200	
New Bal. 6	-300 -100	100				-300	
New Bal. 7	-100					-100	
New Bal. 8	1000						1000.00
New Bal.	-1300	1000	1,800			500	1000.00

1500.00 1500.00

1-4 APPLICATION PROBLEM (LO4, 5, 6), p. 26

Determining how revenue, expense, and withdrawal transactions change an accounting equation

Trans. No.	Assets				= Liabilities	+ Owner's Equity
	Cash +	Accts. Rec.—Eden Wedding Planners	+ Supplies	+ Prepaid Insurance	= Accts. Pay.—Shutter Supplies	+ Shannon O'Bryan, Capital
Beg. Bal. 1	725 −400	0	200	300	200	1,025 −400 (expense)
New Bal. 2	325 −150	0	200	300	200	625 −150.00
New Bal. 3	−175 900	0 0	200 200	300 300	200 200	−475.00 900
New Bal. 4	725 −100	0	200	300	200	425 −100
New Bal. 5	625	0 −400	200	300	200	325 400
New Bal. 6	625 650	−400 0	200 0	300 0	200 0	725 650
New Bal. 7	1275 −35	−400	200	300	200	1375 −35
New Bal. 8	1240 300	−400 −400	200 200	300 300	200 200	1340 1340
New Bal.	1540	−400	200	300	200	1340

Name ______________________ Date ____________ Class ____________

1-M MASTERY PROBLEM (LO4, 5, 6), p. 27

Determining how transactions change an accounting equation

Trans. No.	Assets				= Liabilities +	Owner's Equity
	Cash +	Accts. Rec.— Dr. Shephard +	Supplies +	Prepaid Insurance =	Accts. Pay.— Paws & Claws Co. +	Peter Gentry, Capital
Beg. Bal. 1	2,500 −500	0	200	100	1,300	1,500 −500 (expense)
New Bal. 2	2,000	0	200	100	1,300	1,000
New Bal. 3						
New Bal. 4						
New Bal. 5						
New Bal. 6						
New Bal. 7						
New Bal. 8						
New Bal. 9						
New Bal. 10						
New Bal. 11						
New Bal. 12						
New Bal. 13						
New Bal.						

1-C CHALLENGE PROBLEM (LO4, 5, 6), p. 28

Determining how transactions change an accounting equation

1.

Trans. No.	Assets				= Liabilities	+ Owner's Equity
	Cash	+ Accts. Rec.— 4Kids Daycare	+ Supplies	+ Prepaid Insurance	= Accts. Pay.— Ashley Tech Services	+ Linda Liu, Capital
Beg. Bal. 1	7,542	1,265	1,100	600	3,145	7,362
New Bal. 2						
New Bal. 3						
New Bal. 4						
New Bal.						

2.

Study Guide 2

Name	Perfect Score	Your Score
Identifying Accounting Terms	7 Pts.	
Analyzing Transactions into Debit and Credit Parts	20 Pts.	
Identifying Changes in Accounts	18 Pts.	
Total	45 Pts.	

Part One—Identifying Accounting Terms

Directions: Select the one term in Column I that best fits each definition in Column II. Print the letter identifying your choice in the Answers column.

Column I	Column II	Answers
A. accounts payable	**1.** An accounting device used to analyze transactions. (p. 33)	**1.** ______
B. accounts receivable	**2.** An amount recorded on the left side of an account. (p. 33)	**2.** ______
C. chart of accounts	**3.** An amount recorded on the right side of an account. (p. 33)	**3.** ______
D. credit	**4.** The side of the account that is increased. (p. 33)	**4.** ______
E. debit	**5.** A list of accounts used by a business (p. 36)	**5.** ______
F. normal balance	**6.** Amounts to be paid in the future for goods or services already acquired. (p. 39)	**6.** ______
G. T account	**7.** Amounts to be received in the future due to the sale of goods or services. (p. 44)	**7.** ______

Part Two—Analyzing Transactions into Debit and Credit Parts

Directions: Analyze each of the following transactions into debit and credit parts. Print the letter identifying your choice in the proper Answers columns.

Account Titles

A. Cash
B. Accts. Rec.—Parkview Company
C. Supplies
D. Prepaid Insurance
E. Accts. Pay.—City Supplies
F. N. Lee, Capital
G. N. Lee, Drawing
H. Sales
I. Advertising Expense

	Answers Debit	Answers Credit
1–2. Received cash from owner as an investment. (p. 36)	**1.** ______	**2.** ______
3–4. Paid cash for supplies. (p. 37)	**3.** ______	**4.** ______
5–6. Paid cash for insurance. (p. 38)	**5.** ______	**6.** ______
7–8. Bought supplies on account from City Supplies. (p. 39)	**7.** ______	**8.** ______
9–10. Paid cash on account to City Supplies. (p. 40)	**9.** ______	**10.** ______
11–12. Received cash from sales. (p. 43)	**11.** ______	**12.** ______
13–14. Sold services on account to Parkview Company. (p. 44)	**13.** ______	**14.** ______
15–16. Paid cash for advertising. (p. 45)	**15.** ______	**16.** ______
17–18. Received cash on account from Parkview Company. (p. 46)	**17.** ______	**18.** ______
19–20. Paid cash to owner for personal use. (p. 47)	**19.** ______	**20.** ______

Name ______________________ Date ____________ Class ____________

Part Three—Identifying Changes in Accounts

Directions: For each of the following items, select the choice that best completes the statement. Print the letter identifying your choice in the Answers column.

	Answers
1. The values of all things owned (assets) are on the accounting equation's (A) left side (B) right side (C) credit side (D) none of these. (p. 32)	**1.** ______
2. The values of all equities or claims against the assets (liabilities and owner's equity) are on the accounting equation's (A) left side (B) right side (C) debit side (D) none of these. (p. 32)	**2.** ______
3. An amount recorded on the left side of a T account is a (A) debit (B) credit (C) normal balance (D) none of these. (p. 33)	**3.** ______
4. An amount recorded on the right side of a T account is a (A) debit (B) credit (C) normal balance (D) none of these. (p. 33)	**4.** ______
5. The normal balance side of any asset account is the (A) debit side (B) credit side (C) right side (D) none of these. (p. 33)	**5.** ______
6. The normal balance side of any liability account is the (A) debit side (B) credit side (C) left side (D) none of these. (p. 33)	**6.** ______
7. The normal balance side of an owner's capital account is the (A) debit side (B) credit side (C) left side (D) none of these. (p. 33)	**7.** ______
8. Debits must equal credits (A) in a T account (B) on the equation's left side (C) on the equation's right side (D) for each transaction. (p. 36)	**8.** ______
9. Decreases in an asset account are shown on a T account's (A) debit side (B) credit side (C) left side (D) none of these. (p. 37)	**9.** ______
10. Increases in an asset account are shown on a T account's (A) debit side (B) credit side (C) right side (D) none of these. (p. 37)	**10.** ______
11. Increases in any liability account are shown on the T account's (A) debit side (B) credit side (C) left side (D) none of these. (p. 39)	**11.** ______
12. Decreases in any liability account are shown on a T account's (A) debit side (B) credit side (C) right side (D) none of these. (p. 40)	**12.** ______
13. Increases in a revenue account are shown on a T account's (A) debit side (B) credit side (C) left side (D) none of these. (p. 43)	**13.** ______
14. The normal balance side of any revenue account is the (A) debit side (B) credit side (C) left side (D) none of these. (p. 43)	**14.** ______
15. Increases in an expense account are shown on a T account's (A) debit side (B) credit side (C) right side (D) none of these. (p. 45)	**15.** ______
16. The normal balance side of any expense account is the (A) debit side (B) credit side (C) right side (D) none of these. (p. 45)	**16.** ______
17. The normal balance side of an owner's drawing account is the (A) debit side (B) credit side (C) right side (D) none of these. (p. 47)	**17.** ______
18. Increases in an owner's drawing account are shown on a T account's (A) debit side (B) credit side (C) right side (D) none of these. (p. 47)	**18.** ______

Across

5. An accountant who combines accounting and investigating skills to uncover suspected fraudulent business activity, or to prevent such activity.
6. Amounts to be paid in the future for goods or services already acquired.
7. An amount recorded on the left side of an account.
8. An amount recorded on the right side of an account.

Down

1. A list of accounts used by a business.
2. The side of an account that is increased is called the normal balance of the account.
3. Amounts to be received in the future due to the sale of goods or services.
4. An accounting device used to analyze transactions.

Name ______________________ Date ____________ Class ____________

2-1 WORK TOGETHER, p. 35

Determining the increase and decrease and the normal balance sides for accounts

2-1 ON YOUR OWN, p. 35

Determining the increase and decrease and the normal balance sides for accounts

2-2 WORK TOGETHER, p. 42

Analyzing transactions into debit and credit parts

Mar. 1.

Mar. 6.

Mar. 3.

Mar. 9.

Mar. 4.

2-2 ON YOUR OWN, p. 42

Analyzing transactions into debit and credit parts

June 2.

June 4.

June 5.

June 8.

June 9.

Name ______________________ Date ____________ Class ____________

2-3 WORK TOGETHER, p. 49

Analyzing revenue, expense, and withdrawal transactions into debit and credit parts

Mar. 11.

Mar. 16.

Mar. 13.

Mar. 19.

Mar. 14.

2-3 ON YOUR OWN, p. 49

Analyzing revenue, expense, and withdrawal transactions into debit and credit parts

June 12.

June 14.

June 15.

June 18.

June 19.

Name _______________ Date _______________ Class _______________

2-1 APPLICATION PROBLEM (LO2, 3), p. 52

Determining the increase, decrease, and normal balance side for accounts

1	2	3	4	5	6	7	8
Account	Account Classification	Increase Side		Decrease Side		Account's Normal Balance	
		Debit	Credit	Debit	Credit	Debit	Credit
Cash	Asset	↑			↓	✔	

2-2 APPLICATION PROBLEM (LO4), p. 52

Analyzing transactions into debit and credit parts

June 1.

Cash	
10,000.00	

Sawyer Helfrey, Capital	
	10,000.00

June 2.

June 4.

June 5.

June 8.

Name ______ Date ______ Class ______

2-3 APPLICATION PROBLEM (LO5), p. 53

Analyzing revenue, expense, and withdrawal transactions into debit and credit parts

June 11.

June 18.

June 12.

June 19.

June 14.

2-M MASTERY PROBLEM (LO4, 5), p. 53

Analyzing transactions into debit and credit parts

Name ____________________ Date ____________ Class ____________

2-C CHALLENGE PROBLEM (LO4, 5), p. 54

Analyzing transactions recorded in T accounts

1	2	3	4	5	6
Trans. No.	Accounts Affected	Account Classification	Entered in Account as a		Description of Transaction
			Debit	Credit	
1	Cash	Asset	✔		Received cash from owner as an investment
	Kelsey Guerrero, Capital	Owner's Equity		✔	
2					
3					
4					
5					
6					
7					
8					
9					
10					
11					
12					
13					

Study Guide 3

Name	Perfect Score	Your Score
Identifying Accounting Terms	11 Pts.	
Identifying Accounting Concepts and Practices	19 Pts.	
Recording Transactions in a Multicolumn Journal	20 Pts.	
Total	50 Pts.	

Part One—Identifying Accounting Terms

Directions: Select the one term in Column I that best fits each definition in Column II. Print the letter identifying your choice in the Answers column.

Column I	Column II	Answers
A. check	**1.** A form for recording transactions in chronological order. (p. 58)	**1.** ______
B. double-entry accounting	**2.** Recording transactions in a journal. (p. 58)	**2.** ______
C. entry	**3.** Information for each transaction recorded in a journal. (p. 59)	**3.** ______
D. invoice	**4.** The recording of debit and credit parts of a transaction. (p. 59)	**4.** ______
E. journal	**5.** A business paper from which information is obtained for a journal entry. (p. 59)	**5.** ______
F. journalizing	**6.** A business form ordering a bank to pay cash from a bank account. (p. 60)	**6.** ______
G. memorandum	**7.** A form describing the goods or services sold, the quantity, the price, and the terms of sale. (p. 60)	**7.** ______
H. proving cash	**8.** An invoice used as a source document for recording a sale on account. (p. 60)	**8.** ______
I. receipt	**9.** A business form giving written acknowledgement for cash received. (p. 61)	**9.** ______
J. sales invoice	**10.** A form on which a brief message is written to describe a transaction. (p. 61)	**10.** ______
K. source document	**11.** Determining that the amount of cash agrees with the accounting records. (p. 79)	**11.** ______

Part Two—Identifying Accounting Concepts and Practices

Directions: Place a *T* for True or an *F* for False in the Answers column to show whether each of the following statements is true or false.

	Answers
1. Information in a journal includes the debit and credit parts of each transaction recorded in one place. (p. 59)	**1.** ______
2. In double-entry accounting, each transaction affects at least three accounts. (p. 59)	**2.** ______
3. The Objective Evidence accounting concept requires that there be proof that a transaction did occur. (p. 59)	**3.** ______
4. Examples of source documents include checks, sales invoices, receipts, and memorandums. (p. 59)	**4.** ______
5. The source document for all cash payments is a sales invoice. (p. 60)	**5.** ______
6. A memorandum is the source document used when items are paid in cash. (p. 61)	**6.** ______
7. A receipt is the source document for cash received from transactions other than sales. (p. 61)	**7.** ______
8. A calculator tape is the source document for daily sales. (p. 61)	**8.** ______
9. The source document used when supplies are bought on account is a check. (p. 66)	**9.** ______
10. The journal columns used to record buying supplies on account are General Debit and Cash Credit. (p. 66)	**10.** ______
11. The source document used when supplies bought on account are paid for is a memorandum. (p. 67)	**11.** ______
12. The journal columns used to record receiving cash from sales are Cash Debit and Sales Credit. (p. 70)	**12.** ______
13. The source document *sales invoice* is abbreviated as S in a journal entry. (p. 71)	**13.** ______
14. The journal columns used to record paying cash for equipment rental are General Debit and Cash Credit. (p. 72)	**14.** ______
15. The journal columns used to record paying cash to the owner for a withdrawal of equity are Cash Debit and General Credit. (p. 74)	**15.** ______
16. To prove a journal page, the total debit amounts are compared with the total credit amounts to be sure they are equal. (p. 76)	**16.** ______
17. When a journal page is full, the full page should be proved before a new page is started. (p. 76)	**17.** ______
18. Double lines across column totals mean that the totals have been verified as correct. (p. 77)	**18.** ______
19. To correct an error in a journal, simply erase the incorrect item and write the correct item in the same place. (p. 80)	**19.** ______

Name ______________________ Date ____________ Class ____________

Part Three—Recording Transactions in a Multicolumn Journal

Directions: The columns of the journal below are identified with capital letters. For each of the following transactions, decide which debit and credit amount columns will be used. Print the letters identifying your choice in the proper Answers columns.

JOURNAL PAGE

	DATE	ACCOUNT TITLE	DOC. NO.	POST. REF.	1 GENERAL DEBIT	2 GENERAL CREDIT	3 SALES CREDIT	4 CASH DEBIT	5 CASH CREDIT	
1	A	B	C	D	E	F	G	H	I	1
2										2
3										3

	Answers	
	Debit	***Credit***
1–2. Received cash from owner as an investment. (p. 62)	**1.** ______	**2.** ______
3–4. Paid cash for supplies. (p. 63)	**3.** ______	**4.** ______
5–6. Paid cash for insurance. (p. 65)	**5.** ______	**6.** ______
7–8. Bought supplies on account. (p. 66)	**7.** ______	**8.** ______
9–10. Paid cash on account. (p. 67)	**9.** ______	**10.** ______
11–12. Received cash from sales. (p. 70)	**11.** ______	**12.** ______
13–14. Sold services on account. (p. 71)	**13.** ______	**14.** ______
15–16. Paid cash for an expense. (p. 72)	**15.** ______	**16.** ______
17–18. Received cash on account. (p. 73)	**17.** ______	**18.** ______
19–20. Paid cash to owner as a withdrawal of equity. (p. 74)	**19.** ______	**20.** ______

Across

4. A form on which a brief message is written to describe a transaction.
5. Recording transactions in a journal.
6. Information for each transaction recorded in a journal.
9. An invoice used as a source document for recording a sale on account. This is also referred to as a sales ticket or a sales slip.
10. A business form ordering a bank to pay cash from a bank account.

Down

1. A form for recording transactions in chronological order.
2. Determining that the amount of cash agrees with the accounting records.
3. A business paper from which information is obtained for a journal entry.
7. A business form giving written acknowledgement for cash received.
8. A form describing the goods or services sold, the quantity, the price, and the terms of sale.

Name ______________________ Date ____________ Class ____________

3-1, 3-2, 3-3, and 3-4 WORK TOGETHER, pp. 64, 69, 75, and 81

3-1 Journalizing entries in a multicolumn journal

3-2 Journalizing entries in a multicolumn journal

3-3 Journalizing transactions that affect owner's equity in a multicolumn journal

3-4 Proving and ruling a journal

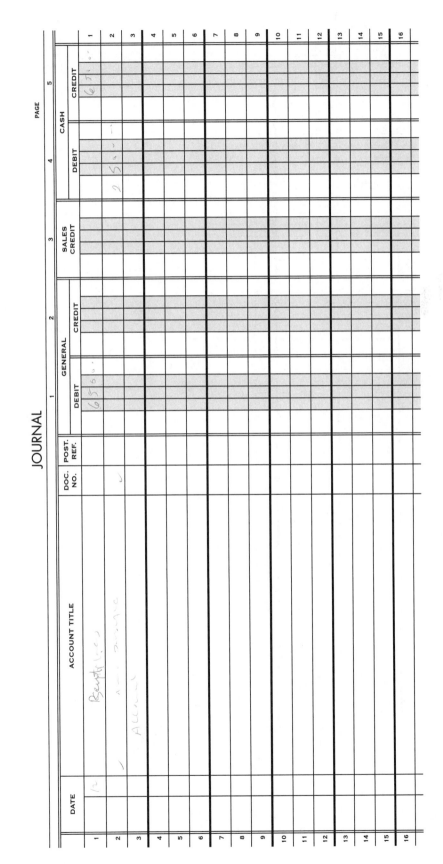

JOURNAL

PAGE

	DATE	ACCOUNT TITLE	DOC. NO.	POST. REF.	1 GENERAL DEBIT	2 GENERAL CREDIT	3 SALES CREDIT	4 CASH DEBIT	5 CASH CREDIT	
1	12	[illegible]			650				650	1
2		[illegible]	✓					250		2
3		[illegible]								3
4										4
5										5
6										6
7										7
8										8
9										9
10										10
11										11
12										12
13										13
14										14
15										15
16										16

JOURNAL

PAGE

	DATE		ACCOUNT TITLE	DOC. NO.	POST. REF.	1 GENERAL DEBIT	2 GENERAL CREDIT	3 SALES CREDIT	4 CASH DEBIT	5 CASH CREDIT	
1											1
2											2
3											3
4											4
5											5
6											6
7											7
8											8
9											9
10											10
11											11

2. *Prove page 1:*

Column	*Debit Column Total*	*Credit Column Total*
General		
Sales.		
Cash.		
Totals		

4. *Prove page 2:*

Column	*Debit Column Total*	*Credit Column Total*
General		
Sales.		
Cash.		
Totals		

5. *Prove cash:*

Cash on hand at the beginning of the month . . . .

\+ Total cash received during the month . . . . ________

Total cash . . . .

– Total cash paid during the month . . . . ________

Cash balance at the end of the month . . . . ________

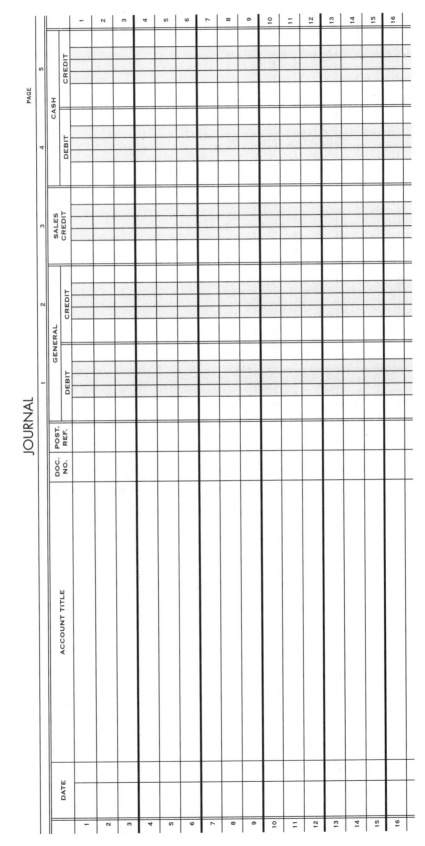

Name ______________________ Date ____________ Class ____________

3-1, 3-2, 3-3, and 3-4 ON YOUR OWN, pp. 64, 69, 75, and 81

3-1 Journalizing entries in a multicolumn journal

3-2 Journalizing entries in a multicolumn journal

3-3 Journalizing transactions that affect owner's equity in a multicolumn journal

3-4 Proving and ruling a journal

JOURNAL

PAGE

					1	2	3	4	5	
					GENERAL		SALES	CASH		
	DATE	ACCOUNT TITLE	DOC. NO.	POST. REF.	DEBIT	CREDIT	CREDIT	DEBIT	CREDIT	
1										1
2										2
3										3
4										4
5										5
6										6
7										7
8										8
9										9
10										10
11										11
12										12
13										13
14										14
15										15
16										16

JOURNAL

PAGE

	DATE	ACCOUNT TITLE	DOC. NO.	POST. REF.	1 GENERAL DEBIT	2 GENERAL CREDIT	3 SALES CREDIT	4 CASH DEBIT	5 CASH CREDIT	
1										1
2										2
3										3
4										4
5										5
6										6
7										7
8										8
9										9
10										10
11										11

2. *Prove page 1:*

Column	*Debit Column Total*	*Credit Column Total*
General		
Sales.		
Cash.		
Totals		

4. *Prove page 2:*

Column	*Debit Column Total*	*Credit Column Total*
General		
Sales.		
Cash.		
Totals		

5. *Prove cash:*

Cash on hand at the beginning of the month . . . .

+ Total cash received during the month . . . .

Total cash . . . .

– Total cash paid during the month . . . .

Cash balance at the end of the month . . . .

Name ______________________ Date ____________ Class ____________

3-1, 3-2, 3-3, and 3-4.1 APPLICATION PROBLEMS, pp. 84–85

3-1 Journalizing transactions in a multicolumn journal (LO3, 4)

3-2 Journalizing buying insurance, buying on account, and paying on account in a multicolumn journal (LO3, 4, 5)

3-3 Journalizing transactions that affect owner's equity and receiving cash on account in a multicolumn journal (LO3, 4, 5, 6, 7)

3-4.1 Proving and ruling a multicolumn journal (LO3, 4, 5, 6, 7, 8, 9)

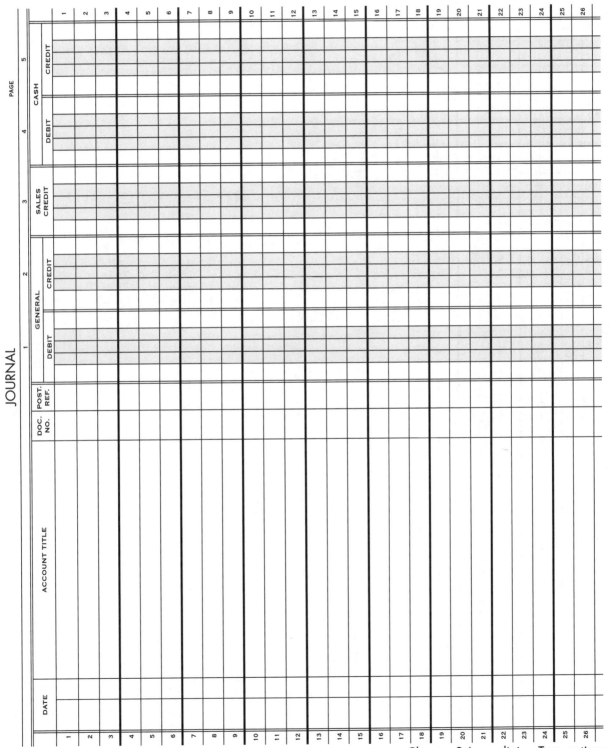

JOURNAL

PAGE

	DATE	ACCOUNT TITLE	DOC. NO.	POST. REF.	1 GENERAL DEBIT	2 GENERAL CREDIT	3 SALES CREDIT	4 CASH DEBIT	5 CASH CREDIT	
1										1
2										2
3										3
4										4
5										5
6										6
7										7
8										8
9										9
10										10
11										11
12										12
13										13
14										14
15										15
16										16
17										17
18										18
19										19
20										20
21										21
22										22
23										23
24										24
25										25
26										26

JOURNAL

PAGE

	DATE	ACCOUNT TITLE	DOC. NO.	POST. REF.	1 GENERAL DEBIT	2 GENERAL CREDIT	3 SALES CREDIT	4 CASH DEBIT	5 CASH CREDIT	
1										1
2										2
3										3
4										4
5										5
6										6
7										7
8										8

2. *Prove page 1:*

Column	*Debit Column Total*	*Credit Column Total*
General		
Sales.		
Cash.		
Totals		

4. *Prove page 2:*

Column	*Debit Column Total*	*Credit Column Total*
General		
Sales.		
Cash.		
Totals		

5. *Prove cash:*

Cash on hand at the beginning of the month . . . .

\+ Total cash received during the month . . . .

Total cash . . . .

– Total cash paid during the month . . . .

Cash balance at the end of the month . . . .

Name ______________________ Date ______________ Class ______________

3-4.2 APPLICATION PROBLEM (LO3, 4, 5, 6, 7, 8, 9), p. 85

Journalizing transactions and proving and ruling a multicolumn journal

JOURNAL PAGE

	DATE	ACCOUNT TITLE	DOC. NO.	POST. REF.	1 GENERAL DEBIT	2 GENERAL CREDIT	3 SALES CREDIT	4 CASH DEBIT	5 CASH CREDIT	
1										1
2										2
3										3
4										4
5										5
6										6
7										7
8										8
9										9
10										10
11										11
12										12
13										13
14										14
15										15
16										16
17										17
18										18

2. *Prove the journal:*

Column	*Debit Column Total*	*Credit Column Total*
General		
Sales.		
Cash.		
Totals.		

3. *Prove cash:*

Cash on hand at the beginning of the month . . . . ________

\+ Total cash received during the month . . . . ________

Total cash . . . . ________

– Total cash paid during the month . . . . ________

Cash balance at the end of the month . . . . ________

3-M MASTERY PROBLEM (LO3, 4, 5, 6, 7, 8, 9), p. 86

Journalizing transactions and proving and ruling a multicolumn journal

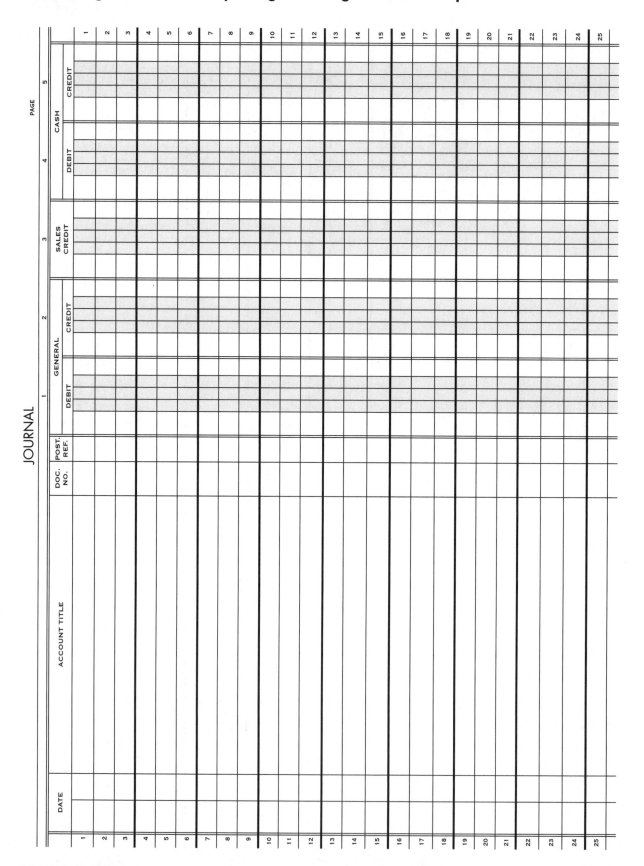

JOURNAL PAGE

DATE	ACCOUNT TITLE	DOC. NO.	POST. REF.	GENERAL DEBIT (1)	GENERAL CREDIT (2)	SALES CREDIT (3)	CASH DEBIT (4)	CASH CREDIT (5)

Name ______________________ Date ____________ Class ____________

3-M MASTERY PROBLEM (concluded)

JOURNAL

PAGE

	DATE	ACCOUNT TITLE	DOC. NO.	POST. REF.	GENERAL DEBIT (1)	GENERAL CREDIT (2)	SALES CREDIT (3)	CASH DEBIT (4)	CASH CREDIT (5)	
1										1
2										2
3										3
4										4
5										5
6										6
7										7
8										8
9										9
10										10
11										11
12										12
13										13
14										14
15										15
16										16

2. *Prove page 1:*

Column	*Debit Column Total*	*Credit Column Total*
General		
Sales.		
Cash.		
Totals.		

4. *Prove page 2:*

Column	*Debit Column Total*	*Credit Column Total*
General		
Sales.		
Cash.		
Totals.		

5. *Prove cash:*

Cash on hand at the beginning of the month . . . . ______
\+ Total cash received during the month . . . . ______
Total cash . . . . ______
– Total cash paid during the month . . . . ______
Cash balance at the end of the month . . . . ______

3-S SOURCE DOCUMENTS PROBLEM (LO2, 3, 4, 5, 6, 7, 8, 9), p. 87

Journalizing transactions

Receipt No. 1
Date June 1, 20--
From Henry White
For Investment
$ 4,000.00

Receipt No. 1 — Form 1
Date June 1 20--
Rec'd from Henry White
For Investment
Four thousand and no/100 Dollars
Amount $ 4,000.00
Henry White
Received by

No. 1 — Form 2
Date June 3 20-- $ 300.00
To Worldwide Supply Company
For Supplies

BALANCE BROUGHT FORWARD		0.00
AMOUNT DEPOSITED	6/1/20-- (Date)	4,000.00
SUBTOTAL		4,000.00
AMOUNT THIS CHECK		300.00
BALANCE CARRIED FORWARD		3,700.00

No. 2 — Form 3
Date June 5 20-- $ 600.00
To NW Management Company
For June rent

BALANCE BROUGHT FORWARD		3,700.00
AMOUNT DEPOSITED	(Date)	
SUBTOTAL		3,700.00
AMOUNT THIS CHECK		600.00
BALANCE CARRIED FORWARD		3,100.00

No. 1 — Form 4
MEMORANDUM

Bought supplies on account from Atlas Supplies, $300.00

Signed: Henry White Date: June 8, 20--

3-S SOURCE DOCUMENTS PROBLEM (continued)

No. 3 Form 5

Date June 9 20-- $ 80.00

To Statewide Electric

For Electric bill

BALANCE BROUGHT FORWARD	3,100	00
AMOUNT DEPOSITED (Date)		
SUBTOTAL	3,100	00
AMOUNT THIS CHECK	80	00
BALANCE CARRIED FORWARD	3,020	00

No. 4 Form 6

Date June 11 20-- $ 300.00

To Atlas Supplies

For Payment on account

BALANCE BROUGHT FORWARD	3,020	00
AMOUNT DEPOSITED (Date)		
SUBTOTAL	3,020	00
AMOUNT THIS CHECK	300	00
BALANCE CARRIED FORWARD	2,720	00

Form 7

June 12, 20--
T12

0.00*
100.00+
500.00+
600.00*

White's Repair Service
11203 Pacific Blvd NW
Albany, OR 97321-7726

SALES INVOICE

Form 8

SOLD TO: J.Puckett
4456 Main Street SW
Albany, OR 97321-4456

No. 1
Date 6/15/--
Terms 30 days

DESCRIPTION	Amount
Repair Water Heater	$ 1,100.00
Total	$ 1,100.00

No. 5 Form 9

Date June 16 20-- $ 300.00

To Oakridge Insurance Co.

For Insurance

BALANCE BROUGHT FORWARD		2,720	00
AMOUNT DEPOSITED	6 12 20-- (Date)	600	00
SUBTOTAL		3,320	00
AMOUNT THIS CHECK		300	00
BALANCE CARRIED FORWARD		3,020	00

Form 10

June 19, 20--
T19

0.00*
300.00
115.00+
285.00+
700.00*

No. 6 Form 11

Date June 23 20-- $ 50.00

To Sunrise Delivery Co.

For Miscellaneous expense

BALANCE BROUGHT FORWARD		3,020	00
AMOUNT DEPOSITED	6 19 20-- (Date)	700	00
SUBTOTAL		3,720	00
AMOUNT THIS CHECK		50	00
BALANCE CARRIED FORWARD		3,670	00

Form 12

June 26, 20--
T26

0.00*
515.00+
386.00+
901.00*

No. 7 Form 13

Date June 29 20-- $ 37.00

To Seaside Cleaning Company

For Miscellaneous expense

BALANCE BROUGHT FORWARD		3,670	00
AMOUNT DEPOSITED	6 26 20-- (Date)	901	00
SUBTOTAL		4,571	00
AMOUNT THIS CHECK		37	00
BALANCE CARRIED FORWARD		4,534	00

Name ________________ Date ________ Class ________

3-S SOURCE DOCUMENTS PROBLEM (continued)

Receipt No. 2
Date June 29, 20--
From J. Puckett
For On account
$ 1,100.00

Receipt No. 2 — Form 14
Date June 29 20--
Rec'd from J. Puckett
For On account
One thousand one hundred and no/100 Dollars
Amount $ 1,100.00
Henry White
Received by

No. 8 — Form 15
Date June 29 20-- $ 110.00
To Salem Telephone Co.
For Cell phone bill

BALANCE BROUGHT FORWARD		4,534	00
AMOUNT DEPOSITED	6 29 20-- (Date)	1,100	00
SUBTOTAL		5,634	00
AMOUNT THIS CHECK		110	00
BALANCE CARRIED FORWARD		5,524	00

No. 9 — Form 16
Date June 30 20-- $ 2,000.00
To Henry White
For Owner withdrawl of equilty

BALANCE BROUGHT FORWARD		5,524	00
AMOUNT DEPOSITED	(Date)		
SUBTOTAL		5,524	00
AMOUNT THIS CHECK		2,000	00
BALANCE CARRIED FORWARD		3,524	00

Form 17

June 30, 20--
T30

0.00*
350.00+
350.00*

No. 10 — Form 18
Date ________ 20__ $ ________
To ________
For ________

BALANCE BROUGHT FORWARD		3,524	00
AMOUNT DEPOSITED	6 30 20-- (Date)	350	00
SUBTOTAL		3,874	00
AMOUNT THIS CHECK			
BALANCE CARRIED FORWARD			

3-S SOURCE DOCUMENTS PROBLEM (concluded)

JOURNAL

PAGE

	DATE		ACCOUNT TITLE	DOC. NO.	POST. REF.	1 GENERAL DEBIT	2 GENERAL CREDIT	3 SALES CREDIT	4 CASH DEBIT	5 CASH CREDIT	
1											1
2											2
3											3
4											4
5											5
6											6
7											7
8											8
9											9
10											10
11											11
12											12
13											13
14											14
15											15
16											16
17											17
18											18
19											19

2. *Prove the journal:*

Column	*Debit Column Total*	*Credit Column Total*
General		
Sales		
Cash		
Totals		

3. *Prove cash:*

Cash on hand at the beginning of the month	
+ Total cash received during the month	
Total cash	
− Total cash paid during the month	
Cash balance at the end of the month	

Name ______________________ Date ____________ Class ____________

3-C CHALLENGE PROBLEM (LO3, 4, 5, 6, 7, 8, 9), p. 88

Journalizing transactions using a variation of the multicolumn journal

JOURNAL PAGE

	1 CASH DEBIT	2 CASH CREDIT	DATE	ACCOUNT TITLE	DOC. NO.	POST. REF.	3 GENERAL DEBIT	4 GENERAL CREDIT	5 SALES CREDIT	
1										1
2										2
3										3
4										4
5										5
6										6
7										7
8										8
9										9
10										10
11										11
12										12
13										13
14										14
15										15
16										16
17										17
18										18
19										19

2. *Prove the journal:*

Column	*Debit Column Total*	*Credit Column Total*
Cash....................		
General....................		
Sales....................		
Totals....................		

3. *Prove cash:*

Cash on hand at the beginning of the month....................	
+ Total cash received during the month....................	
Total cash....................	
– Total cash paid during the month....................	
Cash balance at the end of the month....................	

Study Guide 4

Name	Perfect Score	Your Score
Identifying Accounting Terms	7 Pts.	
Identifying Accounting Concepts and Practices	20 Pts.	
Analyzing Posting from a Journal to a General Ledger	13 Pts.	
Total	40 Pts.	

Part One—Identifying Accounting Terms

Directions: Select the one term in Column I that best fits each definition in Column II. Print the letter identifying your choice in the Answers column.

Column I	*Column II*	*Answers*
A. account	**1.** A group of accounts. (p. 94)	**1.** ______
B. correcting entry	**2.** A ledger that contains all accounts needed to prepare financial statements. (p. 94)	**2.** ______
C. file maintenance	**3.** The number assigned to an account. (p. 94)	**3.** ______
D. general ledger	**4.** The procedure for arranging accounts in a general ledger, assigning account numbers, and keeping records current. (p. 95)	**4.** ______
E. ledger	**5.** Writing an account title and number on the heading of an account. (p. 96)	**5.** ______
F. opening an account	**6.** Transferring information from a journal entry to a ledger account. (p. 98)	**6.** ______
G. posting	**7.** An additional journal entry made to correct an incorrect journal entry. (p. 112)	**7.** ______

Part Two—Identifying Account Concepts and Practices

Directions: Place a *T* for True or an *F* for False in the Answers column to show whether each of the following statements is true or false.

	Answers
1. Because an account form has columns for the debit and credit balance of an account, it is often referred to as the balance-ruled account form. (p. 93)	**1.** _______
2. The asset division accounts for Delgado Web Services are numbered in the 200s. (p. 94)	**2.** _______
3. The cash account for Delgado Web Services is the first asset account and is numbered 110. (p. 94)	**3.** _______
4. The third division of Delgado Web Services chart of accounts is the owner's equity division. (p. 94)	**4.** _______
5. The first digit of account numbers for accounts in the owner's equity ledger division is 4. (p. 94)	**5.** _______
6. The last two digits in a 3-digit account number indicate the general ledger division of the account. (p. 94)	**6.** _______
7. When adding a new expense account between accounts numbered 510 and 520, the new account is assigned the account number 515. (p. 95)	**7.** _______
8. Delgado Web Services arranges expense accounts in chronological order in its general ledger. (p. 95)	**8.** _______
9. The two steps for opening an account are writing the account title and recording the balance. (p. 96)	**9.** _______
10. Separate amounts in special amount columns are not posted individually. (p. 98)	**10.** _______
11. Separate amounts in general amount columns are not posted individually. (p. 98)	**11.** _______
12. The only reason for the Post. Ref. columns of the journal and general ledger is to indicate which entries in the journal still need to be posted if posting is interrupted. (p. 99)	**12.** _______
13. A check mark in parentheses below a General Debit column total indicates that the total is not posted. (p. 103)	**13.** _______
14. The totals of general amount columns in a journal are not posted. (p. 103)	**14.** _______
15. With the exception of the totals lines, the Post. Ref. column is completely filled in with either an account number or a check mark. (p. 103)	**15.** _______
16. Errors discovered before entries are posted must be corrected with a correcting entry. (p. 112)	**16.** _______
17. If an error requires a correcting entry, a memorandum is prepared as the source document describing the correction to be made. (p. 112)	**17.** _______
18. If the payment of cash for rent was journalized and posted in error as a debit to Miscellaneous Expense instead of Rent Expense, the correcting entry will include a credit to Cash. (p. 112)	**18.** _______
19. If an error in posting is made but not discovered until additional postings have been made to the account, the correct posting should be made on the next available line in the correct account. (p. 113)	**19.** _______
20. All corrections for posting errors should be made in a way that leaves no question as to the correct amount. (p. 113)	**20.** _______

Name ____________ Date ________ Class ________

Part Three—Analyzing Posting from a Journal to a General Ledger

Directions: In the journal below, some items are identified with capital letters. In the general ledger accounts, locations to which items are posted are identified with numbers. For each number in a general ledger account, select the letter in the journal that will be posted to the account. Print the letter identifying your choice in the Answers column.

JOURNAL PAGE 1A

	Date		Account Title	Doc. No.	Post. Ref.	1 General Debit	2 General Credit	3 Sales Credit	4 Cash Debit	5 Cash Credit	
1	20-- Mar.	1	R. Rosen, Capital	R1		1,500 00				1,500 00	1
2		2	Supplies	C1		150 00 ← B				150 00	2
3		2	✔	T2	✔		C →	400 00	400 00		3
25		31	Totals			3,200 00	350 00	3,975 00	4,850 00	3,725 00	25
26	D	E			F	G	H	I	J	K	26

ACCOUNT Cash ACCOUNT NO. 110

Date		Item	Post. Ref.	Debit	Credit	Balance Debit	Balance Credit
1	2		3	4			
					5		

ACCOUNT Supplies ACCOUNT NO. 120

Date		Item	Post. Ref.	Debit	Credit	Balance Debit	Balance Credit
6	7		8	9			

ACCOUNT Sales ACCOUNT NO. 410

Date		Item	Post. Ref.	Debit	Credit	Balance Debit	Balance Credit
10	11		12		13		

A through F (pp. 98–100)

G through K (pp. 104–107)

Bold Numbers in Ledger Accounts	**Answers**
1.	
2.	
3.	
4.	
5.	
6.	
7.	
8.	
9.	
10.	
11.	
12.	
13.	

Across

5. The number assigned to an account.
6. The procedure for arranging accounts in a general ledger, assigning account numbers, and keeping records current.

Down

1. A ledger that contains all accounts needed to prepare financial statements.
2. Transferring information from a journal entry to a ledger account.
3. A group of accounts.
4. If a transaction has been improperly journalized and posted to the ledger, the incorrect journal entry should be corrected with this type of additional journal entry.

Name ______________________ Date ____________ Class ____________

4-1 WORK TOGETHER, p. 97

Preparing a chart of accounts and opening an account

1.

2.

3.

ACCOUNT ACCOUNT NO.

DATE		ITEM	POST. REF.	DEBIT	CREDIT	BALANCE	
						DEBIT	CREDIT

4-1 ON YOUR OWN, p. 97

Preparing a chart of accounts and opening an account

1.

2.

3.

ACCOUNT | ACCOUNT NO.

DATE		ITEM	POST. REF.	DEBIT	CREDIT	BALANCE	
						DEBIT	CREDIT

Name ______________________ Date ______________ Class ______________

4-2 and 4-3 WORK TOGETHER, pp. 102 and 111

4-2 Posting separate amounts to a general ledger
4-3 Posting column totals to a general ledger

JOURNAL

PAGE 1

	DATE		ACCOUNT TITLE	DOC. NO.	POST. REF.	1 GENERAL DEBIT	2 GENERAL CREDIT	3 SALES CREDIT	4 CASH DEBIT	5 CASH CREDIT	
1	20– Apr.	1	Omar Boje, Capital	R1			2500 00		2500 00		1
2		3	Prepaid Insurance	C1		330 00				330 00	2
3		4	Supplies	M1		160 00					3
4			Accts. Pay.—Ready Supply				160 00				4
5		8	✔	T8	✔			325 00	325 00		5
6		9	Accts. Rec.—Dan Carroll	S1		122 00		122 00			6
7		12	Rent Expense	C2		260 00				260 00	7
8		15	Accts. Pay.—Ready Supply	C3		80 00				80 00	8
9		16	Accts. Rec.—Dan Carroll	R2			65 00		65 00		9
10		25	Omar Boje, Drawing	C4		500 00				500 00	10
11		30	Totals			1452 00	2725 00	447 00	2890 00	1170 00	11
12						(✔)	(✔)				12
13											13
14											14
15											15
16											16
17											17
18											18
19											19
20											20
21											21
22											22

4-2 and 4-3 **WORK TOGETHER (continued)**

GENERAL LEDGER

ACCOUNT Cash — ACCOUNT NO. 110

DATE		ITEM	POST. REF.	DEBIT	CREDIT	BALANCE DEBIT	BALANCE CREDIT

ACCOUNT Accounts Receivable—Dan Carroll — ACCOUNT NO. 120

DATE		ITEM	POST. REF.	DEBIT	CREDIT	BALANCE DEBIT	BALANCE CREDIT

ACCOUNT Supplies — ACCOUNT NO. 130

DATE		ITEM	POST. REF.	DEBIT	CREDIT	BALANCE DEBIT	BALANCE CREDIT

ACCOUNT Prepaid Insurance — ACCOUNT NO. 140

DATE		ITEM	POST. REF.	DEBIT	CREDIT	BALANCE DEBIT	BALANCE CREDIT

ACCOUNT Accounts Payable—Ready Supply — ACCOUNT NO. 210

DATE		ITEM	POST. REF.	DEBIT	CREDIT	BALANCE DEBIT	BALANCE CREDIT

Name ______________________ Date ____________ Class ____________

4-2 and 4-3 WORK TOGETHER (concluded)

GENERAL LEDGER

ACCOUNT Omar Boje, Capital — ACCOUNT NO. 310

DATE		ITEM	POST. REF.	DEBIT	CREDIT	BALANCE DEBIT	BALANCE CREDIT

ACCOUNT Omar Boje, Drawing — ACCOUNT NO. 320

DATE		ITEM	POST. REF.	DEBIT	CREDIT	BALANCE DEBIT	BALANCE CREDIT

ACCOUNT Sales — ACCOUNT NO. 410

DATE		ITEM	POST. REF.	DEBIT	CREDIT	BALANCE DEBIT	BALANCE CREDIT

ACCOUNT Rent Expense — ACCOUNT NO. 510

DATE		ITEM	POST. REF.	DEBIT	CREDIT	BALANCE DEBIT	BALANCE CREDIT

ACCOUNT — ACCOUNT NO.

DATE		ITEM	POST. REF.	DEBIT	CREDIT	BALANCE DEBIT	BALANCE CREDIT

4-2 Posting separate amounts to a general ledger
4-3 Posting column totals to a general ledger

JOURNAL

PAGE 1

DATE		ACCOUNT TITLE	DOC. NO.	POST. REF.	1 GENERAL DEBIT	2 GENERAL CREDIT	3 SALES CREDIT	4 CASH DEBIT	5 CASH CREDIT
20-- Oct.	1	Helen Orr, Capital	R1			2 250 00		2 250 00	
	4	Supplies	M1		134 00				
		Accts. Pay.—Stein Company				134 00			
	7	Prepaid Insurance	C1		410 00				410 00
	10	Accts. Rec.—K. Green	S1		360 00		360 00		
	13	✔	T13	✔			1 500 00	1 500 00	
	18	Advertising Expense	C2		68 00				68 00
	21	Accts. Pay.—Stein Company	C3		80 00				80 00
	27	Accts. Rec.—K. Green	R2			200 00		200 00	
	30	Helen Orr, Drawing	C4		1 000 00				1 000 00
	31	Totals			2 052 00	2 584 00	1 860 00	3 950 00	1 558 00
					(✔)	(✔)			

Name ______________________ Date ____________ Class ____________

4-2 and 4-3 ON YOUR OWN (continued)

GENERAL LEDGER

ACCOUNT Cash — ACCOUNT NO. 110

DATE		ITEM	POST. REF.	DEBIT	CREDIT	BALANCE DEBIT	BALANCE CREDIT

ACCOUNT Accounts Receivable—K. Green — ACCOUNT NO. 120

DATE		ITEM	POST. REF.	DEBIT	CREDIT	BALANCE DEBIT	BALANCE CREDIT

ACCOUNT Supplies — ACCOUNT NO. 130

DATE		ITEM	POST. REF.	DEBIT	CREDIT	BALANCE DEBIT	BALANCE CREDIT

ACCOUNT Prepaid Insurance — ACCOUNT NO. 140

DATE		ITEM	POST. REF.	DEBIT	CREDIT	BALANCE DEBIT	BALANCE CREDIT

ACCOUNT Accounts Payable—Stein Company — ACCOUNT NO. 210

DATE		ITEM	POST. REF.	DEBIT	CREDIT	BALANCE DEBIT	BALANCE CREDIT

4-2 and 4-3 ON YOUR OWN (concluded)

GENERAL LEDGER

ACCOUNT Helen Orr, Capital ACCOUNT NO. 310

DATE		ITEM	POST. REF.	DEBIT	CREDIT	BALANCE DEBIT	BALANCE CREDIT

ACCOUNT Helen Orr, Drawing ACCOUNT NO. 320

DATE		ITEM	POST. REF.	DEBIT	CREDIT	BALANCE DEBIT	BALANCE CREDIT

ACCOUNT Sales ACCOUNT NO. 410

DATE		ITEM	POST. REF.	DEBIT	CREDIT	BALANCE DEBIT	BALANCE CREDIT

ACCOUNT Advertising Expense ACCOUNT NO. 510

DATE		ITEM	POST. REF.	DEBIT	CREDIT	BALANCE DEBIT	BALANCE CREDIT

ACCOUNT ACCOUNT NO.

DATE		ITEM	POST. REF.	DEBIT	CREDIT	BALANCE DEBIT	BALANCE CREDIT

Name ______________________ Date ____________ Class ____________

4-4 WORK TOGETHER, p. 114

Journalizing correcting entries and correcting posting errors

1.

JOURNAL — PAGE

	DATE		ACCOUNT TITLE	DOC. NO.	POST. REF.	1 GENERAL DEBIT	2 GENERAL CREDIT	3 SALES CREDIT	4 CASH DEBIT	5 CASH CREDIT	
1											1
2											2
3											3
4											4
5											5
6											6
7											7
8											8
9											9

2.

ACCOUNT Art Stevenson, Drawing — ACCOUNT NO. 320

DATE		ITEM	POST. REF.	DEBIT	CREDIT	BALANCE DEBIT	BALANCE CREDIT
20-- Nov.	15		19	450 00		450 00	
	30		20		400 00	150 00	

4-4 ON YOUR OWN, p. 114

Journalizing correcting entries and correcting posting errors

1.

JOURNAL

PAGE

	DATE		ACCOUNT TITLE	DOC. NO.	POST. REF.	1 GENERAL DEBIT	2 GENERAL CREDIT	3 SALES CREDIT	4 CASH DEBIT	5 CASH CREDIT	
1											1
2											2
3											3
4											4
5											5
6											6
7											7
8											8
9											9

2.

ACCOUNT Janet Bies, Capital ACCOUNT NO. 310

DATE		ITEM	POST. REF.	DEBIT	CREDIT	BALANCE DEBIT	BALANCE CREDIT
20-- June	1		10		2 500 00		2 500 00
	15		10	1 000 00			1 500 00

Name ______ Date ______ Class ______

4-1 APPLICATION PROBLEM (LO1, 2, 3, 4), p. 117

Preparing a chart of accounts and opening an account

1.

2.

3.

ACCOUNT ACCOUNT NO.

DATE		ITEM	POST. REF.	DEBIT	CREDIT	BALANCE	
						DEBIT	CREDIT

ACCOUNT ACCOUNT NO.

DATE		ITEM	POST. REF.	DEBIT	CREDIT	BALANCE	
						DEBIT	CREDIT

4-2 Posting separate amounts to a general ledger
4-3 Posting column totals to a general ledger

JOURNAL

PAGE 1

DATE		ACCOUNT TITLE	DOC. NO.	POST. REF.	GENERAL DEBIT (1)	GENERAL CREDIT (2)	SALES CREDIT (3)	CASH DEBIT (4)	CASH CREDIT (5)
20-- July	1	Jing Suen, Capital	R1			4 000 00		4 000 00	
	8	Prepaid Insurance	C1		600 00				600 00
	10	Supplies	M1		180 00				
		Accts. Pay.—Bayou Supply				180 00			
	12	✔	T12	✔			964 00	964 00	
	15	Accts. Rec.—M. Kadam	S1		150 00		150 00		
	19	Advertising Expense	C2		225 00				225 00
	20	Accts. Pay.—Bayou Supply	C3		120 00				120 00
	27	Accts. Rec.—M. Kadam	R2			100 00		100 00	
	31	Jing Suen, Drawing	C4		800 00				800 00
	31	Totals			2 075 00	4 280 00	1 114 00	5 064 00	1 745 00
					(✔)	(✔)			

Name ____________________ Date ____________ Class ____________

4-2 and 4-3 APPLICATION PROBLEMS (continued)

GENERAL LEDGER

ACCOUNT Cash ACCOUNT NO. 110

DATE		ITEM	POST. REF.	DEBIT	CREDIT	BALANCE DEBIT	BALANCE CREDIT

ACCOUNT Accounts Receivable—M. Kadam ACCOUNT NO. 120

DATE		ITEM	POST. REF.	DEBIT	CREDIT	BALANCE DEBIT	BALANCE CREDIT

ACCOUNT Supplies ACCOUNT NO. 130

DATE		ITEM	POST. REF.	DEBIT	CREDIT	BALANCE DEBIT	BALANCE CREDIT

ACCOUNT Prepaid Insurance ACCOUNT NO. 140

DATE		ITEM	POST. REF.	DEBIT	CREDIT	BALANCE DEBIT	BALANCE CREDIT

ACCOUNT Accounts Payable—Bayou Supply ACCOUNT NO. 210

DATE		ITEM	POST. REF.	DEBIT	CREDIT	BALANCE DEBIT	BALANCE CREDIT

GENERAL LEDGER

ACCOUNT Jing Suen, Capital ACCOUNT NO. 310

DATE		ITEM	POST. REF.	DEBIT	CREDIT	BALANCE DEBIT	BALANCE CREDIT

ACCOUNT Jing Suen, Drawing ACCOUNT NO. 320

DATE		ITEM	POST. REF.	DEBIT	CREDIT	BALANCE DEBIT	BALANCE CREDIT

ACCOUNT Sales ACCOUNT NO. 410

DATE		ITEM	POST. REF.	DEBIT	CREDIT	BALANCE DEBIT	BALANCE CREDIT

ACCOUNT Advertising Expense ACCOUNT NO. 510

DATE		ITEM	POST. REF.	DEBIT	CREDIT	BALANCE DEBIT	BALANCE CREDIT

ACCOUNT ACCOUNT NO.

DATE		ITEM	POST. REF.	DEBIT	CREDIT	BALANCE DEBIT	BALANCE CREDIT

Name ______________________ Date ____________ Class ____________

4-4 APPLICATION PROBLEM (LO7, 8), p. 117

Journalizing correcting entries and correcting posting errors

1.

JOURNAL PAGE

	DATE	ACCOUNT TITLE	DOC. NO.	POST. REF.	GENERAL DEBIT (1)	GENERAL CREDIT (2)	SALES CREDIT (3)	CASH DEBIT (4)	CASH CREDIT (5)	
1										1
2										2
3										3
4										4
5										5
6										6
7										7
8										8
9										9

2.

ACCOUNT Supplies ACCOUNT NO. 130

DATE		ITEM	POST. REF.	DEBIT	CREDIT	BALANCE DEBIT	BALANCE CREDIT
20-- July	6		13	260 00		260 00	
	30		14		140 00	120 00	

4-M MASTERY PROBLEM (LO3, 4, 5, 6), p. 118

JOURNAL

PAGE

	DATE		ACCOUNT TITLE	DOC. NO.	POST. REF.	1 GENERAL DEBIT	2 GENERAL CREDIT	3 SALES CREDIT	4 CASH DEBIT	5 CASH CREDIT	
1											1
2											2
3											3
4											4
5											5
6											6
7											7
8											8
9											9
10											10
11											11
12											12
13											13
14											14
15											15
16											16
17											17
18											18
19											19
20											20
21											21

Prove the journal:

Column	*Debit Column Totals*	*Credit Column Totals*
General		
Sales		
Cash		
Totals		

Prove cash:

Cash on hand at the beginning of the month . . . .
+ Total cash received during the month . . . . ______
Total cash . . . .
– Total cash paid during the month . . . . ______
Cash balance at the end of the month . . . . ______
Checkbook balance on the next unused check stub . . . . ______

4-M MASTERY PROBLEM (continued)

GENERAL LEDGER

ACCOUNT Cash ACCOUNT NO. 110

DATE		ITEM	POST. REF.	DEBIT	CREDIT	BALANCE DEBIT	BALANCE CREDIT

ACCOUNT Accounts Receivable—Clara Walthers ACCOUNT NO. 120

DATE		ITEM	POST. REF.	DEBIT	CREDIT	BALANCE DEBIT	BALANCE CREDIT

ACCOUNT Supplies ACCOUNT NO. 130

DATE		ITEM	POST. REF.	DEBIT	CREDIT	BALANCE DEBIT	BALANCE CREDIT

ACCOUNT Accounts Payable—Corner Supplies ACCOUNT NO. 210

DATE		ITEM	POST. REF.	DEBIT	CREDIT	BALANCE DEBIT	BALANCE CREDIT

GENERAL LEDGER

ACCOUNT Brian Ford, Capital — ACCOUNT NO. 310

DATE		ITEM	POST. REF.	DEBIT	CREDIT	BALANCE DEBIT	BALANCE CREDIT

ACCOUNT Brian Ford, Drawing — ACCOUNT NO. 320

DATE		ITEM	POST. REF.	DEBIT	CREDIT	BALANCE DEBIT	BALANCE CREDIT

ACCOUNT Sales — ACCOUNT NO. 410

DATE		ITEM	POST. REF.	DEBIT	CREDIT	BALANCE DEBIT	BALANCE CREDIT

ACCOUNT Advertising Expense — ACCOUNT NO. 510

DATE		ITEM	POST. REF.	DEBIT	CREDIT	BALANCE DEBIT	BALANCE CREDIT

Name ______________________ Date ____________ Class ____________

4-M MASTERY PROBLEM (concluded)

GENERAL LEDGER

ACCOUNT Miscellaneous Expense ACCOUNT NO. 520

DATE		ITEM	POST. REF.	DEBIT	CREDIT	BALANCE DEBIT	BALANCE CREDIT

ACCOUNT Rent Expense ACCOUNT NO. 530

DATE		ITEM	POST. REF.	DEBIT	CREDIT	BALANCE DEBIT	BALANCE CREDIT

ACCOUNT Utilities Expense ACCOUNT NO. 540

DATE		ITEM	POST. REF.	DEBIT	CREDIT	BALANCE DEBIT	BALANCE CREDIT

ACCOUNT ACCOUNT NO.

DATE		ITEM	POST. REF.	DEBIT	CREDIT	BALANCE DEBIT	BALANCE CREDIT

4-S SOURCE DOCUMENTS PROBLEM (LO5, 6), p. 118

Journalizing transactions and posting to a general ledger

Receipt No. 1
Date Sept. 2, 20--
From Darlene Steffens
For Investment

$ 3,500 00

Receipt No. 1 Form 1
Date September 2 20--
Rec'd from Darlene Steffens
For Investment
Thirty-five hundred and no/100 Dollars
Amount $ 3,500 00
Darlene Steffens
Received by

No. 1 Form 2
Date Sept. 3 20-- $ 500.00
To Ready Rental Agency
For September rent

BALANCE BROUGHT FORWARD		0	00
AMOUNT DEPOSITED	9 2 20-- (Date)	3,500	00
SUBTOTAL		3,500	00
AMOUNT THIS CHECK		500	00
BALANCE CARRIED FORWARD		3,000	00

No. 1 Form 3
MEMORANDUM

Bought supplies on account from Atlas Supplies, $650.00

Signed: Darlene Steffens Date: September 6, 20--

4-S SOURCE DOCUMENTS PROBLEM (continued)

No. 2 Form 4

Date Sept. 7 20-- $ 60.00

To Connect Telephone Company

For Telephone bill

BALANCE BROUGHT FORWARD	3,000	00
AMOUNT DEPOSITED (Date)		
SUBTOTAL	3,000	00
AMOUNT THIS CHECK	60	00
BALANCE CARRIED FORWARD	2,940	00

Form 5

Sept. 7, 20--
T7

```
  0.00*
100.00+
300.00+
400.00*
```

Form 6

Darlene's Music Studio
2356 Pacific Blvd. S.
Albany, OR 97321-7726

SOLD TO: K. Hrbek
3088 Pine Street
Albany, OR 97321-4456

No. 1

Date 9/10/--

Terms 30 days

DESCRIPTION	Amount
Guitar lessons	$ 325.00
Total	$ 325.00

No. 3 Form 7

Date Sept. 11 20-- $ 490.00

To Arneson Insurance Agency

For Insurance

BALANCE BROUGHT FORWARD	2,940	00
AMOUNT DEPOSITED 9 7 20-- (Date)	400	00
SUBTOTAL	3,340	00
AMOUNT THIS CHECK	490	00
BALANCE CARRIED FORWARD	2,850	00

Form 8

Sept. 14, 20--
T14

```
  0.00*
175.00+
375.00+
550.00*
```

No. 4 Form 9

Date Sept. 16 20-- $ 163.00

To Sun Newspaper

For Advertising

BALANCE BROUGHT FORWARD		2,850 00
AMOUNT DEPOSITED	9 14 20-- (Date)	550 00
SUBTOTAL		3,400 00
AMOUNT THIS CHECK		163 00
BALANCE CARRIED FORWARD		3,237 00

Form 10

0.00*

Sept. 21, 20--
T21

215.00+
210.00+
425.00*

No. 5 Form 11

Date Sept. 23 20-- $ 500.00

To Atlas Supplies

For On account

BALANCE BROUGHT FORWARD		3,237 00
AMOUNT DEPOSITED	9 21 20-- (Date)	425 00
SUBTOTAL		3,662 00
AMOUNT THIS CHECK		500 00
BALANCE CARRIED FORWARD		3,162 00

Receipt No. 2

Date Sept. 24, 20--

From K. Hrbek

For On account

$ 213 00

Receipt No. 2 Form 12

Date September 24 20--

Rec'd from K. Hrbek

For On account

Two hundred thirteen and no/100 Dollars

Amount $ 213 00

CHF

Received by

4-S SOURCE DOCUMENTS PROBLEM (continued)

No. 6 Form 13

Date Sept. 26 20-- $ 300.00

To Atlas Supplies

For Supplies

BALANCE BROUGHT FORWARD				3,162	00
AMOUNT DEPOSITED	9	24	20--	213	00
		Date			
SUBTOTAL				3,375	00
AMOUNT THIS CHECK				300	00
BALANCE CARRIED FORWARD				3,075	00

Form 14

0.00*

Sept. 28, 20--
T28

250.00+
250.00*

No. 7 Form 15

Date Sept. 29 20-- $ 55.00

To City Electric

For Electric bill

BALANCE BROUGHT FORWARD				3,075	00
AMOUNT DEPOSITED	9	28	20--	250	00
		Date			
SUBTOTAL				3,325	00
AMOUNT THIS CHECK				55	00
BALANCE CARRIED FORWARD				3,270	00

Darlene's Music Studio
2356 Pacific Blvd. S.
Albany, OR 97321-7726

Form 16

SOLD TO: K. Hrbek
3088 Pine Street
Albany, OR 97321-4456

No. 2

Date **9/29/--**
Terms **30 days**

DESCRIPTION	Amount
Guitar lessons	***$ 240.00***
Total	***$ 240.00***

Form *17*

0.00*

Sept. 30, 20--
T30

125.00+
225.00+
350.00*

No. 7 Form *18*

Date *Sept. 30* 20-- $ *500.00*

To *Darlene Steffens*

For *Withdrawal of equity*

BALANCE BROUGHT FORWARD				*3,270*	*00*
AMOUNT DEPOSITED	*9*	*30*	*20--*	*350*	*00*
SUBTOTAL	Date			*3,620*	*00*
AMOUNT THIS CHECK				*500*	*00*
BALANCE CARRIED FORWARD				*3,120*	*00*

No. 8 Form *19*

Date 20-- $

To

For

BALANCE BROUGHT FORWARD			*3,120*	*00*
AMOUNT DEPOSITED				
SUBTOTAL	Date			
AMOUNT THIS CHECK				
BALANCE CARRIED FORWARD				

Name ______________ Date ______________ Class ______________

4-S SOURCE DOCUMENTS PROBLEM (continued)

JOURNAL

PAGE

	DATE	ACCOUNT TITLE	DOC. NO.	POST. REF.	1 GENERAL DEBIT	2 GENERAL CREDIT	3 SALES CREDIT	4 CASH DEBIT	5 CASH CREDIT	
1										1
2										2
3										3
4										4
5										5
6										6
7										7
8										8
9										9
10										10
11										11
12										12
13										13
14										14
15										15
16										16
17										17
18										18
19										19
20										20
21										21
22										22

Prove the journal:

Column	*Debit Column Totals*	*Credit Column Totals*
General		
Sales		
Cash		
Totals		

Prove cash:

Cash on hand at the beginning of the month . . . .
+ Total cash received during the month . . . . ______
Total cash . . . .
– Total cash paid during the month . . . . ______
Cash balance at the end of the month . . . . ______
Checkbook balance on the next unused check stub . . . . ______

GENERAL LEDGER

ACCOUNT Cash ACCOUNT NO. 110

DATE		ITEM	POST. REF.	DEBIT	CREDIT	BALANCE DEBIT	BALANCE CREDIT

ACCOUNT Accounts Receivable—K. Hrbek ACCOUNT NO. 120

DATE		ITEM	POST. REF.	DEBIT	CREDIT	BALANCE DEBIT	BALANCE CREDIT

ACCOUNT Supplies ACCOUNT NO. 130

DATE		ITEM	POST. REF.	DEBIT	CREDIT	BALANCE DEBIT	BALANCE CREDIT

ACCOUNT Prepaid Insurance ACCOUNT NO. 140

DATE		ITEM	POST. REF.	DEBIT	CREDIT	BALANCE DEBIT	BALANCE CREDIT

Name ______ Date ______ Class ______

4-S SOURCE DOCUMENTS PROBLEM (continued)

GENERAL LEDGER

ACCOUNT Accounts Payable—Atlas Supplies ACCOUNT NO. 210

DATE		ITEM	POST. REF.	DEBIT	CREDIT	BALANCE	
						DEBIT	CREDIT

ACCOUNT Darlene Steffens, Capital ACCOUNT NO. 310

DATE		ITEM	POST. REF.	DEBIT	CREDIT	BALANCE	
						DEBIT	CREDIT

ACCOUNT Darlene Steffens, Drawing ACCOUNT NO. 320

DATE		ITEM	POST. REF.	DEBIT	CREDIT	BALANCE	
						DEBIT	CREDIT

ACCOUNT Sales ACCOUNT NO. 410

DATE		ITEM	POST. REF.	DEBIT	CREDIT	BALANCE	
						DEBIT	CREDIT

4-S SOURCE DOCUMENTS PROBLEM (concluded)

GENERAL LEDGER

ACCOUNT Advertising Expense ACCOUNT NO. 510

DATE		ITEM	POST. REF.	DEBIT	CREDIT	BALANCE DEBIT	BALANCE CREDIT

ACCOUNT Rent Expense ACCOUNT NO. 520

DATE		ITEM	POST. REF.	DEBIT	CREDIT	BALANCE DEBIT	BALANCE CREDIT

ACCOUNT Utilities Expense ACCOUNT NO. 530

DATE		ITEM	POST. REF.	DEBIT	CREDIT	BALANCE DEBIT	BALANCE CREDIT

ACCOUNT ACCOUNT NO.

DATE		ITEM	POST. REF.	DEBIT	CREDIT	BALANCE DEBIT	BALANCE CREDIT

4-C CHALLENGE PROBLEM (LO5, 6), p. 119

Posting using a variation of the five-column journal

JOURNAL PAGE 5

	1 DEBIT CASH	2 DEBIT GENERAL	DATE		ACCOUNT TITLE	DOC. NO.	POST. REF.	3 CREDIT GENERAL	4 CREDIT SALES	5 CREDIT CASH	
1	6,000.00		20-- May	1	Lian Liu, Capital	R1		6,000.00			1
2		425.00		3	Rent Expense	C1				425.00	2
3		10.00		5	Miscellaneous Expense	C2				10.00	3
4		500.00		9	Accts. Rec.—Janna Spear	S1			500.00		4
5		800.00		11	Supplies	C3				800.00	5
6	900.00			13	✔	T13	✔		900.00		6
7		400.00		16	Supplies	M1					7
8					Accts. Pay.—Dollar Smart			400.00			8
9		300.00		18	Accts. Pay.—Dollar Smart	C4				300.00	9
10		120.00		19	Utilities Expense	C5				120.00	10
11	2,200.00			20	✔	T20	✔		2,200.00		11
12		100.00		23	Advertising Expense	C6				100.00	12
13		300.00		23	Supplies	C7				300.00	13
14		200.00		27	Supplies	C8				200.00	14
15	3,660.00			27	✔	T27	✔		3,660.00		15
16		2,800.00		30	Lian Liu, Drawing	C9				2,800.00	16
17	820.00			31	✔	T31	✔		820.00		17
18	13,580.00	5,955.00		31	Totals			6,400.00	8,080.00	5,055.00	18
19		(✔)						(✔)			19
20											20
21											21
22											22
23											23

GENERAL LEDGER

ACCOUNT Cash ACCOUNT NO. 110

DATE		ITEM	POST. REF.	DEBIT	CREDIT	BALANCE	
						DEBIT	CREDIT

ACCOUNT Accounts Receivable—Janna Spear ACCOUNT NO. 120

DATE		ITEM	POST. REF.	DEBIT	CREDIT	BALANCE	
						DEBIT	CREDIT

ACCOUNT Supplies ACCOUNT NO. 130

DATE		ITEM	POST. REF.	DEBIT	CREDIT	BALANCE	
						DEBIT	CREDIT

ACCOUNT Accounts Payable—Dollar Smart ACCOUNT NO. 210

DATE		ITEM	POST. REF.	DEBIT	CREDIT	BALANCE	
						DEBIT	CREDIT

ACCOUNT Lian Liu, Capital ACCOUNT NO. 310

DATE		ITEM	POST. REF.	DEBIT	CREDIT	BALANCE	
						DEBIT	CREDIT

Name ______________________ Date ______________ Class ______________

4-C CHALLENGE PROBLEM (concluded)

GENERAL LEDGER

ACCOUNT Lian Liu, Drawing ACCOUNT NO. 320

DATE		ITEM	POST. REF.	DEBIT	CREDIT	BALANCE	
						DEBIT	CREDIT

ACCOUNT Sales ACCOUNT NO. 410

DATE		ITEM	POST. REF.	DEBIT	CREDIT	BALANCE	
						DEBIT	CREDIT

ACCOUNT Advertising Expense ACCOUNT NO. 510

DATE		ITEM	POST. REF.	DEBIT	CREDIT	BALANCE	
						DEBIT	CREDIT

ACCOUNT Miscellaneous Expense ACCOUNT NO. 520

DATE		ITEM	POST. REF.	DEBIT	CREDIT	BALANCE	
						DEBIT	CREDIT

ACCOUNT Rent Expense ACCOUNT NO. 530

DATE		ITEM	POST. REF.	DEBIT	CREDIT	BALANCE	
						DEBIT	CREDIT

ACCOUNT Utilities Expense ACCOUNT NO. 540

DATE		ITEM	POST. REF.	DEBIT	CREDIT	BALANCE	
						DEBIT	CREDIT

Study Guide 5

Name	Perfect Score	Your Score
Identifying Accounting Terms	18 Pts.	
Analyzing Transactions in a Cash Control System	12 Pts.	
Identifying Accounting Concepts and Practices	20 Pts.	
Total	50 Pts.	

Part One—Identifying Accounting Terms

Directions: Select the one term in Column I that best fits each definition in Column II. Print the letter identifying your choice in the Answers column.

Column I	Column II	Answers
A. bank statement	**1.** A bank account from which payments can be ordered by a depositor. (p. 123)	**1.** ______
B. blank endorsement	**2.** A bank form which lists the checks, currency, and coins an account holder is adding to the bank account. (p. 123)	**2.** ______
C. canceled check	**3.** A signature or stamp on the back of a check, transferring ownership. (p. 124)	**3.** ______
D. cash over	**4.** An endorsement consisting only of the endorser's signature. (p. 124)	**4.** ______
E. cash short	**5.** An endorsement indicating a new owner of a check. (p. 124)	**5.** ______
F. checking account	**6.** An endorsement restricting further transfer of a check's ownership. (p. 125)	**6.** ______
G. debit card	**7.** A check with a future date on it. (p. 126)	**7.** ______
H. deposit slip	**8.** A check that cannot be processed because the maker has made it invalid. (p. 127)	**8.** ______
I. dishonored check	**9.** A report of deposits, withdrawals, and bank balances sent to a depositor by a bank. (p. 129)	**9.** ______
J. electronic funds transfer	**10.** A check which has been paid by the bank. (p. 129)	**10.** ______
K. endorsement	**11.** A check that a bank refuses to pay. (p. 135)	**11.** ______
L. NSF check	**12.** A check dishonored by the bank because of insufficient funds in the account of the maker of the check. (p. 135)	**12.** ______
M. petty cash	**13.** A computerized cash payments system that transfers funds without the use of checks, currency, or other paper documents. (p. 137)	**13.** ______
N. petty cash slip	**14.** A bank card that automatically deducts the amount of a purchase from the checking account of the cardholder. (p. 138)	**14.** ______
O. postdated check	**15.** An amount of cash kept on hand and used for making small payments. (p. 140)	**15.** ______
P. restrictive endorsement	**16.** A form showing proof of a petty cash payment. (p. 141)	**16.** ______
Q. special endorsement	**17.** A petty cash on hand amount that is less than a recorded amount. (p. 143)	**17.** ______
R. voided check	**18.** A petty cash on hand amount that is more than a recorded amount. (p. 143)	**18.** ______

Part Two—Analyzing Transactions in a Cash Control System

Directions: Analyze each of the following transactions into debit and credit parts. Print the letter identifying your choice in the proper Answers columns.

Account Titles

A. Cash
B. Petty Cash
C. Accounts Receivable—J. Erlandson
D. Supplies
E. Accounts Payable—Fargo Supplies
F. Cash Short and Over
G. Miscellaneous Expense

	Answers Debit	Answers Credit
1–2. Received bank statement showing bank service charge. (p. 133)	**1.** ______	**2.** ______
3–4. Received notice from the bank of a dishonored check from J. Erlandson. (p. 136)	**3.** ______	**4.** ______
5–6. Paid cash on account to Fargo Supplies using EFT. (p. 137)	**5.** ______	**6.** ______
7–8. Purchased supplies using a debit card. (p. 138)	**7.** ______	**8.** ______
9–10. Paid cash to establish a petty cash fund. (p. 140)	**9.** ______	**10.** ______
11–12. Paid cash to replenish a petty cash fund: $50.00; supplies, $35.00; miscellaneous expense, $14.00; cash short, $1.00. (p. 144)	**11.** ______	**12.** ______

Part Three—Identifying Accounting Concepts and Practices

Directions: Place a *T* for True or *F* for False in the Answers column to show whether each of the following statements is true or false.

Answers

1. Because cash transactions occur more frequently than other transactions, there is more chance for making recording errors affecting cash. (p. 122) — **1.** ______
2. When a deposit is made in a bank account, the bank issues a check. (p. 123) — **2.** ______
3. There are three types of endorsements commonly used: blank, special, and restrictive. (p. 124) — **3.** ______
4. A check with a blank endorsement can be cashed by anyone who has possession of the check. (p. 124) — **4.** ______
5. When writing a check, the first step is to prepare the check. (p. 126) — **5.** ______
6. Most banks do not look at the date the check is written and will withdraw money from the depositor's account anytime. (p. 126) — **6.** ______
7. The amount of a check is written twice on each check. (p. 126) — **7.** ______
8. A check that contains minor errors can be corrected neatly and initialed. (p. 127) — **8.** ______
9. An important aspect of cash control is verifying that the information on a bank statement and a checkbook are in agreement. (p. 130) — **9.** ______
10. An outstanding check is one that has not yet been issued. (p. 130) — **10.** ______
11. Banks deduct service charges from customers' checking accounts without requiring customers to write a check for the amount. (p. 132) — **11.** ______
12. Not only do banks charge a fee for handling a dishonored check, but they also deduct the amount of the check from the account as well. (p. 135) — **12.** ______
13. The journal entry for a payment on account using electronic funds transfer is exactly the same as when the payment is made by debit card. (p. 137) — **13.** ______
14. The source document for an electronic funds transfer is a check number. (p. 137) — **14.** ______
15. The source document for a debit card purchase is a memorandum. (p. 138) — **15.** ______
16. The purpose of a petty cash fund is to make small cash payments without writing checks. (p. 140) — **16.** ______
17. Businesses use petty cash when writing a check is not time or cost effective. (p. 140) — **17.** ______
18. A petty cash report is completed at the end of each business day. (p. 143) — **18.** ______
19. A memorandum is the source document for the entry to record replenishing the petty cash fund. (p. 144) — **19.** ______
20. When the petty cash fund is replenished, the balance of the petty cash account increases. (p. 145) — **20.** ______

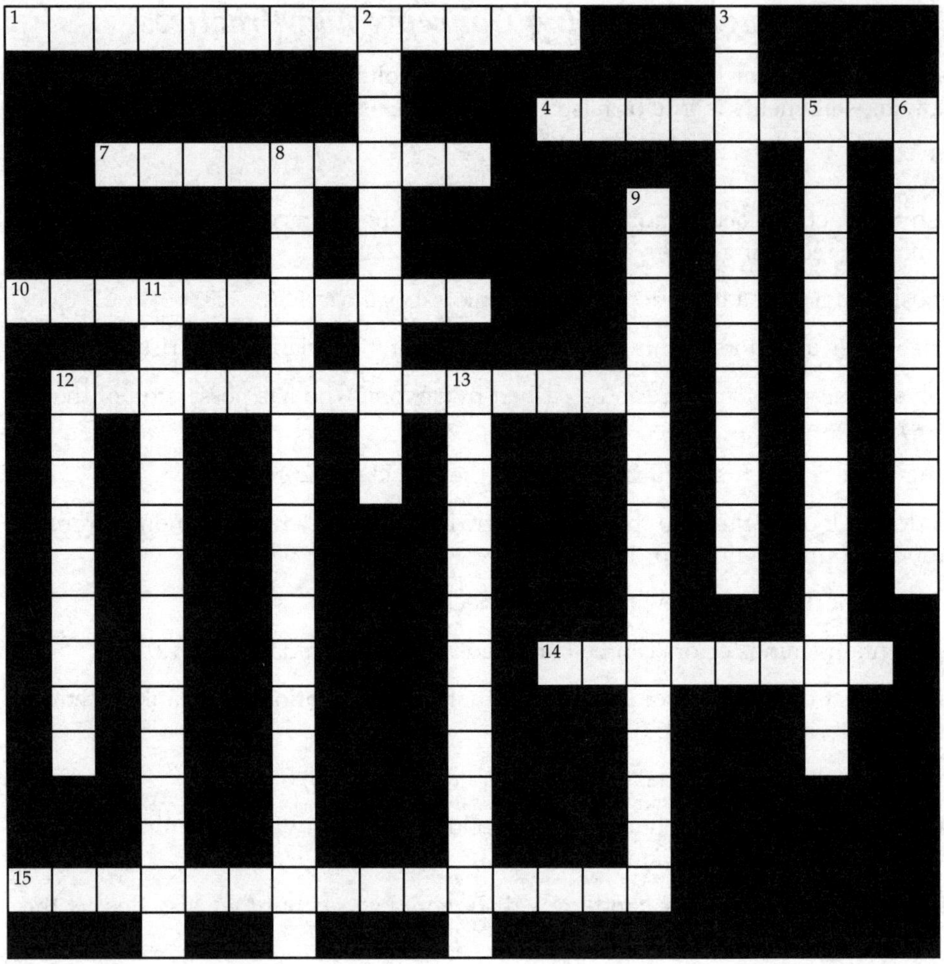

Across

1. A report of deposits, withdrawals, and bank balances sent to a depositor by a bank.
4. A bank card that automatically deducts the amount of a purchase from the checking account of the cardholder.
7. A petty cash on hand amount that is less than the recorded amount.
10. A check that cannot be processed because the maker has made it invalid.
12. A check with a future date on it.
14. A petty cash on hand amount that is more than the recorded amount.
15. A bank account from which payments can be ordered by a depositor.

Down

2. A signature or stamp on the back of a check transferring ownership.
3. A form showing proof of a petty cash payment.
5. An accounting worker who processes routine details about accounting transactions.
6. A bank form which lists the checks, currency, and coins an account holder is adding to a bank account.
8. An endorsement indicating a new owner of a check.
9. An endorsement consisting only of the endorser's signature.
11. A check that a bank refuses to pay.
12. An amount of cash kept on hand and used for making small payments.
13. A check which has been paid by the bank.

Name ____________ Date ________ Class ________

5-1 WORK TOGETHER, p. 128

Endorsing and writing checks

1. a.

ENDORSE HERE
X

DO NOT WRITE, STAMP, OR SIGN BELOW THIS LINE
RESERVED FOR FINANCIAL INSTITUTION USE

b.

ENDORSE HERE
X

DO NOT WRITE, STAMP, OR SIGN BELOW THIS LINE
RESERVED FOR FINANCIAL INSTITUTION USE

c.

ENDORSE HERE
X

DO NOT WRITE, STAMP, OR SIGN BELOW THIS LINE
RESERVED FOR FINANCIAL INSTITUTION USE

2., 3., 4a.

NO. 151 $ ________
Date: ________ 20__
To: ________
For: ________

BALANCE BROUGHT FORWARD		
AMOUNT DEPOSITED (Date)		
SUBTOTAL		
OTHER:		
SUBTOTAL		
AMOUNT THIS CHECK		
BALANCE CARRIED FORWARD		

GRANTSBURG ACCOUNTING NO. **151** 93-552/920
1198 Rose Lane
New Brighton, MN 55112 ________ 20 ____

PAY TO THE ORDER OF ________ $ ________

________ DOLLARS

Northstar Federal Bank
Minneapolis, MN

FOR ________ ________

⑆092005529⑆ 70796631278⑈ 151

4b.

NO. 152 $ ________
Date: ________ 20__
To: ________
For: ________

BALANCE BROUGHT FORWARD		
AMOUNT DEPOSITED (Date)		
SUBTOTAL		
OTHER:		
SUBTOTAL		
AMOUNT THIS CHECK		
BALANCE CARRIED FORWARD		

GRANTSBURG ACCOUNTING NO. **152** 93-552/920
1198 Rose Lane
New Brighton, MN 55112 ________ 20 ____

PAY TO THE ORDER OF ________ $ ________

________ DOLLARS

Northstar Federal Bank
Minneapolis, MN

FOR ________ ________

⑆092005529⑆ 70796631278⑈ 152

5-1 ON YOUR OWN, p. 128

Endorsing and writing checks

1. a.

ENDORSE HERE
X

DO NOT WRITE, STAMP, OR SIGN BELOW THIS LINE
RESERVED FOR FINANCIAL INSTITUTION USE

b.

ENDORSE HERE
X

DO NOT WRITE, STAMP, OR SIGN BELOW THIS LINE
RESERVED FOR FINANCIAL INSTITUTION USE

2., 3., 4a.

NO. 317 $

Date: 20

To:

For:

BALANCE BROUGHT FORWARD		
AMOUNT DEPOSITED (Date)		
SUBTOTAL		
OTHER:		
SUBTOTAL		
AMOUNT THIS CHECK		
BALANCE CARRIED FORWARD		

MILLTOWN HAIR CARE
7921 Main Street
Milltown, WI 54825

NO. **317**

93-109/730

20

PAY TO THE ORDER OF $

DOLLARS

Wisconsin National Bank
Milltown, WI 54825

FOR

⑆073008219⑆ 6079645112780⑈ 317

4b.

NO. 318 $

Date: 20

To:

For:

BALANCE BROUGHT FORWARD		
AMOUNT DEPOSITED (Date)		
SUBTOTAL		
OTHER:		
SUBTOTAL		
AMOUNT THIS CHECK		
BALANCE CARRIED FORWARD		

MILLTOWN HAIR CARE
7921 Main Street
Milltown, WI 54825

NO. **318**

93-109/730

20

PAY TO THE ORDER OF $

DOLLARS

Wisconsin National Bank
Milltown, WI 54825

FOR

⑆073008219⑆ 6079645112780⑈ 318

Name ______________________ Date ____________ Class ____________

5-2 WORK TOGETHER, p. 134

Reconciling a bank statement and recording a bank service charge

1.

RECONCILIATION OF BANK STATEMENT

____
(Date)

Balance On Check Stub No. ___ .... $

DEDUCT BANK CHARGES:

Description	Amount
	$

Total bank charges ▶

Adjusted Check Stub Balance .... $

Balance On Bank Statement .... $

ADD OUTSTANDING DEPOSITS:

Date	Amount
	$

Total outstanding deposits ▶

SUBTOTAL .... $

DEDUCT OUTSTANDING CHECKS:

Ck. No.	Amount	Ck. No.	Amount

Total outstanding checks ▶

Adjusted Bank Balance .... $

2.

NO. **309** $ __________

Date: ____________________ 20__

To: ____________________

____

For: ____________________

____

BALANCE BROUGHT FORWARD		
AMOUNT DEPOSITED (Date)		
SUBTOTAL		
OTHER:		
____________		
____________		
SUBTOTAL		
AMOUNT THIS CHECK		
BALANCE CARRIED FORWARD		

3.

JOURNAL PAGE

	DATE		ACCOUNT TITLE	DOC. NO.	POST. REF.	1 GENERAL DEBIT	2 GENERAL CREDIT	3 SALES CREDIT	4 CASH DEBIT	5 CASH CREDIT	
14											14
15											15

5-2 ON YOUR OWN, p. 134

Reconciling a bank statement and recording a bank service charge

1.

RECONCILIATION OF BANK STATEMENT

_______________ (Date)

Balance On Check Stub No. ___ .... $

DEDUCT BANK CHARGES:

Description	Amount
	$

Total bank charges ▶

Adjusted Check Stub Balance .... $

Balance On Bank Statement .... $

ADD OUTSTANDING DEPOSITS:

Date	Amount
	$

Total outstanding deposits ▶

SUBTOTAL .... $

DEDUCT OUTSTANDING CHECKS:

Ck. No.	Amount	Ck. No.	Amount

Total outstanding checks ▶

Adjusted Bank Balance .... $

2.

NO. **224** $ ____________

Date: ____________ 20__

To: ____________

For: ____________

BALANCE BROUGHT FORWARD	
AMOUNT DEPOSITED (Date)	
SUBTOTAL	
OTHER:	
SUBTOTAL	
AMOUNT THIS CHECK	
BALANCE CARRIED FORWARD	

3.

JOURNAL

PAGE

	DATE	ACCOUNT TITLE	DOC. NO.	POST. REF.	1 GENERAL DEBIT	2 GENERAL CREDIT	3 SALES CREDIT	4 CASH DEBIT	5 CASH CREDIT	
20										20
21										21

Name ______________________ Date ____________ Class ____________

5-3 WORK TOGETHER, p. 139

Recording dishonored checks, electronic funds transfers, and debit card purchases

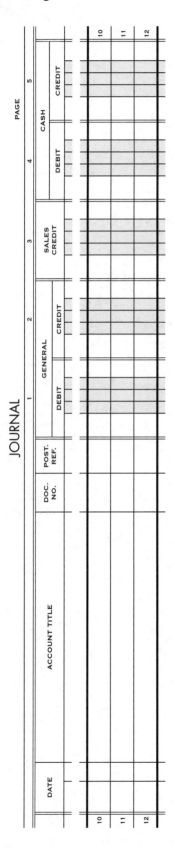

JOURNAL PAGE

	DATE	ACCOUNT TITLE	DOC. NO.	POST. REF.	1 GENERAL DEBIT	2 GENERAL CREDIT	3 SALES CREDIT	4 CASH DEBIT	5 CASH CREDIT	
10										10
11										11
12										12

5-3 ON YOUR OWN, p. 139

Recording dishonored checks, electronic funds transfers, and debit card purchases

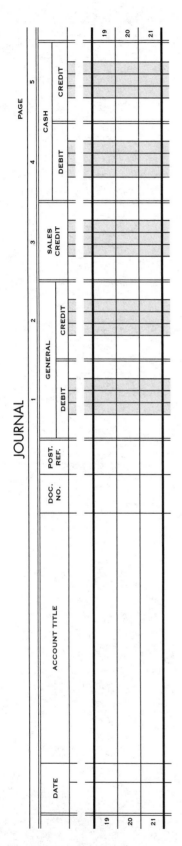

JOURNAL PAGE

					1	2	3	4	5	
					GENERAL		SALES	CASH		
	DATE	ACCOUNT TITLE	DOC. NO.	POST. REF.	DEBIT	CREDIT	CREDIT	DEBIT	CREDIT	
19										19
20										20
21										21

Name ______ Date ______ Class ______

5-4 WORK TOGETHER, p. 146

Establishing and replenishing a petty cash fund

1.

PETTY CASH REPORT

Date: ______ Custodian: ______

Explanation		Reconciliation	Replenish Amount
Fund Total			
Payments:			
Less: Total payments			→
Equals: Recorded amount on hand			
Less: Actual amount on hand			
Equals: Cash short (over)			→
Amount to Replenish			

2.

JOURNAL PAGE

	DATE		ACCOUNT TITLE	DOC. NO.	POST. REF.	1 GENERAL DEBIT	2 GENERAL CREDIT	3 SALES CREDIT	4 CASH DEBIT	5 CASH CREDIT	
1											1
31											31
32											32
33											33

5-4 ON YOUR OWN, p. 146

Establishing and replenishing a petty cash fund

1.

PETTY CASH REPORT

Date: ____________ **Custodian:** ____________

Explanation			Reconciliation	Replenish Amount
Fund Total				
Payments:				
Less:	Total payments			→
Equals:	Recorded amount on hand			
Less:	Actual amount on hand			
Equals:	Cash short (over)			→
Amount to Replenish				

2.

JOURNAL PAGE

	DATE		ACCOUNT TITLE	DOC. NO.	POST. REF.	1 GENERAL DEBIT	2 GENERAL CREDIT	3 SALES CREDIT	4 CASH DEBIT	5 CASH CREDIT	
1											1
28											28
29											29
30											30

Name ______________________ Date ______________ Class ______________

5-1 APPLICATION PROBLEM (LO1, 2, 3), p. 149

Endorsing and writing checks

1. a.

ENDORSE HERE

X

DO NOT WRITE, STAMP, OR SIGN BELOW THIS LINE
RESERVED FOR FINANCIAL INSTITUTION USE

b.

ENDORSE HERE

X

DO NOT WRITE, STAMP, OR SIGN BELOW THIS LINE
RESERVED FOR FINANCIAL INSTITUTION USE

c.

ENDORSE HERE

X

DO NOT WRITE, STAMP, OR SIGN BELOW THIS LINE
RESERVED FOR FINANCIAL INSTITUTION USE

2., 3., 4a.

NO. 410 $ ____________
Date: ____________ 20__
To: ____________
For: ____________

BALANCE BROUGHT FORWARD		
AMOUNT DEPOSITED (Date)		
SUBTOTAL		
OTHER:		
SUBTOTAL		
AMOUNT THIS CHECK		
BALANCE CARRIED FORWARD		

Wash N' Dry
2525 Niles Lane
Centuria, WI 54824

NO. **410** 17-432/965

____________ 20 ______

PAY TO THE ORDER OF ____________ $ ______

____________ DOLLARS

Barron County Bank
Balsam Lake, WI

FOR ____________ ____________

⑆096575527⑆ 7015966317726⑈ 410

4b.

NO. 411 $ ____________
Date: ____________ 20__
To: ____________
For: ____________

BALANCE BROUGHT FORWARD		
AMOUNT DEPOSITED (Date)		
SUBTOTAL		
OTHER:		
SUBTOTAL		
AMOUNT THIS CHECK		
BALANCE CARRIED FORWARD		

Wash N' Dry
2525 Niles Lane
Centuria, WI 54824

NO. **411** 17-432/965

____________ 20 ______

PAY TO THE ORDER OF ____________ $ ______

____________ DOLLARS

Barron County Bank
Balsam Lake, WI

FOR ____________ ____________

⑆096575527⑆ 7015966317726⑈ 411

4c.

NO. 412 $ ____________
Date: ____________ 20__
To: ____________
For: ____________

BALANCE BROUGHT FORWARD		
AMOUNT DEPOSITED (Date)		
SUBTOTAL		
OTHER:		
SUBTOTAL		
AMOUNT THIS CHECK		
BALANCE CARRIED FORWARD		

Wash N' Dry
2525 Niles Lane
Centuria, WI 54824

NO. **412** 17-432/965

____________ 20 ______

PAY TO THE ORDER OF ____________ $ ______

____________ DOLLARS

Barron County Bank
Balsam Lake, WI

FOR ____________ ____________

⑆096575527⑆ 7015966317726⑈ 412

Name ______________________ Date ______________ Class ______________

5-2 APPLICATION PROBLEM (LO4, 5), p. 149

Reconciling a bank statement and recording a bank service charge

1.

RECONCILIATION OF BANK STATEMENT

____
(Date)

Balance On Check Stub No. ___ .... $

DEDUCT BANK CHARGES:

Description	Amount
	$

Total bank charges ▶

Adjusted Check Stub Balance .... $

Balance On Bank Statement .... $

ADD OUTSTANDING DEPOSITS:

Date	Amount
	$

Total outstanding deposits ▶

SUBTOTAL .... $

DEDUCT OUTSTANDING CHECKS:

Ck. No.	Amount	Ck. No.	Amount

Total outstanding checks ▶

Adjusted Bank Balance .... $

2.

NO. **477** $ ______________

Date: ______________________ 20__

To: ______________________

____

For: ______________________

____

BALANCE BROUGHT FORWARD	
AMOUNT DEPOSITED (Date)	
SUBTOTAL	
OTHER:	
______________	
______________	
SUBTOTAL	
AMOUNT THIS CHECK	
BALANCE CARRIED FORWARD	

3.

JOURNAL PAGE

	DATE	ACCOUNT TITLE	DOC. NO.	POST. REF.	1 GENERAL DEBIT	2 GENERAL CREDIT	3 SALES CREDIT	4 CASH DEBIT	5 CASH CREDIT	
20										20
21										21

5-3 APPLICATION PROBLEM (LO6, 7, 8), p. 150

Recording dishonored checks, electronic funds transfers, and debit card purchases

JOURNAL

PAGE

	DATE	ACCOUNT TITLE	DOC. NO.	POST. REF.	1 GENERAL DEBIT	2 GENERAL CREDIT	3 SALES CREDIT	4 CASH DEBIT	5 CASH CREDIT	
10										10
11										11
12										12

Name ____________ Date ________ Class ________

5-4 APPLICATION PROBLEM (LO9, 10, 11), p. 150

Establishing and replenishing a petty cash fund

1.

PETTY CASH REPORT

Date: ____________ **Custodian:** ____________

Explanation		Reconciliation	Replenish Amount
Fund Total			
Payments:			
Less: Total payments			→
Equals: Recorded amount on hand			
Less: Actual amount on hand			
Equals: Cash short (over)			→
Amount to Replenish			

2.

JOURNAL PAGE

	DATE	ACCOUNT TITLE	DOC. NO.	POST. REF.	1 GENERAL DEBIT	2 GENERAL CREDIT	3 SALES CREDIT	4 CASH DEBIT	5 CASH CREDIT	
3										3
28										28
29										29
30										30

5-M MASTERY PROBLEM (LO4, 5, 6, 9, 10, 11), p. 150

Reconciling a bank statement; journalizing a bank service charge, a dishonored check, and petty cash transactions

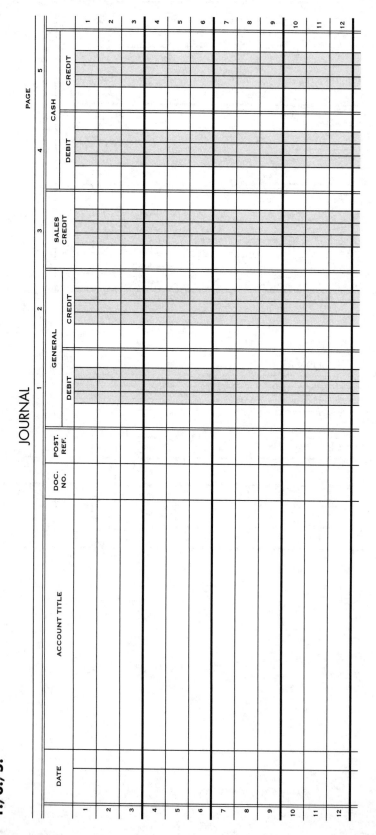

1., 3., 5.

JOURNAL PAGE

	DATE	ACCOUNT TITLE	DOC. NO.	POST. REF.	1 GENERAL DEBIT	2 GENERAL CREDIT	3 SALES CREDIT	4 CASH DEBIT	5 CASH CREDIT	
1										1
2										2
3										3
4										4
5										5
6										6
7										7
8										8
9										9
10										10
11										11
12										12

Name ________________________ Date ____________ Class ____________

5-M MASTERY PROBLEM (concluded)

2.

PETTY CASH REPORT

Date: ____________ **Custodian:** ____________

Explanation		Reconciliation	Replenish Amount
Fund Total			
Payments:			
Less: Total payments			→
Equals: Recorded amount on hand			
Less: Actual amount on hand			
Equals: Cash short (over)			→
Amount to Replenish			

4.

RECONCILIATION OF BANK STATEMENT

____
(Date)

Balance On Check Stub No. ____ .... $

DEDUCT BANK CHARGES:

Description	Amount
	$

Total bank charges

Adjusted Check Stub Balance .... $

Balance On Bank Statement .... $

ADD OUTSTANDING DEPOSITS:

Date	Amount
	$

Total outstanding deposits

SUBTOTAL .... $

DEDUCT OUTSTANDING CHECKS:

Ck. No.	Amount	Ck. No.	Amount

Total outstanding checks

Adjusted Bank Balance .... $

5-C CHALLENGE PROBLEM (LO4, 5, 6), p. 151

Reconciling a bank statement and recording a bank service charge and a dishonored check

1., 2.

Fidelity
NATIONAL BANK
Bonita Springs, FL 34135

STATEMENT OF ACCOUNT FOR
POOL CLEAN
75214 Bonita Beach Road
Bonita Springs, FL 34135

ACCOUNT NUMBER
8524655

STATEMENT DATE
July 28, 20 – –

BALANCE FROM PREVIOUS STATEMENT	NO. OF CHECKS	AMOUNT OF CHECKS	NO. OF DEPOSITS	AMOUNT OF DEPOSITS	SERVICE CHARGES	STATEMENT BALANCE
0.00	11	9,350.00	4	25,910.00	10.00	16,550.00

DATE	CHECK	AMOUNT	CHECK	AMOUNT	DEPOSITS	BALANCE
07/01/– –						0.00
07/01/– –					24,000.00	24,000.00
07/05/– –	251	3,154.00				20,846.00
07/08/– –	252	400.00			250.00	20,696.00
07/15/– –	254	500.00	256	270.00		19,926.00
07/15/– –	253	3,120.00	258	150.00	520.00	17,176.00
07/18/– –	255	410.00	259	196.00		16,570.00
07/18/– –	260	280.00				16,290.00
07/19/– –	257	500.00				15,790.00
07/25/– –					1,140.00	16,930.00
07/25/– –	262	370.00				16,560.00
07/27/– –	SC	10.00				16,550.00

PLEASE EXAMINE AT ONCE • IF NO ERRORS ARE REPORTED WITHIN 10 DAYS, THE ACCOUNT WILL BE CONSIDERED CORRECT. REFER ANY DISCREPANCY TO OUR ACCOUNTING DEPARTMENT IMMEDIATELY.

Pool Clean
75214 Bonita Beach Road
Bonita Springs, FL 34135
NO. 251 13-7552/965
July 1 20 – –
PAY TO THE ORDER OF Industrial Supplies $ 3,154.00

Pool Clean
75214 Bonita Beach Road
Bonita Springs, FL 34135
NO. 252 13-7552/965
July 5 20 – –
PAY TO THE ORDER OF LMC Property Management $ 400.00

Pool Clean
75214 Bonita Beach Road
Bonita Springs, FL 34135
NO. 253 13-7552/965
July 8 20 – –
PAY TO THE ORDER OF Aqua Supplies $ 3,120.00

Pool Clean
75214 Bonita Beach Road
Bonita Springs, FL 34135
NO. 254 13-7552/965
July 8 20 – –
PAY TO THE ORDER OF American Insurance Company $ 500.00

Pool Clean
75214 Bonita Beach Road
Bonita Springs, FL 34135
NO. 255 13-7552/965
July 10 20 – –
PAY TO THE ORDER OF Bonita Springs Electric Company $ 410.00

Pool Clean
75214 Bonita Beach Road
Bonita Springs, FL 34135
NO. 256 13-7552/965
July 10 20 – –
PAY TO THE ORDER OF Fort Myers Supplies $ 270.00
Two hundred seventy dollars and no/100 DOLLARS
Fidelity National Bank
Bonita Springs, FL
FOR Payment on account John Warner
⑆096575527⑆ 8524655⑈ 256

Pool Clean
75214 Bonita Beach Road
Bonita Springs, FL 34135
NO. 257 13-7552/965
July 11 20 – –
PAY TO THE ORDER OF Eduardo Gomez $ 500.00

Pool Clean
75214 Bonita Beach Road
Bonita Springs, FL 34135
NO. 258 13-7552/965
July 11 20 – –
PAY TO THE ORDER OF Century Telephone Company $ 150.00

Pool Clean
75214 Bonita Beach Road
Bonita Springs, FL 34135
NO. 259 13-7552/965
July 15 20 – –
PAY TO THE ORDER OF Sunshine Cleaning Company $ 196.00

Pool Clean
75214 Bonita Beach Road
Bonita Springs, FL 34135
NO. 260 13-7552/965
July 15 20 – –
PAY TO THE ORDER OF Tri-State Agency $ 280.00

Pool Clean
75214 Bonita Beach Road
Bonita Springs, FL 34135
NO. 262 13-7552/965
July 23 20 – –
PAY TO THE ORDER OF Harned Company $ 370.00
Three hundred seventy dollars and no/100 DOLLARS
Fidelity National Bank
Bonita Springs, FL
FOR Payment on account John Warner
⑆096575527⑆ 8524655⑈ 262

Name ______________________ Date ____________ Class ____________

5-C CHALLENGE PROBLEM (continued)

1., 2., 3.

NO. 251 $ 3,154.00
Date: July 1 20--
To: Industrial Supplies
For: Supplies

BALANCE BROUGHT FORWARD	0	00
AMOUNT DEPOSITED 07 01 -- (Date)	24,000	00
SUBTOTAL	24,000	00
OTHER:		
SUBTOTAL	24,000	00
AMOUNT THIS CHECK	3,154	00
BALANCE CARRIED FORWARD	20,846	00

NO. 252 $ 400.00
Date: July 5 20--
To: LMC Property Management
For: Rent

BALANCE BROUGHT FORWARD	20,846	00
AMOUNT DEPOSITED (Date)		
SUBTOTAL	20,846	00
OTHER:		
SUBTOTAL	20,846	00
AMOUNT THIS CHECK	400	00
BALANCE CARRIED FORWARD	20,446	00

NO. 253 $ 3,120.00
Date: July 8 20--
To: Aqua Supplies
For: Supplies

BALANCE BROUGHT FORWARD	20,446	00
AMOUNT DEPOSITED 07 08 -- (Date)	250	00
SUBTOTAL	20,696	00
OTHER:		
SUBTOTAL	20,696	00
AMOUNT THIS CHECK	3,120	00
BALANCE CARRIED FORWARD	17,576	00

NO. 254 $ 500.00
Date: July 8 20--
To: American Insurance Company
For: Insurance

BALANCE BROUGHT FORWARD	17,576	00
AMOUNT DEPOSITED (Date)		
SUBTOTAL	17,576	00
OTHER:		
SUBTOTAL	17,576	00
AMOUNT THIS CHECK	500	00
BALANCE CARRIED FORWARD	17,076	00

NO. 255 $ 410.00
Date: July 10 20--
To: Bonita Springs Electric Company
For: Utilities

BALANCE BROUGHT FORWARD	17,076	00
AMOUNT DEPOSITED (Date)		
SUBTOTAL	17,076	00
OTHER:		
SUBTOTAL	17,076	00
AMOUNT THIS CHECK	410	00
BALANCE CARRIED FORWARD	16,666	00

NO. 256 $ 270.00
Date: July 10 20--
To: Fort Myers Supplies
For: Payment on account

BALANCE BROUGHT FORWARD	16,666	00
AMOUNT DEPOSITED (Date)		
SUBTOTAL	16,666	00
OTHER:		
SUBTOTAL	16,666	00
AMOUNT THIS CHECK	270	00
BALANCE CARRIED FORWARD	16,396	00

NO. 257 $ 500.00
Date: July 11 20--
To: Eduardo Gomez
For: Owner's withdrawal

BALANCE BROUGHT FORWARD	16,396	00
AMOUNT DEPOSITED (Date)		
SUBTOTAL	16,396	00
OTHER:		
SUBTOTAL	16,396	00
AMOUNT THIS CHECK	500	00
BALANCE CARRIED FORWARD	15,896	00

NO. 258 $ 150.00
Date: July 11 20--
To: Century Telephone Company
For: Utilities

BALANCE BROUGHT FORWARD	15,896	00
AMOUNT DEPOSITED (Date)		
SUBTOTAL	15,896	00
OTHER:		
SUBTOTAL	15,896	00
AMOUNT THIS CHECK	150	00
BALANCE CARRIED FORWARD	15,746	00

NO. 259 $ 196.00
Date: July 15 20--
To: Sunshine Cleaning Company
For: Cleaning

BALANCE BROUGHT FORWARD	15,746	00
AMOUNT DEPOSITED (Date)		
SUBTOTAL	15,746	00
OTHER:		
SUBTOTAL	15,746	00
AMOUNT THIS CHECK	196	00
BALANCE CARRIED FORWARD	15,550	00

5-C CHALLENGE PROBLEM (continued)

1., 2., 3.

NO. **260** $ 280.00
Date: July 15 20--
To: Tri-State Agency
For: Miscellaneous

BALANCE BROUGHT FORWARD	15,550	00
AMOUNT DEPOSITED 07 15 -- (Date)	520	00
SUBTOTAL	16,070	00
OTHER:		
SUBTOTAL	16,070	00
AMOUNT THIS CHECK	280	00
BALANCE CARRIED FORWARD	15,790	00

NO. **261** $ 750.00
Date: July 22 20--
To: Naples Press
For: Advertising

BALANCE BROUGHT FORWARD	15,790	00
AMOUNT DEPOSITED (Date)		
SUBTOTAL	15,790	00
OTHER:		
SUBTOTAL	15,790	00
AMOUNT THIS CHECK	750	00
BALANCE CARRIED FORWARD	15,040	00

NO. **262** $ 370.00
Date: July 23 20--
To: Harned Company
For: Payment on account

BALANCE BROUGHT FORWARD	15,040	00
AMOUNT DEPOSITED 07 25 -- (Date)	1,140	00
SUBTOTAL	16,180	00
OTHER:		
SUBTOTAL	16,180	00
AMOUNT THIS CHECK	370	00
BALANCE CARRIED FORWARD	15,810	00

NO. **263** $ 34.00
Date: July 23 20--
To: Amy West
For: Miscellaneous

BALANCE BROUGHT FORWARD	15,810	00
AMOUNT DEPOSITED (Date)		
SUBTOTAL	15,810	00
OTHER:		
SUBTOTAL	15,810	00
AMOUNT THIS CHECK	34	00
BALANCE CARRIED FORWARD	15,776	00

NO. **264** $ 500.00
Date: July 28 20--
To: Eduardo Gomez
For: Owner's withdrawal

BALANCE BROUGHT FORWARD	15,776	00
AMOUNT DEPOSITED 07 28 -- (Date)	860	00
SUBTOTAL	16,636	00
OTHER:		
SUBTOTAL	16,636	00
AMOUNT THIS CHECK	500	00
BALANCE CARRIED FORWARD	16,136	00

4.

NO. **265** $
Date: 20
To:
For:

BALANCE BROUGHT FORWARD	16,136	00
AMOUNT DEPOSITED (Date)		
SUBTOTAL	16,136	00
OTHER:		
SUBTOTAL		
AMOUNT THIS CHECK		
BALANCE CARRIED FORWARD		

Name ______________________ Date ____________ Class ____________

5-C CHALLENGE PROBLEM (concluded)

2.

RECONCILIATION OF BANK STATEMENT

____
(Date)

Balance On Check Stub No. ___ .... $

DEDUCT BANK CHARGES:

Description	Amount
	$

Total bank charges ▶

Adjusted Check Stub Balance .... $

Balance On Bank Statement .... $

ADD OUTSTANDING DEPOSITS:

Date	Amount
	$

Total outstanding deposits ▶

SUBTOTAL .... $

DEDUCT OUTSTANDING CHECKS:

Ck. No.	Amount	Ck. No.	Amount

Total outstanding checks ▶

Adjusted Bank Balance .... $

3.

JOURNAL PAGE

	DATE	ACCOUNT TITLE	DOC. NO.	POST. REF.	1 GENERAL DEBIT	2 GENERAL CREDIT	3 SALES CREDIT	4 CASH DEBIT	5 CASH CREDIT	
1										1
2										2
3										3

Name ______________________ Date ____________ Class ____________

REINFORCEMENT ACTIVITY 1, Part A, p. 153

An Accounting Cycle for a Proprietorship: Journalizing and Posting Transactions

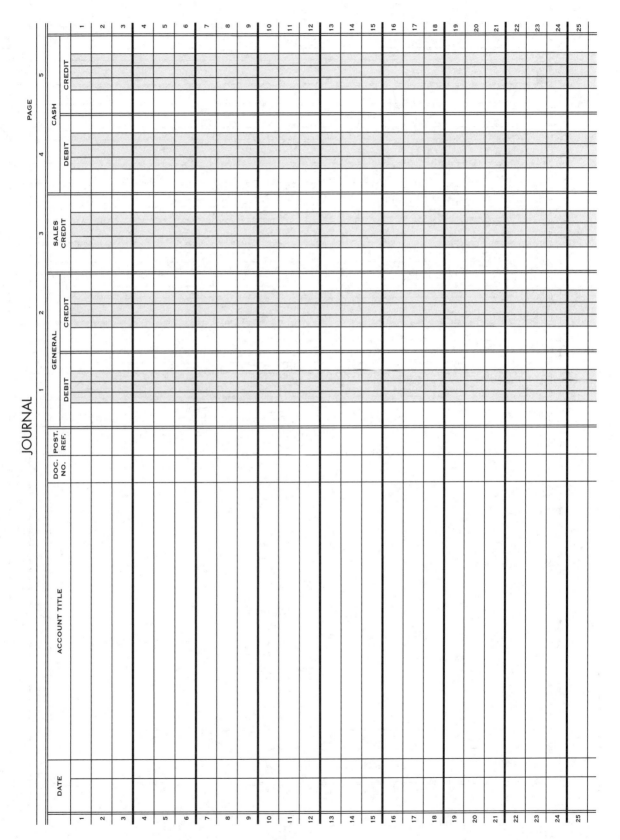

1., 2., 3.

JOURNAL

PAGE

	DATE	ACCOUNT TITLE	DOC. NO.	POST. REF.	1 GENERAL DEBIT	2 GENERAL CREDIT	3 SALES CREDIT	4 CASH DEBIT	5 CASH CREDIT	
1										1
2										2
3										3
4										4
5										5
6										6
7										7
8										8
9										9
10										10
11										11
12										12
13										13
14										14
15										15
16										16
17										17
18										18
19										19
20										20
21										21
22										22
23										23
24										24
25										25

2., 4., 6., 7., 9., 10., 11.

JOURNAL

PAGE

	DATE	ACCOUNT TITLE	DOC. NO.	POST. REF.	1 GENERAL DEBIT	2 GENERAL CREDIT	3 SALES CREDIT	4 CASH DEBIT	5 CASH CREDIT	
1										1
2										2
3										3
4										4
5										5
6										6
7										7
8										8
9										9
10										10
11										11
12										12
13										13
14										14
15										15
16										16
17										17
18										18
19										19
20										20
21										21
22										22
23										23
24										24
25										25

Name ______________________ Date ____________ Class ____________

REINFORCEMENT ACTIVITY 1, Part A (continued)

The general ledger prepared in Reinforcement Activity 1, Part A, is needed to complete Reinforcement Activity 1, Part B.

3., 10., 11., 17., 20.

NOTE: August 31 postings from page 3 of the journal are part of the solution to Part B.

ACCOUNT ______________________ ACCOUNT NO. ________

DATE		ITEM	POST. REF.	DEBIT	CREDIT	BALANCE	
						DEBIT	CREDIT

ACCOUNT ______________________ ACCOUNT NO. ________

DATE		ITEM	POST. REF.	DEBIT	CREDIT	BALANCE	
						DEBIT	CREDIT

ACCOUNT ______________________ ACCOUNT NO. ________

DATE		ITEM	POST. REF.	DEBIT	CREDIT	BALANCE	
						DEBIT	CREDIT

ACCOUNT ______________________ ACCOUNT NO. ________

DATE		ITEM	POST. REF.	DEBIT	CREDIT	BALANCE	
						DEBIT	CREDIT

REINFORCEMENT ACTIVITY 1, Part A (continued)

ACCOUNT ACCOUNT NO.

DATE		ITEM	POST. REF.	DEBIT	CREDIT	BALANCE	
						DEBIT	CREDIT

ACCOUNT ACCOUNT NO.

DATE		ITEM	POST. REF.	DEBIT	CREDIT	BALANCE	
						DEBIT	CREDIT

ACCOUNT ACCOUNT NO.

DATE		ITEM	POST. REF.	DEBIT	CREDIT	BALANCE	
						DEBIT	CREDIT

ACCOUNT ACCOUNT NO.

DATE		ITEM	POST. REF.	DEBIT	CREDIT	BALANCE	
						DEBIT	CREDIT

Name ______________________________ Date ______________ Class ______________

REINFORCEMENT ACTIVITY 1, Part A (continued)

ACCOUNT ACCOUNT NO.

DATE		ITEM	POST. REF.	DEBIT	CREDIT	BALANCE	
						DEBIT	CREDIT

ACCOUNT ACCOUNT NO.

DATE		ITEM	POST. REF.	DEBIT	CREDIT	BALANCE	
						DEBIT	CREDIT

ACCOUNT ACCOUNT NO.

DATE		ITEM	POST. REF.	DEBIT	CREDIT	BALANCE	
						DEBIT	CREDIT

ACCOUNT ACCOUNT NO.

DATE		ITEM	POST. REF.	DEBIT	CREDIT	BALANCE	
						DEBIT	CREDIT

REINFORCEMENT ACTIVITY 1, Part A (continued)

ACCOUNT ACCOUNT NO.

DATE		ITEM	POST. REF.	DEBIT	CREDIT	BALANCE DEBIT	BALANCE CREDIT

ACCOUNT ACCOUNT NO.

DATE		ITEM	POST. REF.	DEBIT	CREDIT	BALANCE DEBIT	BALANCE CREDIT

ACCOUNT ACCOUNT NO.

DATE		ITEM	POST. REF.	DEBIT	CREDIT	BALANCE DEBIT	BALANCE CREDIT

ACCOUNT ACCOUNT NO.

DATE		ITEM	POST. REF.	DEBIT	CREDIT	BALANCE DEBIT	BALANCE CREDIT

Name ______________________ Date ____________ Class ____________

REINFORCEMENT ACTIVITY 1, Part A (continued)

ACCOUNT ______________________ ACCOUNT NO. ______

DATE		ITEM	POST. REF.	DEBIT	CREDIT	BALANCE	
						DEBIT	CREDIT

ACCOUNT ______________________ ACCOUNT NO. ______

DATE		ITEM	POST. REF.	DEBIT	CREDIT	BALANCE	
						DEBIT	CREDIT

ACCOUNT ______________________ ACCOUNT NO. ______

DATE		ITEM	POST. REF.	DEBIT	CREDIT	BALANCE	
						DEBIT	CREDIT

ACCOUNT ______________________ ACCOUNT NO. ______

DATE		ITEM	POST. REF.	DEBIT	CREDIT	BALANCE	
						DEBIT	CREDIT

2. *Prove page 1 of the journal:*

Column	*Debit Column Total*	*Credit Column Total*
General	$	$
Sales		
Cash		
Totals	$	$

5.

RECONCILIATION OF BANK STATEMENT

______________________ (Date)

Balance On Check Stub No. ___ .... $

DEDUCT BANK CHARGES:

Description	Amount
	$

Total bank charges ▶

Adjusted Check Stub Balance .... $

Balance On Bank Statement .... $

ADD OUTSTANDING DEPOSITS:

Date	Amount
	$

Total outstanding deposits ▶

SUBTOTAL .... $

DEDUCT OUTSTANDING CHECKS:

Ck. No.	Amount	Ck. No.	Amount

Total outstanding checks ▶

Adjusted Bank Balance .... $

Name ______________________ Date ____________ Class ____________

REINFORCEMENT ACTIVITY 1, Part A (concluded)

7. *Prove page 2 of the journal:*

Column	*Debit Column Total*	*Credit Column Total*
General	$	$
Sales		
Cash		
Totals	$	$

8. *Prove cash:*

Cash on hand at the beginning of the month	$
+ Total cash received during the month	
Total cash	$
– Total cash paid during the month	
Cash balance at the end of the month	$
Checkbook balance on the next unused check stub	$

Study Guide 6

Name	Perfect Score	Your Score
Identifying Accounting Terms	13 Pts.	
Analyzing Accounting Practices Related to a Work Sheet and Adjusting Entries	20 Pts.	
Analyzing Adjustments and Extending Account Balances on a Work Sheet	17 Pts.	
Total	50 Pts.	

Part One—Identifying Accounting Terms

Directions: Select the one term in Column I that best fits each definition in Column II. Print the letter identifying your choice in the Answers column.

Column I	*Column II*	*Answers*
A. accrual basis of accounting	**1.** The length of time for which a business summarizes its financial information and reports its financial performance. (p. 159)	**1.** ________
B. adjusting entries	**2.** A fiscal period consisting of 12 consecutive months. (p. 159)	**2.** ________
C. adjustments	**3.** A columnar accounting form used to summarize the general ledger information needed to prepare financial statements. (p. 159)	**3.** ________
D. balance sheet	**4.** A proof of equality of debits and credits in a general ledger. (p. 160)	**4.** ________
E. cash basis of accounting	**5.** Cash paid for an expense in one fiscal period that is not used until a later period. (p. 163)	**5.** ________
F. fiscal period	**6.** Reporting income when it is earned and expenses when they are incurred. (p. 163)	**6.** ________
G. fiscal year	**7.** Reporting income when the cash is received and expenses when the cash is paid. (p. 163)	**7.** ________
H. income statement	**8.** Changes recorded on a work sheet to update general ledger accounts at the end of a fiscal period. (p. 163)	**8.** ________
I. net income	**9.** A financial statement that reports assets, liabilities, and owner's equity on a specific date. (p. 169)	**9.** ________
J. net loss	**10.** A financial statement showing the revenue and expenses for a fiscal period. (p. 170)	**10.** ________
K. prepaid expense	**11.** The difference between total revenue and total expenses when total revenue is greater. (p. 171)	**11.** ________
L. trial balance	**12.** The difference between total revenue and total expenses when total expenses are greater. (p. 172)	**12.** ________
M. work sheet	**13.** Journal entries recorded to update general ledger accounts at the end of a fiscal period. (p. 176)	**13.** ________

Part Two—Analyzing Accounting Practices Related to a Work Sheet and Adjusting Entries

Directions: Place a *T* for True or an *F* for False in the Answers column to show whether each of the following statements is true or false.

	Answers
1. The accounting concept Consistent Reporting is being applied when a delivery business reports revenue for the number of deliveries made one year and the amount of revenue received for the deliveries made the next year. (p. 158)	**1.** ______
2. A fiscal period must be 12 months in length. (p. 159)	**2.** ______
3. Journals, ledgers, and work sheets are considered permanent records. (p. 159)	**3.** ______
4. The heading on a work sheet contains the name of the business, the name of the report, and the date of the report. (p. 159)	**4.** ______
5. Only accounts with a balance are listed on a trial balance. (p. 160)	**5.** ______
6. The four questions asked when analyzing an adjustment are: Why? Where? When? and How? (p. 164)	**6.** ______
7. The two accounts affected by the adjustment for supplies are Supplies and Supplies Expense. (p. 164)	**7.** ______
8. The two accounts affected by the adjustment for insurance are Prepaid Insurance Expense and Insurance. (p. 165)	**8.** ______
9. The balance in Prepaid Insurance after adjusting entries are recorded represents the amount of insurance premium still remaining. (p. 165)	**9.** ______
10. Totaling and ruling the Adjustments columns of a work sheet are necessary to prove the equality of debits and credits. (p. 166)	**10.** ______
11. The income statement and balance sheet are prepared from the Trial Balance columns on the work sheet. (p. 169)	**11.** ______
12. Net income on a work sheet is calculated by subtracting the Income Statement Debit column total from the Income Statement Credit column total. (p. 171)	**12.** ______
13. If errors are found on a work sheet, they must be erased and corrected before any further work is completed. (p. 173)	**13.** ______
14. When two column totals are not in balance on the work sheet, the difference between the two totals is calculated and checked. (p. 173)	**14.** ______
15. If the difference between the totals of Debit and Credit columns on a work sheet can be evenly divided by 9, then the error is most likely a transposed number. (p. 173)	**15.** ______
16. If there are errors in the work sheet's Trial Balance columns, it might be because a general ledger account balance was recorded in the wrong Trial Balance column. (p. 174)	**16.** ______
17. Most errors occur in doing arithmetic. (p. 174)	**17.** ______
18. The best way to prevent errors is to use a calculator. (p. 174)	**18.** ______
19. Adjusting entries must be posted to the general ledger accounts. (p. 176)	**19.** ______
20. The balance in Supplies Expense after adjusting entries are recorded represents the amount of supplies used during the fiscal period. (p. 176)	**20.** ______

Name ______________________ Date ____________ Class ____________

Part Three—Analyzing Adjustments and Extending Account Balances on a Work Sheet

Directions: For each account listed below, determine in which work sheet column(s) an amount typically will be written. Place a check mark in the proper Answers column to show your answer.

	Adjustments		Income Statement		Balance Sheet	
	Debit	Credit	Debit	Credit	Debit	Credit
	(pp. 164–166)		(p. 170)		(p. 169)	
1. Cash	____	____	____	____	____	____
2. Petty Cash	____	____	____	____	____	____
3. Accounts Receivable—Corner Bakery	____	____	____	____	____	____
4. Supplies	____	____	____	____	____	____
5. Prepaid Insurance	____	____	____	____	____	____
6. Accounts Payable—Suburban Office Supplies	____	____	____	____	____	____
7. K. Strand, Capital	____	____	____	____	____	____
8. K. Strand, Drawing	____	____	____	____	____	____
9. Income Summary	____	____	____	____	____	____
10. Sales	____	____	____	____	____	____
11. Advertising Expense	____	____	____	____	____	____
12. Cash Short and Over (Debit Balance)	____	____	____	____	____	____
13. Insurance Expense	____	____	____	____	____	____
14. Miscellaneous Expense	____	____	____	____	____	____
15. Rent Expense	____	____	____	____	____	____
16. Supplies Expense	____	____	____	____	____	____
17. Utilities Expense	____	____	____	____	____	____

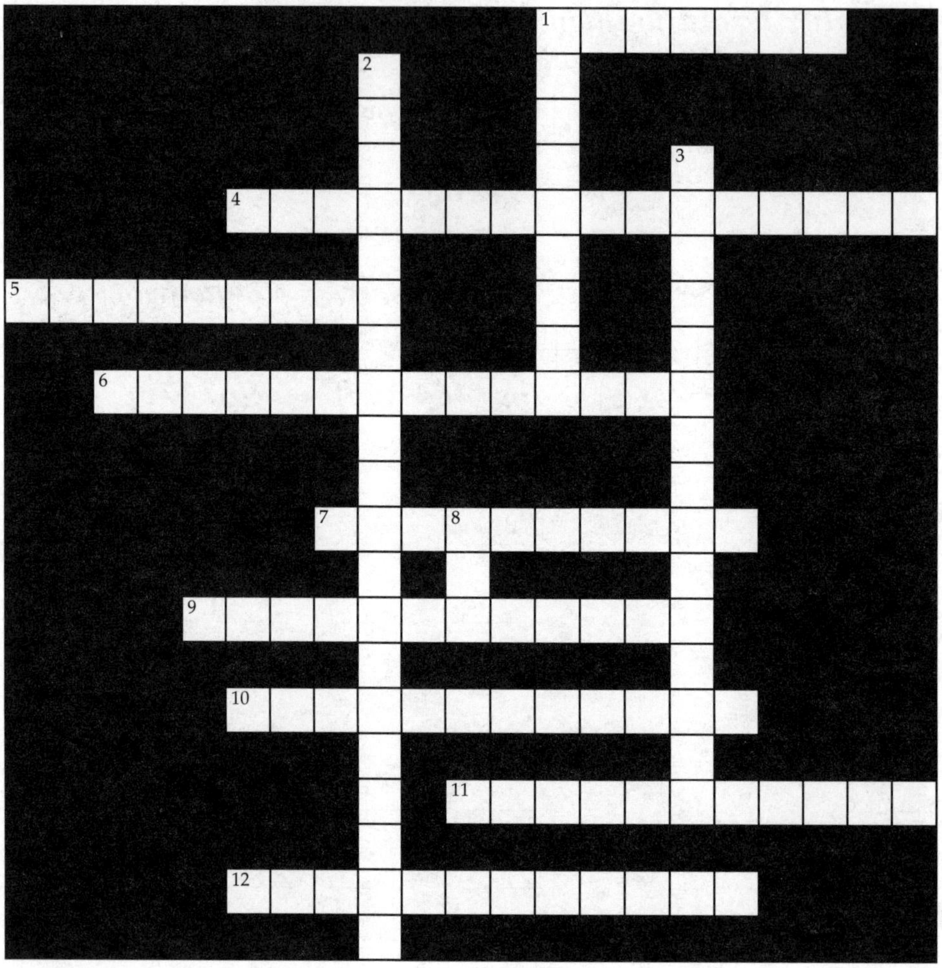

Across

1. The difference between total revenue and total expenses when total expenses are greater.
4. Journal entries recorded to update general ledger accounts at the end of a fiscal period.
5. A columnar accounting form used to summarize the general ledger information needed to prepare financial statements.
6. Cash paid for an expense in one fiscal period that is not used until a later period.
7. A fiscal period consisting of 12 consecutive months.
9. A proof of the equality of debits and credits in a general ledger.
10. A financial statement that reports assets, liabilities, and owner's equity on a specific date.
11. Changes recorded on a work sheet to update general ledger accounts at the end of a fiscal period.
12. The length of time for which a business summarizes its financial information and reports its financial performance.

Down

1. The difference between total revenue and total expenses when total revenue is greater.
2. A trial balance prepared after adjusting entries are posted.
3. A financial statement showing the revenue and expenses for a fiscal period.
8. An accountant who has passed the uniform certified public accounting exam and met the licensing requirement for a state. (Note: Please enter into the puzzle as an acronym.)

6-1, 6-2, and 6-3 WORK TOGETHER, pp. 162, 168, and 175

6-1 Recording the trial balance on a work sheet
6-2 Planning adjustments on a work sheet
6-3 Completing a work sheet

Sales Revenue
Expenses

Work Sheet
April 30 2015

	ACCOUNT TITLE	1 TRIAL BALANCE DEBIT	2 TRIAL BALANCE CREDIT	3 ADJUSTMENTS DEBIT	4 ADJUSTMENTS CREDIT	5 INCOME STATEMENT DEBIT	6 INCOME STATEMENT CREDIT	7 BALANCE SHEET DEBIT	8 BALANCE SHEET CREDIT	
1	Cash	4 900 00						4 900 00		1
2	Petty Cash	75 00						75 00		2
3	Account Receivable - B.Wi	1 387 00						1 387 00		3
4	Supplies	228 00			a 153 00			75 00		4
5	Prepaid Insurance	375 00			b 125 00			250 00		5
6	Accounts Payable southside		267 00						267 00	6
7	Connor whithey Capital		7 443 00						7 443 00	7
8	Connor whithny Drawing	1 700 00						1 700 00		8
9	Income Summary									9
10	Sales		2 160 00				2 160 00			10
11	Advertising Exp	460 00				460 00				11
12	Cash short and over	6 00				6 00				12
13	Insurance Expense			b 125 00		125 00				13
14	Misc. Expense	189 00				189 00				14
15	Supplie Expense			a 153 00		153 00				15
16	Utilities Expense	550 00				550 00				16
17						1 483 00	2 160 00	8 387 00	7 710 00	17
18	Total	9 870 00	9 870 00			677 00			677 00	18
19	Net income					2 160 00			8 387 00	19
20										20

6-1, 6-2, and 6-3 ON YOUR OWN, pp. 162, 168, and 175

6-1 Recording the trial balance on a work sheet
6-2 Planning adjustments on a work sheet
6-3 Completing a work sheet

(Revenue) Sales → Income
Expense →

work sheet
April 30, 2015

	Account Title	1 Trial Balance Debit	2 Trial Balance Credit	3 Adjustments Debit	4 Adjustments Credit	5 Income Statement Debit	6 Income Statement Credit	7 Balance Sheet Debit	8 Balance Sheet Credit	
1	Cash	13 600 00						13 600 00		1
2	Petty Cash	150 00						150 00		2
3	Account Rec. Stephen Coat	2 996 00						2 996 00		3
4	Supplies	476 00			a 236 00			240 00		4
5	Prepaid Insurance	650 00			b 130 00			520 00		5
6	Accounts payable Jill stra		596 00						596 00	6
7	Isiah Clausen, Capital		14 886 00						14 886 00	7
8	Isaiah Clausen, Drawing	3 400 00						3 400 00		8
9	Income Summary									9
10	Sales		8 280 00				8 280 00			10
11	Adve. Expen.	910 00				910 00				11
12	Cash short and over	2 00				2 00				12
13	Insurance Exp.			b 130 00		130 00				13
14	Misc. Expense	378 00				378 00				14
15	Supplies Exp.			a 236 00		236 00				15
16	Utilities Exp	1 200 00				1 200 00				16
17		23 762 00	23 762 00	366 00	366 00	2 856 00	8 280 00	20 906 00	15 482 00	17
18	Net Income					5 424 00			5 424 00	18
19						8 280 00	8 280 00	20 906 00	20 966 00	19
20										20

Name ______________ Date ______________ Class ______________

6-4 WORK TOGETHER, p. 179

Journalizing and posting adjusting entries

1.

JOURNAL PAGE

	DATE		ACCOUNT TITLE	DOC. NO.	POST. REF.	1 GENERAL DEBIT	2 GENERAL CREDIT	3 SALES CREDIT	4 CASH DEBIT	5 CASH CREDIT	
1			Adjusting Entries								1
2	Dec	31	Supplies Expense		550	236 00					2
3			Supplies		140		236 00				3
4		31	Insurance Expense		538	130 00					4
5			Prepaid Insurance		150		130 00				5
6											6
7											7
8											8
9											9
10											10
11											11
12											12
13											13
14											14
15											15
16											16
17											17
18											18
19											19
20											20
21											21
22											22
23											23

GENERAL LEDGER

ACCOUNT Supplies — ACCOUNT NO. 140

DATE 20--		ITEM	POST. REF.	DEBIT	CREDIT	BALANCE DEBIT	BALANCE CREDIT
Apr.	30	Balance	✔	228 00		228 00	
					153 00	75 00	

ACCOUNT Prepaid Insurance — ACCOUNT NO. 150

DATE 20--		ITEM	POST. REF.	DEBIT	CREDIT	BALANCE DEBIT	BALANCE CREDIT
Apr.	30	Balance	✔	375 00		375 00	
					125 00	250 00	

ACCOUNT Insurance Expense — ACCOUNT NO. 530

DATE		ITEM	POST. REF.	DEBIT	CREDIT	BALANCE DEBIT	BALANCE CREDIT
Apr.	30	Balance		125 00		125 00	

ACCOUNT Supplies Expense — ACCOUNT NO. 550

DATE		ITEM	POST. REF.	DEBIT	CREDIT	BALANCE DEBIT	BALANCE CREDIT
Apr.	30	Balance		153 00		153 00	

Name ______________________ Date ____________ Class ____________

6-4 ON YOUR OWN, p. 179

Journalizing and posting adjusting entries

1.

JOURNAL PAGE

	DATE	ACCOUNT TITLE	DOC. NO.	POST. REF.	1 GENERAL DEBIT	2 GENERAL CREDIT	3 SALES CREDIT	4 CASH DEBIT	5 CASH CREDIT	
1										1
2										2
3										3
4										4
5										5
6										6
7										7
8										8
9										9
10										10
11										11
12										12
13										13
14										14
15										15
16										16
17										17
18										18
19										19
20										20
21										21
22										22
23										23

6-4 ON YOUR OWN (concluded)

GENERAL LEDGER

ACCOUNT Supplies — ACCOUNT NO. 140

DATE		ITEM	POST. REF.	DEBIT	CREDIT	BALANCE DEBIT	BALANCE CREDIT
20-- Dec.	31	Balance	✔	476 00		476 00	
					236 00	240 00	

ACCOUNT Prepaid Insurance — ACCOUNT NO. 150

DATE		ITEM	POST. REF.	DEBIT	CREDIT	BALANCE DEBIT	BALANCE CREDIT
20-- Dec.	31	Balance	✔	650 00		650 00	
					130 00	520 00	

ACCOUNT Insurance Expense — ACCOUNT NO. 530

DATE		ITEM	POST. REF.	DEBIT	CREDIT	BALANCE DEBIT	BALANCE CREDIT
				130 00		130 00	

ACCOUNT Supplies Expense — ACCOUNT NO. 550

DATE		ITEM	POST. REF.	DEBIT	CREDIT	BALANCE DEBIT	BALANCE CREDIT
Dec	31	Balance		236 00		236 00	

Name ______________________ Date ____________ Class ____________

6-1, 6-2, and 6-3 APPLICATION PROBLEM (LO1, 2, 3, 4, 5, 6), p. 183

6-1 Recording the trial balance on a work sheet
6-2 Planning adjustments on a work sheet
6-3 Completing a work sheet

	ACCOUNT TITLE	TRIAL BALANCE 1 DEBIT	TRIAL BALANCE 2 CREDIT	ADJUSTMENTS 3 DEBIT	ADJUSTMENTS 4 CREDIT	INCOME STATEMENT 5 DEBIT	INCOME STATEMENT 6 CREDIT	BALANCE SHEET 7 DEBIT	BALANCE SHEET 8 CREDIT	
1										1
2										2
3										3
4										4
5										5
6										6
7										7
8										8
9										9
10										10
11										11
12										12
13										13
14										14
15										15
16										16
17										17
18										18
19										19
20										20

6-4 APPLICATION PROBLEM (LO8), p. 184

Journalizing and posting adjusting entries

1.

JOURNAL PAGE

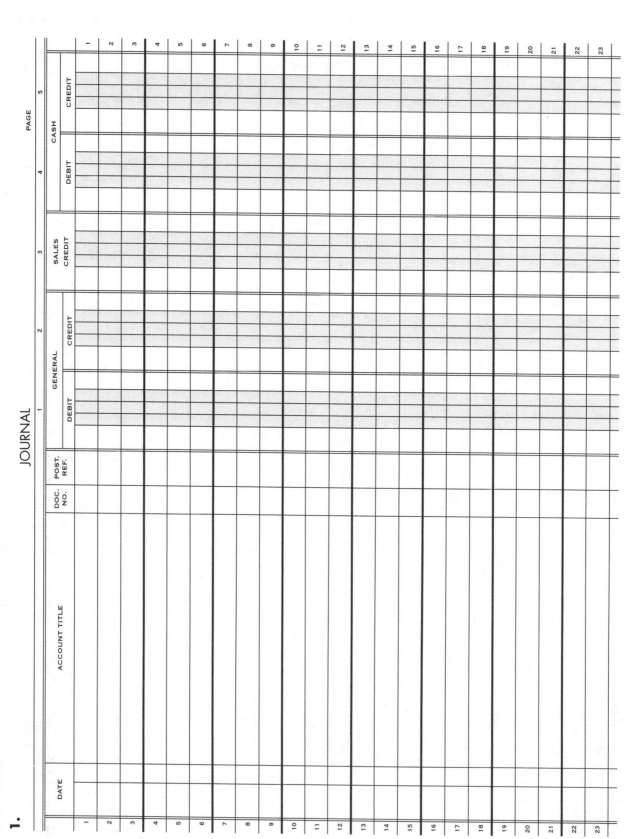

	DATE	ACCOUNT TITLE	DOC. NO.	POST. REF.	GENERAL DEBIT (1)	GENERAL CREDIT (2)	SALES CREDIT (3)	CASH DEBIT (4)	CASH CREDIT (5)	
1										1
2										2
3										3
4										4
5										5
6										6
7										7
8										8
9										9
10										10
11										11
12										12
13										13
14										14
15										15
16										16
17										17
18										18
19										19
20										20
21										21
22										22
23										23

Name ______________________ Date ____________ Class ____________

6-4 APPLICATION PROBLEM (concluded)

GENERAL LEDGER

ACCOUNT Supplies ACCOUNT NO. 140

DATE		ITEM	POST. REF.	DEBIT	CREDIT	BALANCE DEBIT	BALANCE CREDIT
20-- June	30	Balance	✔	518 00		518 00	

ACCOUNT Prepaid Insurance ACCOUNT NO. 150

DATE		ITEM	POST. REF.	DEBIT	CREDIT	BALANCE DEBIT	BALANCE CREDIT
20-- June	30	Balance	✔	675 00		675 00	

ACCOUNT Insurance Expense ACCOUNT NO. 530

DATE		ITEM	POST. REF.	DEBIT	CREDIT	BALANCE DEBIT	BALANCE CREDIT

ACCOUNT Supplies Expense ACCOUNT NO. 550

DATE		ITEM	POST. REF.	DEBIT	CREDIT	BALANCE DEBIT	BALANCE CREDIT

6-M MASTERY PROBLEM (LO1, 2, 3, 4, 5, 6, 8), p. 184

Completing a work sheet; journalizing and posting adjusting entries

1., 2., 3., 4., 5., 6.

		1	2	3	4	5	6	7	8	
	ACCOUNT TITLE	TRIAL BALANCE		ADJUSTMENTS		INCOME STATEMENT		BALANCE SHEET		
		DEBIT	CREDIT	DEBIT	CREDIT	DEBIT	CREDIT	DEBIT	CREDIT	
1										1
2										2
3										3
4										4
5										5
6										6
7										7
8										8
9										9
10										10
11										11
12										12
13										13
14										14
15										15
16										16
17										17
18										18
19										19
20										20
21										21

Name ______________________ Date ____________ Class ____________

6-M MASTERY PROBLEM (continued)

7.

JOURNAL

PAGE

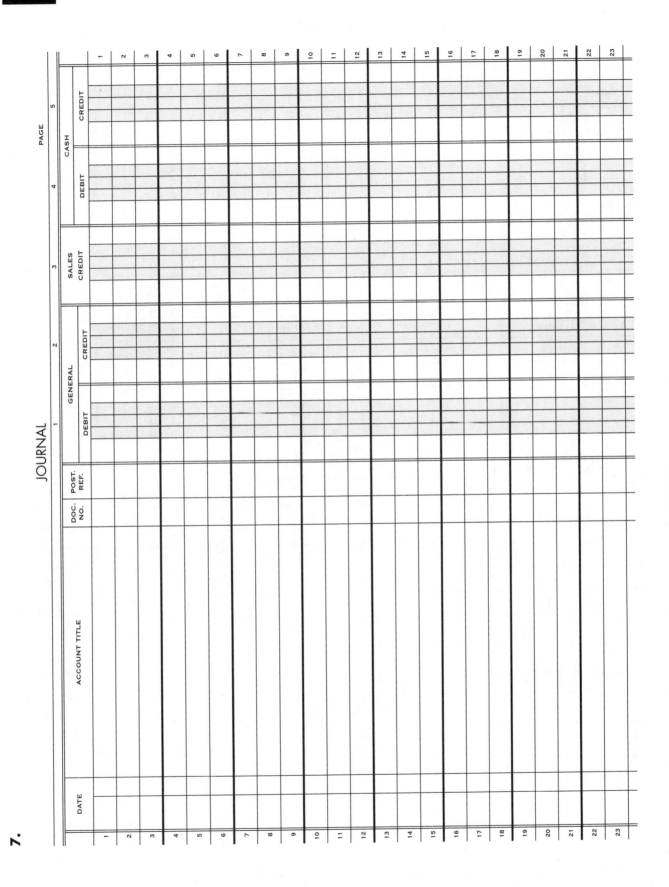

	DATE	ACCOUNT TITLE	DOC. NO.	POST. REF.	GENERAL DEBIT (1)	GENERAL CREDIT (2)	SALES CREDIT (3)	CASH DEBIT (4)	CASH CREDIT (5)	
1										1
2										2
3										3
4										4
5										5
6										6
7										7
8										8
9										9
10										10
11										11
12										12
13										13
14										14
15										15
16										16
17										17
18										18
19										19
20										20
21										21
22										22
23										23

6-M MASTERY PROBLEM (concluded)

GENERAL LEDGER

ACCOUNT Supplies — ACCOUNT NO. 140

DATE		ITEM	POST. REF.	DEBIT	CREDIT	BALANCE DEBIT	BALANCE CREDIT
20-- Apr.	30	Balance	✔	1 7 1 0 00		1 7 1 0 00	

ACCOUNT Prepaid Insurance — ACCOUNT NO. 150

DATE		ITEM	POST. REF.	DEBIT	CREDIT	BALANCE DEBIT	BALANCE CREDIT
20-- Apr.	30	Balance	✔	2 2 0 0 00		2 2 0 0 00	

ACCOUNT Insurance Expense — ACCOUNT NO. 530

DATE		ITEM	POST. REF.	DEBIT	CREDIT	BALANCE DEBIT	BALANCE CREDIT

ACCOUNT Supplies Expense — ACCOUNT NO. 560

DATE		ITEM	POST. REF.	DEBIT	CREDIT	BALANCE DEBIT	BALANCE CREDIT

Name ______________________ Date ____________ Class ____________

6-C CHALLENGE PROBLEM (LO1, 2, 3, 4, 5, 6), p. 185

Completing a work sheet

1., 2.

	ACCOUNT TITLE	1 TRIAL BALANCE	2	3 ADJUSTMENTS	4	5 INCOME STATEMENT	6	7 BALANCE SHEET	8	
		DEBIT	CREDIT	DEBIT	CREDIT	DEBIT	CREDIT	DEBIT	CREDIT	
1										1
2										2
3										3
4										4
5										5
6										6
7										7
8										8
9										9
10										10
11										11
12										12
13										13
14										14
15										15
16										16
17										17
18										18
19										19

Study Guide 7

Name	Perfect Score	Your Score
Identifying Accounting Concepts and Practices	20 Pts.	
Analyzing an Income Statement	15 Pts.	
Analyzing Balance Sheet Procedures	5 Pts.	
Total	40 Pts.	

Part One—Identifying Accounting Concepts and Practices

Directions: Place a *T* for True or an *F* for False in the Answers column to show whether each of the following statements is true or false.

Answers

1. The Full Disclosure accounting concept is applied when a company always prepares financial statements at the end of each monthly fiscal period. (p. 190) 1. ________
2. Internal users of accounting information include company managers, officers, and creditors. (p. 190) 2. ________
3. An income statement reports information on a specific date indicating the financial condition of a business. (p. 192) 3. ________
4. The Matching Expenses with Revenue accounting concept is applied when the revenue earned and the expenses incurred to earn that revenue are reported in the same fiscal period. (p. 192) 4. ________
5. Information needed to prepare an income statement comes from the Account Title column and the Income Statement columns of a work sheet. (p. 192) 5. ________
6. The income statement for a service business has five sections: heading, Revenue, Expenses, Net Income or Net Loss, and Capital. (p. 192) 6. ________
7. The income statement's account balances are obtained from the work sheet's Income Statement columns. (p. 192) 7. ________
8. The net income on an income statement is verified by checking the balance sheet. (p. 194) 8. ________
9. Double lines ruled across both amount columns of an income statement indicate that the amount has been verified. (p. 194) 9. ________
10. A financial ratio is a comparison between two components of financial information. (p. 195) 10. ________
11. Financial ratios on an income statement are calculated by dividing sales and total expenses by net income. (p. 195) 11. ________
12. No company should have a vertical analysis ratio for total expenses higher than 48.0%. (p. 196) 12. ________
13. When a business has two different sources of revenue, both revenue accounts are listed on the income statement. (p. 197) 13. ________
14. An amount written in parentheses on a financial statement indicates a negative amount. (p. 197) 14. ________
15. A balance sheet reports financial information on a specific date and includes the assets, liabilities, and owner's equity. (p. 199) 15. ________
16. A balance sheet reports information about the elements of the accounting equation. (p. 201) 16. ________
17. The owner's capital amount reported on a balance sheet is calculated as: capital account balance plus drawing account balance, less net income. (p. 202) 17. ________
18. The position of the total asset line on the balance sheet is determined after the Equities section is prepared. (p. 202) 18. ________
19. Double lines are ruled across the Balance Sheet columns to show that the column totals have been verified as correct. (p. 202) 19. ________
20. The Owner's Equity section of a balance sheet is the same for all businesses. (p. 203) 20. ________

Part Two—Analyzing an Income Statement

Directions: The parts of the income statement below are identified with capital letters. Decide the location of each of the following items. Print the letter identifying your choice in the Answers column.

A

B

C

			% OF SALES
D			
E		F	
G			
H	I		
J		K	N
L		M	O

(pp. 192–195)

Answers

1. Date of the income statement. 1. ______
2. Heading of Expenses section. 2. ______
3. Statement name. 3. ______
4. Expense account titles. 4. ______
5. Expense account balances. 5. ______
6. The amount of net income or loss. 6. ______
7. Heading of Revenue section. 7. ______
8. Net income ratio (or return on sales). 8. ______
9. Revenue account title. 9. ______
10. Words *Total Expenses.* 10. ______
11. Business name. 11. ______
12. Total amount of revenue. 12. ______
13. Total amount of expenses. 13. ______
14. Words *Net Income* or *Net Loss.* 14. ______
15. Total expenses ratio. 15. ______

Name ______________________ Date ____________ Class ____________

Part Three—Analyzing Balance Sheet Procedures

Directions: For each of the following items, select the choice that best completes the statement. Print the letter identifying your choice in the Answers column.

Answers

1. The date on a monthly balance sheet prepared on July 31 is written as (A) For Month Ended July 31, 20-- (B) July 31, 20-- (C) 20--, July 31 (D) none of the above. (p. 199) — 1. ______
2. Information needed to prepare a balance sheet's Assets section is obtained from a work sheet's Account Title column and (A) Income Statement Debit column (B) Income Statement Credit column (C) Balance Sheet Debit column (D) Balance Sheet Credit column. (p. 201) — 2. ______
3. Information needed to prepare a balance sheet's Liabilities section is obtained from a work sheet's Account Title column and (A) Income Statement Debit column (B) Income Statement Credit column (C) Balance Sheet Debit column (D) Balance Sheet Credit column. (p. 201) — 3. ______
4. The amount of capital reported on a balance sheet is calculated as (A) Capital Account Balance + Net Income – Drawing Account Balance (B) Capital Account Balance – Net Income – Drawing Account Balance (C) Capital Account Balance + Net Income + Drawing Account Balance (D) Capital Account Balance – Net Income + Drawing Account Balance. (p. 202) — 4. ______
5. If a business wanted to show how the current capital balance was calculated, it would (A) only list net income on the balance sheet (B) only list net income and withdrawals on the balance sheet (C) list only the beginning capital balance on the balance sheet (D) list the beginning capital balance, the net income, the withdrawals, and the ending capital balance on the balance sheet. (p. 203) — 5. ______

Across

6. A negative balance that remains after total expenses are subtracted from total income.
8. The ratio of net income to total sales.
9. Reporting an amount on a financial statement as a percentage of another item on the same financial statement.
10. Any persons or groups who will be affected by an action.
11. The area of accounting which focuses on reporting information to internal users.

Down

1. The calculation and interpretation of a financial ratio.
2. The area of accounting which focuses on reporting information to external users.
3. A budgeting strategy of setting aside at least 10% of after-tax income for saving and investing.
4. A financial road map used by individuals and companies as a guide for spending and saving.
5. A comparison between two components of financial information.
7. A positive balance that remains after total expenses are subtracted from total income.

Name ______________ Date ______________ Class ______________

7-1 WORK TOGETHER, p. 198

Preparing an income statement

	ACCOUNT TITLE	5 INCOME STATEMENT DEBIT	6 INCOME STATEMENT CREDIT	7 BALANCE SHEET DEBIT	8 BALANCE SHEET CREDIT	
12	Sales		5,800.00			12
13	Advertising Expense	750.00				13
14	Cash Short and Over	3.00				14
15	Insurance Expense	610.00				15
16	Miscellaneous Expense	167.00				16
17	Supplies Expense	540.00				17
18	Utilities Expense	300.00				18
19		2,370.00	5,800.00	7,554.00	4,124.00	19
20	Net Income	3,430.00			3,430.00	20
21		5,800.00	5,800.00	7,554.00	7,554.00	21
22						22
23						23

			% OF SALES

7-1 ON YOUR OWN, p. 198

Preparing an income statement

	ACCOUNT TITLE	5 INCOME STATEMENT DEBIT	6 INCOME STATEMENT CREDIT	7 BALANCE SHEET DEBIT	8 BALANCE SHEET CREDIT	
12	Sales		3,400.00			12
13	Advertising Expense	225.00				13
14	Cash Short and Over	1.00				14
15	Insurance Expense	340.00				15
16	Miscellaneous Expense	210.00				16
17	Supplies Expense	98.00				17
18	Utilities Expense	140.00				18
19		1,014.00	3,400.00	3,620.00	1,234.00	19
20	Net Income	2,386.00			2,386.00	20
21		3,400.00	3,400.00	3,620.00	3,620.00	21
22						22
23						23

plumbing solution
income stat
For Month ended

			% OF SALES
Revenue			
Sales			
Expenses		3400 00	100.0
Adv.	225		
cash short	1		
Insur.	340		
Misc.	210		
supplies	98 00		
Utiti	140 00		
Total		1014 00	29.8
net income		2386 00	70.2

Name ____________________ Date ____________ Class ____________

7-2 WORK TOGETHER, p. 205

Preparing a balance sheet

	ACCOUNT TITLE	BALANCE SHEET DEBIT (7)	BALANCE SHEET CREDIT (8)	
1	Cash	4 750 00		1
2	Petty Cash	75 00		2
3	Accounts Receivable—G. Mackermann	825 00		3
4	Accounts Receivable—R. Whu	715 00		4
5	Supplies	110 00		5
6	Prepaid Insurance	320 00		6
7	Accounts Payable—Belmont Supplies		275 00	7
8	Accounts Payable—Lurgert Paints		490 00	8
9	Dwight Sundeen, Capital		3 500 00	9
10	Dwight Sundeen, Drawing	1 200 00		10
20		7 995 00	4 265 00	20
21	Net Income		3 730 00	21
22		7 995 00	7 995 00	22
23				23

3500+

Pro Painter

work sheet

April 30, 2015

Assets		Liabilities	
Cash	4 750 00	Accounts payable-Belmont suppl	275 00
Petty cash	75 00	Accounts Payable-Lurgert Paints	490 00
Account receivable-G. Makerman	825 00		765 00
Account receivable-R.Whu	715 00	Owner's Equity	
Supplies	110 00	Dwight sundeen Capital	3500 00
Prepaid Insurance	320 00	Net Income	3730 00
			– 7230 00
Total Assets	6795 00	Dwight – Drawing	– 1200 00
			6030 00

7-2 ON YOUR OWN, p. 205

Preparing a balance sheet

Capital Account Balance − Net Loss − Drawing Account Balance = Current Capital

	ACCOUNT TITLE	BALANCE SHEET DEBIT (7)	BALANCE SHEET CREDIT (8)	
1	Cash	2,650.00		1
2	Petty Cash	200.00		2
3	Accounts Receivable—Sunshine Café	250.00		3
4	Accounts Receivable—Dependable Cleaners	130.00		4
5	Supplies	350.00		5
6	Prepaid Insurance	290.00		6
7	Accounts Payable—Computer Supplies Co.		340.00	7
8	Accounts Payable—Westside Supplies		120.00	8
9	Eva Nelsen, Capital		3,950.00	9
10	Eva Nelsen, Drawing	1,500.00		10
20		5,370.00	4,410.00	20
21	Net Income		960.00	21
22		5,370.00	5,370.00	22
23				23

Capital Account Balance + Net Income − Drawing Account Balance = Current Capital

Computer Repair

Work Sheet

October 31, 2015

Assets		Liabilities	
Cash	2,650.00	A/P - Computer supplies	340.00
Petty Cash	200.00	A/P - Westside Supplies	120.00
A/R - Sunshine Cafe	250.00	Total liabilities	460.00
A/R - Dependable cleaners	130.00	O. E	
Supplies	350.00	Eva Nelson, Capital	3,950.00
Prepaid Insurance	290.00	Net Income	960.00
Total Assets	3,870.00		4,910.00
		Eva Nelson, Drawing	1,500.00
		Current Capital	3,410.00

Name ______________________ Date ______________ Class ______________

7-1 APPLICATION PROBLEM (LO1, 2), p. 208

Preparing an income statement

1., 2.

			% OF SALES

7-2 APPLICATION PROBLEM (LO3), p. 208

Preparing a balance sheet

Name ______________________ Date ____________ Class ____________

7-M MASTERY PROBLEM (LO1, 2, 3), p. 209

Preparing financial statements with a net loss

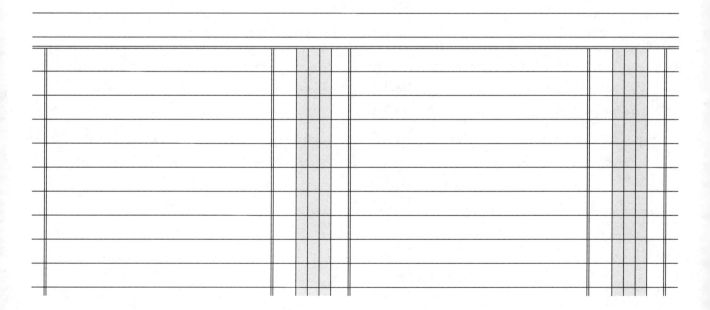

1., 2.

			% OF SALES

3.

7-C CHALLENGE PROBLEM (LO1, 2, 3), p. 210

Preparing financial statements with two sources of revenue and a net loss

1., 2.

			% OF SALES

3.

Study Guide 8	Name	Perfect Score	Your Score
	Identifying Accounting Terms	5 Pts.	
	Analyzing Accounts Affected by Adjusting and Closing Entries	10 Pts.	
	Analyzing Closing Entries	10 Pts.	
	Identifying the Accounting Cycle for a Service Business	8 Pts.	
	Total	33 Pts.	

Part One—Identifying Accounting Terms

Directions: Select the one term in Column I that best fits each definition in Column II. Print the letter identifying your choice in the Answers column.

Column I	***Column II***	***Answers***
A. accounting cycle	**1.** Accounts used to accumulate information from one fiscal period to the next. (p. 214)	**1.** ________
B. closing entries	**2.** Accounts used to accumulate information until it is transferred to the owner's capital account. (p. 214)	**2.** ________
C. permanent accounts	**3.** Journal entries used to prepare temporary accounts for a new fiscal period. (p. 214)	**3.** ________
D. post-closing trial balance	**4.** A trial balance prepared after the closing entries are posted. (p. 227)	**4.** ________
E. temporary accounts	**5.** The series of accounting activities included in recording financial information for a fiscal period. (p. 228)	**5.** ________

Part Two—Analyzing Accounts Affected by Adjusting and Closing Entries

Directions: Use the partial chart of accounts given below. For each closing entry described, decide which accounts are debited and credited. Write the account numbers identifying your choice in the proper Answers column.

Account Titles	Acct. No.
K. Schenk, Capital	310
K. Schenk, Drawing	320
Income Summary	330
Sales	410
Advertising Expense	510
Insurance Expense	520
Supplies Expense	550

	Accounts to Be Debited	Accounts to Be Credited
1–2. Closing entry for Sales. (p. 217)	**1.** ________	**2.** ________
3–4. Closing entry for all expense accounts. (p. 219)	**3.** ________	**4.** ________
5–6. Closing entry for Income Summary with a net income. (p. 220)	**5.** ________	**6.** ________
7–8. Closing entry for Income Summary with a net loss. (p. 220)	**7.** ________	**8.** ________
9–10. Closing entry for owner's drawing account. (p. 221)	**9.** ________	**10.** ________

Name ______________________________ Date ______________ Class ______________

Part Three—Analyzing Closing Entries

Directions: For each of the following items, select the choice that best completes the statement. Print the letter identifying your choice in the Answers column.

Answers

1. Which accounting concept applies when a work sheet is prepared at the end of each fiscal cycle to summarize the general ledger information needed to prepare financial statements? (A) Business Entity (B) Accounting Period Cycle (C) Going Concern (D) Full Disclosure. (p. 214) **1.** ______

2. The ending account balances of permanent accounts for one fiscal period are (A) the same as the prior period's ending balance (B) equal to the capital account balance (C) all equal to zero (D) the beginning account balances for the next fiscal period. (p. 214) **2.** ______

3. Which of the following accounts is a temporary account? (A) Cash (B) Accounts Payable (C) Clyde Sullivan, Capital (D) Rent Expense. (p. 214) **3.** ______

4. Which accounting concept applies when expenses are reported in the same fiscal period that they are used to produce revenue? (A) Business Entity (B) Going Concern (C) Matching Expenses with Revenue (D) Full Disclosure. (p. 214) **4.** ______

5. When revenue is greater than total expenses, resulting in a net income, the Income Summary account has a (A) debit balance (B) credit balance (C) normal debit balance (D) normal credit balance. (p. 216) **5.** ______

6. Information needed for recording the closing entries is obtained from the (A) general ledger accounts' Debit Balance columns (B) work sheet's Income Statement and Balance Sheet columns (C) balance sheet (D) income statement. (p. 216) **6.** ______

7. Income Summary is (A) an asset account (B) a liability account (C) a temporary account (D) a permanent account. (p. 216) **7.** ______

8. After the closing entries are posted, the Sales account balance should be (A) equal to the Sales account balance on the unadjusted trial balance (B) equal to the Sales account balance on the adjusted trial balance (C) zero (D) the same as the beginning balance for that same fiscal period. (p. 218) **8.** ______

9. After the closing entries are posted, the owner's capital account balances should be the same as shown (A) on the balance sheet for the fiscal period (B) in the work sheet's Balance Sheet Debit column (C) in the work sheet's Balance Sheet Credit column (D) in the work sheet's Income Statement Debit column. (p. 221) **9.** ______

10. The accounts listed on a post-closing trial balance are (A) general ledger accounts with balances after the closing entries are posted (B) all general ledger accounts (C) those that have no balances after adjusting and closing entries (D) those that appear in the work sheet's Trial Balance columns. (p. 227) **10.** ______

Part Four—Identifying the Accounting Cycle for a Service Business

Directions: Arrange the series of accounting activities listed below for the accounting cycle for a service business. Indicate the sequence of the steps by writing a number from 1 to 8 to the left of each activity. (p. 228)

Answers

1. _______ A work sheet, including a trial balance, is prepared from the general ledger.

2. _______ Transactions, from information on source documents, are recorded in a journal.

3. _______ Source documents are checked for accuracy, and transactions are analyzed into debit and credit parts.

4. _______ Adjusting entries are journalized and posted to the general ledger.

5. _______ Financial statements are prepared from the work sheet.

6. _______ Closing entries are journalized and posted to the general ledger.

7. _______ A post-closing trial balance of the general ledger is prepared.

8. _______ Journal entries are posted to the general ledger.

8-1 WORK TOGETHER, p. 222

Journalizing and posting closing entries

	ACCOUNT TITLE	5 INCOME STATEMENT DEBIT	6 INCOME STATEMENT CREDIT	7 BALANCE SHEET DEBIT	8 BALANCE SHEET CREDIT	
1	Cash			4 900 00		1
2	Petty Cash			75 00		2
3	Accounts Receivable—B. Widell			1 387 00		3
4	Supplies			75 00		4
5	Prepaid Insurance			250 00		5
6	Accounts Payable—Southside Supplies				267 00	6
7	Connor Whitney, Capital				7 443 00	7
8	Connor Whitney, Drawing			1 700 00		8
9	Income Summary					9
10	Sales		2 160 00			10
11	Advertising Expense	460 00				11
12	Cash Short and Over	6 00				12
13	Insurance Expense	125 00				13
14	Miscellaneous Expense	189 00				14
15	Supplies Expense	153 00				15
16	Utilities Expense	550 00				16
17		1 483 00	2 160 00	8 387 00	7 710 00	17
18	Net Income	677 00			677 00	18
19		2 160 00	2 160 00	8 387 00	8 387 00	19
20						20
21						21
22						22
23						23
24						24
25						25
26						26
27						27
28						28
29						29
30						30
31						31
32						32

8-1 WORK TOGETHER (continued)

JOURNAL

PAGE

	DATE	ACCOUNT TITLE	DOC. NO.	POST. REF.	GENERAL DEBIT (1)	GENERAL CREDIT (2)	SALES CREDIT (3)	CASH DEBIT (4)	CASH CREDIT (5)	
		Closing Entries								
6										6
7	30	Sales			2 160 00					7
8		Income Summary				2 160 00				8
9	30	Income Summary			1 483 00					9
10		Advertising Expense				460 00				10
11		Cash Short and Over				6 00				11
12		Insur. Exp				125 00				12
13		Misc. Exp				189 00				13
14		Supplies Exp				153 00				14
15		Utilities Exp				550 00				15
16	30	Income Summary			677 00					16
17		Connor — Capital				677 00				17
18	30	/ / /			1 700 00					18
19		/ / Drawing				1 700 00				19
20										20
21										21
22										22
23										23
24										24
25										25
26										26
27										27
28										28

Name ____________ Date ________ Class ________

8-1 WORK TOGETHER (continued)

GENERAL LEDGER

ACCOUNT Cash — ACCOUNT NO. 110

DATE		ITEM	POST. REF.	DEBIT	CREDIT	BALANCE DEBIT	BALANCE CREDIT
20-- Apr.	30	Balance	✔			4 900 00	

ACCOUNT Petty Cash — ACCOUNT NO. 120

DATE		ITEM	POST. REF.	DEBIT	CREDIT	BALANCE DEBIT	BALANCE CREDIT
20-- Apr.	30	Balance	✔			75 00	

ACCOUNT Accounts Receivable—B. Widell — ACCOUNT NO. 130

DATE		ITEM	POST. REF.	DEBIT	CREDIT	BALANCE DEBIT	BALANCE CREDIT
20-- Apr.	30	Balance	✔			1 387 00	

ACCOUNT Supplies — ACCOUNT NO. 140

DATE		ITEM	POST. REF.	DEBIT	CREDIT	BALANCE DEBIT	BALANCE CREDIT
20-- Apr.	30	Balance	✔			75 00	

ACCOUNT Prepaid Insurance — ACCOUNT NO. 150

DATE		ITEM	POST. REF.	DEBIT	CREDIT	BALANCE DEBIT	BALANCE CREDIT
20-- Apr.	30	Balance	✔			250 00	

ACCOUNT Accounts Payable—Southside Supplies ACCOUNT NO. 210

DATE		ITEM	POST. REF.	DEBIT	CREDIT	BALANCE DEBIT	BALANCE CREDIT
20– Apr.	30	Balance	✔				2 6 7 00

ACCOUNT Connor Whitney, Capital ACCOUNT NO. 310

DATE		ITEM	POST. REF.	DEBIT	CREDIT	BALANCE DEBIT	BALANCE CREDIT
20– Apr.	30	Balance	✔				7 4 4 3 00
	30				6 7 7 0 00		8 1 2 0 00
	30			1 7 0 0 00			6 4 2 0 00

ACCOUNT Connor Whitney, Drawing ACCOUNT NO. 320

DATE		ITEM	POST. REF.	DEBIT	CREDIT	BALANCE DEBIT	BALANCE CREDIT
20– Apr.	30	Balance	✔			1 7 0 0 00	
	30				1 7 0 0 00	—	—

ACCOUNT Income Summary ACCOUNT NO. 330

DATE		ITEM	POST. REF.	DEBIT	CREDIT	BALANCE DEBIT	BALANCE CREDIT
Apr	30				2 1 6 0 00		2 1 6 0 00
	30			1 4 8 3			6 7 7
	30			6 7 7		—	—

ACCOUNT Sales ACCOUNT NO. 410

DATE		ITEM	POST. REF.	DEBIT	CREDIT	BALANCE DEBIT	BALANCE CREDIT
20– Apr.	30	Balance	✔				2 1 6 0 00
	30			2 1 6 0 00		—	—

Name ______________________ Date ____________ Class ____________

8-1 WORK TOGETHER (concluded)

ACCOUNT Advertising Expense ACCOUNT NO. 510

DATE		ITEM	POST. REF.	DEBIT	CREDIT	BALANCE DEBIT	BALANCE CREDIT
20-- Apr.	30	Balance	✔			460 00	
	30				460 00	—	—

ACCOUNT Cash Short and Over ACCOUNT NO. 520

DATE		ITEM	POST. REF.	DEBIT	CREDIT	BALANCE DEBIT	BALANCE CREDIT
20-- Apr.	30	Balance	✔			6 00	
	30				6 00	—	—

ACCOUNT Insurance Expense ACCOUNT NO. 530

DATE		ITEM	POST. REF.	DEBIT	CREDIT	BALANCE DEBIT	BALANCE CREDIT
20-- Apr.	30	Balance	✔			125 00	
	30				125 00	—	—

ACCOUNT Miscellaneous Expense ACCOUNT NO. 540

DATE		ITEM	POST. REF.	DEBIT	CREDIT	BALANCE DEBIT	BALANCE CREDIT
20-- Apr.	30	Balance	✔			189 00	
	30				189	—	—

ACCOUNT Supplies Expense ACCOUNT NO. 550

DATE		ITEM	POST. REF.	DEBIT	CREDIT	BALANCE DEBIT	BALANCE CREDIT
20-- Apr.	30	Balance	✔			153 00	
	30				153 00	—	—

ACCOUNT Utilities Expense ACCOUNT NO. 560

DATE		ITEM	POST. REF.	DEBIT	CREDIT	BALANCE DEBIT	BALANCE CREDIT
20-- Apr.	30	Balance	✔			550 00	
	30				550	—	—

8-1 ON YOUR OWN, p. 222

Journalizing and posting closing entries

	ACCOUNT TITLE	5 INCOME STATEMENT DEBIT	6 INCOME STATEMENT CREDIT	7 BALANCE SHEET DEBIT	8 BALANCE SHEET CREDIT	
1	Cash			13 600 00		1
2	Petty Cash			150 00		2
3	Accounts Receivable—Eat Right Eatery			2 996 00		3
4	Supplies			240 00		4
5	Prepaid Insurance			520 00		5
6	Accounts Payable—Lakeville Supplies				596 00	6
7	Sawyer Parker, Capital				14 886 00	7
8	Sawyer Parker, Drawing			3 400 00		8
9	Income Summary					9
10	Sales		8 280 00			10
11	Advertising Expense	910 00				11
12	Cash Short and Over	2 00				12
13	Insurance Expense	130 00				13
14	Miscellaneous Expense	378 00				14
15	Supplies Expense	236 00				15
16	Utilities Expense	1 200 00				16
17		2 856 00	8 280 00	20 906 00	15 482 00	17
18	Net Income	5 424 00			5 424 00	18
19		8 280 00	8 280 00	20 906 00	20 906 00	19
20						20
21						21
22						22
23						23
24						24
25						25
26						26
27						27
28						28
29						29
30						30
31						31
32						32

Name ______________________ Date ____________ Class ____________

8-1 ON YOUR OWN (continued)

JOURNAL PAGE

	DATE	ACCOUNT TITLE	DOC. NO.	POST. REF.	GENERAL DEBIT (1)	GENERAL CREDIT (2)	SALES CREDIT (3)	CASH DEBIT (4)	CASH CREDIT (5)	
6		Closing Entries								6
7		Sales			8 280 00					7
8		Income Summary				8 280 00				8
9	30	Income Summary								9
10										10
11										11
12										12
13										13
14										14
15										15
16										16
17										17
18										18
19										19
20										20
21										21
22										22
23										23
24										24
25										25
26										26
27										27
28										28

8-1 ON YOUR OWN (continued)

GENERAL LEDGER

ACCOUNT Cash — ACCOUNT NO. 110

DATE		ITEM	POST. REF.	DEBIT	CREDIT	BALANCE DEBIT	BALANCE CREDIT
20-- Dec.	31	Balance	✔			13,600.00	

ACCOUNT Petty Cash — ACCOUNT NO. 120

DATE		ITEM	POST. REF.	DEBIT	CREDIT	BALANCE DEBIT	BALANCE CREDIT
20-- Dec.	31	Balance	✔			150.00	

ACCOUNT Accounts Receivable—Eat Right Eatery — ACCOUNT NO. 130

DATE		ITEM	POST. REF.	DEBIT	CREDIT	BALANCE DEBIT	BALANCE CREDIT
20-- Dec.	31	Balance	✔			2,996.00	

ACCOUNT Supplies — ACCOUNT NO. 140

DATE		ITEM	POST. REF.	DEBIT	CREDIT	BALANCE DEBIT	BALANCE CREDIT
20-- Dec.	31	Balance	✔			240.00	

ACCOUNT Prepaid Insurance — ACCOUNT NO. 150

DATE		ITEM	POST. REF.	DEBIT	CREDIT	BALANCE DEBIT	BALANCE CREDIT
20-- Dec.	31	Balance	✔			520.00	

ACCOUNT Accounts Payable—Lakeville Supplies — ACCOUNT NO. 210

DATE		ITEM	POST. REF.	DEBIT	CREDIT	BALANCE DEBIT	BALANCE CREDIT
20-- Dec.	31	Balance	✔				596.00

Name ______________________ Date ____________ Class ____________

8-1 ON YOUR OWN (continued)

ACCOUNT Sawyer Parker, Capital ACCOUNT NO. 310

DATE		ITEM	POST. REF.	DEBIT	CREDIT	BALANCE DEBIT	BALANCE CREDIT
20-- Dec.	31	Balance	✔				14 886 00 capital →
				net income	5 424 00		20 310 00
				3 400 00			16 910 00

withdraw

ACCOUNT Sawyer Parker, Drawing ACCOUNT NO. 320

DATE		ITEM	POST. REF.	DEBIT	CREDIT	BALANCE DEBIT	BALANCE CREDIT
20-- Dec.	31	Balance	✔			3 400 00	
					3 400 00	—	—

ACCOUNT Income Summary ACCOUNT NO. 330

DATE		ITEM	POST. REF.	DEBIT	CREDIT	BALANCE DEBIT	BALANCE CREDIT
Dec	31				sales 8 280 00		8 280 00
		Total Exp.		2 856 00			5 424 00
				5 424 00		—	—

ACCOUNT Sales ACCOUNT NO. 410

DATE		ITEM	POST. REF.	DEBIT	CREDIT	BALANCE DEBIT	BALANCE CREDIT
20-- Dec.	31	Balance	✔				8 280 00
				8 280 00		—	—

ACCOUNT Advertising Expense ACCOUNT NO. 510

DATE		ITEM	POST. REF.	DEBIT	CREDIT	BALANCE DEBIT	BALANCE CREDIT
20-- Dec.	31	Balance	✔			910 00	
					910 00	—	—

ACCOUNT Cash Short and Over ACCOUNT NO. 520

DATE		ITEM	POST. REF.	DEBIT	CREDIT	BALANCE DEBIT	BALANCE CREDIT
20-- Dec.	31	Balance	✔			2 00	

ACCOUNT Insurance Expense ACCOUNT NO. 530

DATE		ITEM	POST. REF.	DEBIT	CREDIT	BALANCE DEBIT	BALANCE CREDIT
20-- Dec.	31	Balance	✔			130 00	

ACCOUNT Miscellaneous Expense ACCOUNT NO. 540

DATE		ITEM	POST. REF.	DEBIT	CREDIT	BALANCE DEBIT	BALANCE CREDIT
20-- Dec.	31	Balance	✔			378 00	

ACCOUNT Supplies Expense ACCOUNT NO. 550

DATE		ITEM	POST. REF.	DEBIT	CREDIT	BALANCE DEBIT	BALANCE CREDIT
20-- Dec.	31	Balance	✔			236 00	

ACCOUNT Utilities Expense ACCOUNT NO. 560

DATE		ITEM	POST. REF.	DEBIT	CREDIT	BALANCE DEBIT	BALANCE CREDIT
20-- Dec.	31	Balance	✔			1 200 00	

Name ______________________ Date ______________ Class ______________

8-2 WORK TOGETHER, p. 230

Preparing a post-closing trial balance

ACCOUNT TITLE	DEBIT	CREDIT
Cash	4 900 00	
petty Cash	75 00	
Account Rec. B-Widell	1 387 00	
Supplies	75 00	
PrePaid Insurance	250 00	
Accounts Payable – Southside supplies		267 00
Connor Whitney – Capital		6 420 00
	6 687 00	6 687 00

8-2 ON YOUR OWN, p. 230

Preparing a post-closing trial balance

6
9
15
24

Repair World
Post-closing Trial Balance
Dec. 31, 20

ACCOUNT TITLE	DEBIT	CREDIT
Cash	13 600 00	
Petty cash	150 00	
Account Receivable - Eat Right Eatery	2 996 00	
supplies	240 00	
Prepaid Insu.	520 00	
Acc. Payable - Lakeville supplies		596 00
Sawyer Parker Capital		16 910 00
	17 506 00	17 506 00

Name ______________________ Date ____________ Class ____________

8-1 APPLICATION PROBLEM (LO1), p. 233

Journalizing and posting closing entries

JOURNAL PAGE

	DATE	ACCOUNT TITLE	DOC. NO.	POST. REF.	GENERAL DEBIT (1)	GENERAL CREDIT (2)	SALES CREDIT (3)	CASH DEBIT (4)	CASH CREDIT (5)	
		Closing entries								
6										6
7	30	Sales			1 704 00					7
8		Income summary				1 704 00				8
9		Income summary			1 132 00					9
10		Advertising Exp.				255				10
11		Cash short and over				22 00				11
12		Insurance Expense				135				12
13		Misc. Exp.				138				13
14		Supplies Exp.				330				14
15		Utilities Exp				272				15
16	30	Income summary			572 00					16
17		Akbar Sharma, Capital				572				17
18	30	" " "			375					18
19		Akbar Sharma Drawing				375				19
20										20
21										21
22										22
23										23
24										24
25										25
26										26
27										27
28										28

8-1 APPLICATION PROBLEM (continued)

GENERAL LEDGER

ACCOUNT Cash ACCOUNT NO. 110

DATE		ITEM	POST. REF.	DEBIT	CREDIT	BALANCE DEBIT	BALANCE CREDIT
20-- June	30	Balance	✔			8 715 00	

ACCOUNT Petty Cash ACCOUNT NO. 120

DATE		ITEM	POST. REF.	DEBIT	CREDIT	BALANCE DEBIT	BALANCE CREDIT
20-- June	30	Balance	✔			75 00	

ACCOUNT Accounts Receivable—Raymond O'Neil ACCOUNT NO. 130

DATE		ITEM	POST. REF.	DEBIT	CREDIT	BALANCE DEBIT	BALANCE CREDIT
20-- June	30	Balance	✔			642 00	

ACCOUNT Supplies ACCOUNT NO. 140

DATE		ITEM	POST. REF.	DEBIT	CREDIT	BALANCE DEBIT	BALANCE CREDIT
20-- June	30	Balance	✔			188 00	

ACCOUNT Prepaid Insurance ACCOUNT NO. 150

DATE		ITEM	POST. REF.	DEBIT	CREDIT	BALANCE DEBIT	BALANCE CREDIT
20-- June	30	Balance	✔			540 00	

Name ____________________ Date __________ Class __________

8-1 APPLICATION PROBLEM (continued)

ACCOUNT Accounts Payable—Western Supplies ACCOUNT NO. 210

DATE		ITEM	POST. REF.	DEBIT	CREDIT	BALANCE DEBIT	BALANCE CREDIT
20-- June	30	Balance	✔				268 00

ACCOUNT Akbar Sharma, Capital ACCOUNT NO. 310

DATE		ITEM	POST. REF.	DEBIT	CREDIT	BALANCE DEBIT	BALANCE CREDIT
20-- June	30	Balance	✔				9 695 00

ACCOUNT Akbar Sharma, Drawing ACCOUNT NO. 320

DATE		ITEM	POST. REF.	DEBIT	CREDIT	BALANCE DEBIT	BALANCE CREDIT
20-- June	30	Balance	✔			375 00	

ACCOUNT Income Summary ACCOUNT NO. 330

DATE		ITEM	POST. REF.	DEBIT	CREDIT	BALANCE DEBIT	BALANCE CREDIT

ACCOUNT Sales ACCOUNT NO. 410

DATE		ITEM	POST. REF.	DEBIT	CREDIT	BALANCE DEBIT	BALANCE CREDIT
20-- June	30	Balance	✔				1 704 00

8-1 APPLICATION PROBLEM (concluded)

ACCOUNT Advertising Expense — ACCOUNT NO. 510

DATE		ITEM	POST. REF.	DEBIT	CREDIT	BALANCE DEBIT	BALANCE CREDIT
20-- June	30	Balance	✔			255 00	

ACCOUNT Cash Short and Over — ACCOUNT NO. 520

DATE		ITEM	POST. REF.	DEBIT	CREDIT	BALANCE DEBIT	BALANCE CREDIT
20-- June	30	Balance	✔			2 00	

ACCOUNT Insurance Expense — ACCOUNT NO. 530

DATE		ITEM	POST. REF.	DEBIT	CREDIT	BALANCE DEBIT	BALANCE CREDIT
20-- June	30	Balance	✔			135 00	

ACCOUNT Miscellaneous Expense — ACCOUNT NO. 540

DATE		ITEM	POST. REF.	DEBIT	CREDIT	BALANCE DEBIT	BALANCE CREDIT
20-- June	30	Balance	✔			138 00	

ACCOUNT Supplies Expense — ACCOUNT NO. 550

DATE		ITEM	POST. REF.	DEBIT	CREDIT	BALANCE DEBIT	BALANCE CREDIT
20-- June	30	Balance	✔			330 00	

ACCOUNT Utilities Expense — ACCOUNT NO. 560

DATE		ITEM	POST. REF.	DEBIT	CREDIT	BALANCE DEBIT	BALANCE CREDIT
20-- June	30	Balance	✔			272 00	

Name ______________________ Date ______________ Class ______________

8-2 APPLICATION PROBLEM (LO2), p. 233

Preparing a post-closing trial balance

ACCOUNT TITLE	DEBIT	CREDIT

8-M MASTERY PROBLEM (LO1, 2), p. 234

Journalizing and posting closing entries with a net loss; preparing a post-closing trial balance

1.

JOURNAL PAGE

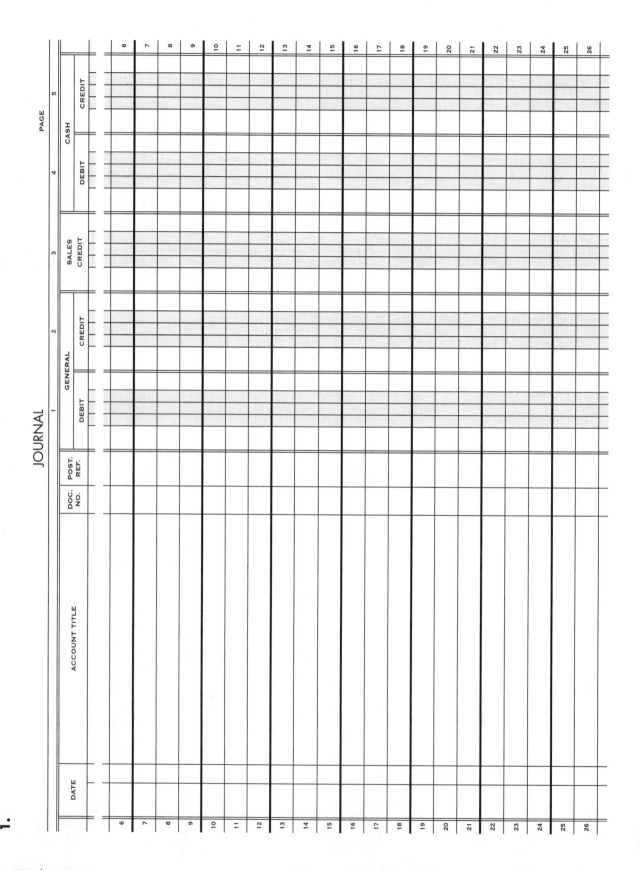

				1	2	3	4	5	
	DATE	ACCOUNT TITLE	DOC. NO.	POST. REF.	GENERAL DEBIT	GENERAL CREDIT	SALES CREDIT	CASH DEBIT	CASH CREDIT
6									
7									
8									
9									
10									
11									
12									
13									
14									
15									
16									
17									
18									
19									
20									
21									
22									
23									
24									
25									
26									

Name ______________________ Date ____________ Class ____________

8-M MASTERY PROBLEM (continued)

GENERAL LEDGER

1.

ACCOUNT Cash — ACCOUNT NO. 110

DATE		ITEM	POST. REF.	DEBIT	CREDIT	BALANCE DEBIT	BALANCE CREDIT
20-- May	31	Balance	✔			3,475.00	

ACCOUNT Petty Cash — ACCOUNT NO. 120

DATE		ITEM	POST. REF.	DEBIT	CREDIT	BALANCE DEBIT	BALANCE CREDIT
20-- May	31	Balance	✔			200.00	

ACCOUNT Accounts Receivable—M. Monesrud — ACCOUNT NO. 130

DATE		ITEM	POST. REF.	DEBIT	CREDIT	BALANCE DEBIT	BALANCE CREDIT
20-- May	31	Balance	✔			375.00	

ACCOUNT Supplies — ACCOUNT NO. 140

DATE		ITEM	POST. REF.	DEBIT	CREDIT	BALANCE DEBIT	BALANCE CREDIT
20-- May	31	Balance	✔			390.00	

ACCOUNT Prepaid Insurance — ACCOUNT NO. 150

DATE		ITEM	POST. REF.	DEBIT	CREDIT	BALANCE DEBIT	BALANCE CREDIT
20-- May	31	Balance	✔			400.00	

8-M MASTERY PROBLEM (continued)

ACCOUNT Accounts Payable—Lexington Supply ACCOUNT NO. 210

DATE		ITEM	POST. REF.	DEBIT	CREDIT	BALANCE DEBIT	BALANCE CREDIT
20-- May	31	Balance	✔				300 00

ACCOUNT Rhonda Rausch, Capital ACCOUNT NO. 310

DATE		ITEM	POST. REF.	DEBIT	CREDIT	BALANCE DEBIT	BALANCE CREDIT
20-- May	31	Balance	✔				5,012 00

ACCOUNT Rhonda Rausch, Drawing ACCOUNT NO. 320

DATE		ITEM	POST. REF.	DEBIT	CREDIT	BALANCE DEBIT	BALANCE CREDIT
20-- May	31	Balance	✔			300 00	

ACCOUNT Income Summary ACCOUNT NO. 330

DATE		ITEM	POST. REF.	DEBIT	CREDIT	BALANCE DEBIT	BALANCE CREDIT

ACCOUNT Sales ACCOUNT NO. 410

DATE		ITEM	POST. REF.	DEBIT	CREDIT	BALANCE DEBIT	BALANCE CREDIT
20-- May	31	Balance	✔				1,790 00

Name ______ Date ______ Class ______

8-M MASTERY PROBLEM (continued)

ACCOUNT Advertising Expense — ACCOUNT NO. 510

DATE		ITEM	POST. REF.	DEBIT	CREDIT	BALANCE DEBIT	BALANCE CREDIT
20-- May	31	Balance	✔			225 00	

ACCOUNT Cash Short and Over — ACCOUNT NO. 520

DATE		ITEM	POST. REF.	DEBIT	CREDIT	BALANCE DEBIT	BALANCE CREDIT
20-- May	31	Balance	✔			2 00	

ACCOUNT Insurance Expense — ACCOUNT NO. 530

DATE		ITEM	POST. REF.	DEBIT	CREDIT	BALANCE DEBIT	BALANCE CREDIT
20-- May	31	Balance	✔			175 00	

ACCOUNT Miscellaneous Expense — ACCOUNT NO. 540

DATE		ITEM	POST. REF.	DEBIT	CREDIT	BALANCE DEBIT	BALANCE CREDIT
20-- May	31	Balance	✔			40 00	

ACCOUNT Supplies Expense — ACCOUNT NO. 550

DATE		ITEM	POST. REF.	DEBIT	CREDIT	BALANCE DEBIT	BALANCE CREDIT
20-- May	31	Balance	✔			700 00	

ACCOUNT Utilities Expense — ACCOUNT NO. 560

DATE		ITEM	POST. REF.	DEBIT	CREDIT	BALANCE DEBIT	BALANCE CREDIT
20-- May	31	Balance	✔			820 00	

8-M MASTERY PROBLEM (concluded)

2.

ACCOUNT TITLE	DEBIT	CREDIT

Name ______________________ Date ____________ Class ____________

8-C CHALLENGE PROBLEM (LO1, 2), p. 235

Journalizing and posting closing entries with two revenue accounts and a net loss; preparing a post-closing trial balance

1.

JOURNAL PAGE

	DATE	ACCOUNT TITLE	DOC. NO.	POST. REF.	1 GENERAL DEBIT	2 GENERAL CREDIT	3 SALES CREDIT	4 CASH DEBIT	5 CASH CREDIT	
6										6
7										7
8										8
9										9
10										10
11										11
12										12
13										13
14										14
15										15
16										16
17										17
18										18
19										19
20										20
21										21
22										22
23										23
24										24
25										25
26										26
27										27

8-C CHALLENGE PROBLEM (continued)

GENERAL LEDGER

1.

ACCOUNT Cash — ACCOUNT NO. 110

DATE		ITEM	POST. REF.	DEBIT	CREDIT	BALANCE DEBIT	BALANCE CREDIT
20-- June	30	Balance	✔			3 796 00	

ACCOUNT Accounts Receivable—V. Mathaney — ACCOUNT NO. 120

DATE		ITEM	POST. REF.	DEBIT	CREDIT	BALANCE DEBIT	BALANCE CREDIT
20-- June	30	Balance	✔			190 00	

ACCOUNT Supplies — ACCOUNT NO. 130

DATE		ITEM	POST. REF.	DEBIT	CREDIT	BALANCE DEBIT	BALANCE CREDIT
20-- June	30	Balance	✔			1 300 00	

ACCOUNT Prepaid Insurance — ACCOUNT NO. 140

DATE		ITEM	POST. REF.	DEBIT	CREDIT	BALANCE DEBIT	BALANCE CREDIT
20-- June	30	Balance	✔			2 400 00	

ACCOUNT Accounts Payable—Eveleth Repair — ACCOUNT NO. 210

DATE		ITEM	POST. REF.	DEBIT	CREDIT	BALANCE DEBIT	BALANCE CREDIT
20-- June	30	Balance	✔				116 00

Name ______________________ Date ______________ Class ______________

8-C CHALLENGE PROBLEM (continued)

ACCOUNT Accounts Payable—Fremont Supplies ACCOUNT NO. 220

DATE		ITEM	POST. REF.	DEBIT	CREDIT	BALANCE DEBIT	BALANCE CREDIT
20– June	30	Balance	✔				220 00

ACCOUNT Accounts Payable—Olmstad Company ACCOUNT NO. 230

DATE		ITEM	POST. REF.	DEBIT	CREDIT	BALANCE DEBIT	BALANCE CREDIT
20– June	30	Balance	✔				430 00

ACCOUNT Jon Yanta, Capital ACCOUNT NO. 310

DATE		ITEM	POST. REF.	DEBIT	CREDIT	BALANCE DEBIT	BALANCE CREDIT
20– June	30	Balance	✔				8 000 00

ACCOUNT Jon Yanta, Drawing ACCOUNT NO. 320

DATE		ITEM	POST. REF.	DEBIT	CREDIT	BALANCE DEBIT	BALANCE CREDIT
20– June	30	Balance	✔			200 00	

ACCOUNT Income Summary ACCOUNT NO. 330

DATE		ITEM	POST. REF.	DEBIT	CREDIT	BALANCE DEBIT	BALANCE CREDIT

ACCOUNT Sales—Lawn Care ACCOUNT NO. 410

DATE		ITEM	POST. REF.	DEBIT	CREDIT	BALANCE DEBIT	BALANCE CREDIT
20– June	30	Balance	✔				980 00

ACCOUNT Sales—Shrub Care ACCOUNT NO. 420

DATE		ITEM	POST. REF.	DEBIT	CREDIT	BALANCE DEBIT	BALANCE CREDIT
20-- June	30	Balance	✔				5,000.00

ACCOUNT Advertising Expense ACCOUNT NO. 510

DATE		ITEM	POST. REF.	DEBIT	CREDIT	BALANCE DEBIT	BALANCE CREDIT
20-- June	30	Balance	✔			780.00	

ACCOUNT Insurance Expense ACCOUNT NO. 520

DATE		ITEM	POST. REF.	DEBIT	CREDIT	BALANCE DEBIT	BALANCE CREDIT
20-- June	30	Balance	✔			800.00	

ACCOUNT Miscellaneous Expense ACCOUNT NO. 530

DATE		ITEM	POST. REF.	DEBIT	CREDIT	BALANCE DEBIT	BALANCE CREDIT
20-- June	30	Balance	✔			1,100.00	

ACCOUNT Rent Expense ACCOUNT NO. 540

DATE		ITEM	POST. REF.	DEBIT	CREDIT	BALANCE DEBIT	BALANCE CREDIT
20-- June	30	Balance	✔			6,600.00	

ACCOUNT Supplies Expense ACCOUNT NO. 550

DATE		ITEM	POST. REF.	DEBIT	CREDIT	BALANCE DEBIT	BALANCE CREDIT
20-- June	30	Balance	✔			6,400.00	

8-C CHALLENGE PROBLEM (continued)

2.

ACCOUNT TITLE	DEBIT	CREDIT

8-C CHALLENGE PROBLEM (concluded)

3.

Name ______________________ Date ____________ Class ____________

REINFORCEMENT ACTIVITY 1, Part B, p. 238

An Accounting Cycle for a Proprietorship: End-of-Fiscal-Period Work

The general ledger prepared in Reinforcement Activity 1, Part A, is needed to complete Reinforcement Activity 1, Part B.

12., 13., 14., 15., 16.

	ACCOUNT TITLE	1 TRIAL BALANCE DEBIT	2 TRIAL BALANCE CREDIT	3 ADJUSTMENTS DEBIT	4 ADJUSTMENTS CREDIT	5 INCOME STATEMENT DEBIT	6 INCOME STATEMENT CREDIT	7 BALANCE SHEET DEBIT	8 BALANCE SHEET CREDIT	
1										1
2										2
3										3
4										4
5										5
6										6
7										7
8										8
9										9
10										10
11										11
12										12
13										13
14										14
15										15
16										16
17										17
18										18
19										19
20										20
21										21
22										22
23										23

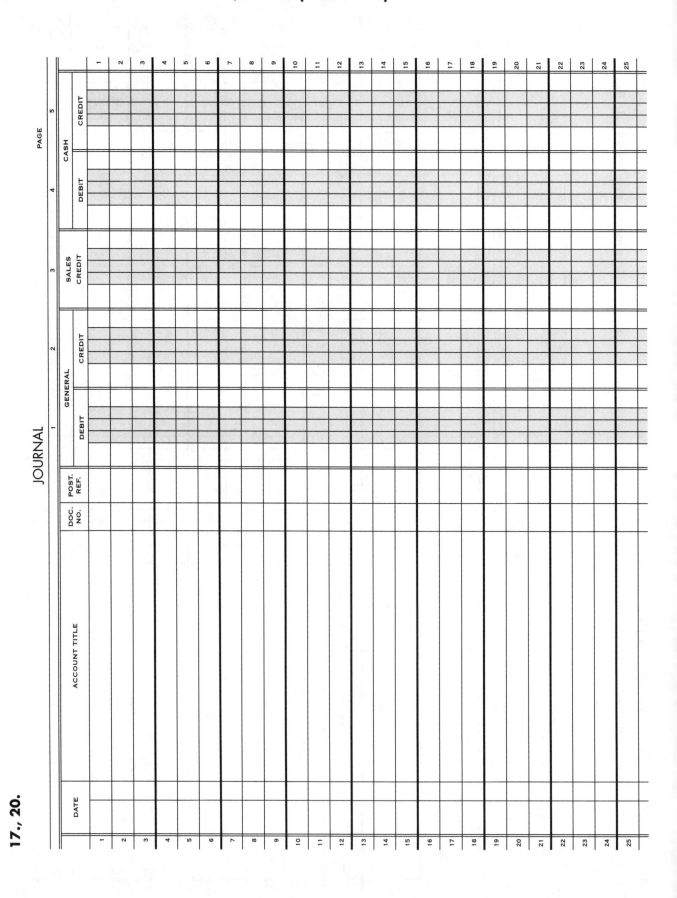

REINFORCEMENT ACTIVITY 1, Part B (continued)

17., 20.

JOURNAL

PAGE

					1	2	3	4	5	
	DATE	ACCOUNT TITLE	DOC. NO.	POST. REF.	GENERAL DEBIT	GENERAL CREDIT	SALES CREDIT	CASH DEBIT	CASH CREDIT	
1										1
2										2
3										3
4										4
5										5
6										6
7										7
8										8
9										9
10										10
11										11
12										12
13										13
14										14
15										15
16										16
17										17
18										18
19										19
20										20
21										21
22										22
23										23
24										24
25										25

Name ______________________ Date ______________ Class ______________

REINFORCEMENT ACTIVITY 1, Part B (continued)

18.

			% OF SALES

REINFORCEMENT ACTIVITY 1, Part B (continued)

19.

Name ______________________ Date ____________ Class ____________

REINFORCEMENT ACTIVITY 1, Part B (concluded)

21.

____

____

____

ACCOUNT TITLE	DEBIT	CREDIT

Study Guide 9	**Name**	**Perfect Score**	**Your Score**
	Identifying Accounting Terms	41 Pts.	
	Analyzing Accounting Concepts and Practices	20 Pts.	
	Analyzing Transactions Recorded in Special Journals	21 Pts.	
	Total	82 Pts.	

Part One—Identifying Accounting Terms

Directions: Select the one term in Column I that best fits each definition in Column II. Print the letter identifying your choice in the Answers column.

Contains accounting terms for Lessons 9-1.

Column I	Column II	Answers
A. accounts payable ledger	**1.** Goods that a business purchases in order to sell. (p. 244)	**1.** ______
B. articles of incorporation	**2.** A business that purchases and resells goods. (p. 244)	**2.** ______
C. capital	**3.** A merchandising business that sells to those who use or consume the goods. (p. 244)	**3.** ______
D. capital stock	**4.** A business that buys and resells merchandise primarily to other merchandising businesses. (p. 244)	**4.** ______
E. charter	**5.** An organization with the legal rights of a person which many persons or other corporations may own. (p. 244)	**5.** ______
F. controlling account	**6.** The assets or other financial resources available to a business. (p. 244)	**6.** ______
G. corporation	**7.** Each unit of ownership in a corporation. (p. 244)	**7.** ______
H. merchandise	**8.** The owner of one or more shares of stock. (p. 244)	**8.** ______
I. merchandising business	**9.** The total shares of ownership in a corporation. (p. 244)	**9.** ______
J. retail merchandising business	**10.** A legal document that identifies basic characteristics of a corporation. (p. 244)	**10.** ______
K. share of stock	**11.** The legal right for a business to conduct operations as a corporation. (p. 244)	**11.** ______
L. stockholder	**12.** A business from which merchandise, supplies, or other assets are purchased. (p. 246)	**12.** ______
M. subsidiary ledger	**13.** A ledger that is summarized in a single general ledger account. (p. 246)	**13.** ______
N. vendor	**14.** The subsidiary ledger containing vendor accounts. (p. 246)	**14.** ______
O. wholesale merchandising business	**15.** An account in a general ledger that summarizes all accounts in a subsidiary ledger. (p. 246)	**15.** ______

Accounting terms for Lessons 9-2 through 9-5 are presented on the following page.

Directions: Select the one term in Column I that best fits each definition in Column II. Print the letter identifying your choice in the Answers column.

Contains accounting terms for Lessons 9-2 through 9-5.

Column I	Column II	Answers
A. cash discount	**1.** A list of assets, usually containing the value of individual items. (p. 249)	**1.** ________
B. cash payments journal	**2.** The goods a business has on hand for sale to customers. (p. 249)	**2.** ________
C. contra account	**3.** An inventory determined by keeping a continuous record of increases, decreases, and the balance on hand of each item of merchandise. (p. 249)	**3.** ________
D. cost of merchandise	**4.** A merchandise inventory evaluated at the end of a fiscal period. (p. 249)	**4.** ________
E. credit limit	**5.** When a periodic inventory is conducted by counting, weighing, or measuring items of merchandise on hand. (p. 249)	**5.** ________
F. discount period	**6.** The amount a business pays for goods it purchases to sell. (p. 250)	**6.** ________
G. due date	**7.** A form requesting the purchase of merchandise. (p. 251)	**7.** ________
H. general amount column	**8.** A form requesting that a vendor sell merchandise to a business. (p. 251)	**8.** ________
I. inventory	**9.** A journal used to record only one kind of transaction. (p. 251)	**9.** ________
J. list price	**10.** A transaction in which the items purchased are to be paid for later. (p. 252)	**10.** ________
K. merchandise inventory	**11.** A special journal used to record only purchases of merchandise on account. (p. 252)	**11.** ________
L. net price	**12.** A journal amount column headed with an account title. (p. 252)	**12.** ________
M. periodic inventory	**13.** An invoice used as a source document for recording a purchase on account transaction. (p. 252)	**13.** ________
N. perpetual inventory	**14.** An agreement between a buyer and a seller about payment for merchandise. (p. 252)	**14.** ________
O. physical inventory	**15.** The date by which an invoice must be paid. (p. 252)	**15.** ________
P. purchase invoice	**16.** A special journal used to record only cash payment transactions. (p. 260)	**16.** ________
Q. purchase on account	**17.** The retail price listed in a catalog or on an Internet site. (p. 260)	**17.** ________
R. purchase order	**18.** A reduction in the list price granted to a merchandising business. (p. 260)	**18.** ________
S. purchases discount	**19.** The price after the trade discount has been deducted from the list price. (p. 260)	**19.** ________
T. purchases journal	**20.** A deduction that a vendor allows on an invoice amount to encourage prompt payment. (p. 260)	**20.** ________
U. requisition	**21.** A journal amount column that is not headed with an account title. (p. 260)	**21.** ________
V. schedule of accounts payable	**22.** The period of time during which a customer may take a cash discount. (p. 263)	**22.** ________
W. special amount column	**23.** When a company that has purchased merchandise on account takes a cash discount. (p. 263)	**23.** ________
X. special journal	**24.** An account that reduces a related account on a financial statement. (p. 263)	**24.** ________
Y. terms of sale	**25.** The maximum outstanding balance allowed to a customer by a vendor. (p. 267)	**25.** ________
Z. trade discount	**26.** A listing of vendor accounts, account balances, and the total amount due to all vendors. (p. 272)	**26.** ________

Name ______________________ Date ____________ Class ____________

Part Two—Analyzing Accounting Concepts and Practices

Directions: Place a *T* for True or an *F* for False in the Answers column to show whether each of the following statements is true or false.

	Answers
1. A corporation can incur liabilities but cannot own property. (p. 244)	**1.** ______
2. The articles of incorporation typically include the name and address of the business, its purpose for operating, any limitations on its activities and rules for dissolving the corporation. (p. 244)	**2.** ______
3. Unlike a proprietorship, a corporation exists independent of its owners. (p. 245)	**3.** ______
4. The total of accounts in the accounts payable ledger equals the balance of the controlling account, Accounts Payable. (p. 246)	**4.** ______
5. The accounts payable ledger form contains the same columns as the general ledger except that it lacks a Credit Balance column. (p. 247)	**5.** ______
6. When a perpetual inventory system is used, purchases of merchandise are accounted for directly to Merchandise Inventory. (p. 249)	**6.** ______
7. The perpetual inventory method is easier to maintain than the periodic method. The perpetual method does not require records of the quantity and cost of individual goods. (p. 249)	**7.** ______
8. When a periodic inventory system is used, the cost of merchandise is recorded to Purchases. (p. 250)	**8.** ______
9. The income statement of a merchandising business places Purchases in a section titled Cost of Goods Sold, separate from other expenses. (p. 250)	**9.** ______
10. A purchase invoice lists the quantity, the description, and the price of each item and shows the total amount of the purchase. (p. 253)	**10.** ______
11. A transaction to record merchandise purchased with a trade discount would include a credit to Merchandise Discount. (p. 260)	**11.** ______
12. When journalizing a cash payment for advertising, the vendor's name is written in the Account Title column of the cash payments journal. (p. 261)	**12.** ______
13. When supplies are purchased for use in the business, the amount is recorded as a debit to Purchases. (p. 262)	**13.** ______
14. The terms of sale 2/15, n/30 mean that 2% of the invoice amount may be deducted if paid within 15 days of the invoice date or the total invoice amount must be paid within 30 days. (p. 263)	**14.** ______
15. The contra account Purchases Discount has a normal credit balance. (p. 263)	**15.** ______
16. The petty cash account Cash Short and Over is a permanent account. (p. 265)	**16.** ______
17. Exceeding a vendor's credit limit can cause a disruption in the company's ability to purchase merchandise. (p. 267)	**17.** ______
18. A journal is proved and ruled whenever a journal page is filled, and always at the end of a month. (p. 269)	**18.** ______
19. The totals of the General amount columns of a cash payments journal are posted to the general ledger. (p. 270)	**19.** ______
20. The total of an accounts payable trial balance should equal the total of Accounts Payable. (p. 272)	**20.** ______

Part Three—Analyzing Transactions Recorded in Special Journals

Directions: In Answers Column 1, print the abbreviation for the journal in which each transaction is to be recorded. In Answers Columns 2 and 3, print the letters identifying the accounts to be debited and credited for each transaction.

PJ—Purchases journal; **CPJ**—Cash payments journal

Account Titles	Transactions	Answers: Journal	Debit	Credit
A. Accounts Payable	**1-2-3**. Purchased merchandise on account from Walner Electric. (p. 253)	1. ____	2. ____	3. ____
B. Cash	**4-5-6**. Paid cash for rent. (p. 261)	4. ____	5. ____	6. ____
C. Cash Short and Over	**7-8-9**. Paid cash to Triangle Suppliers for supplies. (pp. 261 and 262)	7. ____	8. ____	9. ____
D. Miscellaneous Expense	**10-11-12**. Purchased merchandise from Zaben Corp. for cash. (p. 262)	10. ____	11. ____	12. ____
E. Petty Cash	**13-14-15**. Paid cash on account to Walner Electric, less purchases discount. (p. 263)	13. ____	14. ____	15. ____
F. Purchases	**16-17-18**. Paid cash on account to Triangle Suppliers. (p. 264)	16. ____	17. ____	18. ____
G. Purchases Discount	**19-20-21**. Paid cash to replenish the petty cash fund: supplies, miscellaneous, cash over. (p. 265)	19. ____	20. ____	21. ____
H. Purchases Returns and Allowances				
I. Rent Expense				
J. Supplies				
K. Triangle Suppliers				
L. Walner Electric				
M. Zaben Corp.				

Name ______________________ Date ____________ Class ____________

9-1 WORK TOGETHER, p. 248

Starting an accounts payable ledger form

1.

VENDOR ______________________ VENDOR NO. ______

DATE		ITEM	POST. REF.	DEBIT	CREDIT	CREDIT BALANCE

2.

VENDOR ______________________ VENDOR NO. ______

DATE		ITEM	POST. REF.	DEBIT	CREDIT	CREDIT BALANCE

9-1 ON YOUR OWN, p. 248

Starting an accounts payable ledger form

1.

VENDOR VENDOR NO.

DATE		ITEM	POST. REF.	DEBIT	CREDIT	CREDIT BALANCE

2.

VENDOR VENDOR NO.

DATE		ITEM	POST. REF.	DEBIT	CREDIT	CREDIT BALANCE

Name ______________________________ Date ______________ Class ______________

9-2, 9-3, 9-4, and 9-5 WORK TOGETHER, pp. 254, 259, 266, and 273

9-2 Journalizing purchases using a purchases journal
9-3 Posting from a purchases journal
9-4 Journalizing cash payments using a cash payments journal
9-5 Posting from a cash payments journal

1., 2., 3.

PURCHASES JOURNAL

PAGE

	DATE	ACCOUNT CREDITED	PURCH. NO.	POST. REF.	PURCHASES DR. ACCTS. PAY. CR.	
1						1
2						2
3						3
4						4
5						5
6						6
7						7

CASH PAYMENTS JOURNAL

PAGE

					1	2	3	4	5	
	DATE	ACCOUNT TITLE	CK. NO.	POST. REF.	GENERAL		ACCOUNTS PAYABLE DEBIT	PURCHASES DISCOUNT CREDIT	CASH CREDIT	
					DEBIT	CREDIT				
1										1
2										2
3										3
4										4
5										5
6										6
7										7
8										8
9										9
10										10
11										11
12										12

1.

VENDOR Coastal Company VENDOR NO. 210

DATE		ITEM	POST. REF.	DEBIT	CREDIT	CREDIT BALANCE
20-- Oct.	1	Balance	✔			1 6 9 8 88

VENDOR Grey Manufacturing, Inc. VENDOR NO. 220

DATE		ITEM	POST. REF.	DEBIT	CREDIT	CREDIT BALANCE
20-- Oct.	1	Balance	✔			1 6 4 0 00

VENDOR Pacific Supply VENDOR NO. 230

DATE		ITEM	POST. REF.	DEBIT	CREDIT	CREDIT BALANCE
20-- Oct.	1	Balance	✔			9 2 5 65

VENDOR Westland Supply VENDOR NO. 240

DATE		ITEM	POST. REF.	DEBIT	CREDIT	CREDIT BALANCE
20-- Oct.	1	Balance	✔			9 9 2 00

VENDOR Yeatman Designs VENDOR NO. 250

DATE		ITEM	POST. REF.	DEBIT	CREDIT	CREDIT BALANCE
20-- Oct.	1	Balance	✔			8 7 7 00

Name ______________________ Date ____________ Class ____________

9-2, 9-3, 9-4, and 9-5 WORK TOGETHER (continued)

3.

ACCOUNT Cash ACCOUNT NO. 1110

DATE		ITEM	POST. REF.	DEBIT	CREDIT	BALANCE DEBIT	BALANCE CREDIT
20-- Oct.	1	Balance	✔			16 455 19	

ACCOUNT Supplies—Office ACCOUNT NO. 1145

DATE		ITEM	POST. REF.	DEBIT	CREDIT	BALANCE DEBIT	BALANCE CREDIT
20-- Oct.	1	Balance	✔			3 184 17	

ACCOUNT Supplies—Store ACCOUNT NO. 1150

DATE		ITEM	POST. REF.	DEBIT	CREDIT	BALANCE DEBIT	BALANCE CREDIT
20-- Oct.	1	Balance	✔			4 180 18	

ACCOUNT Accounts Payable ACCOUNT NO. 2110

DATE		ITEM	POST. REF.	DEBIT	CREDIT	BALANCE DEBIT	BALANCE CREDIT
20-- Oct.	1	Balance	✔				6 133 53

ACCOUNT Purchases ACCOUNT NO. 5110

DATE		ITEM	POST. REF.	DEBIT	CREDIT	BALANCE DEBIT	BALANCE CREDIT
20-- Oct.	1	Balance	✔			89 478 25	

ACCOUNT Purchases Discount — ACCOUNT NO. 5120

DATE		ITEM	POST. REF.	DEBIT	CREDIT	BALANCE DEBIT	BALANCE CREDIT
20-- Oct.	1	Balance	✔				621 48

ACCOUNT Cash Short and Over — ACCOUNT NO. 6110

DATE		ITEM	POST. REF.	DEBIT	CREDIT	BALANCE DEBIT	BALANCE CREDIT
20-- Oct.	1	Balance	✔			19 95	

ACCOUNT Miscellaneous Expense — ACCOUNT NO. 2110

DATE		ITEM	POST. REF.	DEBIT	CREDIT	BALANCE DEBIT	BALANCE CREDIT
20-- Oct.	1	Balance	✔			2,489 97	

ACCOUNT Utilities Expense — ACCOUNT NO. 6170

DATE		ITEM	POST. REF.	DEBIT	CREDIT	BALANCE DEBIT	BALANCE CREDIT
20-- Oct.	1	Balance	✔			948 59	

Name ______________________ Date ____________ Class ____________

9-2, 9-3, 9-4, and 9-5 WORK TOGETHER (concluded)

PETTY CASH REPORT

Date: October 31, 20--

Custodian: John Sandersen

Explanation			Reconciliation		Replenish Amount
Fund Total			200.00		
Payments:	Supplies—Office	48.15			
	Supplies—Store	57.18			
	Miscellaneous	47.64			
Less:	Total payments		152.97	→	152.97
Equals:	Recorded amount on hand		47.03		
Less:	Actual amount on hand		45.98		
Equals:	Cash short (over)		1.05	→	1.05
Amount to Replenish					154.02

4.

9-2, 9-3, 9-4, and 9-5 ON YOUR OWN, pp. 254, 259, 266, and 273

9-2 Journalizing purchases using a purchases journal
9-3 Posting from a purchases journal
9-4 Journalizing cash payments using a cash payments journal
9-5 Posting from a cash payments journal

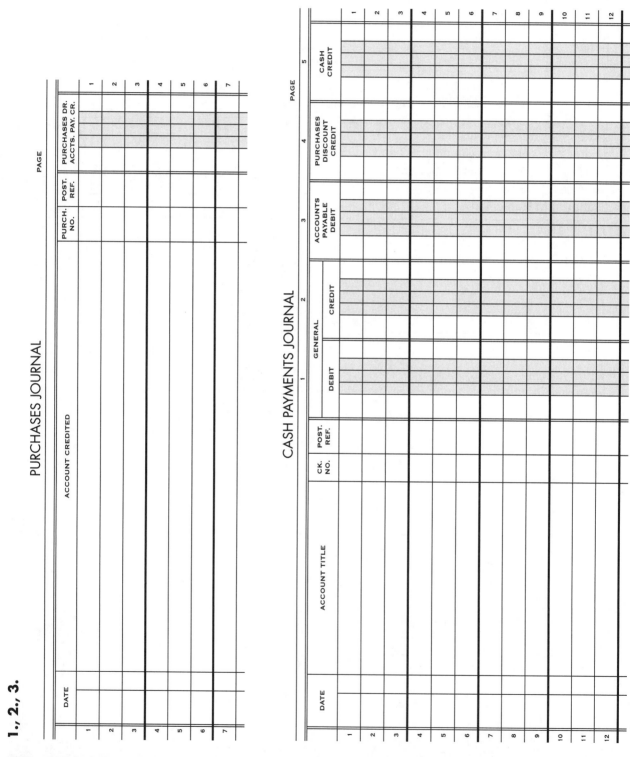

1., 2., 3.

PURCHASES JOURNAL

PAGE

	DATE	ACCOUNT CREDITED	PURCH. NO.	POST. REF.	1 PURCHASES DR. ACCTS. PAY. CR.	
1						1
2						2
3						3
4						4
5						5
6						6
7						7

CASH PAYMENTS JOURNAL

PAGE

	DATE	ACCOUNT TITLE	CK. NO.	POST. REF.	1 GENERAL DEBIT	2 GENERAL CREDIT	3 ACCOUNTS PAYABLE DEBIT	4 PURCHASES DISCOUNT CREDIT	5 CASH CREDIT	
1										1
2										2
3										3
4										4
5										5
6										6
7										7
8										8
9										9
10										10
11										11
12										12

Name ____________ Date ________ Class ________

9-2, 9-3, 9-4, and 9-5 ON YOUR OWN (continued)

1.

VENDOR Gillis Glass Co. VENDOR NO. 210

DATE		ITEM	POST. REF.	DEBIT	CREDIT	CREDIT BALANCE
20-- Nov.	1	Balance	✔			2 1 2 0 00

VENDOR Lawes Imports VENDOR NO. 220

DATE		ITEM	POST. REF.	DEBIT	CREDIT	CREDIT BALANCE
20-- Nov.	1	Balance	✔			1 9 0 8 35

VENDOR McKell Supply, Inc. VENDOR NO. 230

DATE		ITEM	POST. REF.	DEBIT	CREDIT	CREDIT BALANCE
20-- Nov.	1	Balance	✔			6 4 8 50

VENDOR Sheng Industries VENDOR NO. 240

DATE		ITEM	POST. REF.	DEBIT	CREDIT	CREDIT BALANCE
20-- Nov.	1	Balance	✔			2 1 6 9 00

VENDOR Tresler Corporation VENDOR NO. 250

DATE		ITEM	POST. REF.	DEBIT	CREDIT	CREDIT BALANCE
20-- Nov.	1	Balance	✔			2 9 1 3 00

9-2, 9-3, 9-4, and 9-5 ON YOUR OWN (continued)

3.

ACCOUNT Cash — ACCOUNT NO. 1110

DATE		ITEM	POST. REF.	DEBIT	CREDIT	BALANCE DEBIT	BALANCE CREDIT
20-- Nov.	1	Balance	✔			9 1 8 3 10	

ACCOUNT Supplies—Office — ACCOUNT NO. 1145

DATE		ITEM	POST. REF.	DEBIT	CREDIT	BALANCE DEBIT	BALANCE CREDIT
20-- Nov.	1	Balance	✔			2 4 9 8 21	

ACCOUNT Accounts Payable — ACCOUNT NO. 2110

DATE		ITEM	POST. REF.	DEBIT	CREDIT	BALANCE DEBIT	BALANCE CREDIT
20-- Nov.	1	Balance	✔				9 7 5 8 85

ACCOUNT Purchases — ACCOUNT NO. 5110

DATE		ITEM	POST. REF.	DEBIT	CREDIT	BALANCE DEBIT	BALANCE CREDIT
20-- Nov.	1	Balance	✔			92 1 8 4 11	

ACCOUNT Purchases Discount — ACCOUNT NO. 5120

DATE		ITEM	POST. REF.	DEBIT	CREDIT	BALANCE DEBIT	BALANCE CREDIT
20-- Nov.	1	Balance	✔				7 0 1 57

Name ______________________ Date ____________ Class ____________

9-2, 9-3, 9-4, and 9-5 ON YOUR OWN (continued)

ACCOUNT Advertising Expense — ACCOUNT NO. 6105

DATE		ITEM	POST. REF.	DEBIT	CREDIT	BALANCE DEBIT	BALANCE CREDIT
20-- Nov.	1	Balance	✔			16 554 69	

ACCOUNT Cash Short and Over — ACCOUNT NO. 6110

DATE		ITEM	POST. REF.	DEBIT	CREDIT	BALANCE DEBIT	BALANCE CREDIT
20-- Nov.	1	Balance	✔			16 99	

ACCOUNT Miscellaneous Expense — ACCOUNT NO. 6135

DATE		ITEM	POST. REF.	DEBIT	CREDIT	BALANCE DEBIT	BALANCE CREDIT
20-- Nov.	1	Balance	✔			1 092 05	

ACCOUNT Utilities Expense — ACCOUNT NO. 6170

DATE		ITEM	POST. REF.	DEBIT	CREDIT	BALANCE DEBIT	BALANCE CREDIT
20-- Nov.	1	Balance	✔			9 105 40	

9-2, 9-3, 9-4, and 9-5 ON YOUR OWN (concluded)

PETTY CASH REPORT

Date: November 30, 20--

Custodian: Aimee Smith

Explanation			Reconciliation		Replenish Amount
Fund Total			250.00		
Payments:	Supplies—Office	56.21			
	Advertising	82.25			
	Miscellaneous	36.17			
Less:	Total payments		174.63	→	174.63
Equals:	Recorded amount on hand		75.37		
Less:	Actual amount on hand		76.82		
Equals:	Cash short (over)		(1.45)	→	(1.45)
Amount to Replenish					173.18

4.

Name ________________ Date ________ Class ________

9-1 APPLICATION PROBLEM (LO3), p. 277

Starting an accounts payable ledger form

1., 2.

VENDOR ________________ VENDOR NO. ________

DATE		ITEM	POST. REF.	DEBIT	CREDIT	CREDIT BALANCE

VENDOR ________________ VENDOR NO. ________

DATE		ITEM	POST. REF.	DEBIT	CREDIT	CREDIT BALANCE

9-2, 9-3, 9-4, and 9-5 APPLICATION PROBLEMS (LO6, 7, 8, 10), pp. 277 and 278

9-2 Journalizing purchases using a purchases journal
9-3 Posting from a purchases journal
9-4 Journalizing cash payments using a cash payments journal
9-5 Posting from a cash payments journal

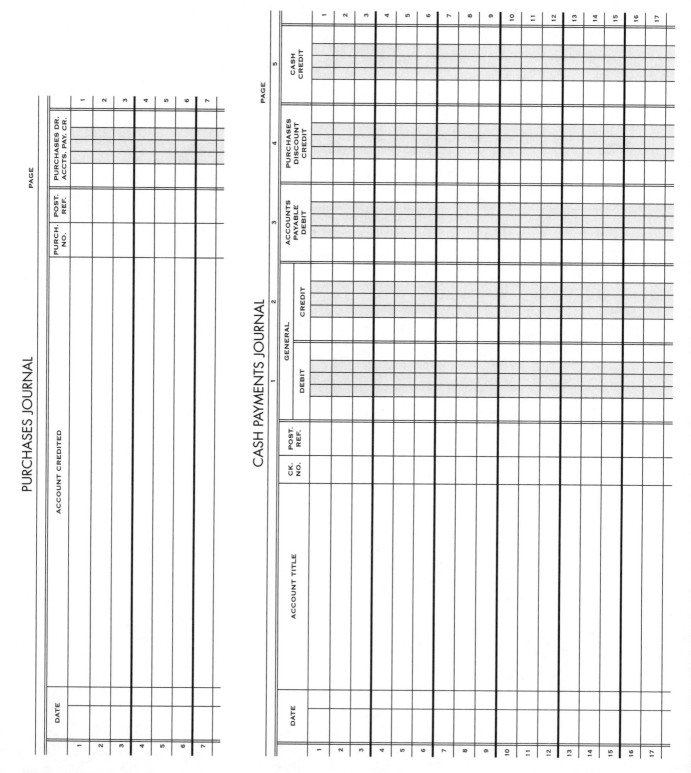

PURCHASES JOURNAL

PAGE

DATE	ACCOUNT CREDITED	PURCH. NO.	POST. REF.	PURCHASES DR. ACCTS. PAY. CR.

CASH PAYMENTS JOURNAL

PAGE

				1	2	3	4	5
				GENERAL				
DATE	ACCOUNT TITLE	CK. NO.	POST. REF.	DEBIT	CREDIT	ACCOUNTS PAYABLE DEBIT	PURCHASES DISCOUNT CREDIT	CASH CREDIT

9-2, 9-3, 9-4, and 9-5 APPLICATION PROBLEMS (continued)

VENDOR Atlanta Systems VENDOR NO. 210

DATE		ITEM	POST. REF.	DEBIT	CREDIT	CREDIT BALANCE
20-- Sept.	1	Balance	✔			2 621 48

VENDOR Henson Audio VENDOR NO. 220

DATE		ITEM	POST. REF.	DEBIT	CREDIT	CREDIT BALANCE
20-- Sept.	1	Balance	✔			2 489 00

VENDOR Lester Corporation VENDOR NO. 230

DATE		ITEM	POST. REF.	DEBIT	CREDIT	CREDIT BALANCE
20-- Sept.	1	Balance	✔			638 00

VENDOR Masonville Music VENDOR NO. 240

DATE		ITEM	POST. REF.	DEBIT	CREDIT	CREDIT BALANCE
20-- Sept.	1	Balance	✔			1 189 00

VENDOR Peterson Electronics VENDOR NO. 250

DATE		ITEM	POST. REF.	DEBIT	CREDIT	CREDIT BALANCE
20-- Sept.	1	Balance	✔			3 484 00

9-2, 9-3, 9-4, and 9-5 APPLICATION PROBLEMS (continued)

3.

ACCOUNT Cash — ACCOUNT NO. 1110

DATE		ITEM	POST. REF.	DEBIT	CREDIT	BALANCE DEBIT	BALANCE CREDIT
20-- Sept.	1	Balance	✔			22 189 18	

ACCOUNT Supplies—Office — ACCOUNT NO. 1145

DATE		ITEM	POST. REF.	DEBIT	CREDIT	BALANCE DEBIT	BALANCE CREDIT
20-- Sept.	1	Balance	✔			4 224 18	

ACCOUNT Supplies—Store — ACCOUNT NO. 1150

DATE		ITEM	POST. REF.	DEBIT	CREDIT	BALANCE DEBIT	BALANCE CREDIT
20-- Sept.	1	Balance	✔			3 914 11	

ACCOUNT Accounts Payable — ACCOUNT NO. 2110

DATE		ITEM	POST. REF.	DEBIT	CREDIT	BALANCE DEBIT	BALANCE CREDIT
20-- Sept.	1	Balance	✔				10 421 48

ACCOUNT Purchases — ACCOUNT NO. 5110

DATE		ITEM	POST. REF.	DEBIT	CREDIT	BALANCE DEBIT	BALANCE CREDIT
20-- Sept.	1	Balance	✔			241 947 18	

Name ______________________ Date ____________ Class ____________

9-2, 9-3, 9-4, and 9-5 APPLICATION PROBLEMS (continued)

ACCOUNT Purchases Discount ACCOUNT NO. 5120

DATE		ITEM	POST. REF.	DEBIT	CREDIT	BALANCE DEBIT	BALANCE CREDIT
20-- Sept.	1	Balance	✔				1 487 17

ACCOUNT Advertising Expense ACCOUNT NO. 6105

DATE		ITEM	POST. REF.	DEBIT	CREDIT	BALANCE DEBIT	BALANCE CREDIT
20-- Sept.	1	Balance	✔			9 209 61	

ACCOUNT Cash Short and Over ACCOUNT NO. 6110

DATE		ITEM	POST. REF.	DEBIT	CREDIT	BALANCE DEBIT	BALANCE CREDIT
20-- Sept.	1	Balance	✔			22 04	

ACCOUNT Miscellaneous Expense ACCOUNT NO. 6135

DATE		ITEM	POST. REF.	DEBIT	CREDIT	BALANCE DEBIT	BALANCE CREDIT
20-- Sept.	1	Balance	✔			8 649 31	

ACCOUNT Utilities Expense ACCOUNT NO. 6170

DATE		ITEM	POST. REF.	DEBIT	CREDIT	BALANCE DEBIT	BALANCE CREDIT
20-- Sept.	1	Balance	✔			6 749 89	

PETTY CASH REPORT

Date: September 30, 20--

Custodian: Eddie Henderson

Explanation			Reconciliation	Replenish Amount
Fund Total			200.00	
Payments:	Advertising	60.00		
	Miscellaneous	26.50		
	Supplies—Store	35.00		
	Supplies—Office	23.24		
Less:	Total payments		144.74 →	144.74
Equals:	Recorded amount on hand		55.26	
Less:	Actual amount on hand		55.14	
Equals:	Cash short (over)		0.12 →	0.12
Amount to Replenish				144.86

4.

Name ______________________ Date __________ Class __________

9-M MASTERY PROBLEM (LO6, 7, 8, 10), p. 279

Journalizing purchases, cash payments, and other transactions

1., 2., 3.

PURCHASES JOURNAL PAGE

	DATE		ACCOUNT CREDITED	PURCH. NO.	POST. REF.	PURCHASES DR. ACCTS. PAY. CR.	
1							1
2							2
3							3
4							4
5							5
6							6
7							7
8							8
9							9
10							10
11							11
12							12
13							13
14							14
15							15
16							16
17							17
18							18
19							19
20							20
21							21
22							22
23							23
24							24
25							25
26							26
27							27
28							28
29							29
30							30
31							31
32							32

9-M MASTERY PROBLEM (continued)

1., 4., 5.

CASH PAYMENTS JOURNAL

PAGE

	DATE	ACCOUNT TITLE	CK. NO.	POST. REF.	1 GENERAL DEBIT	2 GENERAL CREDIT	3 ACCOUNTS PAYABLE DEBIT	4 PURCHASES DISCOUNT CREDIT	5 CASH CREDIT	
1										1
2										2
3										3
4										4
5										5
6										6
7										7
8										8
9										9
10										10
11										11
12										12
13										13
14										14
15										15
16										16
17										17
18										18
19										19
20										20
21										21
22										22

Name ______________________ Date ______________ Class ______________

9-M MASTERY PROBLEM (continued)

1.

VENDOR Delmar, Inc. VENDOR NO. 210

DATE		ITEM	POST. REF.	DEBIT	CREDIT	CREDIT BALANCE
20-- July	1	Balance	✔			3,049.00

VENDOR Helms Supply VENDOR NO. 220

DATE		ITEM	POST. REF.	DEBIT	CREDIT	CREDIT BALANCE
20-- July	1	Balance	✔			1,280.00

VENDOR Kelsay Parts VENDOR NO. 230

DATE		ITEM	POST. REF.	DEBIT	CREDIT	CREDIT BALANCE
20-- July	1	Balance	✔			3,940.00

VENDOR Rackley Industries VENDOR NO. 240

DATE		ITEM	POST. REF.	DEBIT	CREDIT	CREDIT BALANCE
20-- July	1	Balance	✔			2,119.00

9-M MASTERY PROBLEM (continued)

1., 3., 5.

ACCOUNT Cash — ACCOUNT NO. 1110

DATE		ITEM	POST. REF.	DEBIT	CREDIT	BALANCE DEBIT	BALANCE CREDIT
20-- July	1	Balance	✔			18 499 17	

ACCOUNT Supplies—Office — ACCOUNT NO. 1145

DATE		ITEM	POST. REF.	DEBIT	CREDIT	BALANCE DEBIT	BALANCE CREDIT
20-- July	1	Balance	✔			3 418 07	

ACCOUNT Supplies—Store — ACCOUNT NO. 1150

DATE		ITEM	POST. REF.	DEBIT	CREDIT	BALANCE DEBIT	BALANCE CREDIT
20-- July	1	Balance	✔			4 184 17	

ACCOUNT Accounts Payable — ACCOUNT NO. 2110

DATE		ITEM	POST. REF.	DEBIT	CREDIT	BALANCE DEBIT	BALANCE CREDIT
20-- July	1	Balance	✔				10 388 00

ACCOUNT Purchases — ACCOUNT NO. 5110

DATE		ITEM	POST. REF.	DEBIT	CREDIT	BALANCE DEBIT	BALANCE CREDIT
20-- July	1	Balance	✔			294 184 14	

Name ______________________ Date ____________ Class ____________

9-M MASTERY PROBLEM (continued)

ACCOUNT Purchases Discount ACCOUNT NO. 5120

DATE		ITEM	POST. REF.	DEBIT	CREDIT	BALANCE DEBIT	BALANCE CREDIT
20-- July	1	Balance	✔				3,148.14

ACCOUNT Advertising Expense ACCOUNT NO. 6105

DATE		ITEM	POST. REF.	DEBIT	CREDIT	BALANCE DEBIT	BALANCE CREDIT
20-- July	1	Balance	✔			12,495.16	

ACCOUNT Cash Short and Over ACCOUNT NO. 6110

DATE		ITEM	POST. REF.	DEBIT	CREDIT	BALANCE DEBIT	BALANCE CREDIT
20-- July	1	Balance	✔			34.18	

ACCOUNT Miscellaneous Expense ACCOUNT NO. 6135

DATE		ITEM	POST. REF.	DEBIT	CREDIT	BALANCE DEBIT	BALANCE CREDIT
20-- July	1	Balance	✔			14,088.63	

ACCOUNT Utilities Expense ACCOUNT NO. 6170

DATE		ITEM	POST. REF.	DEBIT	CREDIT	BALANCE DEBIT	BALANCE CREDIT
20-- July	1	Balance	✔			7,633.69	

9-M MASTERY PROBLEM (concluded)

PETTY CASH REPORT

Date: July 31, 20-- Custodian: Sean Williams

Explanation			Reconciliation		Replenish Amount
Fund Total			200.00		
Payments:	Supplies—Office	45.60			
	Supplies—Store	67.30			
	Miscellaneous	23.89			
Less:	Total payments		136.79	→	136.79
Equals:	Recorded amount on hand		63.21		
Less:	Actual amount on hand		61.98		
Equals:	Cash short (over)		1.23	→	1.23
Amount to Replenish					138.02

6.

Name ______________________ Date ____________ Class ____________

9-S SOURCE DOCUMENTS PROBLEM (LO6, 8), p. 280

Journalizing purchases, cash payments, and other transactions from source documents

Coastal Sailing, Inc.
1423 Commerical Road
Bell City, LA 70630

INVOICE

REC'D 10/04/-- P324

TO: Messler Sailing
142 River Street
Naperville, IL 60540

DATE: 9/30/--
INV. NO. 6234
TERMS: 30 days
ACCT. NO. 2450

QUANTITY	CAT. NO.	DESCRIPTION	UNIT PRICE	TOTAL
25	4323	jib sheet	$ 45.00	$ 1,125.00
20	4233	jib halyard	165.00	3,300.00
		TOTAL		$ 4,425.00

Aquatic Manufacturing
42 Industrial Road
Stratford, CA 93266

INVOICE

REC'D 10/11/-- P325

TO: Messler Sailing
142 River Street
Naperville, IL 60540

DATE: 10/08/--
INV. NO. 15484
TERMS: 2/10,n/30
ACCT. NO. 1420

QUANTITY	CAT. NO.	DESCRIPTION	UNIT PRICE	TOTAL
10	532	Fiberglass repair kit	$ 83.00	$ 830.00
35	6346	U-bolts, 1"	16.00	560.00
40	6347	U-bolts, 2"	23.00	920.00
		TOTAL		$ 2,310.00

Northern Sail Company
253 Beach Blvd.
Boston, MA 02169

INVOICE

REC'D 10/20/-- P326

TO: Messler Sailing
142 River Street
Naperville, IL 60540

DATE: 10/18/--
INV. NO. 895
TERMS: 30 days
ACCT. NO. 1820

QUANTITY	CAT. NO.	DESCRIPTION	UNIT PRICE	TOTAL
2	B-23	Viking-16 mainsail	$ 1,599.00	$ 3,198.00
4	B-44	Sunset-13 mainsail	459.00	1,836.00
		TOTAL		$ 5,034.00

9-S SOURCE DOCUMENTS PROBLEM (continued)

NO. **621** $ 1,725.00
Date: October 4 20--
To: Seaside Manufacturing
For: On account

BALANCE BROUGHT FORWARD		12,485	25
AMOUNT DEPOSITED	Date		
SUBTOTAL		12,485	25
OTHER:			
SUBTOTAL		12,485	25
AMOUNT THIS CHECK		1,725	00
BALANCE CARRIED FORWARD		10,760	25

NO. **622** $ 668.75
Date: October 10 20--
To: Willcutt & Bishop
For: Supplies

BALANCE BROUGHT FORWARD		10,760	25
AMOUNT DEPOSITED	10 9 20-- (Date)	1,264	00
SUBTOTAL		12,024	25
OTHER:			
SUBTOTAL		12,024	25
AMOUNT THIS CHECK		668	75
BALANCE CARRIED FORWARD		11,355	50

NO. **623** $ 321.15
Date: October 15 20--
To: Northern Electric
For: Utilities

BALANCE BROUGHT FORWARD		11,355	50
AMOUNT DEPOSITED	Date		
SUBTOTAL		11,355	50
OTHER:			
SUBTOTAL		11,355	50
AMOUNT THIS CHECK		321	15
BALANCE CARRIED FORWARD		11,034	35

NO. **624** $ 2,263.80
Date: October 19 20--
To: Aquatic Manufacturing
For: On account

BALANCE BROUGHT FORWARD		11,034	35
AMOUNT DEPOSITED	10 18 20-- (Date)	546	50
SUBTOTAL		11,580	85
OTHER:			
SUBTOTAL		11,580	85
AMOUNT THIS CHECK		2,263	80
BALANCE CARRIED FORWARD		9,317	05

Name ______________________ Date ____________ Class ____________

9-S SOURCE DOCUMENTS PROBLEM (continued)

NO. **625** $ *2,560.00*
Date: *October 20* 20--
To: *WRRX Radio*
For: *Advertising*

BALANCE BROUGHT FORWARD	9,317	05
AMOUNT DEPOSITED (Date)		
SUBTOTAL	9,317	05
OTHER:		
SUBTOTAL	9,317	05
AMOUNT THIS CHECK	2,560	00
BALANCE CARRIED FORWARD	6,757	05

NO. **627** $ *4,425.00*
Date: *October 29* 20--
To: *Coastal Sailing, Inc.*
For: *On account*

BALANCE BROUGHT FORWARD	7,954	13
AMOUNT DEPOSITED (Date)		
SUBTOTAL	7,954	13
OTHER:		
SUBTOTAL	7,954	13
AMOUNT THIS CHECK	4,425	00
BALANCE CARRIED FORWARD	3,529	13

NO. **626** $ *224.00*
Date: *October 22* 20--
To: *Michigan Sail Co.*
For: *Purchases*

BALANCE BROUGHT FORWARD	6,757	05
AMOUNT DEPOSITED 10/21/20-- (Date)	1,421	08
SUBTOTAL	8,178	13
OTHER:		
SUBTOTAL	8,178	13
AMOUNT THIS CHECK	224	00
BALANCE CARRIED FORWARD	7,954	13

NO. **628** $ *112.94*
Date: *October 31* 20--
To: *Mary Donovan, Petty Cash*
For: *Petty cash*

BALANCE BROUGHT FORWARD	3,529	13
AMOUNT DEPOSITED 10/18/20-- (Date)	648	22
SUBTOTAL	4,177	35
OTHER:		
SUBTOTAL	4,177	35
AMOUNT THIS CHECK	112	94
BALANCE CARRIED FORWARD	4,064	41

Willcutt & Bishop
132 Washington Street
Naperville, IL 60540

INVOICE

TO: Messler Sailing
142 River Street
Naperville, IL 60540

DATE: 10/10/20--
INV. NO. 1548

QUANTITY	CAT. NO.	DESCRIPTION	UNIT PRICE	TOTAL
6	4818	computer paper	$ 25.00	$ 150.00
5	5518	pen packs	5.00	25.00
3	1548	jump drive	50.00	150.00
1	n/a	custom document print job #126	300.00	300.00
		SUBTOTAL		$ 625.00
		TAX		43.75
		TOTAL		$ 668.75

Northern Electric
125 Burlington Drive
Aurora, IL 60507-1523

October 13, 20-- 43643

Messler Sailing
142 River Street
Naperville, IL 60540

	This Month	Last Month
Kilowatts	1548	1613
per Day	50	52

Paid this amount → $ 321.15

Serving Your Energy Needs Since 1897

Name ______________________ Date ____________ Class ____________

9-S SOURCE DOCUMENTS PROBLEM (continued)

WRRX Radio

The Voice of the Fox River Valley
P.O. Box 1223
Aurora, IL 60507-1223

TO: Messler Sailing
142 River Street
Naperville, IL 60540

October 20, 20--
Invoice No. 2355

Advertising spots for October, 60 30-second spots at various times during prime-time commuting periods	$ 2,160.00
Recording of radio spot by Kenneth Black	400.00
	$ 2,560.00

Thank you for your business!

Michigan Sail Company
1442 Lakefront Avenue
Evanston, IL 60204

INVOICE

48448

TO: Messler Sailing
142 River Street
Naperville, IL 60540

DATE: 10/22/20--

QUANTITY	CAT. NO.	DESCRIPTION	UNIT PRICE	TOTAL
1	18-235	Sunlight 13' mainsail	$224.00	$ 224.00
		TOTAL		$ 224.00

PETTY CASH REPORT

Date: October 31, 20-- Custodian: Mary Donovan

Explanation			Reconciliation		Replenish Amount
Fund Total			250.00		
Payments:	Supplies—Office	23.45			
	Supplies—Store	65.25			
	Miscellaneous	26.14			
Less:	Total payments		114.84	→	114.84
Equals:	Recorded amount on hand		135.16		
Less:	Actual amount on hand		137.06		
Equals:	Cash short (over)		(1.90)	→	(1.90)
Amount to Replenish					112.94

Name ______________________ Date ______________ Class ______________

9-S SOURCE DOCUMENTS PROBLEM (continued)

1., 2.

PURCHASES JOURNAL

PAGE

	DATE		ACCOUNT CREDITED	PURCH. NO.	POST. REF.	PURCHASES DR. ACCTS. PAY. CR.	
1							1
2							2
3							3
4							4
5							5
6							6
7							7
8							8
9							9
10							10
11							11
12							12
13							13
14							14
15							15
16							16
17							17
18							18
19							19
20							20
21							21
22							22
23							23
24							24
25							25
26							26
27							27
28							28
29							29
30							30
31							31
32							32

9-S SOURCE DOCUMENTS PROBLEM (concluded)

1., 3.

CASH PAYMENTS JOURNAL

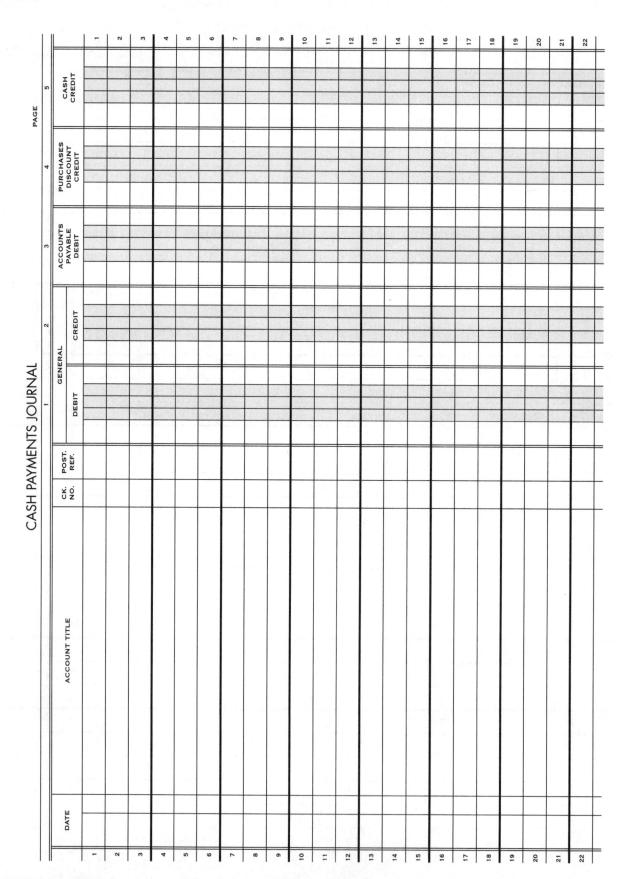

PAGE

					1	2	3	4	5	
					GENERAL					
	DATE	ACCOUNT TITLE	CK. NO.	POST. REF.	DEBIT	CREDIT	ACCOUNTS PAYABLE DEBIT	PURCHASES DISCOUNT CREDIT	CASH CREDIT	
1										1
2										2
3										3
4										4
5										5
6										6
7										7
8										8
9										9
10										10
11										11
12										12
13										13
14										14
15										15
16										16
17										17
18										18
19										19
20										20
21										21
22										22

Name ______________________ Date ____________ Class ____________

9-C CHALLENGE PROBLEM (LO6, 8), p. 280

Journalizing purchases and cash payments

1.

PURCHASES JOURNAL PAGE

DATE		ACCOUNT CREDITED	PURCH. NO.	POST. REF.	PURCHASES DR. ACCTS. PAY. CR.

9-C CHALLENGE PROBLEM (continued)

1.

CASH PAYMENTS JOURNAL

PAGE

	DATE		ACCOUNT TITLE	CK. NO.	POST. REF.	1 GENERAL DEBIT	2 GENERAL CREDIT	3 ACCOUNTS PAYABLE DEBIT	4 PURCHASES DISCOUNT CREDIT	5 CASH CREDIT	
1	20-- Dec.	1	Pacific Guitar	82	230			5 486 00	1 09 72	5 376 28	1
2											2
3											3
4											4
5											5
6											6
7											7
8											8
9											9
10											10
11											11
12											12
13											13
14											14
15											15
16											16
17											17
18											18
19											19
20											20
21											21
22											22

Name ______________________ Date ____________ Class ____________

9-C CHALLENGE PROBLEM (continued)

1.

VENDOR Abraham Instruments VENDOR NO. 210

DATE		ITEM	POST. REF.	DEBIT	CREDIT	CREDIT BALANCE
20-- Nov.	13		P11		1 485 00	1 485 00

VENDOR Brassworks VENDOR NO. 220

DATE		ITEM	POST. REF.	DEBIT	CREDIT	CREDIT BALANCE
20-- Nov.	15		P11		628 00	628 00
	24		P11		248 00	876 00

VENDOR Pacific Guitar VENDOR NO. 230

DATE		ITEM	POST. REF.	DEBIT	CREDIT	CREDIT BALANCE
20-- Nov.	24		P11		5 486 00	5 486 00
	29		P11		3 690 00	9 176 00
Dec.	1		CP12	5 486 00		3 690 00

VENDOR Pratt Publishing VENDOR NO. 240

DATE		ITEM	POST. REF.	DEBIT	CREDIT	CREDIT BALANCE
20-- Nov.	16		P11		2 478 00	2 478 00

VENDOR Southern Music Supply VENDOR NO. 250

DATE		ITEM	POST. REF.	DEBIT	CREDIT	CREDIT BALANCE
20-- Nov.	5		P11		4 810 00	4 810 00
	30		P11		2 490 00	7 300 00

Name ______ Date ______ Class ______

9-C CHALLENGE PROBLEM (concluded)

2.

Study Guide 10

Name	Perfect Score	Your Score
Identifying Accounting Terms	13 Pts.	
Analyzing Accounting Concepts and Practices	20 Pts.	
Analyzing Transactions Recorded in Special Journals	12 Pts.	
Total	45 Pts.	

Part One—Identifying Accounting Terms

Directions: Select the one term in Column I that best fits each definition in Column II. Print the letter identifying your choice in the Answers column.

Column I	Column II	Answers
A. accounts receivable ledger	**1.** The amount a business receives from the sale of an item of merchandise. (p. 284)	1. ________
B. batch report	**2.** The amount a business adds to the cost of merchandise to arrive at the selling price. (p. 284)	2. ________
C. batching out	**3.** A subsidiary ledger containing all accounts for charge customers. (p. 284)	3. ________
D. cash receipts journal	**4.** A tax on a sale of merchandise or services. (p. 286)	4. ________
E. cash sale	**5.** A special journal used to record only sales of merchandise on account. (p. 287)	5. ________
F. markup	**6.** A sale in which the customer pays for the total amount of the sale at the time of the transaction. (p. 294)	6. ________
G. point-of-sale (POS) terminal	**7.** A specialized computer used to collect, store, and report all the information about a sales transaction. (p. 294)	7. ________
H. sales discount	**8.** The report that summarizes the cash and credit card sales of a point-of-sale terminal. (p. 294)	8. ________
I. sales journal	**9.** A report of credit card sales produced by a point-of-sale terminal. (p. 295)	9. ________
J. sales tax	**10.** The process of preparing a batch report from a point-of-sale terminal. (p. 295)	10. ________
K. schedule of accounts receivable	**11.** A special journal used to record only cash receipt transactions. (p. 296)	11. ________
L. selling price	**12.** A cash discount on a sale taken by the customer. (p. 296)	12. ________
M. terminal summary	**13.** A listing of customer accounts, account balances, and total amount due from all customers. (p. 308)	13. ________

Part Two—Analyzing Accounting Concepts and Practices

Directions: Place a *T* for True or an *F* for False in the Answers column to show whether each of the following statements is true or false.

	Answers
1. Regardless of when payment is received, the revenue should be recorded when a sale is made, not on the date cash is received. (p. 284)	**1.** ________
2. The accounts receivable ledger form is based on the general ledger form and contains the same columns, except the Credit balance amount column. (p. 286)	**2.** ________
3. Most states do not require a business to collect sales tax from customers. (p. 286)	**3.** ________
4. Sales tax rates are usually stated as a percentage of sales. (p. 286)	**4.** ________
5. The amount of sales tax collected is an expense of operating a business. (p. 286)	**5.** ________
6. Only the federal government can exempt from sales taxes some types of merchandise or sales to certain types of customers. (p. 286)	**6.** ________
7. An invoice is a form that describes the goods or services sold, the quantity and the price, and the terms of the sale. (p. 287)	**7.** ________
8. The invoice used as a source document for recording a sale on account is often referred to as a sales invoice, a sales ticket, or a sales slip. (p. 287)	**8.** ________
9. While the seller considers an invoice for a sale on account to be a sales invoice, the same invoice is considered by the customer to be a purchase invoice. (p. 287)	**9.** ________
10. Credit card and debit card sales are treated as cash sales because the business receives its cash in a very short time. (p. 294)	**10.** ________
11. A terminal summary is also known as a *T tape*. (p. 294)	**11.** ________
12. A batch report can be detailed, showing every credit card sale. Or, the batch report can be a summary, showing only the number and total of sales by credit card type. (p. 295)	**12.** ________
13. Separate transactions are recorded for cash, credit card, and debit card totals listed on a terminal summary. (p. 297)	**13.** ________
14. Sales Tax Payable has a normal debit balance. (p. 297)	**14.** ________
15. When a sales discount is taken, a customer pays less cash than the invoice amount previously recorded in the sales account. (p. 299)	**15.** ________
16. Maintaining a separate account for sales discounts provides business managers with information to evaluate whether a sales discount is a cost-effective method. (p. 300)	**16.** ________
17. The posting references on the accounts receivable ledger form enable the company to locate the sales invoices and receipts supporting each transaction. (p. 302)	**17.** ________
18. The total of each general amount column of a cash receipts journal is posted to the corresponding general ledger account. (p. 302)	**18.** ________
19. A schedule of accounts receivable contains a complete listing of each sales invoice owed by customers. (p. 308)	**19.** ________
20. Some businesses call the schedule of accounts receivable the *accounts receivable trial balance*. (p. 308)	**20.** ________

Name ______________________ Date ______________ Class ______________

Part Three—Analyzing Transactions Recorded in Special Journals

Directions: In Answers Column 1, print the abbreviation for the journal in which each transaction is to be recorded. In Answers Columns 2 and 3, print the letters identifying the accounts to be debited and credited for each transaction. For transactions affecting accounts receivable, be sure to also include the subsidiary ledger account affected.

SJ—Sales journal; **CRJ**—Cash receipts journal

Account Titles	**Transactions**	**Answers 1 Journal**	**2 Debit**	**3 Credit**
A. Accounts Receivable	**1-2-3**. Sold merchandise on account to Doris Edwards, plus sales tax. (p. 288)	1.____	2.____	3.____
B. Cash	**4-5-6**. Recorded cash and credit card sales, plus sales tax. (p. 297)	4.____	5.____	6.____
C. Doris Edwards	**7-8-9**. Received cash on account from Jim North. (p. 298)	7.____	8.____	9.____
D. Jim North	**10-11-12**. Received cash on account from Doris Edwards, less sales discount. (p. 300)	10.____	11.____	12.____
E. Sales				
F. Sales Discount				
G. Sales Returns and Allowances				
H. Sales Tax Payable				

Across

2. A report of credit card sales produced by a point-of-sale terminal.
3. A special journal used to record only cash receipt transactions.
6. A special journal used to record only sales of merchandise on account.
7. The amount a business receives from the sale of an item of merchandise.
8. A tax on a sale of merchandise or services.
9. A cash discount on a sale taken by the customer.

Down

1. The amount a business adds to the cost of merchandise to establish the selling price.
2. The process of preparing a batch report from a point-of-sale terminal.
4. A sale in which the customer pays for the total amount of the sale at the time of the transaction.
5. The report that summarizes the cash and credit card sales of a point-of-sale terminal. This is also known as a Z tape.

Name ______________________ Date ______________ Class ______________

10-1, 10-2, and 10-4 WORK TOGETHER, pp. 289, 293, and 309

10-1 Accounting for sales on account

10-2 Posting from a sales journal

10-4 Posting from a cash receipts journal

ACCOUNTS RECEIVABLE LEDGER

CUSTOMER Lenny Stanford CUSTOMER NO. 110

DATE		ITEM	POST. REF.	DEBIT	CREDIT	DEBIT BALANCE
20-- Sept.	1	Balance	✔			2 189 36

CUSTOMER CUSTOMER NO.

DATE		ITEM	POST. REF.	DEBIT	CREDIT	DEBIT BALANCE

CUSTOMER Washington City Schools CUSTOMER NO. 130

DATE		ITEM	POST. REF.	DEBIT	CREDIT	DEBIT BALANCE
20-- Sept.	1	Balance	✔			1 509 45

SALES JOURNAL

PAGE

	DATE		ACCOUNT DEBITED	SALE. NO.	POST. REF.	1 ACCOUNTS RECEIVABLE DEBIT	2 SALES CREDIT	3 SALES TAX PAYABLE CREDIT	
1									1
2									2
3									3
4									4
5									5
6									6

10-2 and 10-4 WORK TOGETHER

Column Title	Debit Totals	Credit Totals
Accounts Receivable Debit		
Sales Credit		
Sales Tax Payable Credit		
Totals		

ACCOUNT Cash — ACCOUNT NO. 1110

DATE		ITEM	POST. REF.	DEBIT	CREDIT	BALANCE DEBIT	BALANCE CREDIT
20-- Sept.	1	Balance	✔			11 486 16	
	30		CP9		9 484 24	2 001 92	

ACCOUNT Accounts Receivable — ACCOUNT NO. 1130

DATE		ITEM	POST. REF.	DEBIT	CREDIT	BALANCE DEBIT	BALANCE CREDIT
20-- Sept.	1	Balance	✔			4 089 15	

ACCOUNT Sales Tax Payable — ACCOUNT NO. 2120

DATE		ITEM	POST. REF.	DEBIT	CREDIT	BALANCE DEBIT	BALANCE CREDIT
20-- Sept.	1	Balance	✔				2 484 18

ACCOUNT Sales — ACCOUNT NO. 4110

DATE		ITEM	POST. REF.	DEBIT	CREDIT	BALANCE DEBIT	BALANCE CREDIT
20-- Sept.	1	Balance	✔				185 196 31

ACCOUNT Sales Discount — ACCOUNT NO. 4120

DATE		ITEM	POST. REF.	DEBIT	CREDIT	BALANCE DEBIT	BALANCE CREDIT
20-- Sept.	1	Balance	✔			721 06	

Name ______________________ Date ______________ Class ______________

10-3 and 10-4 WORK TOGETHER, p. 301

10-3 Accounting for cash and credit card sales

10-4 Posting from a cash receipts journal

CASH RECEIPTS JOURNAL

PAGE

					1	2	3	4	5	6	7	
					GENERAL							
	DATE	ACCOUNT TITLE	DOC. NO.	POST. REF.	DEBIT	CREDIT	ACCOUNTS RECEIVABLE CREDIT	SALES CREDIT	SALES TAX PAYABLE CREDIT	SALES DISCOUNT DEBIT	CASH DEBIT	
1												1
2												2
3												3
4												4
5												5
6												6
7												7
8												8
9												9

10-4 WORK TOGETHER (concluded)

2.

Column Title	Debit Totals	Credit Totals
General Debit		
General Credit		
Accounts Receivable Credit		
Sales Credit		
Sales Tax Payable Credit		
Sales Discount Debit		
Cash Debit		
Totals		

3.

Cash on hand at the beginning of the month	
(Sept. 1 balance of general ledger Cash account)	
Plus total cash received during the month	
(Cash Debit column total, cash receipts journal)	
Equal total	
Less total cash paid during the month	
(General ledger posting in Cash account)	
Equals cash balance on hand at the end of the month	
Checkbook balance on the next unused check stub	

6.

Name ______________________ Date ____________ Class ____________

10-1, 10-2, and 10-4 ON YOUR OWN, pp. 289, 293, and 309

10-1 Accounting for sales on account

10-2 Posting from a sales journal

10-4 Posting from a cash receipts journal

ACCOUNTS RECEIVABLE LEDGER

CUSTOMER ______________________ CUSTOMER NO. ______

DATE		ITEM	POST. REF.	DEBIT	CREDIT	DEBIT BALANCE

CUSTOMER FJT Plumbing CUSTOMER NO. 120

DATE		ITEM	POST. REF.	DEBIT	CREDIT	DEBIT BALANCE
20-- June	1	Balance	✔			2 9 8 9 20

CUSTOMER Roberts College CUSTOMER NO. 130

DATE		ITEM	POST. REF.	DEBIT	CREDIT	DEBIT BALANCE
20-- June	1	Balance	✔			3 8 1 60

SALES JOURNAL PAGE ______

	DATE		ACCOUNT DEBITED	SALE. NO.	POST. REF.	1 ACCOUNTS RECEIVABLE DEBIT	2 SALES CREDIT	3 SALES TAX PAYABLE CREDIT	
1									1
2									2
3									3
4									4
5									5
6									6

10-2 and 10-4 ON YOUR OWN

Column Title	Debit Totals	Credit Totals
Accounts Receivable Debit		
Sales Credit		
Sales Tax Payable Credit		
Totals		

ACCOUNT Cash — ACCOUNT NO. 1110

DATE		ITEM	POST. REF.	DEBIT	CREDIT	BALANCE DEBIT	BALANCE CREDIT
20-- June	1	Balance	✔			8,617.01	
	30		CP6		6,948.15	1,668.86	

ACCOUNT Accounts Receivable — ACCOUNT NO. 1130

DATE		ITEM	POST. REF.	DEBIT	CREDIT	BALANCE DEBIT	BALANCE CREDIT
20-- June	1	Balance	✔			3,555.80	

ACCOUNT Sales Tax Payable — ACCOUNT NO. 2120

DATE		ITEM	POST. REF.	DEBIT	CREDIT	BALANCE DEBIT	BALANCE CREDIT
20-- June	1	Balance	✔				648.18

ACCOUNT Sales — ACCOUNT NO. 4110

DATE		ITEM	POST. REF.	DEBIT	CREDIT	BALANCE DEBIT	BALANCE CREDIT
20-- June	1	Balance	✔				94,818.25

ACCOUNT Sales Discount — ACCOUNT NO. 4120

DATE		ITEM	POST. REF.	DEBIT	CREDIT	BALANCE DEBIT	BALANCE CREDIT
20-- June	1	Balance	✔			612.18	

Name ______________________ Date ______________ Class ______________

10-3 and 10-4 ON YOUR OWN, p. 301

10-3 Accounting for cash and credit card sales

10-4 Posting from a cash receipts journal

CASH RECEIPTS JOURNAL

PAGE

					1	2	3	4	5	6	7	
	DATE	ACCOUNT TITLE	DOC. NO.	POST. REF.	GENERAL DEBIT	GENERAL CREDIT	ACCOUNTS RECEIVABLE CREDIT	SALES CREDIT	SALES TAX PAYABLE CREDIT	SALES DISCOUNT DEBIT	CASH DEBIT	
1												1
2												2
3												3
4												4
5												5
6												6
7												7
8												8
9												9

10-4 ON YOUR OWN (concluded)

2.

Column Title	Debit Totals	Credit Totals
General Debit		
General Credit		
Accounts Receivable Credit		
Sales Credit		
Sales Tax Payable Credit		
Sales Discount Debit		
Cash Debit		
Totals		

3.

Cash on hand at the beginning of the month (June 1 balance of general ledger Cash account)	
Plus total cash received during the month (Cash Debit column total, cash receipts journal)	
Equal total	
Less total cash paid during the month (General ledger posting in Cash account)	
Equals cash balance on hand at the end of the month	
Checkbook balance on the next unused check stub	

6.

Name ______________________ Date ______________ Class ______________

10-1, 10-2, and 10-4 APPLICATION PROBLEMS (LO2, 3, 6, 7), pp. 313 and 314

10-1 Journalizing sales on account

10-2 Posting from a sales journal

10-4 Posting from a cash receipts journal

SALES JOURNAL PAGE

	DATE	ACCOUNT DEBITED	SALE NO.	POST. REF.	2 ACCOUNTS RECEIVABLE DEBIT	3 SALES CREDIT	4 SALES TAX PAYABLE CREDIT	
1								1
2								2
3								3
4								4
5								5
6								6
7								7
8								8
9								9

10-2 and 10-4 APPLICATION PROBLEMS (LO3, 6, 7), pp. 313 and 314

10-2 Posting from a sales journal

10-4 Posting from a cash receipts journal

ACCOUNTS RECEIVABLE LEDGER

CUSTOMER Central Medical Clinic — CUSTOMER NO. 110

DATE		ITEM	POST. REF.	DEBIT	CREDIT	DEBIT BALANCE
20-- Nov.	1	Balance	✔			1 6 4 8 96

CUSTOMER Fairview Hospital — CUSTOMER NO. 120

DATE		ITEM	POST. REF.	DEBIT	CREDIT	DEBIT BALANCE
20-- Nov.	1	Balance	✔			4 2 1 8 19

CUSTOMER Mason College — CUSTOMER NO. 130

DATE		ITEM	POST. REF.	DEBIT	CREDIT	DEBIT BALANCE
20-- Nov.	1	Balance	✔			6 7 9 19

CUSTOMER Paulson Medical Clinic — CUSTOMER NO. 140

DATE		ITEM	POST. REF.	DEBIT	CREDIT	DEBIT BALANCE
20-- Nov.	1	Balance	✔			1 5 4 7 15

CUSTOMER Trannon Emergency Center — CUSTOMER NO. 150

DATE		ITEM	POST. REF.	DEBIT	CREDIT	DEBIT BALANCE
20-- Nov.	1	Balance	✔			2 1 8 4 14

Name ______________________ Date ____________ Class ____________

10-2 and 10-4 APPLICATION PROBLEMS

Column Title	Debit Totals	Credit Totals
Accounts Receivable Debit.	______	
Sales Credit.		______
Sales Tax Payable Credit.		______
Totals	______	______

GENERAL LEDGER

ACCOUNT Cash ACCOUNT NO. 1110

DATE		ITEM	POST. REF.	DEBIT	CREDIT	BALANCE DEBIT	BALANCE CREDIT
20-- Nov.	1	Balance	✔			16 489 36	
	30		CP11		14 474 63	2 014 73	

ACCOUNT Accounts Receivable ACCOUNT NO. 1130

DATE		ITEM	POST. REF.	DEBIT	CREDIT	BALANCE DEBIT	BALANCE CREDIT
20-- Nov.	1	Balance	✔			10 277 63	

ACCOUNT Sales Tax Payable ACCOUNT NO. 2120

DATE		ITEM	POST. REF.	DEBIT	CREDIT	BALANCE DEBIT	BALANCE CREDIT
20-- Nov.	1	Balance	✔				945 18

ACCOUNT Sales ACCOUNT NO. 4110

DATE		ITEM	POST. REF.	DEBIT	CREDIT	BALANCE DEBIT	BALANCE
20-- Nov.	1	Balance	✔				194 735 26

ACCOUNT Sales Discount ACCOUNT NO. 4120

DATE		ITEM	POST. REF.	DEBIT	CREDIT	BALANCE DEBIT	BALANCE CREDIT
20-- Nov.	1	Balance	✔			418 19	

10-3 and 10-4 APPLICATION PROBLEMS (LO4, 5, 6, 7), p. 314

10-3 Journalizing cash receipts
10-4 Posting from a cash receipts journal

CASH RECEIPTS JOURNAL

PAGE

					1	2	3	4	5	6	7	
	DATE	ACCOUNT TITLE	DOC. NO.	POST. REF.	GENERAL DEBIT	GENERAL CREDIT	ACCOUNTS RECEIVABLE CREDIT	SALES CREDIT	SALES TAX PAYABLE CREDIT	SALES DISCOUNT DEBIT	CASH DEBIT	
1												1
2												2
3												3
4												4
5												5
6												6
7												7
8												8
9												9
10												10
11												11

Name ____________ Date ________ Class ________

10-4 APPLICATION PROBLEMS (concluded)

2.

Column Title	Debit Totals	Credit Totals
General Debit	______	
General Credit		______
Accounts Receivable Credit		______
Sales Credit		______
Sales Tax Payable Credit		______
Sales Discount Debit	______	
Cash Debit	______	
Totals	______	______

3.

Cash on hand at the beginning of the month (Nov. 1 balance of general ledger Cash account)	
Plus total cash received during the month (Cash Debit column total, cash receipts journal)	______
Equal total	
Less total cash paid during the month (General ledger posting in Cash account)	______
Equals cash balance on hand at the end of the month	______
Checkbook balance on the next unused check stub	______

6.

10-M MASTERY PROBLEM (LO2, 3, 4, 5, 6, 7), p. 314

Journalizing sales and cash receipts transactions

1., 2., 3.

SALES JOURNAL PAGE

	DATE		ACCOUNT DEBITED	SALE. NO.	POST. REF.	1 ACCOUNTS RECEIVABLE DEBIT	2 SALES CREDIT	3 SALES TAX PAYABLE CREDIT	
1									1
2									2
3									3
4									4
5									5
6									6

2.

Column Title	Debit Totals	Credit Totals
Accounts Receivable Debit.		
Sales Credit.		
Sales Tax Payable Credit.		
Totals		

10-M MASTERY PROBLEM (continued)

1., 4., 6., 7.

CASH RECEIPTS JOURNAL

PAGE

	DATE		ACCOUNT TITLE	DOC. NO.	POST. REF.	1 GENERAL DEBIT	2 GENERAL CREDIT	3 ACCOUNTS RECEIVABLE CREDIT	4 SALES CREDIT	5 SALES TAX PAYABLE CREDIT	6 SALES DISCOUNT DEBIT	7 CASH DEBIT	
1													1
2													2
3													3
4													4
5													5
6													6
7													7
8													8
9													9
10													10
11													11

4.

Column Title	Debit Totals	Credit Totals
General Debit		
General Credit		
Accounts Receivable Credit		
Sales Credit		
Sales Tax Payable Credit		
Sales Discount Debit		
Cash Debit		
Totals		

1.

ACCOUNTS RECEIVABLE LEDGER

CUSTOMER Daniel Smith Promotions — CUSTOMER NO. 110

DATE		ITEM	POST. REF.	DEBIT	CREDIT	DEBIT BALANCE
20-- Mar.	1	Balance	✔			3 115 08

CUSTOMER Jenkins & Sanders LLP — CUSTOMER NO. 120

DATE		ITEM	POST. REF.	DEBIT	CREDIT	DEBIT BALANCE
20-- Mar.	1	Balance	✔			1 849 00

CUSTOMER Luxury Suites — CUSTOMER NO. 130

DATE		ITEM	POST. REF.	DEBIT	CREDIT	DEBIT BALANCE
20-- Mar.	1	Balance	✔			4 219 00

CUSTOMER Southwestern University — CUSTOMER NO. 140

DATE		ITEM	POST. REF.	DEBIT	CREDIT	DEBIT BALANCE
20-- Mar.	1	Balance	✔			948 00

CUSTOMER Trailor Stores — CUSTOMER NO. 150

DATE		ITEM	POST. REF.	DEBIT	CREDIT	DEBIT BALANCE

5.

Cash on hand at the beginning of the month
(Mar. 1 balance of general ledger Cash account) . . . .
Plus total cash received during the month
(Cash Debit column total, cash receipts journal) . . . . ________
Equal total. . . . .
Less total cash paid during the month
(General ledger posting in Cash account) . . . . ________
Equals cash balance on hand at the end of the month. . . . . ========
Checkbook balance on the next unused check stub. . . . . ========

Name ______________________ Date ____________ Class ____________

10-M MASTERY PROBLEM (continued)

3., 7.

ACCOUNT Cash — ACCOUNT NO. 1110

DATE		ITEM	POST. REF.	DEBIT	CREDIT	BALANCE DEBIT	BALANCE CREDIT
20-- Mar.	1	Balance	✔			6,544.15	
	31		CP3		4,174.46	2,369.69	

ACCOUNT Accounts Receivable — ACCOUNT NO. 1130

DATE		ITEM	POST. REF.	DEBIT	CREDIT	BALANCE DEBIT	BALANCE CREDIT
20-- Mar.	1	Balance	✔			10,131.08	

ACCOUNT Sales Tax Payable — ACCOUNT NO. 2120

DATE		ITEM	POST. REF.	DEBIT	CREDIT	BALANCE DEBIT	BALANCE CREDIT
20-- Mar.	1	Balance	✔				489.18

ACCOUNT Sales — ACCOUNT NO. 4110

DATE		ITEM	POST. REF.	DEBIT	CREDIT	BALANCE DEBIT	BALANCE CREDIT
20-- Mar.	1	Balance	✔				24,159.15

ACCOUNT Sales Discount — ACCOUNT NO. 4120

DATE		ITEM	POST. REF.	DEBIT	CREDIT	BALANCE DEBIT	BALANCE CREDIT
20-- Mar.	1	Balance	✔			194.03	

8.

Name ____________ Date ________ Class ________

10-S SOURCE DOCUMENTS PROBLEM (LO2, 3, 4, 5, 6), p. 315

Journalizing sales and cash receipts transactions; proving and ruling journals

Golfer's Paradise
142 Glade Road
Crossville, TN 38555-8102

RECEIPT

FROM: Mary Ann Ingram

DATE: 11/13/--
RECEIPT NO.: 528

PAYMENT METHOD	CHECK NO.	CUSTOMER ACCT. NO.	RECEIVED BY
Check	5326	150	Tom Andrews

DESCRIPTION	INVOICE	GROSS AMOUNT	DISCOUNT	CASH RECEIVED
On account	428	$ 150.00	$ —	$ 150.00
		TOTAL DISCOUNT		
			TOTAL	$ 150.00

Golfer's Paradise
142 Glade Road
Crossville, TN 38555-8102

RECEIPT

FROM: Adams Driving Range

DATE: 11/24/--
RECEIPT NO.: 529

PAYMENT METHOD	CHECK NO.	CUSTOMER ACCT. NO.	RECEIVED BY
Check	481	110	Sally Richards

DESCRIPTION	INVOICE	GROSS AMOUNT	DISCOUNT	CASH RECEIVED
On account	444	$ 435.91	$ 8.72	$ 427.19
		TOTAL DISCOUNT	$ 8.72	
			TOTAL	$ 427.19

Golfer's Paradise
142 Glade Road
Crossville, TN 38555-8102

INVOICE

SOLD TO: Daniel Pearson
2345 Lakeview Drive
Crossville, TN 38555-5819

DATE: 11/5/--
INV. NO.: 443
TERMS: n/30
CUST. NO.: 260

QUANTITY	PART NO.	DESCRIPTION	UNIT PRICE	TOTAL
1	2432	9 degree titanium driver	$439.50	**$439.50**
5	745	Practice golf balls, dz.	10.00	**50.00**
		SUBTOTAL		**$489.50**
		TAX		**36.71**
		TOTAL		**$526.21**

Serving Crossville and Fairfield Glade with all your recreational equipment

Golfer's Paradise
142 Glade Road
Crossville, TN 38555-8102

INVOICE

SOLD TO: Adams Driving Range
594 Eagles Nest Road
Crossville, TN 38555-5819

DATE: 11/16/--
INV. NO.: 444
TERMS: 2/10, n/30
CUST. NO.: 110

QUANTITY	PART NO.	DESCRIPTION	UNIT PRICE	TOTAL
1	BG-34	Oversized irons, graphite shafts	$405.50	**$405.50**
		SUBTOTAL		**$405.50**
		TAX		**30.41**
		TOTAL		**$435.91**

Serving Crossville and Fairfield Glade with all your recreational equipment

Name ______________________ Date ____________ Class ____________

10-S SOURCE DOCUMENTS PROBLEM (continued)

Golfer's Paradise
142 Glade Road
Crossville, TN 38555-8102

INVOICE

SOLD TO: Mountain View Golf
1001 Lakeview Drive
Crossville, TN 38555-5819

DATE: 11/26/--
INV. NO.: 445
TERMS: 2/10, n/30
CUST. NO.: 490

QUANTITY	PART NO.	DESCRIPTION	UNIT PRICE	TOTAL
75	9448	X-out golf balls, dz.	$6.50	**$487.50**
35	490	Gloves	5.50	**192.50**
		SUBTOTAL		**$680.00**
		TAX		
		TOTAL		**$680.00**

Serving Crossville and Fairfield Glade with all your recreational equipment

1., 2.

SALES JOURNAL PAGE

	DATE		ACCOUNT DEBITED	SALE. NO.	POST. REF.	1 ACCOUNTS RECEIVABLE DEBIT	2 SALES CREDIT	3 SALES TAX PAYABLE CREDIT	
1									1
2									2
3									3
4									4
5									5
6									6
7									7
8									8

10-S SOURCE DOCUMENTS PROBLEM (continued)

TERMINAL SUMMARY
Golfer's Paradise

CODE:		36
DATE:		11/4/--
TIME:		18:34
VISA	028	
Sales		1,548.95
Sales Tax		92.94
Total		1,641.89
MasterCard	031	
Sales		2,458.08
Sales Tax		147.48
Total		2,605.56
Debit Cards	048	
Sales		1,947.63
Sales Tax		116.86
Total		2,064.49
Cash	158	
Sales		3,154.14
Sales Tax		189.25
Total		3,343.39
Totals		
Sales		9,108.80
Sales Tax		546.53
Total		9,655.33

BATCH REPORT

MERCHANT:	498418 145
TERMINAL:	1548
DATE:	11/4/-- 18:34
BATCH:	36
VISA	
COUNT	028
SALES	1,704.04
RETURNS	62.15
NET	1,641.89
MASTERCARD	
COUNT	031
SALES	2,651.45
RETURNS	45.89
NET	2,605.56
DEBIT CARDS	
COUNT	048
SALES	2,222.64
RETURNS	158.15
NET	2,064.49
TOTALS	
COUNT	107
SALES	6,578.13
RETURNS	266.19
NET	6,311.94

CONTROL NUMBER: 001486486

Name ______________________ Date ______________ Class ______________

10-S SOURCE DOCUMENTS PROBLEM (continued)

TERMINAL SUMMARY
Golfer's Paradise

CODE:		37
DATE:		11/23/--
TIME:		18:34
VISA	033	
Sales		1,648.21
Sales Tax		98.89
Total		1,747.10
MasterCard	025	
Sales		1,473.19
Sales Tax		88.39
Total		1,561.58
Debit Cards	044	
Sales		1,497.21
Sales Tax		89.83
Total		1,587.04
Cash	173	
Sales		2,849.16
Sales Tax		170.95
Total		3,020.11
Totals		
Sales		7,467.77
Sales Tax		448.06
Total		7,915.83

BATCH REPORT

MERCHANT:	498418 145
TERMINAL:	1548
DATE:	11/23/-- 18:48
BATCH:	37
VISA	
COUNT	033
SALES	1,809.25
RETURNS	62.15
NET	1,747.10
MASTERCARD	
COUNT	025
SALES	1,607.47
RETURNS	45.89
NET	1,561.58
DEBIT CARDS	
COUNT	044
SALES	1,745.19
RETURNS	158.15
NET	1,587.04
TOTALS	
COUNT	102
SALES	5,161.91
RETURNS	266.19
NET	4,895.72

CONTROL NUMBER: 001489875

10-S SOURCE DOCUMENTS PROBLEM (concluded)

1., 3.

CASH RECEIPTS JOURNAL

PAGE

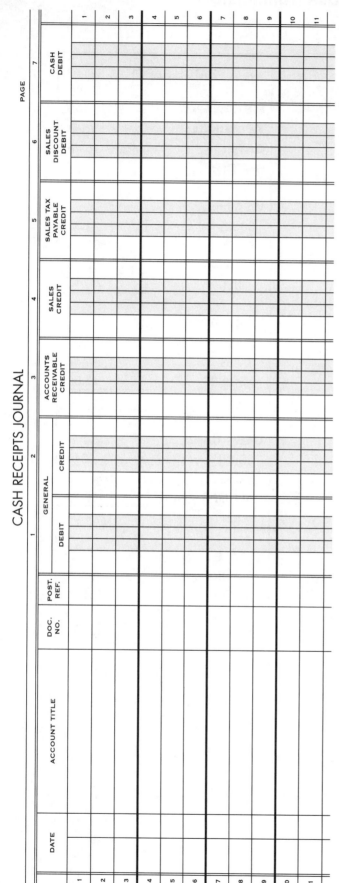

				1	2	3	4	5	6	7	
	DATE	ACCOUNT TITLE	DOC. NO.	POST. REF.	GENERAL DEBIT	GENERAL CREDIT	ACCOUNTS RECEIVABLE CREDIT	SALES CREDIT	SALES TAX PAYABLE CREDIT	SALES DISCOUNT DEBIT	CASH DEBIT	
1												1
2												2
3												3
4												4
5												5
6												6
7												7
8												8
9												9
10												10
11												11

Name ____________ Date ________ Class ________

10-C CHALLENGE PROBLEM (LO2, 3, 4, 5, 6), p. 316

Journalizing sales and cash receipts transactions

1., 2.

SALES JOURNAL PAGE

	DATE		ACCOUNT DEBITED	SALE. NO.	POST. REF.	1 ACCOUNTS RECEIVABLE DEBIT	2 SALES CREDIT	3 SALES TAX PAYABLE CREDIT	
1									1
2									2
3									3
4									4
5									5
6									6
7									7
8									8
9									9

2.

Column Title	Debit Totals	Credit Totals
Accounts Receivable Debit	______	
Sales Credit		______
Sales Tax Payable Credit		______
Totals	======	======

1., 2.

CASH RECEIPTS JOURNAL

PAGE

	DATE	ACCOUNT TITLE	DOC. NO.	POST. REF.	1 GENERAL DEBIT	2 GENERAL CREDIT	3 ACCOUNTS RECEIVABLE CREDIT	4 SALES CREDIT	5 SALES TAX PAYABLE CREDIT	UNEARNED SALES DISCOUNT DEBIT	6 SALES DISCOUNT DEBIT	7 CASH DEBIT	
1													1
2													2
3													3
4													4
5													5
6													6
7													7
8													8
9													9
10													10
11													11

2.

Column Title	Debit Totals	Credit Totals
General Debit		
General Credit		
Accounts Receivable Credit		
Sales Credit		
Sales Tax Payable Credit		
Unearned Sales Discount Debit		
Sales Discount Debit		
Cash Debit		
Totals		

Name ______________________ Date ______________ Class ______________

10-C CHALLENGE PROBLEM (continued)

1.

ACCOUNTS RECEIVABLE LEDGER

CUSTOMER Andersen & Smith LLP — CUSTOMER NO. 110

DATE		ITEM	POST. REF.	DEBIT	CREDIT	DEBIT BALANCE
20-- Nov.	1	Balance	✔			4,209.40
	12		CR11		2,819.41	1,389.99
	20		CR11		1,389.99	—
	22	S893	S11	1,586.69		1,586.69

CUSTOMER Jenson College — CUSTOMER NO. 120

DATE		ITEM	POST. REF.	DEBIT	CREDIT	DEBIT BALANCE
20-- Nov.	1	Balance	✔			6,247.25
	24	S894	S11	3,007.93		9,255.18
	28		CR11		6,247.25	3,007.93

CUSTOMER Northern Regional Airlines — CUSTOMER NO. 130

DATE		ITEM	POST. REF.	DEBIT	CREDIT	DEBIT BALANCE
20-- Nov.	1	Balance	✔			3,481.47
	28	S896	S11	6,184.02		9,665.49
	30		CR11		3,481.47	6,184.02

CUSTOMER Olsen Manufacturing CUSTOMER NO. 140

DATE		ITEM	POST. REF.	DEBIT	CREDIT	DEBIT BALANCE
20-- Nov.	1	Balance	✔			1,549.01
	14	S892	S11	648.08		2,197.09
	25		CR11		1,549.01	648.08
	29	S897	S11	329.99		978.07

CUSTOMER Randle Distribution Centers CUSTOMER NO. 150

DATE		ITEM	POST. REF.	DEBIT	CREDIT	DEBIT BALANCE
20-- Nov.	1	Balance	✔			3,470.59
	4		CR11		3,470.59	—
	28	S895	S11	4,219.64		4,219.64

Name ______________________ Date ____________ Class ____________

10-C CHALLENGE PROBLEM (concluded)

3.

TO:

CC:

BC:

SUBJECT: Analysis of unearned sales discounts

Customers took $236.72 of unearned sales discounts during December, as compared to only $127.98 of earned sales discounts. The unearned discounts represent a 1.3% ($236.72 / $18,235.21) loss in collections from accounts receivable. Many of the unearned discounts were for payments received four or less days late. However, a check received from Randle Distribution Centers was 25 days late.

SEND | SAVE | CANCEL | PRINT

Study Guide 11

Name	Perfect Score	Your Score
Identifying Accounting Terms	11 Pts.	
Analyzing Accounting Concepts and Practices	20 Pts.	
Analyzing Transactions Recorded in Journals	15 Pts.	
Total	46 Pts.	

Part One—Identifying Accounting Terms

Directions: Select the one term in Column I that best fits each definition in Column II. Print the letter identifying your choice in the Answers column.

Column I	***Column II***	***Answers***
A. board of directors	**1.** A journal with two amount columns in which all kinds of entries can be recorded. (p. 320)	**1.** ________
B. credit memorandum	**2.** Credit allowed for the purchase price of returned merchandise, resulting in a decrease in the customer's account payable to the vendor. (p. 322)	**2.** ________
C. debit memorandum	**3.** Credit allowed for part of the purchase price of merchandise that is not returned, resulting in a decrease in the customer's account payable to the vendor. (p. 322)	**3.** ________
D. declaring a dividend	**4.** A form prepared by the customer showing the price deduction taken by the customer for a return or an allowance. (p. 322)	**4.** ________
E. dividends	**5.** Credit allowed to a customer for the sales price of returned merchandise, resulting in a decrease in the accounts receivable of the merchandising business. (p. 327)	**5.** ________
F. general journal	**6.** Credit allowed to a customer for part of the sales price of merchandise that is not returned, resulting in a decrease in the accounts receivable of the merchandising business. (p. 327)	**6.** ________
G. purchases allowance	**7.** A form prepared by the vendor showing the amount deducted for returns and allowances. (p. 327)	**7.** ________
H. purchases return	**8.** An amount earned by a corporation and not yet distributed to stockholders. (p. 332)	**8.** ________
I. retained earnings	**9.** Earnings distributed to stockholders. (p. 332)	**9.** ________
J. sales allowance	**10.** A group of persons elected by the stockholders to govern a corporation. (p. 333)	**10.** ________
K. sales return	**11.** Action by a board of directors to distribute corporate earnings to stockholders. (p. 333)	**11.** ________

Part Two—Analyzing Accounting Concepts and Practices

Directions: Place a *T* for True or an *F* for False in the Answers column to show whether each of the following statements is true or false.

	Answers
1. Transactions that cannot be recorded in a special journal are recorded in a general journal. (p. 320)	**1.** ________
2. A general journal entry posted to Accounts Payable will also be posted to a subsidiary ledger account. (p. 321)	**2.** ________
3. Credit allowed for part of the purchase price of merchandise that is not returned results in an increase in the customer's account. (p. 322)	**3.** ________
4. A debit memorandum prepared by a customer results in the customer recording a debit to the vendor account. (p. 322)	**4.** ________
5. An entry recorded in a general journal will either increase all accounts or decrease all accounts affected by the entry. (p. 323)	**5.** ________
6. The normal account balance of Purchases Returns and Allowances is a debit. (p. 323)	**6.** ________
7. An entry in the general journal that affects Accounts Payable also affects a vendor's account in the accounts payable ledger. (p. 324)	**7.** ________
8. In a computerized accounting system, transactions recorded in a general journal are posted immediately after they are entered. (p. 325)	**8.** ________
9. A completed general journal page should always be reviewed to be sure that all postings have been made. (p. 325)	**9.** ________
10. A credit memorandum issued by a vendor results in the vendor recording a debit to the customer's account. (p. 327)	**10.** ________
11. The normal account balance of Sales Returns and Allowances is a debit. (p. 327)	**11.** ________
12. A sales return that credits the customer's account is not recorded in a cash receipts journal because the transaction does not involve cash. (p. 328)	**12.** ________
13. Entries in the general journal only affect account balances in general ledger accounts. (p. 329)	**13.** ________
14. The correcting entry to correct a sale on account recorded to the wrong customer in the sales journal involves only subsidiary ledger accounts. (p. 330)	**14.** ________
15. Net income increases a corporation's total stockholders' equity. (p. 332)	**15.** ________
16. A corporation's Dividends account is a permanent account similar to a proprietorship's drawing account. (p. 332)	**16.** ________
17. Dividends can be distributed to stockholders only by formal action of a corporation's chief financial officer. (p. 333)	**17.** ________
18. All corporations are required to declare dividends. (p. 333)	**18.** ________
19. The stockholders' equity account, Dividends, has a normal debit balance. (p. 333)	**19.** ________
20. Most corporations pay a dividend by writing a single check to an agent, such as a bank, that distributes checks to individual stockholders. (p. 334)	**20.** ________

Name ____________________ Date __________ Class __________

Part Three—Analyzing Transactions Recorded in Journals

Directions: In Answers Column 1, print the abbreviation for the journal in which each transaction is to be recorded. In Answers Columns 2 and 3, print the letters identifying the subsidiary and general ledger accounts to be debited and credited for each transaction.

GJ—General journal; **CPJ**—Cash payments journal

Account Titles

A. Accounts Payable
B. Accounts Receivable
C. Cash
D. Dividends
E. Dividends Payable
F. Purchases
G. Purchases Returns and Allowances
H. Sales
I. Sales Return and Allowances
J. Sales Tax Payable
K. Supplies—Office
L. Tim Thorton
M. Walton Supply
N. Yeats Corporation

Transactions	Answers 1 Journal	Answers 2 Debit	Answers 3 Credit
1-2-3. Bought office supplies on account from Walton Supply. (p. 321)	1. ____	2. ____	3. ____
4-5-6. Returned merchandise to Yeats Corporation. (p. 323)	4. ____	5. ____	6. ____
7-8-9. Granted credit to Tim Thorton for merchandise returned, plus sales tax. (p. 328)	7. ____	8. ____	9. ____
10-11-12. The board of directors declared a quarterly dividend. (p. 333)	10. ____	11. ____	12. ____
13-14-15. Paid cash for quarterly dividend declared December 15. (p. 334)	13. ____	14. ____	15. ____

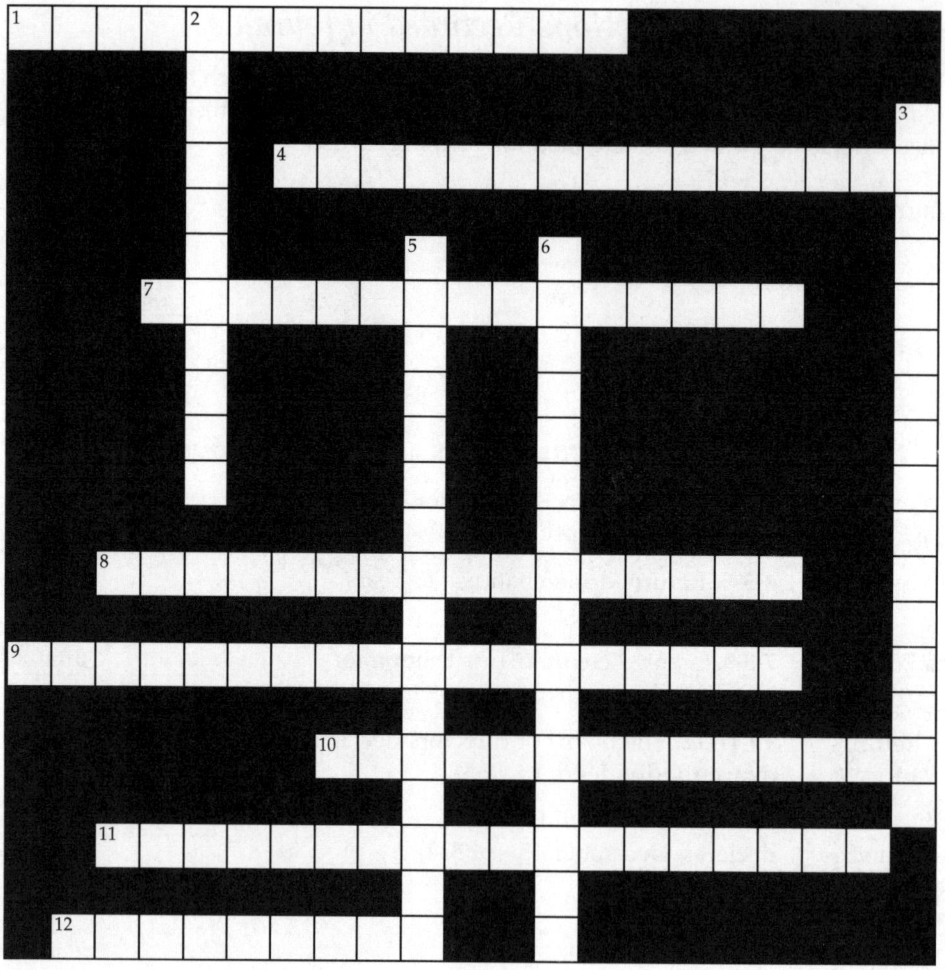

Across

1. Credit allowed to a customer for part of the sales price of merchandise that is not returned, resulting in a decrease in the accounts receivable of the merchandising business.
4. Credit allowed for the purchase price of returned merchandise, resulting in a decrease in the customer's account.
7. A form prepared by the customer showing the price deduction taken by the customer for a return or an allowance.
8. A group of persons elected by the stockholders to govern a corporation.
9. Credit allowed for part of the purchase price of merchandise that is not returned, resulting in a decrease in the customer's account.
10. A journal with two amount columns in which all kinds of entries can be recorded.
11. Action by a board of directors to distribute corporate earnings to stockholders.
12. Earnings distributed to stockholders.

Down

2. Credit allowed to a customer for the sales price of returned merchandise, resulting in a decrease in the accounts receivable of the merchandising business.
3. Processes and procedures employed within a business to ensure that its operations are conducted ethically, accurately, and reliably.
5. An amount earned by a corporation and not yet distributed to stockholders.
6. A form prepared by the vendor showing the amount deducted for returns and allowances.

Name ______________________ Date ____________ Class ____________

11-1 WORK TOGETHER, p. 326

Journalizing and posting transactions using a general journal

1., 2.

GENERAL JOURNAL PAGE

	DATE		ACCOUNT TITLE	DOC. NO.	POST. REF.	DEBIT	CREDIT	
1								1
2								2
3								3
4								4
5								5

2.

VENDOR Griffin, Inc. VENDOR NO. 220

DATE		ITEM	POST. REF.	DEBIT	CREDIT	CREDIT BALANCE
20-- Dec.	1	Balance	✔			958 00

VENDOR Milam Corp. VENDOR NO. 250

DATE		ITEM	POST. REF.	DEBIT	CREDIT	CREDIT BALANCE
20-- Dec.	1	Balance	✔			1 443 00

2.

ACCOUNT Supplies—Office — ACCOUNT NO. 1145

DATE		ITEM	POST. REF.	DEBIT	CREDIT	BALANCE DEBIT	BALANCE CREDIT
20-- Dec.	1	Balance	✔			2,948.00	

ACCOUNT Accounts Payable — ACCOUNT NO. 2110

DATE		ITEM	POST. REF.	DEBIT	CREDIT	BALANCE DEBIT	BALANCE CREDIT
20-- Dec.	1	Balance	✔				8,493.50

ACCOUNT Purchases Returns and Allowances — ACCOUNT NO. 5130

DATE		ITEM	POST. REF.	DEBIT	CREDIT	BALANCE DEBIT	BALANCE CREDIT
20-- Dec.	1	Balance	✔				4,194.60

Name ______________________ Date ____________ Class ____________

11-1 ON YOUR OWN, p. 326

Journalizing and posting transactions using a general journal

1., 2.

GENERAL JOURNAL PAGE

	DATE		ACCOUNT TITLE	DOC. NO.	POST. REF.	DEBIT	CREDIT	
1								1
2								2
3								3
4								4
5								5
6								6
7								7
8								8
9								9

2.

VENDOR Branker Supply VENDOR NO. 210

DATE		ITEM	POST. REF.	DEBIT	CREDIT	CREDIT BALANCE
20-- Dec.	1	Balance	✓			348 00

VENDOR Gould Depot VENDOR NO. 220

DATE		ITEM	POST. REF.	DEBIT	CREDIT	CREDIT BALANCE
20-- Dec.	1	Balance	✓			694 00

VENDOR Olen, Inc. VENDOR NO. 230

DATE		ITEM	POST. REF.	DEBIT	CREDIT	CREDIT BALANCE
20-- Dec.	1	Balance	✓			819 00

VENDOR Plette Corp. VENDOR NO. 240

DATE		ITEM	POST. REF.	DEBIT	CREDIT	CREDIT BALANCE
20-- Dec.	1	Balance	✓			1 183 00

11-1 ON YOUR OWN (concluded)

2.

ACCOUNT Supplies—Office ACCOUNT NO. 1145

DATE		ITEM	POST. REF.	DEBIT	CREDIT	BALANCE DEBIT	BALANCE CREDIT
20-- Dec.	1	Balance	✔			3 0 4 9 60	

ACCOUNT Supplies—Store ACCOUNT NO. 1150

DATE		ITEM	POST. REF.	DEBIT	CREDIT	BALANCE DEBIT	BALANCE CREDIT
20-- Dec.	1	Balance	✔			4 1 8 30	

ACCOUNT Accounts Payable ACCOUNT NO. 2110

DATE		ITEM	POST. REF.	DEBIT	CREDIT	BALANCE DEBIT	BALANCE CREDIT
20-- Dec.	1	Balance	✔				3 0 4 4 00

ACCOUNT Purchases Returns and Allowances ACCOUNT NO. 5130

DATE		ITEM	POST. REF.	DEBIT	CREDIT	BALANCE DEBIT	BALANCE CREDIT
20-- Dec.	1	Balance	✔				6 4 9 8 10

Name ______________ Date ______________ Class ______________

11-2 WORK TOGETHER, p. 331

Accounting for sales returns and allowances using a general journal

1., 2.

GENERAL JOURNAL PAGE

	DATE		ACCOUNT TITLE	DOC. NO.	POST. REF.	DEBIT	CREDIT	
1								1
2								2
3								3
4								4
5								5
6								6
7								7
8								8
9								9
10								10
11								11

2.

CUSTOMER Abraham Corporation — CUSTOMER NO. 110

DATE		ITEM	POST. REF.	DEBIT	CREDIT	DEBIT BALANCE
20-- June	1	Balance	✔			1,649.50

CUSTOMER Ashston & Lindsay LLP — CUSTOMER NO. 120

DATE		ITEM	POST. REF.	DEBIT	CREDIT	DEBIT BALANCE
20-- June	1	Balance	✔			684.25

CUSTOMER Karson Properties — CUSTOMER NO. 130

DATE		ITEM	POST. REF.	DEBIT	CREDIT	DEBIT BALANCE
20-- June	1	Balance	✔			1,647.60

CUSTOMER Keller Associates — CUSTOMER NO. 140

DATE		ITEM	POST. REF.	DEBIT	CREDIT	DEBIT BALANCE
20-- June	1	Balance	✔			1,716.40

CUSTOMER Lambert Schools — CUSTOMER NO. 150

DATE		ITEM	POST. REF.	DEBIT	CREDIT	DEBIT BALANCE
20-- June	1	Balance	✔			3,490.00

Name ______________________ Date ____________ Class ____________

11-2 WORK TOGETHER (concluded)

2.

ACCOUNT Accounts Receivable ACCOUNT NO. 1130

DATE		ITEM	POST. REF.	DEBIT	CREDIT	BALANCE DEBIT	BALANCE CREDIT
20-- June	1	Balance	✔			9 187 75	

ACCOUNT Sales Tax Payable ACCOUNT NO. 2120

DATE		ITEM	POST. REF.	DEBIT	CREDIT	BALANCE DEBIT	BALANCE CREDIT
20-- June	1	Balance	✔				648 10

ACCOUNT Sales Returns and Allowances ACCOUNT NO. 4130

DATE		ITEM	POST. REF.	DEBIT	CREDIT	BALANCE DEBIT	BALANCE CREDIT
20-- June	1	Balance	✔			2 487 60	

11-2 ON YOUR OWN, p. 331

Accounting for sales returns and allowances using a general journal

1., 2.

GENERAL JOURNAL PAGE

	DATE		ACCOUNT TITLE	DOC. NO.	POST. REF.	DEBIT	CREDIT	
1								1
2								2
3								3
4								4
5								5
6								6
7								7
8								8
9								9
10								10
11								11

Name ______________________ Date ____________ Class ____________

11-2 ON YOUR OWN (continued)

2.

CUSTOMER Bettsworth Hospital — CUSTOMER NO. 110

DATE		ITEM	POST. REF.	DEBIT	CREDIT	DEBIT BALANCE
20-- July	1	Balance	✔			1 6 4 9 50

CUSTOMER City Food Bank — CUSTOMER NO. 120

DATE		ITEM	POST. REF.	DEBIT	CREDIT	DEBIT BALANCE
20-- July	1	Balance	✔			6 8 4 25

CUSTOMER Learning Playhouse — CUSTOMER NO. 130

DATE		ITEM	POST. REF.	DEBIT	CREDIT	DEBIT BALANCE
20-- July	1	Balance	✔			1 6 4 7 60

CUSTOMER Paulson Café — CUSTOMER NO. 140

DATE		ITEM	POST. REF.	DEBIT	CREDIT	DEBIT BALANCE
20-- July	1	Balance	✔			1 7 1 6 40

CUSTOMER RPL Corporation — CUSTOMER NO. 150

DATE		ITEM	POST. REF.	DEBIT	CREDIT	DEBIT BALANCE
20-- July	1	Balance	✔			3 4 9 0 00

11-2 ON YOUR OWN (concluded)

2.

ACCOUNT Accounts Receivable ACCOUNT NO. 1130

DATE		ITEM	POST. REF.	DEBIT	CREDIT	BALANCE DEBIT	BALANCE CREDIT
20-- July	1	Balance	✔			9 1 8 7 75	

ACCOUNT Sales Tax Payable ACCOUNT NO. 2120

DATE		ITEM	POST. REF.	DEBIT	CREDIT	BALANCE DEBIT	BALANCE CREDIT
20-- July	1	Balance	✔				6 4 8 10

ACCOUNT Sales Returns and Allowances ACCOUNT NO. 4130

DATE		ITEM	POST. REF.	DEBIT	CREDIT	BALANCE DEBIT	BALANCE CREDIT
20-- July	1	Balance	✔			2 4 8 7 60	

Name ______________________ Date ____________ Class ____________

11-3 WORK TOGETHER, p. 336

Journalizing the declaration and payment of dividends

GENERAL JOURNAL

PAGE

	DATE		ACCOUNT TITLE	DOC. NO.	POST. REF.	DEBIT	CREDIT	
13								13
14								14
15								15
16								16

CASH PAYMENTS JOURNAL

PAGE

						1	2	3	4	5	
						GENERAL		ACCOUNTS PAYABLE DEBIT	PURCHASES DISCOUNT CREDIT	CASH CREDIT	
	DATE		ACCOUNT TITLE	CK. NO.	POST. REF.	DEBIT	CREDIT				
16											16
17											17
18											18

11-3 ON YOUR OWN, p. 336

Journalizing the declaration and payment of dividends

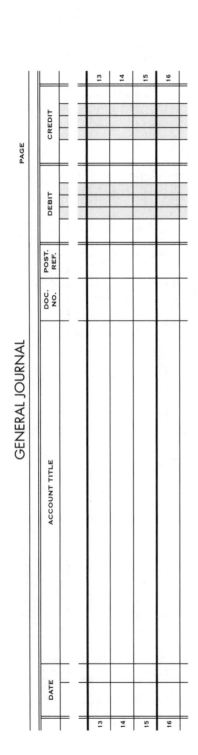

GENERAL JOURNAL

PAGE

	DATE	ACCOUNT TITLE	DOC. NO.	POST. REF.	DEBIT	CREDIT	
13							13
14							14
15							15
16							16

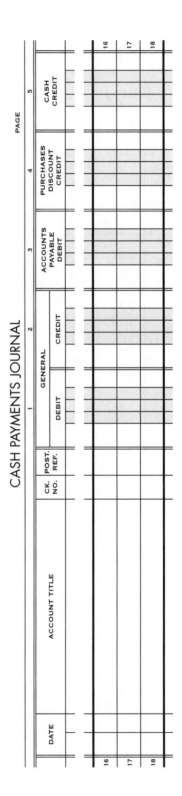

CASH PAYMENTS JOURNAL

PAGE

					1	2	3	4	5	
	DATE	ACCOUNT TITLE	CK. NO.	POST. REF.	GENERAL		ACCOUNTS PAYABLE DEBIT	PURCHASES DISCOUNT CREDIT	CASH CREDIT	
					DEBIT	CREDIT				
16										16
17										17
18										18

Name ______ Date ______ Class ______

11-1 APPLICATION PROBLEM (LO2, 3), p. 339

Journalizing and posting purchases transactions using a general journal

1., 2.

GENERAL JOURNAL PAGE

	DATE		ACCOUNT TITLE	DOC. NO.	POST. REF.	DEBIT	CREDIT	
1								1
2								2
3								3
4								4
5								5
6								6
7								7
8								8
9								9

2.

VENDOR Daniels Supply — VENDOR NO. 210

DATE		ITEM	POST. REF.	DEBIT	CREDIT	CREDIT BALANCE
20-- Dec.	1	Balance	✔			1 123 00

VENDOR Harris Paints — VENDOR NO. 220

DATE		ITEM	POST. REF.	DEBIT	CREDIT	CREDIT BALANCE
20-- Dec.	1	Balance	✔			1 560 00

VENDOR Mason Molds — VENDOR NO. 230

DATE		ITEM	POST. REF.	DEBIT	CREDIT	CREDIT BALANCE
20-- Dec.	1	Balance	✔			640 00

VENDOR Office Zone — VENDOR NO. 240

DATE		ITEM	POST. REF.	DEBIT	CREDIT	CREDIT BALANCE
20-- Dec.	1	Balance	✔			795 00

Name ______________________ Date ____________ Class ____________

11-1 APPLICATION PROBLEM (concluded)

2.

ACCOUNT Supplies—Office ACCOUNT NO. 1145

DATE		ITEM	POST. REF.	DEBIT	CREDIT	BALANCE DEBIT	BALANCE CREDIT
20-- Dec.	1	Balance	✔			4 260 00	

ACCOUNT Supplies—Store ACCOUNT NO. 1150

DATE		ITEM	POST. REF.	DEBIT	CREDIT	BALANCE DEBIT	BALANCE CREDIT
20-- Dec.	1	Balance	✔			1 570 00	

ACCOUNT Accounts Payable ACCOUNT NO. 2110

DATE		ITEM	POST. REF.	DEBIT	CREDIT	BALANCE DEBIT	BALANCE CREDIT
20-- Dec.	1	Balance	✔				6 491 00

ACCOUNT Purchases Returns and Allowances ACCOUNT NO. 5130

DATE		ITEM	POST. REF.	DEBIT	CREDIT	BALANCE DEBIT	BALANCE CREDIT
20-- Dec.	1	Balance	✔				3 047 25

11-2 APPLICATION PROBLEM (LO4, 5, 6), p. 339

Accounting for sales returns and allowances using a general journal

1., 2.

GENERAL JOURNAL PAGE

	DATE		ACCOUNT TITLE	DOC. NO.	POST. REF.	DEBIT	CREDIT	
1								1
2								2
3								3
4								4
5								5
6								6
7								7
8								8
9								9
10								10
11								11

Name ______________________ Date ______________ Class ______________

11-2 APPLICATION PROBLEM (continued)

2.

CUSTOMER John Auburn CUSTOMER NO. 110

DATE		ITEM	POST. REF.	DEBIT	CREDIT	DEBIT BALANCE
20-- Sept.	1	Balance	✔			589 15

CUSTOMER Mary Best CUSTOMER NO. 120

DATE		ITEM	POST. REF.	DEBIT	CREDIT	DEBIT BALANCE
20-- Sept.	1	Balance	✔			1 562 00

CUSTOMER Burns & Associates CUSTOMER NO. 130

DATE		ITEM	POST. REF.	DEBIT	CREDIT	DEBIT BALANCE
20-- Sept.	1	Balance	✔			489 58

CUSTOMER Cassidy Corporation CUSTOMER NO. 140

DATE		ITEM	POST. REF.	DEBIT	CREDIT	DEBIT BALANCE
20-- Sept.	1	Balance	✔			2 199 19

CUSTOMER Anna Jackson CUSTOMER NO. 150

DATE		ITEM	POST. REF.	DEBIT	CREDIT	DEBIT BALANCE
20-- Sept.	1	Balance	✔			1 948 25

CUSTOMER Metsville Schools CUSTOMER NO. 160

DATE		ITEM	POST. REF.	DEBIT	CREDIT	DEBIT BALANCE
20-- Sept.	1	Balance	✔			2 794 18

2.

ACCOUNT Accounts Receivable — ACCOUNT NO. 1130

DATE		ITEM	POST. REF.	DEBIT	CREDIT	BALANCE DEBIT	BALANCE CREDIT
20– Sept.	1	Balance	✔			9 582 35	

ACCOUNT Sales Tax Payable — ACCOUNT NO. 2120

DATE		ITEM	POST. REF.	DEBIT	CREDIT	BALANCE DEBIT	BALANCE CREDIT
20– Sept.	1	Balance	✔				648 10

ACCOUNT Sales Returns and Allowances — ACCOUNT NO. 4130

DATE		ITEM	POST. REF.	DEBIT	CREDIT	BALANCE DEBIT	BALANCE CREDIT
20– Sept.	1	Balance	✔			2 487 60	

Name ______________________ Date ____________ Class ____________

11-3 APPLICATION PROBLEM (LO8), p. 339

Journalizing the declaration and payment of dividends

GENERAL JOURNAL

PAGE

	DATE		ACCOUNT TITLE	DOC. NO.	POST. REF.	DEBIT	CREDIT	
13								13
14								14
15								15
16								16

CASH PAYMENTS JOURNAL

PAGE

	DATE		ACCOUNT TITLE	CK. NO.	POST. REF.	1 GENERAL DEBIT	2 GENERAL CREDIT	3 ACCOUNTS PAYABLE DEBIT	4 PURCHASES DISCOUNT CREDIT	5 CASH CREDIT	
16											16
17											17
18											18

11-M.1 MASTERY PROBLEM (LO2, 3, 4, 5, 6, 8), p. 340

Journalizing and posting transactions using a general journal and a cash payments journal

1., 2.

GENERAL JOURNAL PAGE

	DATE		ACCOUNT TITLE	DOC. NO.	POST. REF.	DEBIT	CREDIT	
1								1
2								2
3								3
4								4
5								5
6								6
7								7
8								8
9								9
10								10
11								11
12								12
13								13
14								14
15								15
16								16

1., 3.

CASH PAYMENTS JOURNAL PAGE

	DATE		ACCOUNT TITLE	CK. NO.	POST. REF.	1 GENERAL DEBIT	2 GENERAL CREDIT	3 ACCOUNTS PAYABLE DEBIT	4 PURCHASES DISCOUNT CREDIT	5 CASH CREDIT	
16											16
17											17
18											18

Name ____________________ Date ____________ Class ____________

11-M.1 MASTERY PROBLEM (continued)

2. **ACCOUNTS PAYABLE LEDGER**

VENDOR Century Foods VENDOR NO. 220

DATE		ITEM	POST. REF.	DEBIT	CREDIT	CREDIT BALANCE
20-- Dec.	1	Balance	✔			1 9 4 8 25

VENDOR Great Lakes Produce VENDOR NO. 260

DATE		ITEM	POST. REF.	DEBIT	CREDIT	CREDIT BALANCE
20-- Dec.	1	Balance	✔			3 1 8 4 26

VENDOR Kelsar Supply VENDOR NO. 280

DATE		ITEM	POST. REF.	DEBIT	CREDIT	CREDIT BALANCE
20-- Dec.	1	Balance	✔			9 6 8 28

2.

ACCOUNTS RECEIVABLE LEDGER

CUSTOMER Connie's Bakery — CUSTOMER NO. 120

DATE		ITEM	POST. REF.	DEBIT	CREDIT	DEBIT BALANCE
20-- Dec.	1	Balance	✔			589 15

CUSTOMER JD's Café — CUSTOMER NO. 160

DATE		ITEM	POST. REF.	DEBIT	CREDIT	DEBIT BALANCE
20-- Dec.	1	Balance	✔			1 562 00

CUSTOMER Restaurant Deville — CUSTOMER NO. 180

DATE		ITEM	POST. REF.	DEBIT	CREDIT	DEBIT BALANCE
20-- Dec.	1	Balance	✔			970 36

CUSTOMER Rib Shack — CUSTOMER NO. 190

DATE		ITEM	POST. REF.	DEBIT	CREDIT	DEBIT BALANCE
20-- Dec.	1	Balance	✔			574 05

Name ______________________ Date __________ Class __________

11-M.1 MASTERY PROBLEM (continued)

2., 3.

GENERAL LEDGER

ACCOUNT Accounts Receivable ACCOUNT NO. 1130

DATE		ITEM	POST. REF.	DEBIT	CREDIT	BALANCE DEBIT	BALANCE CREDIT
20-- Dec.	1	Balance	✔			16 482 15	

ACCOUNT Supplies—Store ACCOUNT NO. 1150

DATE		ITEM	POST. REF.	DEBIT	CREDIT	BALANCE DEBIT	BALANCE CREDIT
20-- Dec.	1	Balance	✔			3 049 24	

ACCOUNT Accounts Payable ACCOUNT NO. 2110

DATE		ITEM	POST. REF.	DEBIT	CREDIT	BALANCE DEBIT	BALANCE CREDIT
20-- Dec.	1	Balance	✔				18 431 18

ACCOUNT Sales Tax Payable ACCOUNT NO. 2120

DATE		ITEM	POST. REF.	DEBIT	CREDIT	BALANCE DEBIT	BALANCE CREDIT
20-- Dec.	1	Balance	✔				894 17

11-M.1 MASTERY PROBLEM (concluded)

2., 3.

ACCOUNT Dividends Payable — ACCOUNT NO. 2180

DATE		ITEM	POST. REF.	DEBIT	CREDIT	BALANCE DEBIT	BALANCE CREDIT

ACCOUNT Dividends — ACCOUNT NO. 3130

DATE		ITEM	POST. REF.	DEBIT	CREDIT	BALANCE DEBIT	BALANCE CREDIT
20-- Dec.	1	Balance	✔			8,772.00	

ACCOUNT Sales Returns and Allowances — ACCOUNT NO. 4130

DATE		ITEM	POST. REF.	DEBIT	CREDIT	BALANCE DEBIT	BALANCE CREDIT
20-- Dec.	1	Balance	✔			8,417.10	

ACCOUNT Purchases Returns and Allowances — ACCOUNT NO. 5130

DATE		ITEM	POST. REF.	DEBIT	CREDIT	BALANCE DEBIT	BALANCE CREDIT
20-- Dec.	1	Balance	✔				4,189.94

Name ________________ Date ________ Class ________

11-M.2 MASTERY PROBLEM (Review of Chapters 9, 10, and 11), p. 340

Journalizing and posting transactions

1.

GENERAL JOURNAL PAGE

	DATE		ACCOUNT TITLE	DOC. NO.	POST. REF.	DEBIT	CREDIT	
1								1
2								2
3								3
4								4
5								5
6								6
7								7
8								8
9								9
10								10
11								11
12								12
13								13
14								14

11-M.2 MASTERY PROBLEM (continued)

1., 2.

SALES JOURNAL PAGE

	DATE		ACCOUNT DEBITED	SALE NO.	POST. REF.	1 ACCOUNTS RECEIVABLE DEBIT	2 SALES CREDIT	3 SALES TAX PAYABLE CREDIT	
1									1
2									2
3									3
4									4
5									5
6									6
7									7

2. Sales Journal Proof

Column Title	Debit Totals	Credit Totals
Accounts Receivable Debit		
Sales Credit		
Sales Tax Payable Credit		
Totals		

1., 3.

PURCHASES JOURNAL PAGE

	DATE		ACCOUNT CREDITED	PURCH. NO.	POST. REF.	PURCHASES DR. ACCTS. PAY. CR.	
1							1
2							2
3							3
4							4
5							5
6							6
7							7
8							8
9							9

Name ______________________ Date ____________ Class ____________

11-M.2 MASTERY PROBLEM (continued)

1., 4.

CASH RECEIPTS JOURNAL

PAGE

					1	2	3	4	5	6	7	
					GENERAL							
	DATE	ACCOUNT TITLE	DOC. NO.	POST. REF.	DEBIT	CREDIT	ACCOUNTS RECEIVABLE CREDIT	SALES CREDIT	SALES TAX PAYABLE CREDIT	SALES DISCOUNT DEBIT	CASH DEBIT	
1												1
2												2
3												3
4												4
5												5
6												6
7												7
8												8
9												9
10												10
11												11
12												12
13												13
14												14
15												15

4. Cash Receipts Journal Proof

Column Title	Debit Totals	Credit Totals
General Debit		
General Credit		
Accounts Receivable Credit		
Sales Credit		
Sales Tax Payable Credit		
Sales Discount Debit		
Cash Debit		
Totals		

1., 5.

CASH PAYMENTS JOURNAL

PAGE

	DATE	ACCOUNT TITLE	CK. NO.	POST. REF.	1 GENERAL DEBIT	2 GENERAL CREDIT	3 ACCOUNTS PAYABLE DEBIT	4 PURCHASES DISCOUNT CREDIT	5 CASH CREDIT	
1										1
2										2
3										3
4										4
5										5
6										6
7										7
8										8
9										9
10										10
11										11
12										12
13										13
14										14
15										15

5. Cash Payments Journal Proof

Column Title	Debit Totals	Credit Totals
General Debit		
General Credit		
Accounts Payable Debit		
Purchases Discount Credit		
Cash Debit		
Totals		

Name ______________________ Date ____________ Class ____________

11-M.2 MASTERY PROBLEM (continued)

1.

ACCOUNTS RECEIVABLE LEDGER

CUSTOMER LaDonna Atkins CUSTOMER NO. 110

DATE		ITEM	POST. REF.	DEBIT	CREDIT	DEBIT BALANCE
20-- Dec.	1	Balance	✔			2 2 1 1 98

CUSTOMER Coastal County Schools CUSTOMER NO. 120

DATE		ITEM	POST. REF.	DEBIT	CREDIT	DEBIT BALANCE
20-- Dec.	1	Balance	✔			1 6 4 7 50

CUSTOMER Joseph Greggs CUSTOMER NO. 130

DATE		ITEM	POST. REF.	DEBIT	CREDIT	DEBIT BALANCE
20-- Dec.	1	Balance	✔			3 4 9 4 50

CUSTOMER Kelsey Pittman CUSTOMER NO. 140

DATE		ITEM	POST. REF.	DEBIT	CREDIT	DEBIT BALANCE
20-- Dec.	1	Balance	✔			2 4 1 7 50

CUSTOMER Larry Simpson CUSTOMER NO. 150

DATE		ITEM	POST. REF.	DEBIT	CREDIT	DEBIT BALANCE

7.

11-M.2 MASTERY PROBLEM (continued)

1.

ACCOUNTS PAYABLE LEDGER

VENDOR Barger Office Supply VENDOR NO. 210

DATE		ITEM	POST. REF.	DEBIT	CREDIT	CREDIT BALANCE
20-- Dec.	1	Balance	✔			2 284 00

VENDOR Francis Industries VENDOR NO. 220

DATE		ITEM	POST. REF.	DEBIT	CREDIT	CREDIT BALANCE
20-- Dec.	1	Balance	✔			1 595 00

VENDOR Jing Corporation VENDOR NO. 230

DATE		ITEM	POST. REF.	DEBIT	CREDIT	CREDIT BALANCE
20-- Dec.	1	Balance	✔			3 290 00

VENDOR Quitman Manufacturing VENDOR NO. 240

DATE		ITEM	POST. REF.	DEBIT	CREDIT	CREDIT BALANCE
20-- Dec.	1	Balance	✔			1 589 00

VENDOR Wilson Metals VENDOR NO. 250

DATE		ITEM	POST. REF.	DEBIT	CREDIT	CREDIT BALANCE

7.

Name ______________________ Date ____________ Class ____________

11-M.2 MASTERY PROBLEM (continued)

1., 2., 3., 4., 5.

GENERAL LEDGER

ACCOUNT Cash — ACCOUNT NO. 1110

DATE		ITEM	POST. REF.	DEBIT	CREDIT	BALANCE DEBIT	BALANCE CREDIT
20-- Dec.	1	Balance	✔			21 359 50	

ACCOUNT Petty Cash — ACCOUNT NO. 1120

DATE		ITEM	POST. REF.	DEBIT	CREDIT	BALANCE DEBIT	BALANCE CREDIT
20-- Dec.	1	Balance	✔			150 00	

ACCOUNT Accounts Receivable — ACCOUNT NO. 1130

DATE		ITEM	POST. REF.	DEBIT	CREDIT	BALANCE DEBIT	BALANCE CREDIT
20-- Dec.	1	Balance	✔			9 771 48	

ACCOUNT Supplies—Office — ACCOUNT NO. 1145

DATE		ITEM	POST. REF.	DEBIT	CREDIT	BALANCE DEBIT	BALANCE CREDIT
20-- Dec.	1	Balance	✔			1 648 66	

ACCOUNT Accounts Payable — ACCOUNT NO. 2110

DATE		ITEM	POST. REF.	DEBIT	CREDIT	BALANCE DEBIT	BALANCE CREDIT
20-- Dec.	1	Balance	✔				8 758 00

11-M.2 MASTERY PROBLEM (continued)

ACCOUNT Sales Tax Payable — ACCOUNT NO. 2120

DATE		ITEM	POST. REF.	DEBIT	CREDIT	BALANCE DEBIT	BALANCE CREDIT
20-- Dec.	1	Balance	✔				4 1 8 05

ACCOUNT Dividends Payable — ACCOUNT NO. 2180

DATE		ITEM	POST. REF.	DEBIT	CREDIT	BALANCE DEBIT	BALANCE CREDIT

ACCOUNT Dividends — ACCOUNT NO. 3130

DATE		ITEM	POST. REF.	DEBIT	CREDIT	BALANCE DEBIT	BALANCE CREDIT

ACCOUNT Sales — ACCOUNT NO. 4110

DATE		ITEM	POST. REF.	DEBIT	CREDIT	BALANCE DEBIT	BALANCE CREDIT
20-- Dec.	1	Balance	✔				162 7 8 9 11

ACCOUNT Sales Discount — ACCOUNT NO. 4120

DATE		ITEM	POST. REF.	DEBIT	CREDIT	BALANCE DEBIT	BALANCE CREDIT
20-- Dec.	1	Balance	✔			6 1 8 90	

Name ______________________ Date ____________ Class ____________

11-M.2 MASTERY PROBLEM (continued)

ACCOUNT Sales Returns and Allowances ACCOUNT NO. 4130

DATE		ITEM	POST. REF.	DEBIT	CREDIT	BALANCE DEBIT	BALANCE CREDIT
20-- Dec.	1	Balance	✔			3 491 10	

ACCOUNT Purchases ACCOUNT NO. 5110

DATE		ITEM	POST. REF.	DEBIT	CREDIT	BALANCE DEBIT	BALANCE CREDIT
20-- Dec.	1	Balance	✔			114 910 84	

ACCOUNT Purchases Discount ACCOUNT NO. 5120

DATE		ITEM	POST. REF.	DEBIT	CREDIT	BALANCE DEBIT	BALANCE CREDIT
20-- Dec.	1	Balance	✔				3 471 80

ACCOUNT Purchases Returns and Allowances ACCOUNT NO. 5130

DATE		ITEM	POST. REF.	DEBIT	CREDIT	BALANCE DEBIT	BALANCE CREDIT
20-- Dec.	1	Balance	✔				2 471 62

ACCOUNT Advertising Expense ACCOUNT NO. 6105

DATE		ITEM	POST. REF.	DEBIT	CREDIT	BALANCE DEBIT	BALANCE CREDIT
20-- Dec.	1	Balance	✔			8 497 20	

11-M.2 MASTERY PROBLEM (concluded)

ACCOUNT Cash Short and Over ACCOUNT NO. 6110

DATE		ITEM	POST. REF.	DEBIT	CREDIT	BALANCE DEBIT	BALANCE CREDIT
20-- Dec.	1	Balance	✔			6 15	

ACCOUNT Miscellaneous Expense ACCOUNT NO. 6135

DATE		ITEM	POST. REF.	DEBIT	CREDIT	BALANCE DEBIT	BALANCE CREDIT
20-- Dec.	1	Balance	✔			4 1 7 3 56	

ACCOUNT Rent Expense ACCOUNT NO. 6145

DATE		ITEM	POST. REF.	DEBIT	CREDIT	BALANCE DEBIT	BALANCE CREDIT
20-- Dec.	1	Balance	✔			8 8 0 0 00	

ACCOUNT Utilities Expense ACCOUNT NO. 6170

DATE		ITEM	POST. REF.	DEBIT	CREDIT	BALANCE DEBIT	BALANCE CREDIT
20-- Dec.	1	Balance	✔			4 4 8 1 19	

6. Cash Proof

Cash on hand at the beginning of the month . . . .
Plus total cash received during the month . . . . ________
Equals total. . . . .
Less total cash paid during the month. . . . . ________
Equals cash balance on hand at the end of the month . . . . ________
Checkbook balance on the next unused check stub. . . . . ________

Name ______________________ Date ____________ Class ____________

11-C CHALLENGE PROBLEM (LO2, 6), p. 341

Journalizing business transactions

GENERAL JOURNAL PAGE

	DATE		ACCOUNT TITLE	DOC. NO.	POST. REF.	DEBIT	CREDIT	
1								1
2								2
3								3
4								4
5								5
6								6
7								7
8								8
9								9
10								10
11								11
12								12
13								13

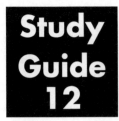

Study Guide 12

Name	Perfect Score	Your Score
Identifying Accounting Terms	24 Pts.	
Analyzing Payroll Procedures	5 Pts.	
Identifying Accounting Practices	25 Pts.	
Total	54 Pts.	

Part One—Identifying Accounting Terms

Directions: Select the one term in Column I that best fits each definition in Column II. Print the letter identifying your choice in the Answers column.

Contains accounting terms for Lessons 12-1 and 12-2.

Column I	Column II	Answers
A. 401(k)	**1.** The amount paid to an employee for every hour worked. (p. 346)	**1.** ________
B. accumulated earnings	**2.** A fixed annual sum of money divided among equal pay periods. (p. 346)	**2.** ________
C. commission	**3.** A method of paying an employee based on the amount of sales the employee generates. (p. 346)	**3.** ________
D. individual retirement account	**4.** The total amount paid by a business for an employee's work, earned by a wage, salary, or commission. (p. 346)	**4.** ________
E. Medicare tax	**5.** The number of days or weeks of work covered by an employee's paycheck. (p. 346)	**5.** ________
F. pay period	**6.** The total amount earned by all employees for a pay period. (p. 346)	**6.** ________
G. payroll	**7.** The accounting staff position that compiles and computes payroll data, then prepares, journalizes, and posts payroll transactions. (p. 346)	**7.** ________
H. payroll clerk	**8.** A device used to record the dates and times of every employee's arrivals and departures. (p. 347)	**8.** ________
I. payroll deduction	**9.** Taxes based on the payroll of a business. (p. 351)	**9.** ________
J. payroll taxes	**10.** A deduction from total earnings for each person legally supported by a taxpayer, including the employee. (p. 352)	**10.** ________
K. qualified retirement plan	**11.** Any amount withheld from an employee's gross earnings. (p. 352)	**11.** ________
L. Roth individual retirement account	**12.** A federal tax paid for old-age, survivors, and disability insurance. (p. 355)	**12.** ________
M. salary	**13.** A federal tax paid for hospital insurance. (p. 355)	**13.** ________
N. social security tax	**14.** The total gross earnings year to date for an employee. (p. 355)	**14.** ________
O. tax base	**15.** The maximum amount of gross earnings on which a tax is calculated. (p. 355)	**15.** ________
P. time clock	**16.** A retirement savings plan approved by the Internal Revenue Service that provides individuals with a tax benefit. (p. 356)	**16.** ________
Q. total earnings	**17.** A qualified retirement plan sponsored by an employer. (p. 356)	**17.** ________
R. wage	**18.** A qualified retirement plan that provides most individuals with a deferred federal income tax benefit. (p. 356)	**18.** ________
S. withholding allowance	**19.** A qualified retirement plan that allows tax-free withdrawals from the account. (p. 356)	**19.** ________

Directions: Select the one term in Column I that best fits each definition in Column II. Print the letter identifying your choice in the Answers column.

Contains accounting terms for Lessons 12-3 and 12-4.

Column I	Column II	Answers
A. direct deposit	**1.** An accounting form that summarizes the earnings, deductions, and net pay of all employees for one pay period. (p. 358)	**1.** ______
B. employee earnings record	**2.** The total earnings paid to an employee after payroll taxes and other deductions. (p. 359)	**2.** ______
C. net pay	**3.** A business form used to record details of an employee's earnings and deductions. (p. 360)	**3.** ______
D. payroll register	**4.** A check with a detachable check stub that contains detailed information about the cash payment. (p. 364)	**4.** ______
E. voucher check	**5.** The payment of an employee's net pay using electronic funds transfer. (p. 366)	**5.** ______

Part Two—Analyzing Payroll Procedures

Directions: For each of the following items, select the choice that best completes the statement. Print the letter of your choice in the Answers column.

	Answers
1. How many hours were worked by an employee who arrived at 8:10 A.M. and departed at 12:10 P.M.? (A) 4 hours (B) 5 hours (C) 4 hours and 10 minutes (D) none of these. (p. 347)	**1.** ______
2. How many hours were worked by an employee who arrived at 7:05 A.M. and departed at 6:05 P.M. with one hour off for lunch? (A) 11 hours (B) 10 hours (C) 12 hours (D) none of these. (p. 347)	**2.** ______
3. Employee regular earnings are calculated as (A) regular hours times regular rate (B) total hours divided by regular rate (C) total hours plus overtime rate (D) overtime hours minus overtime rate. (p. 349)	**3.** ______
4. Social security tax is calculated on (A) total earnings and marital status (B) number of withholding allowances (C) total earnings and number of withholding allowances (D) employee earnings up to a maximum paid in a calendar year. (p. 355)	**4.** ______
5. A separate payroll checking account is used primarily to (A) simplify the payroll accounting system (B) help reduce the cost of preparing a payroll (C) provide additional protection and control payroll payments (D) eliminate employer earnings records. (p. 364)	**5.** ______

Name ________________________________ Date ____________ Class ____________

Part Three—Identifying Accounting Practices

Directions: Place a *T* for True or an *F* for False in the Answers column to show whether each of the following statements is true or false.

	Answers
1. A business may decide to pay employee salaries every week, every two weeks, twice a month, or once a month. (p. 346)	**1.** _______
2. Today's time clocks can feed data directly into a company's computer system. (p. 348)	**2.** _______
3. Total earnings are sometimes referred to as net pay or net earnings. (p. 346)	**3.** _______
4. An hourly employee's total earnings are calculated as regular hours × regular rate, plus overtime hours × overtime rate. (p. 349)	**4.** _______
5. Payroll taxes withheld represent a liability for an employer until payment is made to the government. (p. 351)	**5.** _______
6. Employers are required to have a current Form W-4, Employee's Withholding Allowance Certificate, for all employees. (p. 352)	**6.** _______
7. Federal income tax is one example of a payroll deduction. (p. 352)	**7.** _______
8. The amount of income tax withheld from each employee's total earnings is determined from the number of withholding allowances and by the employee's marital status. (p. 352)	**8.** _______
9. A single person will have less income tax withheld than a married employee earning the same amount. (p. 352)	**9.** _______
10. The larger the number of withholding allowances claimed, the larger the amount of income tax withheld. (p. 352)	**10.** _______
11. An employee can be exempt from having federal income tax withheld under certain conditions. (p. 352)	**11.** _______
12. Social security tax is only paid by the employer. (p. 355)	**12.** _______
13. An act of Congress can change the social security tax base and tax rate at any time. (p. 355)	**13.** _______
14. When an employee's accumulated earnings exceed the tax base, no more social security tax is deducted. (p. 355)	**14.** _______
15. Qualified retirement plans are approved by the Internal Revenue Service (p. 356)	**15.** _______
16. Employee contributions to a 401(k) reduce the amount of earnings subject to payroll taxes. (p. 356)	**16.** _______
17. The investment income of a 401(k) account is taxable to the employee in the year earned. (p. 356)	**17.** _______
18. Taxes on the contributions and investment income of an IRA are deferred until the funds are withdrawn. (p. 356)	**18.** _______
19. Contributions to a Roth IRA do not provide a current tax benefit. (p. 356)	**19.** _______
20. The investment income in a Roth IRA is subject to federal income taxes when withdrawn. (p. 356)	**20.** _______

Answers

21. The columns of the employee earnings record consist of the amount columns in a payroll register and an Accumulated Earnings column. (p. 360) **21.** ______

22. A check for each employee's total net pay is written on the general checking account of the business. (p. 364) **22.** ______

23. The original voucher check, with the voucher attached, is mailed to the vendor. (p. 365) **23.** ______

24. The voucher of a payroll check contains current pay period and year-to-date earnings and deduction information. (p. 365) **24.** ______

25. When EFT is used, the employee does not receive an individual check. (p. 366) **25.** ______

Name ______________________________ Date ______________ Class ______________

12-1 WORK TOGETHER, p. 350

Calculating hourly employee total earnings

1.

EMPLOYEE NO. 4

NAME Alice R. Webster

PAY PERIOD ENDED October 15, 20--

Day	MORNING		AFTERNOON		EVENING		HOURS	
	IN	OUT	IN	OUT	IN	OUT	REG	OT
Mon 01	7^{54}	11^{57}	12^{56}	5^{02}				
Tue 02	8^{00}	11^{52}	1^{06}	5^{02}				
Wed 03	7^{56}	12^{01}	1^{04}	5^{01}				
Thu 04	7^{59}	11^{57}	12^{59}	4^{59}	6^{01}	9^{33}		
Fri 05			12^{58}	4^{56}	6^{01}	10^{10}		
Mon 08	8^{01}	11^{57}	1^{00}	4^{53}				
Tue 09	8^{01}	12^{03}	12^{57}	6^{06}				
Wed 10	7^{54}	11^{52}	1^{02}	5^{03}				
Thu 11	7^{58}	12^{01}	12^{58}	5^{00}				
Fri 12	8^{01}	1^{04}	2^{02}	5^{05}				
Sat 13	10^{05}	1^{05}						
Mon 15	7^{52}	12^{00}	12^{59}	4^{53}				
						PERIOD TOTALS		

APPROVED BY ______________________

2.

Employee Number	Hours Worked		Regular Rate	Earnings		Total Earnings
	Regular	Overtime		Regular	Overtime	
1	80	5	$ 9.00	________	________	________
2	80	3	12.50	________	________	________
3	70	0	9.75	________	________	________
4			11.00	________	________	________

12-1 ON YOUR OWN, p. 350

Calculating hourly employee total earnings

1.

EMPLOYEE NO. 34

NAME Mary Carol Prestwood

PAY PERIOD ENDED June 30, 20--

Day	MORNING IN	MORNING OUT	AFTERNOON IN	AFTERNOON OUT	EVENING IN	EVENING OUT	HOURS REG	HOURS OT
Mon 16	8^{55}	11^{53}	12^{52}	6^{05}				
Tue 17	9^{06}	11^{58}	1^{00}	6^{02}				
Thu 19	8^{57}	12^{00}	1^{00}	6^{03}				
Fri 20	8^{55}	11^{57}	12^{59}	5^{52}	6^{01}	9^{10}		
Sat 21	8^{56}	12^{01}	12^{52}	5^{53}				
Mon 23	9^{04}	11^{55}	1^{01}	5^{53}				
Tue 24	9^{05}	12^{02}	12^{59}	5^{54}				
Thu 26			1^{05}	6^{04}				
Fri 27	8^{58}	12^{00}	12^{55}	6^{00}	7^{05}	9^{05}		
Sat 28	9^{03}	11^{56}	12^{56}	5^{52}				
Mon 30	8^{52}	11^{57}	12^{57}	5^{56}				
PERIOD TOTALS								

APPROVED BY ____________________

2.

Employee Number	Hours Worked Regular	Hours Worked Overtime	Regular Rate	Earnings Regular	Earnings Overtime	Total Earnings
25	88	5	$10.00			
28	72	3	14.50			
32	88	4	13.75			
34			12.50			

Name ______________________ Date ______________ Class ______________

12-2 WORK TOGETHER, p. 357

Determining payroll tax withholding

1., 2.

Employee		Marital Status	Number of Withholding Allowances	Total Earnings	Federal Income Tax Withholding	Social Security Tax Withholding	Medicare Withholding
No.	Name						
1	Clauson, John P.	M	2	$1,360.00			
9	Edison, Janice A.	S	1	980.00			
5	Lambert, Terri C.	M	3	1,510.00			
2	Simpson, Anthony W.	S	2	1,125.00			

12-2 ON YOUR OWN, p. 357

Determining payroll tax withholding

1., 2.

Employee		Marital Status	Number of Withholding Allowances	Total Earnings	Federal Income Tax Withholding	Social Security Tax Withholding	Medicare Withholding
No.	Name						
3	Gilmore, Harris J.	S	2	$1,020.00			
8	Keller, Francis P.	M	3	1,810.00			
4	Millhouse, Gary R.	S	1	1,205.00			
1	Williamson, Mary A.	M	1	1,405.00			

12-3 WORK TOGETHER, p. 363

Preparing payroll records
(Note: The payroll register and employee earnings record used in this problem are also used in Work Together 12-4.)

1., 2.

PAYROLL REGISTER

SEMIMONTHLY PERIOD ENDED ____ DATE OF PAYMENT ____

	EMPL. NO.	EMPLOYEE'S NAME	MARITAL STATUS	NO. OF ALLOWANCES	EARNINGS 1 REGULAR	EARNINGS 2 OVERTIME	EARNINGS 3 TOTAL	DEDUCTIONS 4 FEDERAL INCOME TAX	DEDUCTIONS 5 SOCIAL SECURITY TAX	DEDUCTIONS 6 MEDICARE TAX	DEDUCTIONS 7 HEALTH INSURANCE	DEDUCTIONS 8 RETIREMENT PLAN	DEDUCTIONS 9 TOTAL	10 NET PAY	CHECK NO.	
1	2	Johnson, Edward P.	M	2	1,320.00	112.50	1,432.50									1
2	4	Nelson, Janice E.	S	1	920.00	51.75	971.75									2
3																3
4																4
5																5

3.

EARNINGS RECORD FOR QUARTER ENDED ____

EMPLOYEE NO. ____ ____ (LAST NAME) (FIRST) (MIDDLE INITIAL) MARITAL STATUS ____ WITHHOLDING ALLOWANCES ____

RATE OF PAY ____ PER HOUR SOCIAL SECURITY NO. ____ POSITION ____

PAY PERIOD NO.	PAY PERIOD ENDED	EARNINGS 1 REGULAR	EARNINGS 2 OVERTIME	EARNINGS 3 TOTAL	DEDUCTIONS 4 FEDERAL INCOME TAX	DEDUCTIONS 5 SOCIAL SECURITY TAX	DEDUCTIONS 6 MEDICARE TAX	DEDUCTIONS 7 HEALTH INSURANCE	DEDUCTIONS 8 RETIREMENT PLAN	DEDUCTIONS 9 TOTAL	10 NET PAY	11 ACCUMULATED EARNINGS
1												
7												
TOTALS												

Name ______________ Date ________ Class ________

12-3 ON YOUR OWN, p. 363

Preparing payroll records

(Note: The payroll register used in this problem is also used in On Your Own 12-4.)

1., 2.

PAYROLL REGISTER

SEMIMONTHLY PERIOD ENDED ______ DATE OF PAYMENT ______

	EMPL. NO.	EMPLOYEE'S NAME	MARITAL STATUS	NO. OF ALLOWANCES	EARNINGS 1 REGULAR	2 OVERTIME	3 TOTAL	DEDUCTIONS 4 FEDERAL INCOME TAX	5 SOCIAL SECURITY TAX	6 MEDICARE TAX	7 HEALTH INSURANCE	8 RETIREMENT PLAN	9 TOTAL	10 NET PAY	CHECK NO.	
1	3	Patterson, James T.	S	2	1,601.60	54.60	1,656.20									1
2	6	Reeves, Glenda R.	M	3	1,584.00	94.50	1,678.50									2
3																3
4																4
5																5

3.

EARNINGS RECORD FOR QUARTER ENDED ______

EMPLOYEE NO. ______ LAST NAME ______ FIRST ______ MIDDLE INITIAL ______ MARITAL STATUS ______ WITHHOLDING ALLOWANCES ______

RATE OF PAY ______ PER HOUR SOCIAL SECURITY NO. ______ POSITION ______

PAY PERIOD NO.	ENDED	EARNINGS 1 REGULAR	2 OVERTIME	3 TOTAL	DEDUCTIONS 4 FEDERAL INCOME TAX	5 SOCIAL SECURITY TAX	6 MEDICARE TAX	7 HEALTH INSURANCE	8 RETIREMENT PLAN	9 TOTAL	10 NET PAY	11 ACCUMULATED EARNINGS
1												
7												
TOTALS												

12-4 WORK TOGETHER, p. 368

Preparing payroll checks

(Note: The payroll register used in this problem was also used in Work Together 12-3.)

1.

JUDY'S FASHIONS DATE **No. 895**

PAYEE			
ACCOUNT	TITLE	DESCRIPTION	AMOUNT

JUDY'S FASHIONS
1534 South College Street
Auburn, AL 36830

FIRST COMMUNITY BANK
320 N. Dean Road
Auburn, AL 36830

No. 895

GENERAL ACCOUNT

DATE ______________ AMOUNT $ __________

____ Dollars

FOR CLASSROOM USE ONLY

PAY TO THE ORDER OF

⑆918948616⑆ 518481158⑈ 0895

Name ______________________ Date ____________ Class ____________

12-4 WORK TOGETHER (continued)

2.

EMPLOYEE Edward P. Johnson					DATE June 30, 20--	
TYPE	HOURS	RATE	GROSS PAY	DEDUCTIONS	CURRENT	YTD
				Federal Income Tax	43.00	522.00
Regular	84.00	15.00	1,260.00	Social Security Tax	80.91	1,067.52
Overtime	2.00	22.50	45.00	Medicare Tax	18.92	249.66
				Health Insurance	60.00	720.00
				Retirement	15.00	180.00
Current Total Earnings			1,305.00	Totals	217.83	2,739.18
YTD Total Earnings			17,218.00	Net Pay	1,087.17	14,478.82

EMPLOYEE					DATE	
TYPE	HOURS	RATE	GROSS PAY	DEDUCTIONS	CURRENT	YTD
				Federal Income Tax	______	______
Regular	88.00	15.00	______	Social Security Tax	______	______
Overtime	5.00	22.50	______	Medicare Tax	______	______
				Health Insurance	______	______
				Retirement	______	______
Current Total Earnings			______	Totals	______	______
YTD Total Earnings			______	Net Pay	______	______

PAYROLL ACCOUNT ______________ 66-311/513

JUDY'S FASHIONS

No. 261

PAY TO THE ORDER OF ______________________________ $ ________

____ Dollars

FOR CLASSROOM USE ONLY

FIRST COMMUNITY BANK
AUBURN, AL 36830

____

⑆918948618⑆ 148164118⑈ 261

EMPLOYEE Janice E. Nelson					DATE June 30, 20--	
TYPE	HOURS	RATE	GROSS PAY	DEDUCTIONS	CURRENT	YTD
				Federal Income Tax	79.00	892.00
Regular	82.00	11.50	943.00	Social Security Tax	61.67	736.10
Overtime	3.00	17.25	51.75	Medicare Tax	14.42	172.15
				Health Insurance	60.00	720.00
				Retirement	15.00	180.00
Current Total Earnings			994.75	Totals	230.09	2,700.25
YTD Total Earnings			11,872.50	Net Pay	764.66	9,172.25

EMPLOYEE					DATE	
TYPE	HOURS	RATE	GROSS PAY	DEDUCTIONS	CURRENT	YTD
				Federal Income Tax		
Regular	80.00	11.50		Social Security Tax		
Overtime	3.00	17.25		Medicare Tax		
				Health Insurance		
				Retirement		
Current Total Earnings				Totals		
YTD Total Earnings				Net Pay		

PAYROLL ACCOUNT ______________ 66-311/513

JUDY'S FASHIONS

No. 262

PAY TO THE ORDER OF ______________________________ $ ________

______________________________ Dollars

FOR CLASSROOM USE ONLY

FIRST COMMUNITY BANK
AUBURN, AL 36830

⑆091894861⑆ 148164118⑈ 262

Name ______________________ Date ____________ Class ____________

12-4 ON YOUR OWN, p. 368

Preparing payroll checks

(Note: The payroll register used in this problem was also used in On Your Own 12-3.)

1.

RUSSELL COMPANY DATE No. 921

PAYEE			
ACCOUNT	TITLE	DESCRIPTION	AMOUNT

RUSSELL COMPANY
1534 Military Road
Columbus, MS 39701

FIRST AMERICAN BANK
656 S. 7th Street
Columbus, MS 39701

No. 921

GENERAL ACCOUNT

DATE ____________ AMOUNT $ ____________

______________________________ Dollars

FOR CLASSROOM USE ONLY

PAY TO THE ORDER OF

⑆648188841⑆ 7184848⑈ 0921

2.

EMPLOYEE James T. Patterson **DATE** June 30, 20--

TYPE	HOURS	RATE	GROSS PAY	DEDUCTIONS	CURRENT	YTD
				Federal Income Tax	137.00	1,583.00
Regular	80.00	18.20	1,456.00	Social Security Tax	95.35	1,187.30
Overtime	3.00	27.30	81.90	Medicare Tax	22.30	277.68
				Health Insurance	75.00	900.00
				Retirement	30.00	360.00
Current Total Earnings			1,537.90	Totals	359.65	4,307.98
YTD Total Earnings			19,150.00	Net Pay	1,178.25	14,842.02

EMPLOYEE **DATE**

TYPE	HOURS	RATE	GROSS PAY	DEDUCTIONS	CURRENT	YTD
				Federal Income Tax	______	______
Regular	88.00	18.20	______	Social Security Tax	______	______
Overtime	2.00	27.30	______	Medicare Tax	______	______
				Health Insurance	______	______
				Retirement	______	______
Current Total Earnings			______	Totals	______	______
YTD Total Earnings			______	Net Pay	______	______

PAYROLL ACCOUNT ______________________ 66-311/513

RUSSELL COMPANY **No. 148**

PAY TO THE ORDER OF ____ $ ________

____ Dollars

FOR CLASSROOM USE ONLY

FIRST AMERICAN BANK
Columbus, MS 39701 ______________________

⑆0648108840⑆ 7484767⑈ 148

Name ______________________ Date ____________ Class ____________

12-4 ON YOUR OWN (concluded)

EMPLOYEE Glenda R. Reeves					DATE June 30, 20--	
TYPE	HOURS	RATE	GROSS PAY	DEDUCTIONS	CURRENT	YTD
				Federal Income Tax	44.00	408.00
Regular	80.00	18.00	1,440.00	Social Security Tax	90.95	836.32
Overtime	1.00	27.00	27.00	Medicare Tax	21.27	195.59
				Health Insurance	75.00	675.00
				Retirement	30.00	270.00
Current Total Earnings			1,467.00	Totals	261.22	2,384.91
YTD Total Earnings			13,489.00	Net Pay	1,205.78	11,104.09

EMPLOYEE					DATE	
TYPE	HOURS	RATE	GROSS PAY	DEDUCTIONS	CURRENT	YTD
				Federal Income Tax		
Regular	88.00	18.00		Social Security Tax		
Overtime	3.50	27.00		Medicare Tax		
				Health Insurance		
				Retirement		
Current Total Earnings				Totals		
YTD Total Earnings				Net Pay		

PAYROLL ACCOUNT ____________________ 66-311/513

RUSSELL COMPANY

No. 149

PAY TO THE ORDER OF ________________________________ $ ________

________________________________ Dollars

FOR CLASSROOM USE ONLY

FIRST AMERICAN BANK
Columbus, MS 39701

____

⑆6481884⑆ 7484767⑈ 149

12-1 APPLICATION PROBLEM (LO1, 2), p. 371

Calculating total earnings

1.

EMPLOYEE NO. 7

NAME Marcus T. Groves

PAY PERIOD ENDED December 15, 20--

	MORNING		AFTERNOON		EVENING		HOURS	
Day	IN	OUT	IN	OUT	IN	OUT	REG	OT
Mon 01	5^{58}	11^{53}	12^{59}	3^{54}				
Tue 02	8^{56}	12^{01}	12^{53}	5^{56}	6^{53}	9^{53}		
Wed 03			1^{00}	6^{02}	7^{55}	9^{55}		
Thu 04			12^{54}	5^{56}	6^{53}	10^{06}		
Fri 05			12^{54}	5^{58}				
Sat 06	9^{04}	11^{56}	12^{56}	5^{56}	6^{28}	9^{26}		
Mon 08	6^{04}	12^{02}	12^{59}	3^{54}				
Tue 09	9^{02}	11^{55}	1^{56}	6^{03}				
Wed 10			12^{58}	6^{59}	7^{57}	9^{57}		
Thu 11			12^{57}	5^{56}	6^{54}	10^{04}		
Fri 12			12^{54}	5^{55}				
Sat 13			12^{59}	5^{59}	6^{34}	9^{56}		
Mon 15	9^{01}	11^{55}	1^{03}	6^{00}				
				PERIOD TOTALS				

APPROVED BY ______________

2.

Employee Number	Hours Worked		Regular Rate	Earnings		Total Earnings
	Regular	Overtime		Regular	Overtime	
2	80	12	$15.00			
4	80	2	16.50			
6	60	2.5	18.00			
7			14.50			

Name ____________________ Date __________ Class __________

12-2 APPLICATION PROBLEM (LO3, 4), p. 371

Determining payroll tax withholding

1., 2.

Employee		Marital Status	Number of Withholding Allowances	Total Earnings	Federal Income Tax Withholding	Social Security Tax Withholding	Medicare Withholding
No.	Name						
1	Kelly, Sandra P.	S	3	$1,485.00			
9	Miller, Kelly T.	M	2	1,621.00			
5	Cleveland, Patti A.	S	1	1,595.00			
2	Maxwell, Jon T.	M	4	1,348.00			
3	King, David R.	M	2	1,492.00			
8	Greene, Mary S.	S	0	215.00			
4	Hazelwood, Ellie J.	S	1	1,642.00			
7	Sharpe, Molli E.	M	3	1,489.00			

12-3 APPLICATION PROBLEM (LO6, 7), p. 372

Preparing payroll records

1.

PAYROLL REGISTER

SEMIMONTHLY PERIOD ENDED ________ DATE OF PAYMENT ________

	EMPL. NO.	EMPLOYEE'S NAME	MARITAL STATUS	NO. OF ALLOWANCES	EARNINGS 1 REGULAR	EARNINGS 2 OVERTIME	EARNINGS 3 TOTAL	DEDUCTIONS 4 FEDERAL INCOME TAX	DEDUCTIONS 5 SOCIAL SECURITY TAX	DEDUCTIONS 6 MEDICARE TAX	DEDUCTIONS 7 HEALTH INSURANCE	DEDUCTIONS 8 RETIREMENT PLAN	DEDUCTIONS 9 TOTAL	10 NET PAY	CHECK NO.	
1	9	Gamble, Ed P.	S	1	1,342.00		1,342.00				45.00	10.00			395	1
2	7	Holtz, Thomas E.	M	2	1,058.00	48.50	1,106.50				60.00	25.00			396	2
3	6	Jones, Virginia W.	S	4	1,074.00	84.00	1,158.00				90.00	20.00			397	3
4	8	Lowe, Mary C.	M	2	1,486.00	108.00	1,594.00				60.00	50.00			398	4
5	1	Muldoon, Janice T.	M	2	1,648.00	55.50	1,703.50				60.00	50.00			399	5
6	11	Myers, Samuel L.	S	0	235.00		235.00				45.00	60.00			400	6
7	12	Spiller, Nathan R.	S	3	1,628.00		1,628.00				75.00	40.00			401	7
8	2	Terrell, Mary A.	M	2	1,600.00	30.00	1,630.00				60.00	30.00			402	8
9																9
10																10
11																11
12																12
13																13
14																14
15																15
16																16
17																17
18																18
19																19
20																20
21																21

Name ______________________ Date ____________ Class ____________

12-3 APPLICATION PROBLEM (concluded)

2., 3.

EARNINGS RECORD FOR QUARTER ENDED September 30, 20--

EMPLOYEE NO. 2 — LAST NAME: Terrell — FIRST: Mary — MIDDLE INITIAL: A. — MARITAL STATUS: M — WITHHOLDING ALLOWANCES: 2

RATE OF PAY $20.00 PER HOUR — SOCIAL SECURITY NO. 947-15-4487 — POSITION: Purchasing Manager

PAY PERIOD		EARNINGS			DEDUCTIONS						NET PAY	ACCUMULATED EARNINGS
		1	2	3	4	5	6	7	8	9	10	11
NO.	ENDED	REGULAR	OVERTIME	TOTAL	FEDERAL INCOME TAX	SOCIAL SECURITY TAX	MEDICARE TAX	HEALTH INSURANCE	RETIREMENT PLAN	TOTAL		20640.00
1	7/15	1760.00	60.00	1820.00	121.00	112.84	26.39	60.00	30.00	350.23	1469.77	22460.00
2	7/31	1600.00	90.00	1690.00	100.00	104.78	24.51	60.00	30.00	319.29	1370.71	24150.00
3	8/15	1540.00	75.00	1615.00	88.00	100.13	23.42	60.00	30.00	301.55	1313.45	25765.00
4	8/31	1760.00	108.00	1868.00	127.00	115.82	27.09	60.00	30.00	359.91	1508.09	27633.00
5	9/15	1600.00	55.50	1655.50	94.00	102.64	24.00	60.00	30.00	310.64	1344.86	29288.50
6												
7												
TOTALS												

12-4 APPLICATION PROBLEM (LO9), p. 372

Preparing payroll checks

1.

CASTLE ELECTRONICS DATE No. 1056

PAYEE			
ACCOUNT	TITLE	DESCRIPTION	AMOUNT

CASTLE ELECTRONICS
940 Dean Street
St. Charles, Illinois 60174

THE PEOPLES BANK
180 N. Jefferson Street
Batavia, Illinois 60510

No. 1056

GENERAL ACCOUNT

DATE ____________ AMOUNT $ ________

________________________________ Dollars

FOR CLASSROOM USE ONLY

PAY TO THE ORDER OF

⑆154861 2⑆ 5186644 81⑈ 1056

Name ______ Date ______ Class ______

12-4 APPLICATION PROBLEM (continued)

2.

EMPLOYEE Mitchell R. Haynes					DATE April 30, 20--	
TYPE	HOURS	RATE	GROSS PAY	DEDUCTIONS	CURRENT	YTD
				Federal Income Tax	56.00	409.00
Regular	72.00	16.00	1,152.00	Social Security Tax	77.38	610.20
Overtime	4.00	24.00	96.00	Medicare Tax	18.10	142.71
				Health Insurance	50.00	400.00
				Retirement	25.00	200.00
Current Total Earnings			1,248.00	Totals	226.48	1,761.91
YTD Total Earnings			9,842.00	Net Pay	1,021.52	8,080.09

EMPLOYEE					DATE	
TYPE	HOURS	RATE	GROSS PAY	DEDUCTIONS	CURRENT	YTD
				Federal Income Tax	______	______
Regular	80.00	16.00	______	Social Security Tax	______	______
Overtime	2.50	24.00	______	Medicare Tax	______	______
				Health Insurance	______	______
				Retirement	______	______
Current Total Earnings			______	Totals	______	______
YTD Total Earnings			______	Net Pay	______	______

PAYROLL ACCOUNT ______ 77-126/169

CASTLE ELECTRONICS **No. 658**

PAY TO THE ORDER OF ______ $ ______

______ Dollars

FOR CLASSROOM USE ONLY

THE PEOPLES BANK
Batavia, Illinois 60510 ______

⑆0154861 2⑆ 5184811 48⑈ 658

APPLICATION PROBLEM (concluded)

EMPLOYEE Sharon V. Bricken — **DATE** April 30, 20--

TYPE	HOURS	RATE	GROSS PAY	DEDUCTIONS	CURRENT	YTD
				Federal Income Tax	101.00	792.00
Regular	80.00	14.50	1,160.00	Social Security Tax	80.01	629.80
Overtime	6.00	21.75	130.50	Medicare Tax	18.71	147.29
				Health Insurance	65.00	520.00
				Retirement	40.00	320.00
Current Total Earnings			1,290.50	Totals	304.72	2,409.09
YTD Total Earnings			10,158.00	Net Pay	985.78	7,748.91

EMPLOYEE — **DATE**

TYPE	HOURS	RATE	GROSS PAY	DEDUCTIONS	CURRENT	YTD
				Federal Income Tax		
Regular	80.00	14.50		Social Security Tax		
Overtime	1.70	21.75		Medicare Tax		
				Health Insurance		
				Retirement		
Current Total Earnings				Totals		
YTD Total Earnings				Net Pay		

PAYROLL ACCOUNT ______________ 77-126/169

CASTLE ELECTRONICS

No. 659

PAY TO THE ORDER OF ______________________ $ ________

______________________ Dollars

FOR CLASSROOM USE ONLY

THE PEOPLES BANK
Batavia, Illinois 60510

⑆0154861 2⑆ 518481148⑈ 659

Name ______________________ Date __________ Class __________

12-M MASTERY PROBLEM (LO3, 4, 6, 9), p. 373

Preparing a semimonthly payroll

1., 3.

PAYROLL REGISTER

SEMIMONTHLY PERIOD ENDED August 15, 20-- DATE OF PAYMENT August 15, 20--

	EMPL. NO.	EMPLOYEE'S NAME	MARITAL STATUS	NO. OF ALLOWANCES	EARNINGS 1 REGULAR	EARNINGS 2 OVERTIME	EARNINGS 3 TOTAL	DEDUCTIONS 4 FEDERAL INCOME TAX	DEDUCTIONS 5 SOCIAL SECURITY TAX	DEDUCTIONS 6 MEDICARE TAX	DEDUCTIONS 7 HEALTH INSURANCE	DEDUCTIONS 8 RETIREMENT PLAN	DEDUCTIONS 9 TOTAL	10 NET PAY	CHECK NO.	
1	2	Davis, Henry W.	M	2	1,188.00	131.63	1,319.63				50.00	20.00				1
2	11	Garcia, Juan S.	M	1	1,276.00	97.88	1,373.88				20.00	25.00				2
3	7	Lewis, Jack P.	S	3	940.00	105.75	1,045.75				80.00	20.00				3
4	9	Lopez, Gloria P.	S	2	1,460.00	—	1,460.00				50.00	20.00				4
5	3	Nelson, Evelyn Y.	M	4	1,188.00	178.20	1,366.20				100.00	25.00				5
6	4	Robinson, Joshua T.	S	2	1,500.00	105.00	1,605.00				50.00	60.00				6
7	13	Rodriguez, Jean A.	M	3	1,240.00	171.00	1,411.00				80.00	20.00				7
8	6	Walker, Mildred M.	S	1	1,104.00	—	1,104.00				20.00	35.00				8
9																9
10																10
11																11
12																12
13																13
14																14
15																15
16																16
17																17
18																18
19																19
20																20
21																21

2.

MALONE COMPANY DATE NO. 1895

PAYEE			
ACCOUNT	TITLE	DESCRIPTION	AMOUNT

MALONE COMPANY
1290 N. Fry Road
Katy, Texas 77450

FIRST AMERICAN BANK
2680 S. Mason Road
Katy, Texas 77450

No. 1895

GENERAL ACCOUNT

DATE ____________ AMOUNT $ ________

____ Dollars

FOR CLASSROOM USE ONLY

PAY TO THE ORDER OF

⑆311848991⑆ 6510554888⑈ 1895

Name ______________________ Date ____________ Class ____________

12-M MASTERY PROBLEM (continued)

3.

EMPLOYEE Henry W. Davis					DATE July 31, 20--	
TYPE	HOURS	RATE	GROSS PAY	DEDUCTIONS	CURRENT	YTD
				Federal Income Tax	35.00	525.00
Regular	88.00	13.50	1,188.00	Social Security Tax	76.17	1,130.91
Overtime	2.00	20.25	40.50	Medicare Tax	17.81	264.49
				Health Insurance	50.00	700.00
				Retirement	20.00	280.00
Current Total Earnings			1,228.50	Totals	198.98	2,900.40
YTD Total Earnings			18,240.48	Net Pay	1,029.52	15,340.08

EMPLOYEE					DATE	
TYPE	HOURS	RATE	GROSS PAY	DEDUCTIONS	CURRENT	YTD
				Federal Income Tax	________	________
Regular	88.00	13.50	________	Social Security Tax	________	________
Overtime	6.50	20.25	________	Medicare Tax	________	________
				Health Insurance	________	________
				Retirement	________	________
Current Total Earnings			________	Totals	________	________
YTD Total Earnings			________	Net Pay	________	________

PAYROLL ACCOUNT ____________________ 66-311/513

MALONE COMPANY **No. 452**

PAY TO THE ORDER OF ______________________________________ $ ________

____ Dollars

FOR CLASSROOM USE ONLY

FIRST AMERICAN BANK
Katy, Texas 77450
____

⑆318489⑆ 3455972⑈ 452

12-M MASTERY PROBLEM (concluded)

EMPLOYEE Juan S. Garcia					DATE July 31, 20--	
TYPE	HOURS	RATE	GROSS PAY	DEDUCTIONS	CURRENT	YTD
				Federal Income Tax	80.00	1,085.00
Regular	88.00	14.50	1,276.00	Social Security Tax	87.88	1,150.25
Overtime	6.50	21.75	141.38	Medicare Tax	20.55	269.01
				Health Insurance	20.00	280.00
				Retirement	25.00	350.00
Current Total Earnings			1,417.38	Totals	233.43	3,134.26
YTD Total Earnings			18,552.40	Net Pay	1,183.95	15,418.14

EMPLOYEE					DATE	
TYPE	HOURS	RATE	GROSS PAY	DEDUCTIONS	CURRENT	YTD
				Federal Income Tax		
Regular	88.00	14.50		Social Security Tax		
Overtime	4.50	21.75		Medicare Tax		
				Health Insurance		
				Retirement		
Current Total Earnings				Totals		
YTD Total Earnings				Net Pay		

PAYROLL ACCOUNT ______________ 66-311/513

MALONE COMPANY

No. 453

PAY TO THE ORDER OF ______________________ $ ________

______________________ Dollars

FOR CLASSROOM USE ONLY

FIRST AMERICAN BANK
Katy, Texas 77450

⑆318489⑆ 34559721⑈ 453

Name ______________________ Date __________ Class __________

12-S SOURCE DOCUMENTS PROBLEM (LO2, 3, 4, 6, 7, 9), p. 373

Preparing a semimonthly payroll

Hour Summary

Payroll Period: 12/1/20-- to 12/15/20--

Employee No.: 3 — Hourly Rate: $15.50

Employee Name: Michael P. Hogan

Date	Day	Regular	Overtime	Total
12/1/20--	Mon	8.0		8.0
12/2/20--	Tue	8.0	1.0	9.0
12/3/20--	Wed	8.0	1.0	9.0
12/4/20--	Thu	8.0		8.0
12/5/20--	Fri	8.0		8.0
12/8/20--	Mon	8.0		8.0
12/9/20--	Tue	8.0		8.0
12/10/20--	Wed	8.0		8.0
12/11/20--	Thu	8.0		8.0
12/12/20--	Fri	8.0		8.0
12/13/20--	Sat		4.0	4.0
12/15/20--	Mon	8.0		8.0
Totals		88.0	6.0	94.0

Employee No.: 4 — Hourly Rate: $14.00

Employee Name: Rickey J. McGuire

Date	Day	Regular	Overtime	Total
12/2/20--	Tue	8.0		8.0
12/3/20--	Wed	8.0		8.0
12/4/20--	Thu	8.0	3.0	11.0
12/5/20--	Fri	8.0		8.0
12/8/20--	Mon	8.0		8.0
12/9/20--	Tue	8.0		8.0
12/10/20--	Wed	8.0		8.0
12/11/20--	Thu	8.0		8.0
12/12/20--	Fri	8.0		8.0
12/15/20--	Mon	8.0		8.0
Totals		80.0	3.0	83.0

Employee No.: 5			Hourly Rate:	$15.00
Employee Name: Candace M. Powers				
Date	**Day**	**Regular**	**Overtime**	**Total**
12/2/20--	Tue	4.0		4.0
12/3/20--	Wed	8.0		8.0
12/4/20--	Thu	8.0		8.0
12/5/20--	Fri	4.0		4.0
12/8/20--	Mon	8.0		8.0
12/9/20--	Tue	8.0		8.0
12/10/20--	Wed	8.0		8.0
12/11/20--	Thu	8.0		8.0
12/12/20--	Fri	8.0		8.0
12/13/20--	Sat		6.0	6.0
12/15/20--	Mon	8.0		8.0
Totals		72.0	6.0	78.0

Employee No.: 7			Hourly Rate:	$17.20
Employee Name: Damon B. Whorton				
Date	**Day**	**Regular**	**Overtime**	**Total**
12/2/20--	Tue	4.0		4.0
12/3/20--	Wed	8.0	3.0	11.0
12/4/20--	Thu	8.0	4.0	12.0
12/8/20--	Mon	8.0		8.0
12/9/20--	Tue	8.0		8.0
12/10/20--	Wed	8.0		8.0
12/11/20--	Thu	8.0		8.0
12/12/20--	Fri	8.0		8.0
12/15/20--	Mon	8.0		8.0
Totals		68.0	7.0	75.0

12-S SOURCE DOCUMENTS PROBLEM (continued)

Preparing a semimonthly payroll

1.

PAYROLL REGISTER

SEMIMONTHLY PERIOD ENDED December 15, 20-- DATE OF PAYMENT December 15, 20--

	EMPL. NO.	EMPLOYEE'S NAME	MARITAL STATUS	NO. OF ALLOWANCES	EARNINGS 1 REGULAR	2 OVERTIME	3 TOTAL	DEDUCTIONS 4 FEDERAL INCOME TAX	5 SOCIAL SECURITY TAX	6 MEDICARE TAX	7 HEALTH INSURANCE	8 RETIREMENT PLAN	9 TOTAL	10 NET PAY	CHECK NO.	
1	3	Hogan, Michael P.	S	2							40.00	30.00				1
2	4	McGuire, Rickey J.	M	1							30.00	15.00				2
3	5	Powers, Candace M.	M	3							60.00	40.00				3
4	7	Whorton, Damon B.	M	2							40.00	30.00				4
5		Totals														5
6																6

2.

EARNINGS RECORD FOR QUARTER ENDED December 31, 20--

EMPLOYEE NO. 3 Hogan (LAST NAME) Michael (FIRST) P. (MIDDLE INITIAL) MARITAL STATUS S WITHHOLDING ALLOWANCES 2

RATE OF PAY $15.50 PER HOUR SOCIAL SECURITY NO. 904-51-4891 POSITION Manager

PAY PERIOD NO.	ENDED	EARNINGS 1 REGULAR	2 OVERTIME	3 TOTAL	DEDUCTIONS 4 FEDERAL INCOME TAX	5 SOCIAL SECURITY TAX	6 MEDICARE TAX	7 HEALTH INSURANCE	8 RETIREMENT PLAN	9 TOTAL	10 NET PAY	11 ACCUMULATED EARNINGS
												24,505.50
1	10/15	1,302.00	139.50	1,441.50	125.00	89.37	20.90	40.00	30.00	305.27	1,136.23	25,947.00
2	10/31	1,364.00	—	1,364.00	113.00	84.57	19.78	40.00	30.00	287.35	1,076.65	27,311.00
3	11/15	1,116.00	93.00	1,209.00	89.00	74.96	17.53	40.00	30.00	251.49	957.51	28,520.00
4	11/30	1,116.00	186.00	1,302.00	104.00	80.72	18.88	40.00	30.00	273.60	1,028.40	29,822.00
5												
6												
TOTALS												

12-S SOURCE DOCUMENTS PROBLEM (continued)

EARNINGS RECORD FOR QUARTER ENDED December 31, 20--

EMPLOYEE NO. 4 — LAST NAME McGuire — FIRST Rickey — MIDDLE INITIAL J. — MARITAL STATUS M — WITHHOLDING ALLOWANCES 1

RATE OF PAY $14.00 PER HOUR — SOCIAL SECURITY NO. 987-15-0058 — POSITION Carpenter

PAY PERIOD NO.	ENDED	1 EARNINGS REGULAR	2 EARNINGS OVERTIME	3 EARNINGS TOTAL	4 DEDUCTIONS FEDERAL INCOME TAX	5 SOCIAL SECURITY TAX	6 MEDICARE TAX	7 HEALTH INSURANCE	8 RETIREMENT PLAN	9 TOTAL	10 NET PAY	11 ACCUMULATED EARNINGS
												19,530.00
1	10/15	1,176.00	126.00	1,302.00	65.00	80.72	18.88	30.00	15.00	209.60	1,092.40	20,832.00
2	10/31	1,232.00	42.00	1,274.00	59.00	78.99	18.47	30.00	15.00	201.46	1,072.54	22,106.00
3	11/15	1,092.00	—	1,092.00	37.00	67.70	15.83	30.00	15.00	165.53	926.47	23,198.00
4	11/30	1,008.00	105.00	1,113.00	39.00	69.01	16.14	30.00	15.00	169.15	943.85	24,311.00
5												
6												
TOTALS												

EARNINGS RECORD FOR QUARTER ENDED December 31, 20--

EMPLOYEE NO. 5 — LAST NAME Powers — FIRST Candace — MIDDLE INITIAL M. — MARITAL STATUS M — WITHHOLDING ALLOWANCES 3

RATE OF PAY $15.00 PER HOUR — SOCIAL SECURITY NO. 905-15-1849 — POSITION Office Manager

PAY PERIOD NO.	ENDED	1 EARNINGS REGULAR	2 EARNINGS OVERTIME	3 EARNINGS TOTAL	4 DEDUCTIONS FEDERAL INCOME TAX	5 SOCIAL SECURITY TAX	6 MEDICARE TAX	7 HEALTH INSURANCE	8 RETIREMENT PLAN	9 TOTAL	10 NET PAY	11 ACCUMULATED EARNINGS
												20,160.00
1	10/15	1,260.00	—	1,260.00	24.00	78.12	18.27	60.00	40.00	220.39	1,039.61	21,420.00
2	10/31	1,320.00	—	1,320.00	30.00	81.84	19.14	60.00	40.00	230.98	1,089.02	22,740.00
3	11/15	1,080.00	135.00	1,215.00	18.00	75.33	17.62	60.00	40.00	210.95	1,004.05	23,955.00
4	11/30	1,080.00	180.00	1,260.00	24.00	78.12	18.27	60.00	40.00	220.39	1,039.61	25,215.00
5												
6												
TOTALS												

Name ______________________ Date ______________ Class ______________

12-S SOURCE DOCUMENTS PROBLEM (continued)

EARNINGS RECORD FOR QUARTER ENDED December 31, 20--

EMPLOYEE NO. 7 — LAST NAME: Whorton — FIRST: Damon — MIDDLE INITIAL: B. — MARITAL STATUS: M — WITHHOLDING ALLOWANCES: 2

RATE OF PAY $17.20 PER HOUR — SOCIAL SECURITY NO. 945-06-8473 — POSITION: Carpenter

PAY PERIOD		EARNINGS			DEDUCTIONS						NET PAY	ACCUMULATED EARNINGS
		1	2	3	4	5	6	7	8	9	10	11
NO.	ENDED	REGULAR	OVERTIME	TOTAL	FEDERAL INCOME TAX	SOCIAL SECURITY TAX	MEDICARE TAX	HEALTH INSURANCE	RETIREMENT PLAN	TOTAL		24,355.20
1	10/15	1,444.80	77.40	1,522.20	76.00	94.38	22.07	40.00	30.00	262.45	1,259.75	25,877.40
2	10/31	1,513.60	103.20	1,616.80	88.00	100.24	23.44	40.00	30.00	281.68	1,335.12	27,494.20
3	11/15	1,238.40	51.60	1,290.00	41.00	79.98	18.71	40.00	30.00	209.69	1,080.31	28,784.20
4	11/30	1,238.40	154.80	1,393.20	55.00	86.38	20.20	40.00	30.00	231.58	1,161.62	30,177.40
5												
6												
7												
TOTALS												

12-S SOURCE DOCUMENTS PROBLEM (continued)

3.

JENKINS CABINETS DATE **No. 689**

PAYEE			
ACCOUNT	TITLE	DESCRIPTION	AMOUNT

JENKINS CABINETS
6001 Atlantic Avenue
Florence, CA 90201

First National Savings Bank
890 W. Manchester Blvd.
Inglewood, CA 90045

No. 689

GENERAL ACCOUNT

DATE ____________ AMOUNT $ ________

____ Dollars

FOR CLASSROOM USE ONLY

PAY TO THE ORDER OF

⑆848919841⑆ 84848005⑈ 0689

Name ______________________________ Date ______________ Class ______________

12-S SOURCE DOCUMENTS PROBLEM (continued)

4.

EMPLOYEE Michael P. Hogan					DATE December 1, 20--	
TYPE	HOURS	RATE	GROSS PAY	DEDUCTIONS	CURRENT	YTD
				Federal Income Tax	104.00	2,984.00
Regular	72.00	15.50	1,116.00	Social Security Tax	80.72	1,848.96
Overtime	8.00	23.25	186.00	Medicare Tax	18.88	432.42
				Health Insurance	40.00	880.00
				Retirement	30.00	660.00
Current Total Earnings			1,302.00	Totals	273.60	6,805.38
YTD Total Earnings			29,822.00	Net Pay	1,028.40	23,016.62

EMPLOYEE					DATE	
TYPE	HOURS	RATE	GROSS PAY	DEDUCTIONS	CURRENT	YTD
				Federal Income Tax	______	______
Regular	88.00	15.50	______	Social Security Tax	______	______
Overtime	6.00	23.25	______	Medicare Tax	______	______
				Health Insurance	______	______
				Retirement	______	______
Current Total Earnings			______	Totals	______	______
YTD Total Earnings			______	Net Pay	______	______

PAYROLL ACCOUNT ______________________ 66-311/513

JENKINS CABINETS

No. 234

PAY TO THE ORDER OF ______________________________________ $ __________

____ Dollars

FOR CLASSROOM USE ONLY

First National Savings Bank
Inglewood, CA 90045

____

⑆848919841⑆ 481154488⑈ 234

EMPLOYEE Rickey J. McGuire				DATE December 1, 20--		
TYPE	HOURS	RATE	GROSS PAY	DEDUCTIONS	CURRENT	YTD
				Federal Income Tax	39.00	1,018.00
Regular	72.00	14.00	1,008.00	Social Security Tax	69.01	1,507.28
Overtime	5.00	21.00	105.00	Medicare Tax	16.14	352.51
				Health Insurance	30.00	660.00
				Retirement	15.00	330.00
Current Total Earnings			1,113.00	Totals	169.15	3,867.79
YTD Total Earnings			24,311.00	Net Pay	943.85	20,443.21

EMPLOYEE				DATE		
TYPE	HOURS	RATE	GROSS PAY	DEDUCTIONS	CURRENT	YTD
				Federal Income Tax		
Regular	80.00	14.00		Social Security Tax		
Overtime	3.00	21.00		Medicare Tax		
				Health Insurance		
				Retirement		
Current Total Earnings				Totals		
YTD Total Earnings				Net Pay		

PAYROLL ACCOUNT ______________ 66-311/513

JENKINS CABINETS **No. 235**

PAY TO THE ORDER OF ______________________________ $ ________

______________________________ Dollars

FOR CLASSROOM USE ONLY

First National Savings Bank
Inglewood, CA 90045

____

⑆648188884⑆ 481154488⑈ 235

Name ______________________ Date ____________ Class ____________

12-S SOURCE DOCUMENTS PROBLEM (continued)

EMPLOYEE Candace M. Powers					DATE December 1, 20--	
TYPE	HOURS	RATE	GROSS PAY	DEDUCTIONS	CURRENT	YTD
				Federal Income Tax	24.00	365.00
Regular	72.00	15.00	1,080.00	Social Security Tax	78.12	1,563.33
Overtime	8.00	22.50	180.00	Medicare Tax	18.27	365.62
				Health Insurance	60.00	1,200.00
				Retirement	40.00	800.00
Current Total Earnings			1,260.00	Totals	220.39	4,293.95
YTD Total Earnings			25,215.00	Net Pay	1,039.61	20,921.05

EMPLOYEE					DATE	
TYPE	HOURS	RATE	GROSS PAY	DEDUCTIONS	CURRENT	YTD
				Federal Income Tax	______	______
Regular	72.00	15.00	______	Social Security Tax	______	______
Overtime	6.00	22.50	______	Medicare Tax	______	______
				Health Insurance	______	______
				Retirement	______	______
Current Total Earnings			______	Totals	______	______
YTD Total Earnings			______	Net Pay	______	______

PAYROLL ACCOUNT ______________________ 66-311/513

JENKINS CABINETS **No. 236**

PAY TO THE ORDER OF ______________________________________ $ ________

____ Dollars

FOR CLASSROOM USE ONLY

First National Savings Bank
Inglewood, CA 90045

____

⑆648188846⑆ 481154488⑈ 236

SOURCE DOCUMENTS PROBLEM (concluded)

EMPLOYEE Damon B. Whorton					DATE December 1, 20--	
TYPE	HOURS	RATE	GROSS PAY	DEDUCTIONS	CURRENT	YTD
				Federal Income Tax	55.00	1,402.00
Regular	72.00	17.20	1,238.40	Social Security Tax	86.38	1,870.97
Overtime	6.00	25.80	154.80	Medicare Tax	20.20	437.57
				Health Insurance	40.00	800.00
				Retirement	30.00	600.00
Current Total Earnings			1,393.20	Totals	231.58	5,110.54
YTD Total Earnings			30,177.00	Net Pay	1,161.62	25,066.46

EMPLOYEE					DATE	
TYPE	HOURS	RATE	GROSS PAY	DEDUCTIONS	CURRENT	YTD
				Federal Income Tax	______	______
Regular	68.00	17.20	______	Social Security Tax	______	______
Overtime	7.00	25.80	______	Medicare Tax	______	______
				Health Insurance	______	______
				Retirement	______	______
Current Total Earnings			______	Totals	______	______
YTD Total Earnings			______	Net Pay	______	______

PAYROLL ACCOUNT ________________ 66-311/513

JENKINS CABINETS **No. 237**

PAY TO THE ORDER OF ______________________________ $ ________

____ Dollars

FOR CLASSROOM USE ONLY

First National Savings Bank
Inglewood, CA 90045 ________________

⑆648188841⑆ 481154488⑈ 237

Name ____________________ Date ____________ Class ____________

12-C CHALLENGE PROBLEM (LO3, 4, 6), p. 374

Preparing a semimonthly payroll with pretax medical and retirement plans

1.

PAYROLL REGISTER

SEMIMONTHLY PERIOD ENDED August 15, 20-- DATE OF PAYMENT August 15, 20--

					EARNINGS			DEDUCTIONS									
	EMPL. NO.	EMPLOYEE'S NAME	MARITAL STATUS	NO. OF ALLOWANCES	1 REGULAR	2 OVERTIME	3 TOTAL	4 FEDERAL INCOME TAX	5 SOCIAL SECURITY TAX	6 MEDICARE TAX	7 HEALTH INSURANCE	8 RETIREMENT PLAN	9 TOTAL	10 NET PAY	CHECK NO.	
1	2	Davis, Henry W.	M	2	1,188.00	131.63	1,319.63				50.00	20.00				1
2	11	Garcia, Juan S.	M	1	1,276.00	97.88	1,373.88				20.00	25.00				2
3	7	Lewis, Jack P.	S	3	940.00	105.75	1,045.75				80.00	20.00				3
4	9	Lopez, Gloria P.	S	2	1,460.00	—	1,460.00				50.00	20.00				4
5	3	Nelson, Evelyn Y.	M	4	1,188.00	178.20	1,366.20				100.00	25.00				5
6	4	Robinson, Joshua T.	S	2	1,500.00	105.00	1,605.00				50.00	60.00				6
7	13	Rodriguez, Jean A.	M	3	1,240.00	171.00	1,411.00				80.00	20.00				7
8	6	Walker, Mildred M.	S	1	1,104.00	—	1,104.00				20.00	35.00				8
9																9
10																10
11																11

2.

	Net Pay with Voluntary Deductions		
Employee	Taxable	Nontaxable	Difference
Davis, Henry W.			
Garcia, Juan S.			
Lewis, Jack P.			
Lopez, Gloria P.			
Nelson, Evelyn Y.			
Robinson, Joshua T.			
Rodriguez, Jean A.			
Walker, Mildred M.			

Study Guide 13

Name	Perfect Score	Your Score
Analyzing Payroll Records	15 Pts.	
Analyzing Transactions Affecting Payroll	5 Pts.	
Analyzing Form W-2	10 Pts.	
Total	30 Pts.	

Part One—Analyzing Payroll Records

Directions: For each of the following items, select the choice that best completes the statement. Print the letter identifying your choice in the Answers column.

Answers

1. All the payroll information needed to prepare payroll and tax reports is found on (A) Form W-4 and the employee earnings record (B) Form W-4 and the payroll register (C) the payroll register and the employee earnings record (D) Form W-4. (p. 378) — 1. ______
2. The payroll journal entry is based on the totals of the payroll register (A) Total Earnings column, each deduction column, and the Net Pay column (B) Total Earnings, Earnings Regular, Earnings Overtime, and Deductions Total columns (C) Earnings Regular, Earnings Overtime, and Deductions Total columns (D) Total Earnings, Earnings Regular, and Earnings Overtime Total columns. (p. 379) — 2. ______
3. The Total Earnings column total of a payroll register is journalized as a debit to (A) Cash (B) Salary Expense (C) Employee Income Tax Payable (D) Social Security Tax Payable. (p. 380) — 3. ______
4. The total of the Federal Income Tax column of a payroll register is credited to (A) a revenue account (B) an expense account (C) a liability account (D) an asset account. (p. 380) — 4. ______
5. The total of the Net Pay column of the payroll register is credited to (A) a revenue account (B) an expense account (C) an asset account (D) a liability account. (p. 380) — 5. ______
6. When a semimonthly payroll is paid, the credit to Cash is equal to the (A) total earnings of all employees (B) total deductions for income tax and social security tax (C) total deductions (D) net pay of all employees. (p. 380) — 6. ______
7. Employer payroll taxes are (A) assets (B) expenses (C) revenues (D) none of these. (p. 382) — 7. ______
8. Payroll taxes that are paid by both the employer and the employee are (A) federal unemployment tax and social security tax (B) federal unemployment tax and Medicare tax (C) social security tax and Medicare tax (D) federal income tax, social security tax, and Medicare tax. (p. 382) — 8. ______
9. A tax paid to administer the unemployment program is the (A) social security tax (B) Medicare tax (C) federal unemployment tax (D) state unemployment tax. (p. 382) — 9. ______
10. A state tax used to pay benefits to unemployed workers is the (A) social security tax (B) Medicare tax (C) unemployment tax (D) state unemployment tax. (p. 382) — 10. ______
11. An employee's earnings subject to unemployment taxes are referred to as (A) gross earnings (B) net earnings (C) FUTA earnings (D) accumulated earnings. (p. 383) — 11. ______
12. Each employer who withholds income tax, social security tax, and Medicare tax from employee earnings must furnish each employee an (A) IRS Form W-4 (B) IRS Form W-2 (C) IRS Form W-3 (D) IRS Form 941. (p. 387) — 12. ______
13. Each employer is required by law to report payroll taxes on an (A) IRS Form W-4 (B) IRS Form 941 (C) IRS Form W-2 (D) IRS Form W-3. (p. 389) — 13. ______
14. The form used to report annual earnings and payroll taxes for all employees to the Social Security Administration is the (A) W-2 (B) Form 941 (C) W-3 (D) W-4. (p. 390) — 14. ______
15. To record the payment of federal unemployment tax, the account debited is (A) a revenue account (B) an expense account (C) a liability account (D) an asset account. (p. 396) — 15. ______

Part Two—Analyzing Transactions Affecting Payroll

Directions: Analyze each of the following transactions into debit and credit parts. Print the letters identifying your choices in the proper Answers column.

Account Titles	Transactions	Answers Debit	Answers Credit
A. Cash	1. Paid cash for semimonthly payroll. (p. 380)	______	______
B. Employee Income Tax Payable	2. Recorded employer payroll taxes expense. (p. 384)	______	______
C. Health Insurance Premiums Payable	3. Paid cash for liability for employee income tax, social security tax, and Medicare tax. (p. 394)	______	______
D. Medicare Tax Payable	4. Paid cash for federal unemployment tax liability. (p. 396)	______	______
E. Payroll Taxes Expense	5. Paid cash for state unemployment tax liability. (p. 396)	______	______
F. Retirement Contributions Payable			
G. Salary Expense			
H. Social Security Tax Payable			
I. Unemployment Tax Payable—Federal			
J. Unemployment Tax Payable—State			

Name ________________________________ Date ____________ Class ____________

Part Three—Analyzing Form W-2

Directions: Analyze the following statements about a Form W-2, Wage and Tax Statement. Use the Form W-2 below to answer the specific questions about John Butler. Place a T for True or an F for False in the Answers column to show whether each of the following statements is true or false. (p. 387)

22222	a Employee's social security number 194-81-5823	OMB No. 1545-0008	
b Employer identification number (EIN) 31-0429632		1 Wages, tips, other compensation 30,273.75	2 Federal income tax withheld 620.00
c Employer's name, address, and ZIP code ThreeGreen Products, Inc. 1501 Commerce Street Carlisle, PA 17013		3 Social security wages 30,273.75	4 Social security tax withheld 1,876.97
		5 Medicare wages and tips 30,273.75	6 Medicare tax withheld 438.97
		7 Social security tips	8 Allocated tips
d Control number		9	10 Dependent care benefits
e Employee's first name and initial John P.	Last name Butler Suff.	11 Nonqualified plans	12a
1014 Bosler Ave. Carlisle, PA 17013		13 Statutory employee / Retirement plan / Third-party sick pay	12b
		14 Other	12c
f Employee's address and ZIP code			12d

15 State Employer's state ID number	16 State wages, tips, etc.	17 State income tax	18 Local wages, tips, etc.	19 Local income tax	20 Locality name

Form **W-2** **Wage and Tax Statement** 20- -

Department of the Treasury—Internal Revenue Service

Copy 1—For State, City, or Local Tax Department

Answers

1. John Butler's total salary is more than his total social security salary. 1. ________
2. This Form W-2 shows John Butler's net pay for the entire year. 2. ________
3. The amount withheld for Mr. Butler's social security tax was more than the amount withheld for his federal income tax. 3. ________
4. State income tax was withheld from Mr. Butler's salary. 4. ________
5. All deductions from Mr. Butler's salary for taxes and retirement plan contributions are shown on his Form W-2. 5. ________
6. This Form W-2 would indicate whether Mr. Butler had more than one employer during the year. 6. ________
7. If an employee works for several employers during the year, that employee must receive a Form W-2 from each employer. 7. ________
8. An employer is required to provide employees with a Form W-2 no later than January 31 of the year following the one for which the report has been completed. 8. ________
9. When John Butler files his federal income tax return, he must attach Copy A of Form W-2 to his return. 9. ________
10. Businesses in states with state income tax must prepare additional copies of Form W-2. 10. ________

Across

5. The total of gross earnings for all employees earning hourly wages, salaries, and commissions.
6. The 12-month period that ends on June 30th of the prior year that is used to determine how frequently a business must deposit payroll taxes.

Down

1. A state tax paid by employers that is used to pay benefits to unemployed workers.
2. The payment of payroll taxes to the government.
3. The chief accountant in an organization, having responsibility for both financial and managerial accounting activities. Sometimes called comptroller.
4. A process that requires an employer to withhold a portion of an employee's paycheck to pay a court-ordered debt settlement.16. Earnings paid to an employee after payroll taxes and other deductions.

Name ______________________ Date ____________ Class ____________

13-1 WORK TOGETHER, p. 381

Recording a payroll

1.

Salary Expense

Employee Income Tax Payable

Social Security Tax Payable

Medicare Tax Payable

Cash

2.

CASH PAYMENTS JOURNAL

PAGE

					1	2	3	4	5	
	DATE	ACCOUNT TITLE	CK. NO.	POST. REF.	GENERAL DEBIT	GENERAL CREDIT	ACCOUNTS PAYABLE DEBIT	PURCHASES DISCOUNT CREDIT	CASH CREDIT	
1										1
2										2
3										3
4										4
5										5
6										6

13-1 ON YOUR OWN, p. 381

Recording a payroll

1.

Salary Expense

Employee Income Tax Payable

Social Security Tax Payable

Medicare Tax Payable

Cash

2.

CASH PAYMENTS JOURNAL

PAGE

	DATE	ACCOUNT TITLE	CK. NO.	POST. REF.	1 GENERAL DEBIT	2 GENERAL CREDIT	3 ACCOUNTS PAYABLE DEBIT	4 PURCHASES DISCOUNT CREDIT	5 CASH CREDIT	
1										1
2										2
3										3
4										4
5										5
6										6

Name ______________________ Date ______________ Class ______________

13-2 WORK TOGETHER, p. 386

Recording employer payroll taxes

1., 2.

1	2	3	4	5
Employee Name	**Prior Accumulated Earnings**	**Earnings to Equal FUTA Tax Base**	**Earnings for Current Pay Period**	**FUTA Earnings**
Ellis, Nick C.	$6,100.00	$ 900.00	$ 762.50	
Jennings, Evan P.	7,980.00	0.00	1,040.00	
Powers, Virginia A.	4,380.00	2,620.00	527.00	
Wolfe, Kerry T.	6,850.00	150.00	849.50	
	Totals			

Social Security Tax Payable, 6.2%	
Medicare Tax Payable, 1.45%	
Unemployment Tax Payable—Federal, 0.8%	
Unemployment Tax Payable—State, 5.4%	
Total Payroll Taxes	

3.

GENERAL JOURNAL PAGE

	DATE		ACCOUNT TITLE	DOC. NO.	POST. REF.	DEBIT	CREDIT	
7								7
8								8
9								9
10								10
11								11
12								12
13								13
14								14
15								15
16								16
17								17
18								18
19								19
20								20

13-2 ON YOUR OWN, p. 386

Recording employer payroll taxes

1., 2.

1	2	3	4	5
Employee Name	**Prior Accumulated Earnings**	**Earnings to Equal FUTA Tax Base**	**Earnings for Current Pay Period**	**FUTA Earnings**
Holt, Stephanie L.	$6,380.00	$ 620.00	$ 653.00	
Klein, Jacob S.	3,840.00	3,160.00	521.00	
Singh, Irene M.	7,290.00	0.00	736.50	
Tate, Joyce B.	6,270.00	730.00	614.00	
	Totals			

Social Security Tax Payable, 6.2%	
Medicare Tax Payable, 1.45%	
Unemployment Tax Payable—Federal, 0.8%	
Unemployment Tax Payable—State, 5.4%	
Total Payroll Taxes	

3.

GENERAL JOURNAL PAGE

	DATE	ACCOUNT TITLE	DOC. NO.	POST. REF.	DEBIT	CREDIT	
7							7
8							8
9							9
10							10
11							11
12							12
13							13
14							14
15							15
16							16
17							17
18							18
19							19
20							20

Name ______________________ Date ____________ Class ____________

13-3 WORK TOGETHER, p. 391

Reporting withholding and payroll taxes

1.

Form **941 for 20--: Employer's QUARTERLY Federal Tax Return** 951110
(Rev. October 20--) Department of the Treasury — Internal Revenue Service OMB No. 1545-0029

(EIN) Employer identification number ☐☐ – ☐☐☐☐☐☐☐

Name *(not your trade name)* ____________

Trade name *(if any)* ____________

Address ____________
Number Street Suite or room number
____________ ____ ____
City State ZIP code

Report for this Quarter of 20--
(Check one.)

☐ **1:** January, February, March
☐ **2:** April, May, June
☐ **3:** July, August, September
☐ **4:** October, November, December

Read the separate instructions before you complete Form 941. Type or print within the boxes.

Part 1: Answer these questions for this quarter.

1	Number of employees who received wages, tips, or other compensation for the pay period including: *Mar. 12* (Quarter 1), *June 12* (Quarter 2), *Sept. 12* (Quarter 3), or *Dec. 12* (Quarter 4)		1	
2	Wages, tips, and other compensation		2	.
3	Income tax withheld from wages, tips, and other compensation		3	.
4	If no wages, tips, and other compensation are subject to social security or Medicare tax			☐ Check and go to line 6e.

		Column 1		Column 2	
5a	Taxable social security wages*	.	× .124 =	.	*Report wages/tips for this quarter, including those paid to qualified new employees, on lines 5a–5c. The social security tax exemption on wages/tips will be figured on lines 6c and 6d and will reduce the tax on line 6e.*
5b	Taxable social security tips*	.	× .124 =	.	
5c	Taxable Medicare wages & tips*	.	× .029 =	.	

5d	Add *Column 2* line 5a, *Column 2* line 5b, and *Column 2* line 5c		5d	.
6a	Number of qualified employees *first* paid exempt wages/tips this quarter			See instructions for definitions of qualified employee and exempt wages/tips.
6b	Number of qualified employees paid exempt wages/tips this quarter			
6c	Exempt wages/tips paid to qualified employees this quarter	. × .062 =	6d	.
6e	Total taxes before adjustments (line 3 + line 5d – line 6d = line 6e)		6e	.
7a	Current quarter's adjustment for fractions of cents		7a	.
7b	Current quarter's adjustment for sick pay		7b	.
7c	Current quarter's adjustments for tips and group-term life insurance		7c	.
8	Total taxes after adjustments. Combine lines 6e through 7c		8	.
9	Advance earned income credit (EIC) payments made to employees		9	.
10	Total taxes after adjustment for advance EIC (line 8 – line 9 = line 10)		10	.
11	Total deposits, including prior quarter overpayments		11	.
12a	COBRA premium assistance payments (see instructions)		12a	.
12b	Number of individuals provided COBRA premium assistance			Complete lines 12c, 12d, and 12e only for the 2nd quarter of 20--.
12c	Number of qualified employees paid exempt wages/tips March 19–31			
12d	Exempt wages/tips paid to qualified employees March 19–31	. × .062 =	12e	.
13	Add lines 11, 12a, and 12e		13	.
14	Balance due. If line 10 is more than line 13, enter the difference and see instructions		14	.
15	Overpayment. If line 13 is more than line 10, enter the difference	.	Check one:	☐ Apply to next return. ☐ Send a refund.

▶ **You MUST complete both pages of Form 941 and SIGN it.** Next ▶

For Privacy Act and Paperwork Reduction Act Notice, see the back of the Payment Voucher. Cat. No. 17001Z Form **941** (Rev. 10-20--)

950210

Name *(not your trade name)* | **Employer identification number (EIN)**

Part 2: Tell us about your deposit schedule and tax liability for this quarter.

If you are unsure about whether you are a monthly schedule depositor or a semiweekly schedule depositor, see *Pub. 15 (Circular E),* section 11.

16 ☐☐ **Write the state abbreviation for the state where you made your deposits** OR **write "MU" if you made your deposits in *multiple* states.**

17 Check one: ☐ **Line 10 on this return is less than $2,500 or line 10 on the return for the preceding quarter was less than $2,500, and you did not incur a $100,000 next-day deposit obligation during the current quarter.** Go to Part 3.

☐ **You were a monthly schedule depositor for the entire quarter.** Enter your tax liability for each month and total liability for the quarter.

Tax liability:	**Month 1**	.
	Month 2	.
	Month 3	.
Total liability for quarter		.

Total must equal line 10.

☐ **You were a semiweekly schedule depositor for any part of this quarter.** Complete *Schedule B (Form 941): Report of Tax Liability for Semiweekly Schedule Depositors,* and attach it to Form 941.

Name ______________________ Date ____________ Class ____________

13-3 ON YOUR OWN, p. 391

Reporting withholding and payroll taxes

1.

Form **941 for 20--: Employer's QUARTERLY Federal Tax Return** 951110
(Rev. October 20--) Department of the Treasury — Internal Revenue Service OMB No. 1545-0029

(EIN)
Employer identification number ☐☐ – ☐☐☐☐☐☐☐

Name *(not your trade name)* ____________

Trade name *(if any)* ____________

Address ____________
Number Street Suite or room number
____
City State ZIP code

Report for this Quarter of 20--
(Check one.)

☐ **1:** January, February, March
☐ **2:** April, May, June
☐ **3:** July, August, September
☐ **4:** October, November, December

Read the separate instructions before you complete Form 941. Type or print within the boxes.

Part 1: Answer these questions for this quarter.

1	**Number of employees who received wages, tips, or other compensation for the pay period including:** ***Mar. 12*** **(Quarter 1),** ***June 12*** **(Quarter 2),** ***Sept. 12*** **(Quarter 3), or** ***Dec. 12*** **(Quarter 4)**			1	
2	**Wages, tips, and other compensation**			2	.
3	**Income tax withheld from wages, tips, and other compensation**			3	.
4	**If no wages, tips, and other compensation are subject to social security or Medicare tax**				☐ **Check and go to line 6e.**
		Column 1	*Column 2*		**Report wages/tips for this quarter, including those paid to qualified new employees, on lines 5a–5c. The social security tax exemption on wages/tips will be figured on lines 6c and 6d and will reduce the tax on line 6e.*
5a	**Taxable social security wages***	.	× .124 = .		
5b	**Taxable social security tips***	.	× .124 = .		
5c	**Taxable Medicare wages & tips***	.	× .029 = .		
5d	**Add** ***Column 2*** **line 5a,** ***Column 2*** **line 5b, and** ***Column 2*** **line 5c**			5d	.
6a	**Number of qualified employees** ***first*** **paid exempt wages/tips this quarter**				See instructions for definitions of qualified employee and exempt wages/tips.
6b	**Number of qualified employees paid exempt wages/tips this quarter**				
6c	**Exempt wages/tips paid to qualified employees this quarter**	.	× .062 =	6d	.
6e	**Total taxes before adjustments** (line 3 + line 5d – line 6d = line 6e)			6e	.
7a	**Current quarter's adjustment for fractions of cents**			7a	.
7b	**Current quarter's adjustment for sick pay**			7b	.
7c	**Current quarter's adjustments for tips and group-term life insurance**			7c	.
8	**Total taxes after adjustments.** Combine lines 6e through 7c			8	.
9	**Advance earned income credit (EIC) payments made to employees**			9	.
10	**Total taxes after adjustment for advance EIC** (line 8 – line 9 = line 10)			10	.
11	**Total deposits, including prior quarter overpayments**			11	.
12a	**COBRA premium assistance payments** (see instructions)			12a	.
12b	**Number of individuals provided COBRA premium assistance**				Complete lines 12c, 12d, and 12e only for the 2nd quarter of 20--.
12c	**Number of qualified employees paid exempt wages/tips March 19–31**				
12d	**Exempt wages/tips paid to qualified employees March 19–31**	.	× .062 =	12e	.
13	**Add lines 11, 12a, and 12e**			13	.
14	**Balance due.** If line 10 is more than line 13, enter the difference and see instructions			14	.
15	**Overpayment.** If line 13 is more than line 10, enter the difference	.			Check one: ☐ Apply to next return. ☐ Send a refund.

▶ **You MUST complete both pages of Form 941 and SIGN it.** Next ▶

For Privacy Act and Paperwork Reduction Act Notice, see the back of the Payment Voucher. Cat. No. 17001Z Form **941** (Rev. 10-20--)

13-3 ON YOUR OWN (concluded)

950210

Name *(not your trade name)* | Employer identification number (EIN)

Part 2: Tell us about your deposit schedule and tax liability for this quarter.

If you are unsure about whether you are a monthly schedule depositor or a semiweekly schedule depositor, see *Pub. 15 (Circular E),* section 11.

16 ☐☐ **Write the state abbreviation for the state where you made your deposits** OR **write "MU" if you made your deposits in *multiple* states.**

17 Check one: ☐ **Line 10 on this return is less than $2,500 or line 10 on the return for the preceding quarter was less than $2,500, and you did not incur a $100,000 next-day deposit obligation during the current quarter.** Go to Part 3.

☐ **You were a monthly schedule depositor for the entire quarter.** Enter your tax liability for each month and total liability for the quarter.

Tax liability:	**Month 1**	.
	Month 2	.
	Month 3	.
Total liability for quarter		. **Total must equal line 10.**

☐ **You were a semiweekly schedule depositor for any part of this quarter.** Complete *Schedule B (Form 941): Report of Tax Liability for Semiweekly Schedule Depositors,* and attach it to Form 941.

Name ______________________ Date ____________ Class ____________

13-4 WORK TOGETHER, p. 397

Paying withholding and payroll taxes

1., 2.

CASH PAYMENTS JOURNAL PAGE

					1	2	3	4	5	
	DATE	ACCOUNT TITLE	CK. NO.	POST. REF.	GENERAL DEBIT	GENERAL CREDIT	ACCOUNTS PAYABLE DEBIT	PURCHASES DISCOUNT CREDIT	CASH CREDIT	
1										1
2										2
3										3
4										4
5										5
6										6
7										7
8										8
9										9
10										10
11										11
12										12
13										13
14										14
15										15
16										16
17										17
18										18
19										19
20										20
21										21
22										22
23										23
24										24
25										25

13-4 ON YOUR OWN, p. 397

Paying withholding and payroll taxes

1., 2.

CASH PAYMENTS JOURNAL

PAGE

	DATE	ACCOUNT TITLE	CK. NO.	POST. REF.	1 GENERAL DEBIT	2 GENERAL CREDIT	3 ACCOUNTS PAYABLE DEBIT	4 PURCHASES DISCOUNT CREDIT	5 CASH CREDIT	
1										1
2										2
3										3
4										4
5										5
6										6
7										7
8										8
9										9
10										10
11										11
12										12
13										13
14										14
15										15
16										16
17										17
18										18
19										19
20										20
21										21
22										22
23										23
24										24
25										25

Name ______________________ Date ____________ Class ____________

13-1 APPLICATION PROBLEM (LO2), p. 401

CASH PAYMENTS JOURNAL

PAGE

				1	2	3	4	5	
	DATE	ACCOUNT TITLE	CK. NO.	POST. REF.	GENERAL DEBIT	GENERAL CREDIT	ACCOUNTS PAYABLE DEBIT	PURCHASES DISCOUNT CREDIT	CASH CREDIT	
1										1
2										2
3										3
4										4
5										5
6										6
7										7
8										8
9										9
10										10
11										11
12										12
13										13
14										14
15										15
16										16
17										17
18										18
19										19
20										20
21										21
22										22
23										23
24										24
25										25

13-2 APPLICATION PROBLEM (LO3), p. 401

Recording employer payroll taxes

1., 2., 4.

1	2	3	4	5	6	7	8	9
Employee Name	**Prior Accumulated Earnings**	**Earnings to Equal FUTA Tax Base**	**Earnings for Current Pay Period**	**FUTA Earnings**	**Prior Accumulated Earnings**	**Earnings to Equal FUTA Tax Base**	**Earnings for Current Pay Period**	**FUTA Earnings**
Campos, Regina P.	$4,980.00		$ 830.00				$ 850.00	
Duran, Erica A.	5,490.00		915.00				895.00	
Glover, Brandon T.	7,080.00		1,180.00				1,180.00	
Norton, Authur S.	5,340.00		890.00				795.00	
Rivas, Pearl S.	6,900.00		1,150.00				1,060.00	
	Totals				Totals			
	Social Security Tax Payable, 6.2%							
	Medicare Tax Payable, 1.45%							
	Unemployment Tax Payable—Federal, 0.8%							
	Unemployment Tax Payable—State, 5.4%							
	Total Payroll Taxes							

3., 5.

GENERAL JOURNAL

PAGE

	DATE		ACCOUNT TITLE	DOC. NO.	POST. REF.	DEBIT	CREDIT	
1								1
2								2
3								3
4								4
5								5
6								6
7								7
8								8
9								9
10								10

Name ______________________ Date ____________ Class ____________

13-3 APPLICATION PROBLEM (LO4), p. 402

Reporting withholding and payroll taxes

1.

Form **941 for 20--: Employer's QUARTERLY Federal Tax Return**
(Rev. October 20--)
Department of the Treasury — Internal Revenue Service

951110
OMB No. 1545-0029

(EIN)
Employer identification number ☐☐ – ☐☐☐☐☐☐☐

Name *(not your trade name)* ______________________

Trade name *(if any)* ______________________

Address ______________________
Number Street Suite or room number
____
City State ZIP code

Report for this Quarter of 20--
(Check one.)

☐ **1:** January, February, March
☐ **2:** April, May, June
☐ **3:** July, August, September
☐ **4:** October, November, December

Read the separate instructions before you complete Form 941. Type or print within the boxes.

Part 1: Answer these questions for this quarter.

1	**Number of employees who received wages, tips, or other compensation for the pay period including:** ***Mar. 12*** **(Quarter 1),** ***June 12*** **(Quarter 2),** ***Sept. 12*** **(Quarter 3), or** ***Dec. 12*** **(Quarter 4)**			1	
2	**Wages, tips, and other compensation**			2	.
3	**Income tax withheld from wages, tips, and other compensation**			3	.
4	**If no wages, tips, and other compensation are subject to social security or Medicare tax**				☐ **Check and go to line 6e.**
		Column 1	*Column 2*		**Report wages/tips for this quarter, including those paid to qualified new employees, on lines 5a–5c. The social security tax exemption on wages/tips will be figured on lines 6c and 6d and will reduce the tax on line 6e.*
5a	**Taxable social security wages***	.	× .124 = .		
5b	**Taxable social security tips***	.	× .124 = .		
5c	**Taxable Medicare wages & tips***	.	× .029 = .		
5d	**Add** ***Column 2*** **line 5a,** ***Column 2*** **line 5b, and** ***Column 2*** **line 5c**			5d	.
6a	**Number of qualified employees** ***first*** **paid exempt wages/tips this quarter**				See instructions for definitions of qualified employee and exempt wages/tips.
6b	**Number of qualified employees paid exempt wages/tips this quarter**				
6c	**Exempt wages/tips paid to qualified employees this quarter**	.	× .062 =	6d	.
6e	**Total taxes before adjustments** (line 3 + line 5d – line 6d = line 6e)			6e	.
7a	**Current quarter's adjustment for fractions of cents**			7a	.
7b	**Current quarter's adjustment for sick pay**			7b	.
7c	**Current quarter's adjustments for tips and group-term life insurance**			7c	.
8	**Total taxes after adjustments.** Combine lines 6e through 7c			8	.
9	**Advance earned income credit (EIC) payments made to employees**			9	.
10	**Total taxes after adjustment for advance EIC** (line 8 – line 9 = line 10)			10	.
11	**Total deposits, including prior quarter overpayments**			11	.
12a	**COBRA premium assistance payments** (see instructions)			12a	.
12b	**Number of individuals provided COBRA premium assistance**				Complete lines 12c, 12d, and 12e only for the 2nd quarter of 20--.
12c	**Number of qualified employees paid exempt wages/tips March 19–31**				
12d	**Exempt wages/tips paid to qualified employees March 19–31**	.	× .062 =	12e	.
13	**Add lines 11, 12a, and 12e**			13	.
14	**Balance due.** If line 13 is more than line 10, enter the difference and see instructions			14	.
15	**Overpayment.** If line 13 is more than line 10, enter the difference	.			Check one: ☐ Apply to next return. ☐ Send a refund.

▶ **You MUST complete both pages of Form 941 and SIGN it.** Next ▶

For Privacy Act and Paperwork Reduction Act Notice, see the back of the Payment Voucher. Cat. No. 17001Z Form **941** (Rev. 10-20--)

950210

Name *(not your trade name)* | Employer identification number (EIN)

Part 2: Tell us about your deposit schedule and tax liability for this quarter.

If you are unsure about whether you are a monthly schedule depositor or a semiweekly schedule depositor, see *Pub. 15 (Circular E)*, section 11.

16 ☐☐ **Write the state abbreviation for the state where you made your deposits** OR **write "MU" if you made your deposits in *multiple* states.**

17 Check one: ☐ **Line 10 on this return is less than $2,500 or line 10 on the return for the preceding quarter was less than $2,500, and you did not incur a $100,000 next-day deposit obligation during the current quarter.** Go to Part 3.

☐ **You were a monthly schedule depositor for the entire quarter.** Enter your tax liability for each month and total liability for the quarter.

Tax liability:	**Month 1**	.
	Month 2	.
	Month 3	.
Total liability for quarter		. **Total must equal line 10.**

☐ **You were a semiweekly schedule depositor for any part of this quarter.** Complete *Schedule B (Form 941): Report of Tax Liability for Semiweekly Schedule Depositors,* and attach it to Form 941.

Name ____________________ Date ____________ Class ____________

13-4 APPLICATION PROBLEM (LO5), p. 402

Paying withholding and payroll taxes

1., 2., 3.

CASH PAYMENTS JOURNAL

PAGE

	DATE	ACCOUNT TITLE	CK. NO.	POST. REF.	1 GENERAL DEBIT	2 GENERAL CREDIT	3 ACCOUNTS PAYABLE DEBIT	4 PURCHASES DISCOUNT CREDIT	5 CASH CREDIT	
1										1
2										2
3										3
4										4
5										5
6										6
7										7
8										8

13-M MASTERY PROBLEM (LO2, 3, 5), p. 403

Journalizing payroll transactions

1., 2.

CASH PAYMENTS JOURNAL

PAGE

	DATE	ACCOUNT TITLE	CK. NO.	POST. REF.	1 GENERAL DEBIT	2 GENERAL CREDIT	3 ACCOUNTS PAYABLE DEBIT	4 PURCHASES DISCOUNT CREDIT	5 CASH CREDIT	
1										1
2										2
3										3
4										4
5										5
6										6
7										7
8										8
9										9
10										10
11										11
12										12
13										13
14										14
15										15
16										16
17										17
18										18
19										19
20										20
21										21
22										22
23										23
24										24
25										25

Name ______________________ Date ______________ Class ______________

13-M MASTERY PROBLEM (concluded)

1.

GENERAL JOURNAL PAGE

	DATE		ACCOUNT TITLE	DOC. NO.	POST. REF.	DEBIT	CREDIT	
1								1
2								2
3								3
4								4
5								5
6								6
7								7
8								8
9								9
10								10
11								11
12								12
13								13
14								14
15								15
16								16
17								17
18								18
19								19
20								20
21								21
22								22
23								23
24								24
25								25

13-C CHALLENGE PROBLEM (LO3), p. 403

Projecting employee expense

1.

Salary			
Insurance			
Tax	**Taxable Amount**	**Tax Rate**	
Total expense for employee			

2.

Salary			
Insurance			
Tax	**Taxable Amount**	**Tax Rate**	
Total expense for employee			

3.

Name ______________________ Date ____________ Class ____________

REINFORCEMENT ACTIVITY 2, Part A, p. 406

An Accounting Cycle for a Corporation: Journalizing and Posting Transactions

1.

GENERAL JOURNAL PAGE 12

	DATE		ACCOUNT TITLE	DOC. NO.	POST. REF.	DEBIT	CREDIT	
1								1
2								2
3								3
4								4
5								5
6								6
7								7
8								8
9								9
10								10
11								11
12								12
13								13
14								14
15								15
16								16
17								17
18								18
19								19
20								20
21								21
22								22
23								23

REINFORCEMENT ACTIVITY 2, Part A (continued)

1., 5.

PURCHASES JOURNAL PAGE 12

	DATE		ACCOUNT CREDITED	PURCH. NO.	POST. REF.	PURCHASES DR. ACCTS. PAY. CR.	
1							1
2							2
3							3
4							4
5							5
6							6
7							7
8							8
9							9
10							10
11							11
12							12
13							13
14							14
15							15
16							16
17							17
18							18
19							19
20							20
21							21
22							22
23							23
24							24
25							25

Name ______________________ Date ____________ Class ____________

REINFORCEMENT ACTIVITY 2, Part A (continued)

1., 2., 7., 9.

CASH PAYMENTS JOURNAL

PAGE 23

					1	2	3	4	5	
	DATE	ACCOUNT TITLE	CK. NO.	POST. REF.	GENERAL DEBIT	GENERAL CREDIT	ACCOUNTS PAYABLE DEBIT	PURCHASES DISCOUNT CREDIT	CASH CREDIT	
1										1
2										2
3										3
4										4
5										5
6										6
7										7
8										8
9										9
10										10
11										11
12										12
13										13
14										14
15										15
16										16
17										17
18										18
19										19
20										20
21										21
22										22
23										23
24										24
25										25

REINFORCEMENT ACTIVITY 2, Part A (continued)

1., 3., 6., 7., 9.

CASH PAYMENTS JOURNAL

PAGE 24

	DATE	ACCOUNT TITLE	CK. NO.	POST. REF.	1 GENERAL DEBIT	2 GENERAL CREDIT	3 ACCOUNTS PAYABLE DEBIT	4 PURCHASES DISCOUNT CREDIT	5 CASH CREDIT	
1										1
2										2
3										3
4										4
5										5
6										6
7										7
8										8
9										9
10										10
11										11
12										12
13										13
14										14
15										15

Column Title	Debit Column Totals	Credit Column Totals
General Debit		
General Credit		
Accounts Payable Debit		
Purchases Discount Credit		
Cash Credit		
Totals		

Column Title	Debit Column Totals	Credit Column Totals
General Debit		
General Credit		
Accounts Payable Debit		
Purchases Discount Credit		
Cash Credit		
Totals		

REINFORCEMENT ACTIVITY 2, Part A (continued)

1., 4.

SALES JOURNAL PAGE 12

	DATE		ACCOUNT DEBITED	SALE NO.	POST. REF.	1 ACCOUNTS RECEIVABLE DEBIT	2 SALES CREDIT	3 SALES TAX PAYABLE CREDIT	
1									1
2									2
3									3
4									4
5									5
6									6
7									7
8									8
9									9
10									10
11									11
12									12
13									13
14									14
15									15
16									16
17									17
18									18
19									19
20									20
21									21
22									22
23									23
24									24
25									25

1., 3., 6., 7., 8.

CASH RECEIPTS JOURNAL

PAGE 12

	DATE	ACCOUNT TITLE	DOC. NO.	POST. REF.	1 GENERAL DEBIT	2 GENERAL CREDIT	3 ACCOUNTS RECEIVABLE CREDIT	4 SALES CREDIT	5 SALES TAX PAYABLE CREDIT	6 SALES DISCOUNT DEBIT	7 CASH DEBIT	
1												1
2												2
3												3
4												4
5												5
6												6
7												7
8												8
9												9
10												10
11												11
12												12
13												13
14												14
15												15
16												16

Column Title	Debit Totals	Credit Totals
General Debit		
General Credit		
Accounts Receivable Credit		
Sales Credit		
Sales Tax Payable Credit		
Sales Discount Debit		
Cash Debit		
Totals		

Cash on hand at the beginning of the month
(Dec. 1 balance of general ledger Cash account) ....
Plus total cash received during the month
(Cash Debit column total, cash receipts journal) .... ______
Equal total..
Less total cash paid during the month
(General ledger postings in Cash account) .... ______
Equals cash balance on hand at the end of the month..... ______
Checkbook balance on the next unused check stub........ ______

Name _______________ Date _______________ Class _______________

REINFORCEMENT ACTIVITY 2, Part A (continued)

1., 3., 10.

ACCOUNTS RECEIVABLE LEDGER

CUSTOMER Batesville Manufacturing — CUSTOMER NO. 110

DATE		ITEM	POST. REF.	DEBIT	CREDIT	DEBIT BALANCE
20-- Dec.	1	Balance	✔			5 819 35

CUSTOMER Chandler City Schools — CUSTOMER NO. 120

DATE		ITEM	POST. REF.	DEBIT	CREDIT	DEBIT BALANCE
20-- Dec.	1	Balance	✔			814 80

CUSTOMER Hubbard Medical Clinic — CUSTOMER NO. 130

DATE		ITEM	POST. REF.	DEBIT	CREDIT	DEBIT BALANCE
20-- Dec.	1	Balance	✔			4 649 80

CUSTOMER Musheer Orthopedics — CUSTOMER NO. 140

DATE		ITEM	POST. REF.	DEBIT	CREDIT	DEBIT BALANCE
20-- Dec.	1	Balance	✔			1 643 00

REINFORCEMENT ACTIVITY 2, Part A (continued)

CUSTOMER Pacific Stores CUSTOMER NO. 150

DATE		ITEM	POST. REF.	DEBIT	CREDIT	DEBIT BALANCE

CUSTOMER Western Theaters CUSTOMER NO. 160

DATE		ITEM	POST. REF.	DEBIT	CREDIT	DEBIT BALANCE
20-- Dec.	1	Balance	✔			1 6 9 4 34

Name ______________________ Date ____________ Class ____________

REINFORCEMENT ACTIVITY 2, Part A (continued)

1., 3., 10.

ACCOUNTS PAYABLE LEDGER

VENDOR Alpha Supply VENDOR NO. 210

DATE		ITEM	POST. REF.	DEBIT	CREDIT	CREDIT BALANCE
20-- Dec.	1	Balance	✔			2 284 00

VENDOR Distinctive Garments VENDOR NO. 220

DATE		ITEM	POST. REF.	DEBIT	CREDIT	CREDIT BALANCE
20-- Dec.	1	Balance	✔			1 595 00

VENDOR Klein Industries VENDOR NO. 230

DATE		ITEM	POST. REF.	DEBIT	CREDIT	CREDIT BALANCE
20-- Dec.	1	Balance	✔			3 290 00

VENDOR Medical Clothiers VENDOR NO. 240

DATE		ITEM	POST. REF.	DEBIT	CREDIT	CREDIT BALANCE
20-- Dec.	1	Balance	✔			548 00

REINFORCEMENT ACTIVITY 2, Part A (continued)

VENDOR Singh Imports VENDOR NO. 250

DATE		ITEM	POST. REF.	DEBIT	CREDIT	CREDIT BALANCE
20-- Dec.	1	Balance	✔			1 5 8 9 00

VENDOR Trevino Company VENDOR NO. 260

DATE		ITEM	POST. REF.	DEBIT	CREDIT	CREDIT BALANCE

Name ______________________ Date ____________ Class ____________

REINFORCEMENT ACTIVITY 2, Part A (continued)

1., 2., 3., 4., 5., 8., 9. **GENERAL LEDGER**

ACCOUNT Cash — ACCOUNT NO. 1110

DATE		ITEM	POST. REF.	DEBIT	CREDIT	BALANCE DEBIT	BALANCE CREDIT
20-- Dec.	1	Balance	✔			31,485.25	

ACCOUNT Petty Cash — ACCOUNT NO. 1120

DATE		ITEM	POST. REF.	DEBIT	CREDIT	BALANCE DEBIT	BALANCE CREDIT
20-- Dec.	1	Balance	✔			250.00	

ACCOUNT Accounts Receivable — ACCOUNT NO. 1130

DATE		ITEM	POST. REF.	DEBIT	CREDIT	BALANCE DEBIT	BALANCE CREDIT
20-- Dec.	1	Balance	✔			14,621.29	

ACCOUNT Allowance for Uncollectible Accounts — ACCOUNT NO. 1135

DATE		ITEM	POST. REF.	DEBIT	CREDIT	BALANCE DEBIT	BALANCE CREDIT
20-- Dec.	1	Balance	✔				2,169.25

ACCOUNT Merchandise Inventory — ACCOUNT NO. 1140

DATE		ITEM	POST. REF.	DEBIT	CREDIT	BALANCE DEBIT	BALANCE CREDIT
20-- Dec.	1	Balance	✔			49,154.84	

REINFORCEMENT ACTIVITY 2, Part A (continued)

ACCOUNT Supplies—Office ACCOUNT NO. 1145

DATE		ITEM	POST. REF.	DEBIT	CREDIT	BALANCE DEBIT	BALANCE CREDIT
20-- Dec.	1	Balance	✔			2,598.48	

ACCOUNT Supplies—Store ACCOUNT NO. 1150

DATE		ITEM	POST. REF.	DEBIT	CREDIT	BALANCE DEBIT	BALANCE CREDIT
20-- Dec.	1	Balance	✔			3,481.20	

ACCOUNT Prepaid Insurance ACCOUNT NO. 1160

DATE		ITEM	POST. REF.	DEBIT	CREDIT	BALANCE DEBIT	BALANCE CREDIT
20-- Dec.	1	Balance	✔			14,400.00	

ACCOUNT Notes Receivable ACCOUNT NO. 1170

DATE		ITEM	POST. REF.	DEBIT	CREDIT	BALANCE DEBIT	BALANCE CREDIT
20-- Dec.	1	Balance	✔			4,000.00	

Name ______________________ Date ______________ Class ______________

REINFORCEMENT ACTIVITY 2, Part A (continued)

ACCOUNT Interest Receivable — ACCOUNT NO. 1175

DATE		ITEM	POST. REF.	DEBIT	CREDIT	BALANCE DEBIT	BALANCE CREDIT

ACCOUNT Office Equipment — ACCOUNT NO. 1205

DATE		ITEM	POST. REF.	DEBIT	CREDIT	BALANCE DEBIT	BALANCE CREDIT
20-- Dec.	1	Balance	✔			23 245 97	

ACCOUNT Accumulated Depreciation—Office Equipment — ACCOUNT NO. 1210

DATE		ITEM	POST. REF.	DEBIT	CREDIT	BALANCE DEBIT	BALANCE CREDIT
20-- Dec.	1	Balance	✔				3 210 00

ACCOUNT Store Equipment — ACCOUNT NO. 1215

DATE		ITEM	POST. REF.	DEBIT	CREDIT	BALANCE DEBIT	BALANCE CREDIT
20-- Dec.	1	Balance	✔			36 489 20	

ACCOUNT Accumulated Depreciation—Store Equipment — ACCOUNT NO. 1220

DATE		ITEM	POST. REF.	DEBIT	CREDIT	BALANCE DEBIT	BALANCE CREDIT
20-- Dec.	1	Balance	✔				6 182 00

ACCOUNT Accounts Payable — ACCOUNT NO. 2110

DATE		ITEM	POST. REF.	DEBIT	CREDIT	BALANCE DEBIT	BALANCE CREDIT
20-- Dec.	1	Balance	✔				9 306 00

REINFORCEMENT ACTIVITY 2, Part A (continued)

ACCOUNT Sales Tax Payable ACCOUNT NO. 2120

DATE		ITEM	POST. REF.	DEBIT	CREDIT	BALANCE DEBIT	BALANCE CREDIT
20-- Dec.	1	Balance	✔				324 00

ACCOUNT Employee Income Tax Payable ACCOUNT NO. 2130

DATE		ITEM	POST. REF.	DEBIT	CREDIT	BALANCE DEBIT	BALANCE CREDIT
20-- Dec.	1	Balance	✔				471 00

ACCOUNT Social Security Tax Payable ACCOUNT NO. 2135

DATE		ITEM	POST. REF.	DEBIT	CREDIT	BALANCE DEBIT	BALANCE CREDIT
20-- Dec.	1	Balance	✔				899 00

Name ______________________ Date ____________ Class ____________

REINFORCEMENT ACTIVITY 2, Part A (continued)

ACCOUNT Medicare Tax Payable ACCOUNT NO. 2140

DATE		ITEM	POST. REF.	DEBIT	CREDIT	BALANCE DEBIT	BALANCE CREDIT
20-- Dec.	1	Balance	✔				210 25

ACCOUNT Health Insurance Premiums Payable ACCOUNT NO. 2145

DATE		ITEM	POST. REF.	DEBIT	CREDIT	BALANCE DEBIT	BALANCE CREDIT
20-- Dec.	1	Balance	✔				480 00

ACCOUNT Retirement Benefits Payable ACCOUNT NO. 2150

DATE		ITEM	POST. REF.	DEBIT	CREDIT	BALANCE DEBIT	BALANCE CREDIT
20-- Dec.	1	Balance	✔				120 00

ACCOUNT Unemployment Tax Payable—Federal ACCOUNT NO. 2160

DATE		ITEM	POST. REF.	DEBIT	CREDIT	BALANCE DEBIT	BALANCE CREDIT
20-- Dec.	1	Balance					10 76

REINFORCEMENT ACTIVITY 2, Part A (continued)

ACCOUNT Unemployment Tax Payable—State — ACCOUNT NO. 2165

DATE		ITEM	POST. REF.	DEBIT	CREDIT	BALANCE DEBIT	BALANCE CREDIT
20-- Dec.	1	Balance	✔				72 63

ACCOUNT Federal Income Tax Payable — ACCOUNT NO. 2170

DATE		ITEM	POST. REF.	DEBIT	CREDIT	BALANCE DEBIT	BALANCE CREDIT

ACCOUNT Dividends Payable — ACCOUNT NO. 2180

DATE		ITEM	POST. REF.	DEBIT	CREDIT	BALANCE DEBIT	BALANCE CREDIT

ACCOUNT Capital Stock — ACCOUNT NO. 3110

DATE		ITEM	POST. REF.	DEBIT	CREDIT	BALANCE DEBIT	BALANCE CREDIT
20-- Dec.	1	Balance	✔				60 000 00

ACCOUNT Retained Earnings — ACCOUNT NO. 3120

DATE		ITEM	POST. REF.	DEBIT	CREDIT	BALANCE DEBIT	BALANCE CREDIT
20-- Dec.	1	Balance	✔				23 352 50

Name ______________________ Date ____________ Class ____________

REINFORCEMENT ACTIVITY 2, Part A (continued)

ACCOUNT Dividends ACCOUNT NO. 3130

DATE		ITEM	POST. REF.	DEBIT	CREDIT	BALANCE DEBIT	BALANCE CREDIT

ACCOUNT Income Summary ACCOUNT NO. 3140

DATE		ITEM	POST. REF.	DEBIT	CREDIT	BALANCE DEBIT	BALANCE CREDIT

ACCOUNT Sales ACCOUNT NO. 4110

DATE		ITEM	POST. REF.	DEBIT	CREDIT	BALANCE DEBIT	BALANCE CREDIT
20-- Dec.	1	Balance	✔				381,585.60

ACCOUNT Sales Discount ACCOUNT NO. 4120

DATE		ITEM	POST. REF.	DEBIT	CREDIT	BALANCE DEBIT	BALANCE CREDIT
20-- Dec.	1	Balance	✔			315.00	

ACCOUNT Sales Returns and Allowances ACCOUNT NO. 4130

DATE		ITEM	POST. REF.	DEBIT	CREDIT	BALANCE DEBIT	BALANCE CREDIT
20-- Dec.	1	Balance	✔			2,164.80	

REINFORCEMENT ACTIVITY 2, Part A (continued)

ACCOUNT Purchases — ACCOUNT NO. 5110

DATE		ITEM	POST. REF.	DEBIT	CREDIT	BALANCE DEBIT	BALANCE CREDIT
20-- Dec.	1	Balance	✔			168 411 89	

ACCOUNT Purchases Discount — ACCOUNT NO. 5120

DATE		ITEM	POST. REF.	DEBIT	CREDIT	BALANCE DEBIT	BALANCE CREDIT
20-- Dec.	1	Balance	✔				2 194 89

ACCOUNT Purchases Returns and Allowances — ACCOUNT NO. 5130

DATE		ITEM	POST. REF.	DEBIT	CREDIT	BALANCE DEBIT	BALANCE CREDIT
20-- Dec.	1	Balance	✔				3 184 49

ACCOUNT Advertising Expense — ACCOUNT NO. 6105

DATE		ITEM	POST. REF.	DEBIT	CREDIT	BALANCE DEBIT	BALANCE CREDIT
20-- Dec.	1	Balance	✔			14 915 90	

ACCOUNT Cash Short and Over — ACCOUNT NO. 6110

DATE		ITEM	POST. REF.	DEBIT	CREDIT	BALANCE DEBIT	BALANCE CREDIT
20-- Dec.	1	Balance	✔			6 15	

Name ______________________ Date ____________ Class ____________

REINFORCEMENT ACTIVITY 2, Part A (continued)

ACCOUNT Credit Card Fee Expense — ACCOUNT NO. 6115

DATE		ITEM	POST. REF.	DEBIT	CREDIT	BALANCE DEBIT	BALANCE CREDIT
20-- Dec.	1	Balance	✔			4 518 10	

ACCOUNT Depreciation Expense—Office Equipment — ACCOUNT NO. 6120

DATE		ITEM	POST. REF.	DEBIT	CREDIT	BALANCE DEBIT	BALANCE CREDIT

ACCOUNT Depreciation Expense—Store Equipment — ACCOUNT NO. 6125

DATE		ITEM	POST. REF.	DEBIT	CREDIT	BALANCE DEBIT	BALANCE CREDIT

ACCOUNT Insurance Expense — ACCOUNT NO. 6130

DATE		ITEM	POST. REF.	DEBIT	CREDIT	BALANCE DEBIT	BALANCE CREDIT

ACCOUNT Miscellaneous Expense — ACCOUNT NO. 6135

DATE		ITEM	POST. REF.	DEBIT	CREDIT	BALANCE DEBIT	BALANCE CREDIT
20-- Dec.	1	Balance	✔			5 168 90	

REINFORCEMENT ACTIVITY 2, Part A (continued)

ACCOUNT Payroll Taxes Expense — ACCOUNT NO. 6140

DATE		ITEM	POST. REF.	DEBIT	CREDIT	BALANCE DEBIT	BALANCE CREDIT
20-- Dec.	1	Balance	✓			6,381.20	

ACCOUNT Rent Expense — ACCOUNT NO. 6145

DATE		ITEM	POST. REF.	DEBIT	CREDIT	BALANCE DEBIT	BALANCE CREDIT
20-- Dec.	1	Balance	✓			17,600.00	

ACCOUNT Salary Expense — ACCOUNT NO. 6150

DATE		ITEM	POST. REF.	DEBIT	CREDIT	BALANCE DEBIT	BALANCE CREDIT
20-- Dec.	1	Balance	✓			77,616.00	

ACCOUNT Supplies Expense—Office — ACCOUNT NO. 6155

DATE		ITEM	POST. REF.	DEBIT	CREDIT	BALANCE DEBIT	BALANCE CREDIT

ACCOUNT Supplies Expense—Store — ACCOUNT NO. 6160

DATE		ITEM	POST. REF.	DEBIT	CREDIT	BALANCE DEBIT	BALANCE CREDIT

Name ______ Date ______ Class ______

REINFORCEMENT ACTIVITY 2, Part A (concluded)

ACCOUNT Uncollectible Accounts Expense ACCOUNT NO. 6165

DATE		ITEM	POST. REF.	DEBIT	CREDIT	BALANCE DEBIT	BALANCE CREDIT

ACCOUNT Utilities Expense ACCOUNT NO. 6170

DATE		ITEM	POST. REF.	DEBIT	CREDIT	BALANCE DEBIT	BALANCE CREDIT
20-- Dec.	1	Balance	✔			6 948 20	

ACCOUNT Federal Income Tax Expense ACCOUNT NO. 6205

DATE		ITEM	POST. REF.	DEBIT	CREDIT	BALANCE DEBIT	BALANCE CREDIT
20-- Dec.	1	Balance	✔			10 000 00	

ACCOUNT Interest Income ACCOUNT NO. 7110

DATE		ITEM	POST. REF.	DEBIT	CREDIT	BALANCE DEBIT	BALANCE CREDIT

Study Guide 14

Name	Perfect Score	Your Score
Identifying Accounting Terms	22 Pts.	
Analyzing Accounts Receivable and Notes Receivable	20 Pts.	
Journalizing Accounts Receivable and Notes Receivable Transactions	21 Pts.	
Total	63 Pts.	

Part One—Identifying Accounting Terms

Directions: Select the one term in Column I that best fits each definition in Column II. Print the letter identifying your choice in the Answers column.

Column I	*Column II*	*Answers*
A. aging of accounts receivable	**1.** Accounts receivable that cannot be collected. (p. 412)	1. ______
B. allowance method	**2.** Crediting the estimated value of uncollectible accounts to a contra account. (p. 412)	2. ______
C. book value	**3.** The difference between an asset's account balance and its related contra account balance. (p. 412)	3. ______
D. book value of accounts receivable	**4.** The difference between the balance of Accounts Receivable and its contra account, Allowance for Uncollectible Accounts. (p. 412)	4. ______
E. direct write-off method	**5.** The amount of accounts receivable a business expects to collect. (p. 412)	5. ______
F. dishonored note	**6.** A method used to estimate uncollectible accounts receivable that assumes a percent of credit sales will become uncollectible. (p. 413)	6. ______
G. interest income	**7.** A method used to estimate uncollectible accounts receivable that uses an analysis of accounts receivable to estimate the amount that will be uncollectible. (p. 413)	7. ______
H. interest rate	**8.** Analyzing accounts receivable according to when they are due. (p. 414)	8. ______
I. maker of a note	**9.** Canceling the balance of a customer account because the customer does not pay. (p. 418)	9. ______
J. maturity date	**10.** Recording uncollectible accounts expense only when an amount is actually known to be uncollectible. (p. 419)	10. ______
K. maturity value	**11.** A written and signed promise to pay a sum of money at a specified time. (p. 425)	11. ______
L. net realizable value	**12.** A promissory note signed by a business and given to a creditor. (p. 425)	12. ______
M. note payable	**13.** A promissory note that a business accepts from a person or business. (p. 425)	13. ______
N. note receivable	**14.** The person or business that signs a note, and thus promises to make payment. (p. 425)	14. ______
O. payee	**15.** The person or business to whom the amount of a note is payable. (p. 425)	15. ______

Column I	Column II	Answers
P. percent of accounts receivable method	**16.** The original amount of a note, sometimes referred to as the face amount. (p. 425)	**16.** ________
Q. percent of sales method	**17.** The percentage of the principal that is due for the use of the funds secured by a note. (p. 425)	**17.** ________
R. principal	**18.** The date on which the principal of a note is due to be repaid. (p. 425)	**18.** ________
S. promissory note	**19.** The length of time from the signing date of a note to the maturity date. (p. 425)	**19.** ________
T. time of a note	**20.** The amount that is due on the maturity date of a note. (p. 427)	**20.** ________
U. uncollectible accounts	**21.** The interest earned on money loaned. (p. 428)	**21.** ________
V. writing off an account	**22.** A note that is not paid when due. (p. 429)	**22.** ________

Part Two—Analyzing Accounts Receivable and Notes Receivable

Directions: Place a *T* for True or an *F* for False in the Answers column to show whether each of the following statements is true or false.

	Answers
1. The expense of an uncollectible account should be recorded in the accounting period that the account becomes uncollectible. (p. 412)	**1.** ______
2. The account, Allowance for Uncollectible Accounts, has a normal credit balance. (p. 412)	**2.** ______
3. A business usually knows at the end of the fiscal year which customer accounts will become uncollectible. (p. 412)	**3.** ______
4. The account, Allowance for Uncollectible Accounts, is reported on the income statement. (p. 412)	**4.** ______
5. The book value of accounts receivable must be a reasonable and unbiased estimate of the money the business expects to collect in the future. (p. 413)	**5.** ______
6. The percent of sales method of estimating uncollectible accounts expense assumes that a portion of every dollar of sales on account will become uncollectible. (p. 413)	**6.** ______
7. The accounting concept, Conservatism, is applied when the process of making accounting estimates is free from bias. (p. 413)	**7.** ______
8. The percent of each age group of an accounts receivable aging that is expected to become uncollectible is determined by the Securities and Exchange Commission. (p. 414)	**8.** ______
9. The adjusting entry for uncollectible accounts does not affect the balance of the Accounts Receivable account. (p. 415)	**9.** ______
10. A business having a $300.00 credit balance in Allowance for Uncollectible Accounts and estimating its uncollectible accounts to be $4,000.00 would record a $4,300.00 credit to Allowance for Uncollectible Accounts. (p. 415)	**10.** ______
11. When an account is written off as uncollectible, the business sends the customer a credit memo. (p. 418)	**11.** ______
12. When a customer account is written off under the allowance method, book value of accounts receivable decreases. (p. 418)	**12.** ______
13. The direct write-off method of accounting for uncollectible accounts does not comply with GAAP. (p. 419)	**13.** ______
14. When a previously written-off account is collected, Accounts Receivable is both debited and credited for the amount collected. (pp. 421–422)	**14.** ______
15. A note provides the business with legal evidence of the debt should it be necessary to go to court to collect. (p. 425)	**15.** ______
16. Total assets are reduced when a business accepts a note receivable from a customer needing an extension of time to pay an account receivable. (p. 426)	**16.** ______
17. Interest rates are stated as a percentage of the principal. (p. 427)	**17.** ______
18. Interest income is classified as an Other Revenue account. (p. 428)	**18.** ______
19. The method for calculating interest is the same for notes payable and notes receivable. (p. 428)	**19.** ______
20. Interest income should not be recorded on a dishonored note receivable. (p. 429)	**20.** ______

Part Three—Journalizing Accounts Receivable and Notes Receivable Transactions

Directions: In Answers Column 1, print the abbreviation for the journal in which each transaction is to be recorded. In Answers Columns 2 and 3, print the letters identifying the accounts to be debited and credited for each transaction.

G—General journal CR—Cash receipts journal

Account Titles	Transactions	Answers 1 Journal	Answers 2 Debit	Answers 3 Credit
A. Accounts Receivable	**1-2-3**. Recorded adjusting entry for uncollectible accounts expense. (p. 415)	1. ____	2. ____	3. ____
B. Allowance for Uncollectible Accounts	**4-5-6**. Wrote off Sanderson Company's past-due account as uncollectible. (p. 418)	4. ____	5. ____	6. ____
C. Cash	Received cash in full payment of Sanderson Company's account, previously written off as uncollectible. *(Record two entries, 7-8-9 and 10-11-12, below.)*			
D. Interest Income	**7-8-9**. First entry. (p. 421)	7. ____	8. ____	9. ____
E. Notes Receivable	**10-11-12**. Second entry. (p. 422)	10. ____	11. ____	12. ____
F. Sanderson Company	**13-14-15**. Accepted a note from Sanderson Company for an extension of time on its account. (p. 426)	13. ____	14. ____	15. ____
G. Uncollectible Accounts Expense	**16-17-18**. Collected a note receivable from Sanderson Company. (p. 428)	16. ____	17. ____	18. ____
H. Williams Supply	**19-20-21**. Williams Supply dishonored a note receivable. (p. 429)	19. ____	20. ____	21. ____

Name _______________ Date _______________ Class _______________

14-1 WORK TOGETHER, p. 417

Journalizing the adjusting entry for Allowance for Uncollectible Accounts

1.

Age Group	Amount	Percent	Uncollectible
Current	$16,485.18	2.0%	
1–30	12,489.05	4.0%	
31–60	6,958.18	8.0%	
61–90	4,218.21	20.0%	
Over 90	3,157.10	70.0%	
	$43,307.72		
Current Balance of Allowance for Uncollectible Accounts			
Estimated Addition to Allowance for Uncollectible Accounts			

2.

GENERAL JOURNAL PAGE 13

	DATE		ACCOUNT TITLE	DOC. NO.	POST. REF.	DEBIT	CREDIT	
1								1
2								2
3								3
4								4

14-1 ON YOUR OWN, p. 417

Journalizing the adjusting entry for Allowance for Uncollectible Accounts

1.

Age Group	Amount	Percent	Uncollectible
Current	$25,114.16	1.0%	
1–30	32,458.15	2.5%	
31–60	12,489.58	7.5%	
61–90	6,154.25	30.0%	
Over 90	7,189.28	80.0%	
	$83,405.42		
Current Balance of Allowance for Uncollectible Accounts			
Estimated Addition to Allowance for Uncollectible Accounts			

2.

GENERAL JOURNAL PAGE 13

	DATE		ACCOUNT TITLE	DOC. NO.	POST. REF.	DEBIT	CREDIT	
1								1
2								2
3								3
4								4

Name ______________________ Date ______________ Class ______________

14-2 WORK TOGETHER, p. 424

Recording entries related to uncollectible accounts receivable

1., 2.

GENERAL JOURNAL PAGE 15

	DATE		ACCOUNT TITLE	DOC. NO.	POST. REF.	DEBIT	CREDIT	
1								1
2								2
3								3
4								4
5								5
6								6
7								7
8								8
9								9
10								10
11								11
12								12

1.

ACCOUNTS RECEIVABLE LEDGER

ACCOUNT Fisher Industries CUSTOMER NO. 110

DATE		ITEM	POST. REF.	DEBIT	CREDIT	DEBIT BALANCE
20-- Nov.	1	Balance	✓			1 360 00

14-2 WORK TOGETHER (continued)

ACCOUNT Horne Co. CUSTOMER NO. 120

DATE		ITEM	POST. REF.	DEBIT	CREDIT	DEBIT BALANCE
20-- Nov.	1	Balance	✔			1 548 00

ACCOUNT Mellon Corp. CUSTOMER NO. 130

DATE		ITEM	POST. REF.	DEBIT	CREDIT	DEBIT BALANCE
20-- Nov.	1	Balance	✔			494 00

2.

GENERAL LEDGER

ACCOUNT Accounts Receivable ACCOUNT NO. 1130

DATE		ITEM	POST. REF.	DEBIT	CREDIT	BALANCE	
						DEBIT	CREDIT
20-- Nov.	1	Balance	✔			35 148 85	

ACCOUNT Allowance for Uncollectible Accounts ACCOUNT NO. 1135

DATE		ITEM	POST. REF.	DEBIT	CREDIT	BALANCE	
						DEBIT	CREDIT
20-- Nov.	1	Balance	✔				3 158 47

Name ____________________ Date ____________ Class ____________

14-2 WORK TOGETHER (concluded)

1., 2.

CASH RECEIPTS JOURNAL PAGE 24

	DATE	ACCOUNT TITLE	DOC. NO.	POST. REF.	1 GENERAL DEBIT	2 GENERAL CREDIT	3 ACCOUNTS RECEIVABLE CREDIT	4 SALES CREDIT	5 SALES TAX PAYABLE CREDIT	6 SALES DISCOUNT DEBIT	7 CASH DEBIT	
1												1
2												2
3												3

14-2 ON YOUR OWN, p. 424

Recording entries related to uncollectible accounts receivable

1., 2.

GENERAL JOURNAL PAGE 10

	DATE		ACCOUNT TITLE	DOC. NO.	POST. REF.	DEBIT	CREDIT	
1								1
2								2
3								3
4								4
5								5
6								6
7								7
8								8
9								9
10								10
11								11
12								12

1.

ACCOUNTS RECEIVABLE LEDGER

ACCOUNT Nancy Brown CUSTOMER NO. 110

DATE		ITEM	POST. REF.	DEBIT	CREDIT	DEBIT BALANCE
20-- Oct.	1	Balance	✔			428 00

ACCOUNT Janice Harrell CUSTOMER NO. 120

DATE		ITEM	POST. REF.	DEBIT	CREDIT	DEBIT BALANCE
20-- Oct.	1	Balance	✔			527 00

Name ______________________ Date ____________ Class ____________

14-2 ON YOUR OWN (continued)

ACCOUNT Daniel Pruitt — CUSTOMER NO. 130

DATE		ITEM	POST. REF.	DEBIT	CREDIT	DEBIT BALANCE
20-- Oct.	1	Balance	✔			249 00

ACCOUNT Tom Sloan — CUSTOMER NO. 140

DATE		ITEM	POST. REF.	DEBIT	CREDIT	DEBIT BALANCE

2.

GENERAL LEDGER

ACCOUNT Accounts Receivable — ACCOUNT NO. 1130

DATE		ITEM	POST. REF.	DEBIT	CREDIT	BALANCE	
						DEBIT	CREDIT
20-- Oct.	1	Balance	✔			19,482 58	

ACCOUNT Allowance for Uncollectible Accounts — ACCOUNT NO. 1135

DATE		ITEM	POST. REF.	DEBIT	CREDIT	BALANCE	
						DEBIT	CREDIT
20-- Oct.	1	Balance	✔				3,658 97

1., 2.

CASH RECEIPTS JOURNAL

PAGE 22

					1	2	3	4	5	6	7	
	DATE	ACCOUNT TITLE	DOC. NO.	POST. REF.	GENERAL DEBIT	GENERAL CREDIT	ACCOUNTS RECEIVABLE CREDIT	SALES CREDIT	SALES TAX PAYABLE CREDIT	SALES DISCOUNT DEBIT	CASH DEBIT	
1												1
2												2
3												3

Name ______________________ Date ______________ Class ______________

14-3 WORK TOGETHER, p. 430

Recording notes receivable

1.

Note	Date	Principal	Interest Rate	Time in Days	Interest	Maturity Date	Maturity Value
NR3	June 5	$20,000.00	8%	90			
NR4	June 12	$10,000.00	6%	120			

Calculations:

Note	Maturity Date			Interest	Maturity Value
NR3		Days from the Month	Days Remaining		
	Term of the Note		90		
NR4		Days from the Month	Days Remaining		
	Term of the Note		120		

2., 3.

GENERAL JOURNAL

PAGE 7

	DATE	ACCOUNT TITLE	DOC. NO.	POST. REF.	DEBIT	CREDIT	
4							4
5							5
6							6
7							7
8							8
9							9

2., 3.

CASH RECEIPTS JOURNAL

PAGE 8

					1	2	3	4	5	6	7	
	DATE	ACCOUNT TITLE	DOC. NO.	POST. REF.	GENERAL		ACCOUNTS RECEIVABLE CREDIT	SALES CREDIT	SALES TAX PAYABLE CREDIT	SALES DISCOUNT DEBIT	CASH DEBIT	
					DEBIT	CREDIT						
13												13
14												14
15												15

Name ______________________ Date ____________ Class ____________

14-3 WORK TOGETHER (concluded)

2., 3. **ACCOUNTS RECEIVABLE LEDGER**

ACCOUNT Dennis Craft CUSTOMER NO. 110

DATE		ITEM	POST. REF.	DEBIT	CREDIT	DEBIT BALANCE

ACCOUNT Gary Kinney CUSTOMER NO. 120

DATE		ITEM	POST. REF.	DEBIT	CREDIT	DEBIT BALANCE
20-- July	1	Balance	✔			1 800 00

3. **GENERAL LEDGER**

ACCOUNT Accounts Receivable ACCOUNT NO. 1130

DATE		ITEM	POST. REF.	DEBIT	CREDIT	BALANCE	
						DEBIT	CREDIT
20-- July	1	Balance	✔			42 181 97	

ACCOUNT Notes Receivable ACCOUNT NO. 1170

DATE		ITEM	POST. REF.	DEBIT	CREDIT	BALANCE	
						DEBIT	CREDIT
20-- July	1	Balance	✔			16 200 00	

ACCOUNT Interest Income ACCOUNT NO. 7110

DATE		ITEM	POST. REF.	DEBIT	CREDIT	BALANCE	
						DEBIT	CREDIT
20-- July	1	Balance	✔				458 00

14-3 ON YOUR OWN, p. 430

Recording notes receivable

1.

Note	Date	Principal	Interest Rate	Time in Days	Interest	Maturity Date	Maturity Value
NR12	March 22	$8,000.00	6%	120			
NR13	April 7	$6,000.00	7%	90			

Calculations:

Note	Maturity Date			Interest	Maturity Value
NR12		Days from the Month	Days Remaining		
	Term of the Note		120		
NR13		Days from the Month	Days Remaining		
	Term of the Note		90		

Name ______________________ Date ____________ Class ____________

14-3 ON YOUR OWN (continued)

2., 3.

GENERAL JOURNAL

PAGE 15

	DATE	ACCOUNT TITLE	DOC. NO.	POST. REF.	DEBIT	CREDIT	
7							7
8							8
9							9
10							10
11							11
12							12

2., 3.

CASH RECEIPTS JOURNAL

PAGE 20

	DATE	ACCOUNT TITLE	DOC. NO.	POST. REF.	1 GENERAL DEBIT	2 GENERAL CREDIT	3 ACCOUNTS RECEIVABLE CREDIT	4 SALES CREDIT	5 SALES TAX PAYABLE CREDIT	6 SALES DISCOUNT DEBIT	7 CASH DEBIT	
19												19
20												20
21												21

14-3 ON YOUR OWN (concluded)

2., 3.

ACCOUNTS RECEIVABLE LEDGER

ACCOUNT Roger Hamm CUSTOMER NO. 110

DATE		ITEM	POST. REF.	DEBIT	CREDIT	DEBIT BALANCE

ACCOUNT Marshall Sykes CUSTOMER NO. 120

DATE		ITEM	POST. REF.	DEBIT	CREDIT	DEBIT BALANCE
20-- May	1	Balance	✔			3 2 0 0 00

3.

GENERAL LEDGER

ACCOUNT Accounts Receivable ACCOUNT NO. 1130

DATE		ITEM	POST. REF.	DEBIT	CREDIT	BALANCE DEBIT	BALANCE CREDIT
20-- May	1	Balance	✔			56 1 8 4 50	

ACCOUNT Notes Receivable ACCOUNT NO. 1170

DATE		ITEM	POST. REF.	DEBIT	CREDIT	BALANCE DEBIT	BALANCE CREDIT
20-- May	1	Balance	✔			14 3 0 0 00	

ACCOUNT Interest Income ACCOUNT NO. 7110

DATE		ITEM	POST. REF.	DEBIT	CREDIT	BALANCE DEBIT	BALANCE CREDIT
20-- May	1	Balance	✔				6 4 8 00

Name ______________________ Date ______________ Class ______________

14-1 APPLICATION PROBLEM (LO2, 3), p. 434

Journalizing the adjusting entry for Allowance for Uncollectible Accounts

1.

Age Group	Amount	Percent	Uncollectible
Current	$20,489.15	2.0%	
1–30	16,487.20	6.0%	
31–60	8,415.29	15.0%	
61–90	6,218.47	50.0%	
Over 90	2,584.95	90.0%	
	$54,195.06		
Current Balance of Allowance for Uncollectible Accounts			
Estimated Addition to Allowance for Uncollectible Accounts			

2.

GENERAL JOURNAL PAGE 13

	DATE		ACCOUNT TITLE	DOC. NO.	POST. REF.	DEBIT	CREDIT	
1								1
2								2
3								3
4								4

14-2 APPLICATION PROBLEM (LO4, 5), p. 434

Recording entries related to uncollectible accounts receivable

1., 2.

GENERAL JOURNAL PAGE 6

	DATE		ACCOUNT TITLE	DOC. NO.	POST. REF.	DEBIT	CREDIT	
1								1
2								2
3								3
4								4
5								5
6								6
7								7
8								8
9								9
10								10
11								11
12								12

1., 2. **ACCOUNTS RECEIVABLE LEDGER**

ACCOUNT Durham Supply CUSTOMER NO. 110

DATE		ITEM	POST. REF.	DEBIT	CREDIT	DEBIT BALANCE
20-- May	1	Balance	✔			948 50

ACCOUNT Foley Corp. CUSTOMER NO. 120

DATE		ITEM	POST. REF.	DEBIT	CREDIT	DEBIT BALANCE

14-2 APPLICATION PROBLEM (continued)

ACCOUNT Pennington Co. CUSTOMER NO. 130

DATE		ITEM	POST. REF.	DEBIT	CREDIT	DEBIT BALANCE
20-- May	1	Balance	✔			4 8 8 93

ACCOUNT Suarez Consulting CUSTOMER NO. 140

DATE		ITEM	POST. REF.	DEBIT	CREDIT	DEBIT BALANCE
20-- May	1	Balance	✔			1 6 4 8 11

2.

GENERAL LEDGER

ACCOUNT Accounts Receivable ACCOUNT NO. 1130

DATE		ITEM	POST. REF.	DEBIT	CREDIT	BALANCE DEBIT	BALANCE CREDIT
20-- May	1	Balance	✔			19 4 8 2 58	

ACCOUNT Allowance for Uncollectible Accounts ACCOUNT NO. 1135

DATE		ITEM	POST. REF.	DEBIT	CREDIT	BALANCE DEBIT	BALANCE CREDIT
20-- May	1	Balance	✔				3 4 5 0 00

1., 2.

CASH RECEIPTS JOURNAL

PAGE 11

					1	2	3	4	5	6	7	
	DATE	ACCOUNT TITLE	DOC. NO.	POST. REF.	GENERAL DEBIT	GENERAL CREDIT	ACCOUNTS RECEIVABLE CREDIT	SALES CREDIT	SALES TAX PAYABLE CREDIT	SALES DISCOUNT DEBIT	CASH DEBIT	
1												1
2												2
3												3

Name ______________________ Date ____________ Class ____________

14-3 APPLICATION PROBLEM (LO6, 7, 8), p. 435

Recording notes receivable

1.

Note	Date	Principal	Interest Rate	Time in Days	Interest	Maturity Date	Maturity Value
NR8	April 16	$25,000.00	8%	90			
NR9	May 3	$ 8,000.00	9%	180			

Calculations:

1.

Note	Maturity Date			Interest	Maturity Value
		Days from the Month	Days Remaining		
NR8	Term of the Note		90		
		Days from the Month	Days Remaining		
NR9	Term of the Note		180		

2.

GENERAL JOURNAL

PAGE 16

	DATE	ACCOUNT TITLE	DOC. NO.	POST. REF.	DEBIT	CREDIT	
10							10
11							11
12							12
13							13
14							14
15							15

2.

CASH RECEIPTS JOURNAL

PAGE 23

					1	2	3	4	5	6	7	
	DATE	ACCOUNT TITLE	DOC. NO.	POST. REF.	GENERAL DEBIT	GENERAL CREDIT	ACCOUNTS RECEIVABLE CREDIT	SALES CREDIT	SALES TAX PAYABLE CREDIT	SALES DISCOUNT DEBIT	CASH DEBIT	
22												22
23												23
24												24

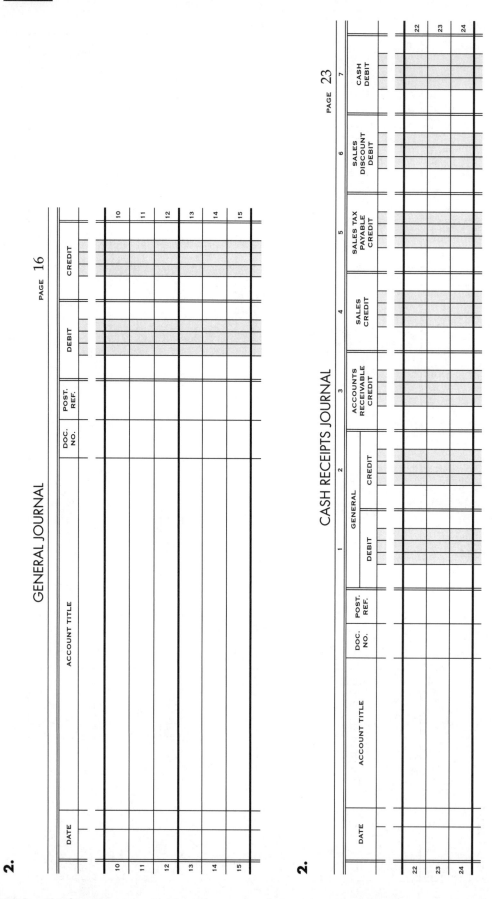

Name ______________________ Date ____________ Class ____________

14-3 APPLICATION PROBLEM (concluded)

2., 3. **ACCOUNTS RECEIVABLE LEDGER**

ACCOUNT Daniel Burris CUSTOMER NO. 110

DATE		ITEM	POST. REF.	DEBIT	CREDIT	DEBIT BALANCE
20-- June	1	Balance	✔			6 800 00

ACCOUNT Maggie Singer CUSTOMER NO. 120

DATE		ITEM	POST. REF.	DEBIT	CREDIT	DEBIT BALANCE

3. **GENERAL LEDGER**

ACCOUNT Accounts Receivable ACCOUNT NO. 1130

DATE		ITEM	POST. REF.	DEBIT	CREDIT	BALANCE DEBIT	BALANCE CREDIT
20-- June	1	Balance	✔			64 081 13	

ACCOUNT Notes Receivable ACCOUNT NO. 1170

DATE		ITEM	POST. REF.	DEBIT	CREDIT	BALANCE DEBIT	BALANCE CREDIT
20-- June	1	Balance	✔			12 850 00	

ACCOUNT Interest Income ACCOUNT NO. 7110

DATE		ITEM	POST. REF.	DEBIT	CREDIT	BALANCE DEBIT	BALANCE CREDIT
20-- June	1	Balance	✔				829 00

14-M MASTERY PROBLEM (LO4, 5, 6, 7, 8), p. 435

Recording entries for uncollectible accounts

1., 2.

GENERAL JOURNAL PAGE 12

	DATE		ACCOUNT TITLE	DOC. NO.	POST. REF.	DEBIT	CREDIT	
1								1
2								2
3								3
4								4
5								5
6								6
7								7
8								8
9								9
10								10
11								11
12								12
13								13
14								14
15								15
16								16

3.

GENERAL JOURNAL PAGE 13

	DATE		ACCOUNT TITLE	DOC. NO.	POST. REF.	DEBIT	CREDIT	
1								1
2								2
3								3
4								4
5								5

Name ____________________ Date ____________ Class ____________

14-M MASTERY PROBLEM (continued)

1., 2.

CASH RECEIPTS JOURNAL PAGE 22

	DATE	ACCOUNT TITLE	DOC. NO.	POST. REF.	1 GENERAL DEBIT	2 GENERAL CREDIT	3 ACCOUNTS RECEIVABLE CREDIT	4 SALES CREDIT	5 SALES TAX PAYABLE CREDIT	6 SALES DISCOUNT DEBIT	7 CASH DEBIT	
1												1
2												2
3												3
4												4
5												5
6												6
7												7

3.

Age Group	Amount	Percent	Uncollectible
Current	$ 52,271.96	1.0%	
1–30	32,581.28	2.5%	
31–60	12,849.15	7.5%	
61–90	9,418.25	25.0%	
Over 90	11,848.15	60.0%	
	$118,968.79		
Current Balance of Allowance for Uncollectible Accounts			
Estimated Addition to Allowance for Uncollectible Accounts			

1., 2., 3.

ACCOUNTS RECEIVABLE LEDGER

ACCOUNT Banda Company — CUSTOMER NO. 110

DATE		ITEM	POST. REF.	DEBIT	CREDIT	DEBIT BALANCE

ACCOUNT Broyles Industries — CUSTOMER NO. 120

DATE		ITEM	POST. REF.	DEBIT	CREDIT	DEBIT BALANCE

ACCOUNT Maples Corporation — CUSTOMER NO. 130

DATE		ITEM	POST. REF.	DEBIT	CREDIT	DEBIT BALANCE
20-- Dec.	1	Balance	✔			4,500 00

ACCOUNT Murrell, Inc. — CUSTOMER NO. 140

DATE		ITEM	POST. REF.	DEBIT	CREDIT	DEBIT BALANCE
20-- Dec.	1	Balance	✔			16,450 00

ACCOUNT Patel Corporation — CUSTOMER NO. 150

DATE		ITEM	POST. REF.	DEBIT	CREDIT	DEBIT BALANCE
20-- Dec.	1	Balance	✔			498 25

Name ______________________ Date ____________ Class ____________

14-M MASTERY PROBLEM (concluded)

3.

GENERAL LEDGER

ACCOUNT Accounts Receivable — ACCOUNT NO. 1130

DATE		ITEM	POST. REF.	DEBIT	CREDIT	BALANCE DEBIT	BALANCE CREDIT
20-- Dec.	1	Balance	✔			120,716 04	

ACCOUNT Allowance for Uncollectible Accounts — ACCOUNT NO. 1135

DATE		ITEM	POST. REF.	DEBIT	CREDIT	BALANCE DEBIT	BALANCE CREDIT
20-- Dec.	1	Balance	✔				2,143 01

ACCOUNT Notes Receivable — ACCOUNT NO. 1170

DATE		ITEM	POST. REF.	DEBIT	CREDIT	BALANCE DEBIT	BALANCE CREDIT
20-- Dec.	1	Balance	✔			22,800 00	

ACCOUNT Uncollectible Accounts Expense — ACCOUNT NO. 6165

DATE		ITEM	POST. REF.	DEBIT	CREDIT	BALANCE DEBIT	BALANCE CREDIT

ACCOUNT Interest Income — ACCOUNT NO. 7110

DATE		ITEM	POST. REF.	DEBIT	CREDIT	BALANCE DEBIT	BALANCE CREDIT
20-- Dec.	1	Balance	✔				1,095 00

14-C CHALLENGE PROBLEM (LO2), p. 436

Estimating uncollectible accounts expense

1., 2.

Wood Company Aging of Accounts Receivable 12/31/20--			
Age Group	**Amount**	**Percent**	**Uncollectible**
Current	$ 70,728.14		
1–30	30,438.99		
31–60	14,563.59		
61–90	8,090.34		
Over 90	14,574.76		
	$138,395.82		
Current Balance of Allowance for Uncollectible Accounts			
Estimated Addition to Allowance for Uncollectible Accounts			

3.

Study Guide 15

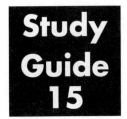

Name	Perfect Score	Your Score
Identifying Accounting Terms	17 Pts.	
Identifying Accounting Concepts and Practices	20 Pts.	
Analyzing Adjustments	12 Pts.	
Total	49 Pts.	

Part One—Identifying Accounting Terms

Directions: Select the one term in Column I that best fits each definition in Column II. Print the letter identifying your choice in the Answers column.

Column I	Column II	Answers
A. accrued interest income	1. A trial balance prepared before adjusting entries are posted. (p. 441)	1. ________
B. accrued revenue	2. The amount of inventory on hand at the beginning of a fiscal period. (p. 446)	2. ________
C. accumulated depreciation	3. The actual count of merchandise at the end of a fiscal period. (p. 446)	3. ________
D. adjusted trial balance	4. Revenue earned in one fiscal period but not received until a later fiscal period. (p. 447)	4. ________
E. beginning inventory	5. Interest earned but not yet received. (p. 448)	5. ________
F. book value of a plant asset	6. Cash and other assets expected to be exchanged for cash or consumed within a year. (p. 450)	6. ________
G. current assets	7. Physical assets that will be used for a number of years in the operation of a business. (p. 450)	7. ________
H. depreciation	8. A loss in the usefulness of a plant asset as a result of wear or obsolescence. (p. 450)	8. ________
I. depreciation expense	9. The portion of a plant asset's cost that is transferred to an expense account in each fiscal period during that asset's useful life. (p. 450)	9. ________
J. ending inventory	10. An estimate of the amount that will be received for an asset at the time of its disposal. (p. 450)	10. ________
K. marginal tax rate	11. The period of time over which an asset contributes to the earnings of a business. (p. 450)	11. ________
L. plant assets	12. Recording an equal amount of depreciation expense for a plant asset in each year of its useful life. (p. 451)	12. ________
M. salvage value	13. The total amount of depreciation expense that has been recorded since the purchase of a plant asset. (p. 451)	13. ________
N. straight-line method of depreciation	14. The original cost of a plant asset minus accumulated depreciation. (p. 451)	14. ________
O. tax bracket	15. A trial balance prepared after adjusting entries are posted. (p. 457)	15. ________
P. unadjusted trial balance	16. Each tax rate and taxable income amount on one line of a tax table. (p. 458)	16. ________
Q. useful life	17. The tax rate associated with a tax bracket. (p. 458)	17. ________

Part Two—Identifying Accounting Concepts and Practices

Directions: Place a *T* for True or an *F* for False in the Answers column to show whether each of the following statements is true or false.

	Answers
1. Businesses must use a 12-month period, or fiscal year, ending on December 31 for reporting their financial performance. (p. 440)	**1.** ________
2. The adjusting entry for Merchandise Inventory is unique to a merchandising business. (p. 440)	**2.** ________
3. The first step in preparing adjusting entries is to prepare an unadjusted trial balance. (p. 441)	**3.** ________
4. A trial balance provides a complete list of accounts that may need to be brought up to date. (p. 441)	**4.** ________
5. Rather than using a worksheet, a business can use an unadjusted trial balance and record adjustments directly to a general journal. (p. 441)	**5.** ________
6. The adjustment for the Supplies—Office account will result in a debit to Supplies Expense—Office. (p. 442)	**6.** ________
7. The amount of the adjustment for Prepaid Insurance represents the value of insurance premium used during the fiscal period. (p. 444)	**7.** ________
8. For a company using the periodic inventory method, the account balance of Merchandise Inventory changes during the fiscal year. (p. 446)	**8.** ________
9. If ending inventory is less than the account balance of Merchandise Inventory, the inventory adjustment will include a credit to Income Summary. (p. 447)	**9.** ________
10. The adjusting entry for accrued revenue increases a revenue account (a credit) and increases a receivable account (a debit). (p. 447)	**10.** ________
11. Estimates of the cost, salvage value, and useful life of a plant asset are used to calculate its annual depreciation. (p. 450)	**11.** ________
12. Functional depreciation occurs when a plant asset becomes inadequate or obsolete. (p. 450)	**12.** ________
13. The annual straight-line depreciation of equipment costing $4,000.00 with a salvage value of $500.00 and a useful life of 5 years would be $700.00. (p. 451)	**13.** ________
14. The adjustment for Accumulated Depreciation—Store Equipment includes a credit to Depreciation Expense—Store Equipment. (p. 452)	**14.** ________
15. The annual straight-line depreciation of land costing $40,000.00 with a salvage value of $10,000.00 and a useful life of 20 years would be $1,500.00. (p. 452)	**15.** ________
16. The adjustment for Federal Income Tax Payable and Federal Income Tax Expense is determined only after all other adjusting entries are posted and the net income before federal income tax is determined. (p. 457)	**16.** ________
17. Corporations anticipating annual federal income taxes of $500.00 or more are required to pay estimated taxes each month. (p. 458)	**17.** ________
18. A corporation using a 35% marginal tax rate must pay income taxes equal to 35% of its income before federal income taxes. (p. 458)	**18.** ________
19. Tax rates for corporations can be changed by an act of Congress. (p. 458)	**19.** ________
20. Any amount of federal income tax owed at the end of the fiscal year is debited to Federal Income Tax Payable. (p. 459)	**20.** ________

Name ______________________ Date ____________ Class ____________

Part Three—Analyzing Adjustments

Directions: For each of the following items, select the choice that best completes the statement. Print the letter identifying your choice in the Answers column.

	Answers
1. The amount in the Supplies—Office account on an unadjusted trial balance represents the value of supplies (A) at the beginning of a fiscal period (B) used during a fiscal period (C) at the beginning of a fiscal period plus office supplies bought during the fiscal period (D) bought during a fiscal period. (p. 442)	**1.** ________
2. The two accounts used to adjust the Office Supplies account are (A) Supplies and Purchases (B) Supplies—Office and Income Summary (C) Supplies—Office and Supplies Expense—Office (D) Supplies Expense—Office and Income Summary. (p. 442)	**2.** ________
3. The portion of the insurance premiums that has expired during a fiscal period is classified as (A) a liability (B) an asset (C) an expense (D) capital. (p. 444)	**3.** ________
4. The two accounts used to adjust the Prepaid Insurance account are (A) Insurance Expense and Income Summary (B) Prepaid Insurance and Insurance Expense (C) Prepaid Insurance and Income Summary (D) Prepaid Insurance Expense and Income Summary. (p. 444)	**4.** ________
5. For a business using the periodic inventory method, the Merchandise Inventory amount on the unadjusted trial balance represents the merchandise inventory (A) at the end of a fiscal period (B) at the beginning of a fiscal period (C) purchased during a fiscal period (D) available during a fiscal period. (p. 446)	**5.** ________
6. The two accounts used to adjust the Merchandise Inventory account are (A) Merchandise Inventory and Supplies (B) Merchandise Inventory and Purchases (C) Merchandise Inventory and Income Summary (D) Merchandise Inventory and Sales. (pp. 446–447)	**6.** ________
7. A credit to Income Summary in the Merchandise Inventory adjustment represents the (A) decrease in Merchandise Inventory (B) increase in Merchandise Inventory (C) beginning Merchandise Inventory (D) ending Merchandise Inventory. (p. 447)	**7.** ________
8. Recording revenue in the accounting period in which the revenue is earned is an application of the accounting concept (A) Realization of Revenue (B) Consistent Reporting (C) Historical Cost (D) Adequate Disclosure. (p. 447)	**8.** ________
9. The two accounts used to adjust for interest income earned on notes receivable are (A) Interest Receivable and Interest Income (B) Accounts Receivable and Interest Income (C) Interest Receivable and Sales (D) Accounts Receivable and Sales. (p. 448)	**9.** ________
10. After recording the adjustment for accumulated depreciation, the book value of plant assets (A) remains unchanged, (B) increases, (C) decreases, (D) cannot be determined. (pp. 451–452)	**10.** ________
11. The two accounts used to adjust the depreciation of store equipment are (A) Store Equipment and Store Equipment Expense (B) Accumulated Depreciation—Store Equipment and Accumulated Depreciation Expense (C) Accumulated Depreciation—Store Equipment and Store Equipment Expense (D) Accumulated Depreciation—Store Equipment and Depreciation Expense—Store Equipment. (p. 452)	**11.** ________
12. The two accounts used to record the adjustment for federal income tax are (A) Federal Income Tax Expense and Prepaid Taxes (B) Federal Income Tax Payable and Federal Income Tax Expense (C) Federal Income Tax Expense and Allowance for Federal Tax Expense (D) Federal Income Tax Expense and Federal Income Tax Adjustments. (p. 459)	**12.** ________

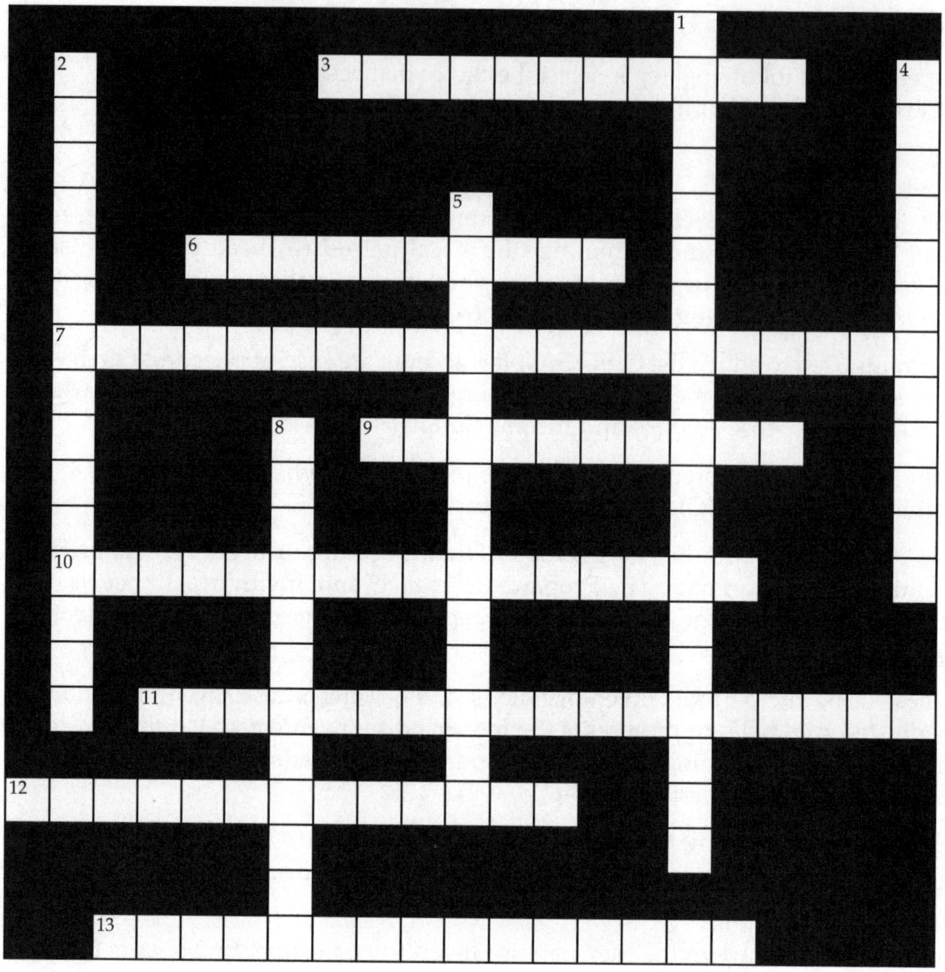

Across

3. Physical assets that will be used for a number of years in the operation of a business.
6. Each tax rate and taxable income amount on one line of a tax table.
7. A trial balance prepared after adjusting entries are posted.
9. The period of time over which an asset contributes to the earnings of a business.
10. Transactions that are set up for automated entry in computerized accounting systems.
11. The amount of inventory on hand at the beginning of a fiscal period.
12. Cash and other assets expected to be exchanged for cash or consumed within a year.
13. The actual count of merchandise at the end of a fiscal period.

Down

1. The portion of a plant asset's cost that is transferred to an expense account in each fiscal period during that asset's useful life.
2. The tax rate associated with a tax bracket.
4. The amount that will be received for an asset at the time of its disposal.
5. Revenue earned in one fiscal period but not received until a later fiscal period.
8. A loss in the usefulness of a plant asset as a result of wear or obsolescence.

Name ______________________ Date ____________ Class ____________

15-1 WORK TOGETHER, p. 445

Journalizing the adjusting entries for supplies and prepaid insurance

(Note: Working papers for 15-1 ON YOUR OWN begin on p. 435.)

1., 2.

ACCOUNT TITLE	DEBIT	CREDIT
Cash	24 194 34	
Petty Cash	250 00	
Accounts Receivable	38 518 56	
Merchandise Inventory	94 845 31	
Supplies—Office	3 108 08	
Supplies—Store		
Prepaid Insurance	11 200 00	
Notes Receivable	8 000 00	
Interest Receivable		
Office Equipment	6 948 88	
Store Equipment	22 461 95	
Accumulated Depreciation—Store Equipment		8 564 00
Accounts Payable		4 462 21
Sales Tax Payable		495 90
Employee Income Tax Payable—Federal		594 00
Social Security Tax Payable		1 266 80
Medicare Tax Payable		296 27
Health Insurance Premiums Payable		288 04
Retirement Benefits Payable		291 17
Unemployment Tax Payable—Federal		185 99
Unemployment Tax Payable—State		92 31
Federal Income Tax Payable		
Dividends Payable		3 000 00
Capital Stock		30 000 00
Retained Earnings		37 129 26
Dividends	12 000 00	

(Note: Trial balance is continued on the next page.)

ACCOUNT TITLE	DEBIT	CREDIT
Income Summary		
Sales		532 371 75
Sales Discount	2 181 0	
Sales Returns and Allowances	1 484 8	
Purchases	223 174 88	
Purchases Discount		922 14
Purchases Returns and Allowances		1 495 01
Advertising Expense	2 182 81	
Credit Card Fee Expense	395 42	
Depreciation Expense—Office Equipment		
Depreciation Expense—Store Equipment		
Miscellaneous Expense	2 382 80	
Payroll Taxes Expense	12 797 20	
Rent Expense	5 714 03	
Salary Expense	115 364 38	
Supplies Expense—Office		
Supplies Expense—Store		
Uncollectible Accounts Expense		
Utilities Expense	3 973 68	
Federal Income Tax Expense	32 000 00	
Interest Income		464 00

Name ____________________ Date ____________ Class ____________

15-1, 15-2, 15-3, and 15-4 WORK TOGETHER, pp. 445, 449, 454, and 462

15-1 Journalizing the adjusting entries for supplies and prepaid insurance
15-2 Journalizing the adjusting entries for merchandise inventory and interest receivable
15-3 Journalizing the adjusting entries for accumulated depreciation
15-4 Preparing the adjusting entry for federal income tax and an adjusted trial balance

GENERAL JOURNAL PAGE 15

	DATE		ACCOUNT TITLE	DOC. NO.	POST. REF.	DEBIT	CREDIT	
1			Adjusting Entries					1
2	20-- Dec.	31	Uncollectible Accounts Expense			3 415 00		2
3			Allowance for Uncollectible Accounts				3 415 00	3
4								4
5								5
6								6
7								7
8								8
9								9
10								10
11								11
12								12
13								13
14								14
15								15
16								16
17								17
18								18
19								19
20								20

15-3 WORK TOGETHER, p. 454

1.

Original Cost	$
Estimated Salvage Value	
Estimated Total Depreciation Expense	$
Years of Estimated Useful Life	
Annual Depreciation Expense	$

2.

Original Cost			$
Depreciation:	Year 1	$	
	Year 2		
Book Value			$

Name ______________________ Date ____________ Class ____________

15-4 WORK TOGETHER, p. 462

GENERAL LEDGER

1., 4.

ACCOUNT Allowance for Uncollectible Accounts — ACCOUNT NO. 1135

DATE		ITEM	POST. REF.	DEBIT	CREDIT	BALANCE DEBIT	BALANCE CREDIT
20-- Dec.	1	Balance	✔				48 67

ACCOUNT Merchandise Inventory — ACCOUNT NO. 1140

DATE		ITEM	POST. REF.	DEBIT	CREDIT	BALANCE DEBIT	BALANCE CREDIT
20-- Dec.	1	Balance	✔			94 845 31	

ACCOUNT Supplies—Office — ACCOUNT NO. 1145

DATE		ITEM	POST. REF.	DEBIT	CREDIT	BALANCE DEBIT	BALANCE CREDIT
20-- Dec.	1	Balance	✔			3 108 08	

ACCOUNT Supplies—Store — ACCOUNT NO. 1150

DATE		ITEM	POST. REF.	DEBIT	CREDIT	BALANCE DEBIT	BALANCE CREDIT
20-- Dec.	1	Balance	✔			4 483 62	

ACCOUNT Prepaid Insurance — ACCOUNT NO. 1160

DATE		ITEM	POST. REF.	DEBIT	CREDIT	BALANCE DEBIT	BALANCE CREDIT
20-- Dec.	1	Balance	✔			11 200 00	

ACCOUNT Interest Receivable — ACCOUNT NO. 1175

DATE		ITEM	POST. REF.	DEBIT	CREDIT	BALANCE DEBIT	BALANCE CREDIT

15-4 WORK TOGETHER (continued)

ACCOUNT Accumulated Depreciation—Office Equipment — ACCOUNT NO. 1210

DATE		ITEM	POST. REF.	DEBIT	CREDIT	BALANCE DEBIT	BALANCE CREDIT
20-- Dec.	1	Balance	✔				2,395.00

ACCOUNT Accumulated Depreciation—Store Equipment — ACCOUNT NO. 1220

DATE		ITEM	POST. REF.	DEBIT	CREDIT	BALANCE DEBIT	BALANCE CREDIT
20-- Dec.	1	Balance	✔				8,564.00

ACCOUNT Federal Income Tax Payable — ACCOUNT NO. 2170

DATE		ITEM	POST. REF.	DEBIT	CREDIT	BALANCE DEBIT	BALANCE CREDIT

ACCOUNT Income Summary — ACCOUNT NO. 3150

DATE		ITEM	POST. REF.	DEBIT	CREDIT	BALANCE DEBIT	BALANCE CREDIT

ACCOUNT Depreciation Expense—Office Equipment — ACCOUNT NO. 6120

DATE		ITEM	POST. REF.	DEBIT	CREDIT	BALANCE DEBIT	BALANCE CREDIT

ACCOUNT Depreciation Expense—Store Equipment — ACCOUNT NO. 6125

DATE		ITEM	POST. REF.	DEBIT	CREDIT	BALANCE DEBIT	BALANCE CREDIT

15-4 WORK TOGETHER (continued)

ACCOUNT Insurance Expense — ACCOUNT NO. 6130

DATE		ITEM	POST. REF.	DEBIT	CREDIT	BALANCE DEBIT	BALANCE CREDIT

ACCOUNT Supplies Expense—Office — ACCOUNT NO. 6155

DATE		ITEM	POST. REF.	DEBIT	CREDIT	BALANCE DEBIT	BALANCE CREDIT

ACCOUNT Supplies Expense—Store — ACCOUNT NO. 6160

DATE		ITEM	POST. REF.	DEBIT	CREDIT	BALANCE DEBIT	BALANCE CREDIT

ACCOUNT Uncollectible Accounts Expense — ACCOUNT NO. 6165

DATE		ITEM	POST. REF.	DEBIT	CREDIT	BALANCE DEBIT	BALANCE CREDIT

ACCOUNT Federal Income Tax Expense — ACCOUNT NO. 6205

DATE		ITEM	POST. REF.	DEBIT	CREDIT	BALANCE DEBIT	BALANCE CREDIT
20-- Dec.	1	Balance	✔			32 000 00	

ACCOUNT Interest Income — ACCOUNT NO. 7110

DATE		ITEM	POST. REF.	DEBIT	CREDIT	BALANCE DEBIT	BALANCE CREDIT
20-- Dec.	1	Balance	✔				464 00

3.

Total of income statement credit accounts	$
Less total of income statement debit accounts excluding federal income tax	
Equals net income before federal income tax	$

Net Income before Federal Income Tax	–	Of the Amount Over	=	Net Income Subject to Marginal Tax Rate	×	Marginal Tax Rate	=	Marginal Income Tax
$	–	$	=	$	×		=	$

Bracket Minimum Income Tax	+	Marginal Income Tax	=	Federal Income Tax
$	+	$	=	$

Name ______________________ Date ____________ Class ____________

15-4 WORK TOGETHER (continued)

2., 5., 6.

ACCOUNT TITLE	DEBIT	CREDIT
Cash	24,194.34	
Petty Cash	250.00	
Accounts Receivable	38,518.56	
Allowance for Uncollectible Accounts		
Merchandise Inventory		
Supplies—Office		
Supplies—Store		
Prepaid Insurance		
Notes Receivable	8,000.00	
Interest Receivable		
Office Equipment	6,948.88	
Accumulated Depreciation—Office Equipment		
Store Equipment	22,461.95	
Accumulated Depreciation—Store Equipment		
Accounts Payable		4,462.21
Sales Tax Payable		495.90
Employee Income Tax Payable—Federal		594.00
Social Security Tax Payable		1,266.80
Medicare Tax Payable		296.27
Health Insurance Premiums Payable		288.04
Retirement Benefits Payable		291.17
Unemployment Tax Payable—Federal		185.99
Unemployment Tax Payable—State		92.31
Federal Income Tax Payable		
Dividends Payable		3,000.00
Capital Stock		30,000.00
Retained Earnings		37,129.26
Dividends	12,000.00	

(Note: Trial balance is continued on the next page.)

15-4 WORK TOGETHER (concluded)

ACCOUNT TITLE	DEBIT	CREDIT
Income Summary		
Sales		532 3 7 1 75
Sales Discount	2 1 8 10	
Sales Returns and Allowances	1 4 8 48	
Purchases	223 1 7 4 88	
Purchases Discount		9 2 2 14
Purchases Returns and Allowances		1 4 9 5 01
Advertising Expense	2 1 8 2 81	
Credit Card Fee Expense	3 9 5 42	
Depreciation Expense—Office Equipment		
Depreciation Expense—Store Equipment		
Insurance Expense		
Miscellaneous Expense	2 3 8 2 80	
Payroll Taxes Expense	12 7 9 7 20	
Rent Expense	5 7 1 4 03	
Salary Expense	115 3 6 4 38	
Supplies Expense—Office		
Supplies Expense—Store		
Uncollectible Accounts Expense		
Utilities Expense	3 9 7 3 68	
Federal Income Tax Expense		
Interest Income		

Name ______________________ Date ____________ Class ____________

15-1 ON YOUR OWN, p. 445

Journalizing the adjusting entries for supplies and prepaid insurance

1., 2.

ACCOUNT TITLE	DEBIT	CREDIT
Cash	18,431.35	
Petty Cash	200.00	
Accounts Receivable	38,148.21	
Merchandise Inventory	165,448.21	
Supplies—Store	5,491.19	
Prepaid Insurance	12,800.00	
Notes Receivable	7,500.00	
Interest Receivable		
Office Equipment	15,495.28	
Accumulated Depreciation—Office Equipment		6,149.00
Store Equipment	28,491.48	
Accounts Payable		8,491.04
Sales Tax Payable		4,915.22
Employee Income Tax Payable—Federal		743.00
Social Security Tax Payable		1,583.34
Medicare Tax Payable		370.30
Health Insurance Premiums Payable		360.02
Retirement Benefits Payable		363.93
Unemployment Tax Payable—Federal		232.46
Unemployment Tax Payable—State		115.38
Federal Income Tax Payable		
Dividends Payable		2,500.00
Capital Stock		50,000.00
Retained Earnings		103,807.14
Dividends	10,000.00	

(Note: Trial balance is continued on the next page.)

15-1 ON YOUR OWN (continued)

ACCOUNT TITLE	DEBIT	CREDIT
Income Summary		
Sales		768,194.26
Sales Discount	2,487.16	
Sales Returns and Allowances	3,149.25	
Purchases	395,419.20	
Purchases Discount		2,947.24
Purchases Returns and Allowances		3,498.11
Advertising Expense	24,200.00	
Credit Card Fee Expense	12,441.80	
Depreciation Expense—Office Equipment		
Depreciation Expense—Store Equipment		
Insurance Expense		
Miscellaneous Expense	6,847.14	
Payroll Taxes Expense	12,977.15	
Rent Expense	34,800.00	
Salary Expense	144,191.15	
Supplies Expense—Office		
Supplies Expense—Store		
Uncollectible Accounts Expense		
Utilities Expense	6,148.25	
Federal Income Tax Expense	18,000.00	

Name ____________________ Date ____________ Class ____________

15-1, 15-2, 15-3, and 15-4 ON YOUR OWN, pp. 445, 449, 454, and 462

15-1 Journalizing the adjusting entries for supplies and prepaid insurance

15-2 Journalizing the adjusting entries for merchandise inventory and interest receivable

15-3 Journalizing the adjusting entries for accumulated depreciation

15-4 Preparing the adjusting entry for federal income tax and an adjusted trial balance

GENERAL JOURNAL PAGE 18

	DATE		ACCOUNT TITLE	DOC. NO.	POST. REF.	DEBIT	CREDIT	
1			Adjusting Entries					1
2	20-- Dec.	31	Uncollectible Accounts Expense			4 2 2 5 00		2
3			Allowance for Uncollectible Accounts				4 2 2 5 00	3
4								4
5								5
6								6
7								7
8								8
9								9
10								10
11								11
12								12
13								13
14								14
15								15
16								16
17								17
18								18
19								19
20								20

15-3 ON YOUR OWN, p. 454

1.

Original Cost	$
Estimated Salvage Value	
Estimated Total Depreciation Expense	$
Years of Estimated Useful Life	
Annual Depreciation Expense	$

2.

Original Cost			$
Depreciation:	Year 1	$	
	Year 2		
Book Value			$

Name ______________________ Date ____________ Class ____________

15-4 ON YOUR OWN, p. 462

GENERAL LEDGER

1., 4.

ACCOUNT Allowance for Uncollectible Accounts — ACCOUNT NO. 1135

DATE		ITEM	POST. REF.	DEBIT	CREDIT	BALANCE DEBIT	BALANCE CREDIT
20-- Dec.	1	Balance	✔			208 50	

ACCOUNT Merchandise Inventory — ACCOUNT NO. 1140

DATE		ITEM	POST. REF.	DEBIT	CREDIT	BALANCE DEBIT	BALANCE CREDIT
20-- Dec.	1	Balance	✔			165 448 21	

ACCOUNT Supplies—Office — ACCOUNT NO. 1145

DATE		ITEM	POST. REF.	DEBIT	CREDIT	BALANCE DEBIT	BALANCE CREDIT
20-- Dec.	1	Balance	✔			4 148 12	

ACCOUNT Supplies—Store — ACCOUNT NO. 1150

DATE		ITEM	POST. REF.	DEBIT	CREDIT	BALANCE DEBIT	BALANCE CREDIT
20-- Dec.	1	Balance	✔			5 491 19	

ACCOUNT Prepaid Insurance — ACCOUNT NO. 1160

DATE		ITEM	POST. REF.	DEBIT	CREDIT	BALANCE DEBIT	BALANCE CREDIT
20-- Dec.	1	Balance	✔			12 800 00	

ACCOUNT Interest Receivable — ACCOUNT NO. 1175

DATE		ITEM	POST. REF.	DEBIT	CREDIT	BALANCE DEBIT	BALANCE CREDIT

15-4 ON YOUR OWN (continued)

ACCOUNT Accumulated Depreciation—Office Equipment — ACCOUNT NO. 1210

DATE		ITEM	POST. REF.	DEBIT	CREDIT	BALANCE DEBIT	BALANCE CREDIT
20-- Dec.	1	Balance	✔				6,149.00

ACCOUNT Accumulated Depreciation—Store Equipment — ACCOUNT NO. 1220

DATE		ITEM	POST. REF.	DEBIT	CREDIT	BALANCE DEBIT	BALANCE CREDIT
20-- Dec.	1	Balance	✔				12,495.00

ACCOUNT Federal Income Tax Payable — ACCOUNT NO. 2170

DATE		ITEM	POST. REF.	DEBIT	CREDIT	BALANCE DEBIT	BALANCE CREDIT

ACCOUNT Income Summary — ACCOUNT NO. 3150

DATE		ITEM	POST. REF.	DEBIT	CREDIT	BALANCE DEBIT	BALANCE CREDIT

ACCOUNT Depreciation Expense—Office Equipment — ACCOUNT NO. 6120

DATE		ITEM	POST. REF.	DEBIT	CREDIT	BALANCE DEBIT	BALANCE CREDIT

ACCOUNT Depreciation Expense—Store Equipment — ACCOUNT NO. 6125

DATE		ITEM	POST. REF.	DEBIT	CREDIT	BALANCE DEBIT	BALANCE CREDIT

Name ______________________ Date ____________ Class ____________

15-4 ON YOUR OWN (continued)

ACCOUNT Insurance Expense — ACCOUNT NO. 6130

DATE		ITEM	POST. REF.	DEBIT	CREDIT	BALANCE DEBIT	BALANCE CREDIT

ACCOUNT Supplies Expense—Office — ACCOUNT NO. 6155

DATE		ITEM	POST. REF.	DEBIT	CREDIT	BALANCE DEBIT	BALANCE CREDIT

ACCOUNT Supplies Expense—Store — ACCOUNT NO. 6160

DATE		ITEM	POST. REF.	DEBIT	CREDIT	BALANCE DEBIT	BALANCE CREDIT

ACCOUNT Uncollectible Accounts Expense — ACCOUNT NO. 6165

DATE		ITEM	POST. REF.	DEBIT	CREDIT	BALANCE DEBIT	BALANCE CREDIT

ACCOUNT Federal Income Tax Expense — ACCOUNT NO. 6205

DATE		ITEM	POST. REF.	DEBIT	CREDIT	BALANCE DEBIT	BALANCE CREDIT
20-- Dec.	1	Balance	✔			18 000 00	

ACCOUNT Interest Income — ACCOUNT NO. 7110

DATE		ITEM	POST. REF.	DEBIT	CREDIT	BALANCE DEBIT	BALANCE CREDIT
20-- Dec.	1	Balance	✔				258 00

15-4 ON YOUR OWN (continued)

3.

Total of income statement credit accounts	$
Less total of income statement debit accounts	
excluding federal income tax..	
Equals net income before federal income tax........................	$

Net Income before Federal Income Tax	–	Of the Amount Over	=	Net Income Subject to Marginal Tax Rate	×	Marginal Tax Rate	=	Marginal Income Tax
$	–	$	=	$	×		=	$

Bracket Minimum Income Tax	+	Marginal Income Tax	=	Federal Income Tax
$	+	$	=	$

Name ______________________ Date ______________ Class ______________

15-4 ON YOUR OWN (continued)

2., 5., 6.

ACCOUNT TITLE	DEBIT	CREDIT
Cash	18 431 35	
Petty Cash	200 00	
Accounts Receivable	38 148 21	
Allowance for Uncollectible Accounts		
Merchandise Inventory		
Supplies—Office		
Supplies—Store		
Prepaid Insurance		
Notes Receivable	7 500 00	
Interest Receivable		
Office Equipment	15 495 28	
Accumulated Depreciation—Office Equipment		
Store Equipment	28 491 48	
Accumulated Depreciation—Store Equipment		
Accounts Payable		8 491 04
Sales Tax Payable		4 915 22
Employee Income Tax Payable—Federal		743 00
Social Security Tax Payable		1 583 34
Medicare Tax Payable		370 30
Health Insurance Premiums Payable		360 02
Retirement Benefits Payable		363 93
Unemployment Tax Payable—Federal		232 46
Unemployment Tax Payable—State		115 38
Federal Income Tax Payable		
Dividends Payable		2 500 00
Capital Stock		50 000 00
Retained Earnings		103 807 14
Dividends	10 000 00	

(Note: Trial balance is continued on the next page.)

15-4 ON YOUR OWN (concluded)

ACCOUNT TITLE	DEBIT	CREDIT
Income Summary		
Sales		768 194 26
Sales Discount	2 487 16	
Sales Returns and Allowances	3 149 25	
Purchases	395 419 20	
Purchases Discount		2 947 24
Purchases Returns and Allowances		3 498 11
Advertising Expense	24 200 00	
Credit Card Fee Expense	12 441 80	
Depreciation Expense—Office Equipment		
Depreciation Expense—Store Equipment		
Insurance Expense		
Miscellaneous Expense	6 847 14	
Payroll Taxes Expense	12 977 15	
Rent Expense	34 800 00	
Salary Expense	144 191 15	
Supplies Expense—Office		
Supplies Expense—Store		
Uncollectible Accounts Expense		
Utilities Expense	6 148 25	
Federal Income Tax Expense		
Interest Income		

Name ______________________ Date ____________ Class ____________

15-1 APPLICATION PROBLEM (LO1, 2), p. 465

Preparing adjusting entries for supplies and prepaid insurance

1., 2.

ACCOUNT TITLE	DEBIT	CREDIT
Cash	16,448.28	
Petty Cash	300.00	
Accounts Receivable	28,419.36	
Allowance for Uncollectible Accounts		332.20
Supplies—Office	3,419.11	
Supplies—Store	4,116.25	
Prepaid Insurance	14,200.00	
Notes Receivable	4,200.00	
Interest Receivable		
Office Equipment	16,447.21	
Store Equipment	42,115.00	
Accumulated Depreciation—Store Equipment		18,441.48
Accounts Payable		7,510.94
Sales Tax Payable		2,448.11
Employee Income Tax Payable—Federal		590.00
Social Security Tax Payable		1,191.20
Medicare Tax Payable		278.59
Health Insurance Premiums Payable		270.85
Retirement Benefits Payable		273.80
Unemployment Tax Payable—Federal		174.89
Unemployment Tax Payable—State		86.80
Federal Income Tax Payable		
Dividends Payable		1,000.00
Capital Stock		20,000.00
Retained Earnings		72,649.37
Dividends	4,000.00	

(Note: Trial balance is continued on the next page.)

ACCOUNT TITLE	DEBIT	CREDIT
Income Summary		
Sales		574,801.40
Sales Discount	3,140.84	
Sales Returns and Allowances	2,479.20	
Purchases	294,418.26	
Purchases Discount		1,847.16
Purchases Returns and Allowances		2,846.51
Advertising Expense	18,200.00	
Credit Card Fee Expense	8,445.63	
Depreciation Expense—Store Equipment		
Insurance Expense		
Miscellaneous Expense	8,114.10	
Payroll Taxes Expense	12,918.25	
Rent Expense	18,200.00	
Salary Expense	108,479.50	
Supplies Expense—Office		
Supplies Expense—Store		
Utilities Expense	7,119.21	
Federal Income Tax Expense	10,000.00	
Interest Income		356.00

15-1, 15-2, 15-3, and 15-4 APPLICATION PROBLEMS, pp. 465–466

15-1 Preparing adjusting entries for supplies and prepaid insurance (LO1, 2)

15-2 Journalizing the adjusting entries for merchandise inventory and interest receivable (LO3, 4)

15-3 Journalizing the adjusting entries for accumulated depreciation (LO5, 6)

15-4 Preparing the adjusting entry for federal income tax and an adjusted trial balance (LO7, 8, 9)

GENERAL JOURNAL PAGE 20

	DATE		ACCOUNT TITLE	DOC. NO.	POST. REF.	DEBIT	CREDIT	
1			Adjusting Entries					1
2	20-- Dec.	31	Uncollectible Accounts Expense			4 225 00		2
3			Allowance for Uncollectible Accounts				4 225 00	3
4								4
5								5
6								6
7								7
8								8
9								9
10								10
11								11
12								12
13								13
14								14
15								15
16								16
17								17
18								18
19								19
20								20

15-3 APPLICATION PROBLEM, p. 465

1.

Original Cost	$
Estimated Salvage Value	
Estimated Total Depreciation Expense	$
Years of Estimated Useful Life	
Annual Depreciation Expense	$

2.

Original Cost			$
Depreciation:	Year 1	$	
	Year 2		
Book Value			$

Name ______________________ Date ______________ Class ______________

15-4 APPLICATION PROBLEM, p. 466

GENERAL LEDGER

1., 4.

ACCOUNT Allowance for Uncollectible Accounts — ACCOUNT NO. 1135

DATE		ITEM	POST. REF.	DEBIT	CREDIT	BALANCE DEBIT	BALANCE CREDIT
20-- Dec.	1	Balance	✓				332.20

ACCOUNT Merchandise Inventory — ACCOUNT NO. 1140

DATE		ITEM	POST. REF.	DEBIT	CREDIT	BALANCE DEBIT	BALANCE CREDIT
20-- Dec.	1	Balance	✓			85,114.10	

ACCOUNT Supplies—Office — ACCOUNT NO. 1145

DATE		ITEM	POST. REF.	DEBIT	CREDIT	BALANCE DEBIT	BALANCE CREDIT
20-- Dec.	1	Balance	✓			3,419.11	

ACCOUNT Supplies—Store — ACCOUNT NO. 1150

DATE		ITEM	POST. REF.	DEBIT	CREDIT	BALANCE DEBIT	BALANCE CREDIT
20-- Dec.	1	Balance	✓			4,116.25	

ACCOUNT Prepaid Insurance — ACCOUNT NO. 1160

DATE		ITEM	POST. REF.	DEBIT	CREDIT	BALANCE DEBIT	BALANCE CREDIT
20-- Dec.	1	Balance	✓			14,200.00	

ACCOUNT Interest Receivable — ACCOUNT NO. 1175

DATE		ITEM	POST. REF.	DEBIT	CREDIT	BALANCE DEBIT	BALANCE CREDIT

ACCOUNT Accumulated Depreciation—Office Equipment ACCOUNT NO. 1210

DATE		ITEM	POST. REF.	DEBIT	CREDIT	BALANCE DEBIT	BALANCE CREDIT
20-- Dec.	1	Balance	✔				5 195 00

ACCOUNT Accumulated Depreciation—Store Equipment ACCOUNT NO. 1220

DATE		ITEM	POST. REF.	DEBIT	CREDIT	BALANCE DEBIT	BALANCE CREDIT
20-- Dec.	1	Balance	✔				18 441 48

ACCOUNT Federal Income Tax Payable ACCOUNT NO. 2170

DATE		ITEM	POST. REF.	DEBIT	CREDIT	BALANCE DEBIT	BALANCE CREDIT

ACCOUNT Income Summary ACCOUNT NO. 3150

DATE		ITEM	POST. REF.	DEBIT	CREDIT	BALANCE DEBIT	BALANCE CREDIT

ACCOUNT Depreciation Expense—Office Equipment ACCOUNT NO. 6120

DATE		ITEM	POST. REF.	DEBIT	CREDIT	BALANCE DEBIT	BALANCE CREDIT

ACCOUNT Depreciation Expense—Store Equipment ACCOUNT NO. 6125

DATE		ITEM	POST. REF.	DEBIT	CREDIT	BALANCE DEBIT	BALANCE CREDIT

15-4 APPLICATION PROBLEM (continued)

ACCOUNT Insurance Expense — ACCOUNT NO. 6130

DATE		ITEM	POST. REF.	DEBIT	CREDIT	BALANCE DEBIT	BALANCE CREDIT

ACCOUNT Supplies Expense—Office — ACCOUNT NO. 6155

DATE		ITEM	POST. REF.	DEBIT	CREDIT	BALANCE DEBIT	BALANCE CREDIT

ACCOUNT Supplies Expense—Store — ACCOUNT NO. 6160

DATE		ITEM	POST. REF.	DEBIT	CREDIT	BALANCE DEBIT	BALANCE CREDIT

ACCOUNT Uncollectible Accounts Expense — ACCOUNT NO. 6165

DATE		ITEM	POST. REF.	DEBIT	CREDIT	BALANCE DEBIT	BALANCE CREDIT

ACCOUNT Federal Income Tax Expense — ACCOUNT NO. 6205

DATE		ITEM	POST. REF.	DEBIT	CREDIT	BALANCE DEBIT	BALANCE CREDIT
20-- Dec.	1	Balance	✔			10 000 00	

ACCOUNT Interest Income — ACCOUNT NO. 7110

DATE		ITEM	POST. REF.	DEBIT	CREDIT	BALANCE DEBIT	BALANCE CREDIT
20-- Dec.	1	Balance	✔				356 00

3.

Total of income statement credit accounts	$
Less total of income statement debit accounts excluding federal income tax..	
Equals net income before federal income tax.........................	$

Net Income before Federal Income Tax	–	Of the Amount Over	=	Net Income Subject to Marginal Tax Rate	×	Marginal Tax Rate	=	Marginal Income Tax
$	–	$	=	$	×		=	$

Bracket Minimum Income Tax	+	Marginal Income Tax	=	Federal Income Tax
$	+	$	=	$

Name ______________________ Date ____________ Class ____________

15-4 APPLICATION PROBLEM (continued)

2., 5., 6.

ACCOUNT TITLE	DEBIT	CREDIT
Cash	16 448 28	
Petty Cash	300 00	
Accounts Receivable	28 419 36	
Allowance for Uncollectible Accounts		
Merchandise Inventory		
Supplies—Office		
Supplies—Store		
Prepaid Insurance		
Notes Receivable	4 200 00	
Interest Receivable		
Office Equipment	16 447 21	
Accumulated Depreciation—Office Equipment		
Store Equipment	42 115 00	
Accumulated Depreciation—Store Equipment		
Accounts Payable		7 510 94
Sales Tax Payable		2 448 11
Employee Income Tax Payable—Federal		590 00
Social Security Tax Payable		1 191 20
Medicare Tax Payable		278 59
Health Insurance Premiums Payable		270 85
Retirement Benefits Payable		273 80
Unemployment Tax Payable—Federal		174 89
Unemployment Tax Payable—State		86 80
Federal Income Tax Payable		
Dividends Payable		1 000 00
Capital Stock		20 000 00
Retained Earnings		72 649 37
Dividends	4 000 00	

(Note: Trial balance is continued on the next page.)

15-4 APPLICATION PROBLEM (concluded)

ACCOUNT TITLE	DEBIT	CREDIT
Income Summary		
Sales		574 8 0 1 40
Sales Discount	3 1 4 0 84	
Sales Returns and Allowances	2 4 7 9 20	
Purchases	294 4 1 8 26	
Purchases Discount		1 8 4 7 16
Purchases Returns and Allowances		2 8 4 6 51
Advertising Expense	18 2 0 0 00	
Credit Card Fee Expense	8 4 4 5 63	
Depreciation Expense—Office Equipment		
Depreciation Expense—Store Equipment		
Insurance Expense		
Miscellaneous Expense	8 1 1 4 10	
Payroll Taxes Expense	12 9 1 8 25	
Rent Expense	18 2 0 0 00	
Salary Expense	108 4 7 9 50	
Supplies Expense—Office		
Supplies Expense—Store		
Uncollectible Accounts Expense		
Utilities Expense	7 1 1 9 21	
Federal Income Tax Expense		
Interest Income		

Name ______________________ Date ____________ Class ____________

15-M MASTERY PROBLEM (LO2, 3, 4, 6, 7, 8, 9), p. 466

Journalizing adjusting entries and preparing an adjusted trial balance

1., 2., 4., 5.

GENERAL JOURNAL PAGE 16

	DATE		ACCOUNT TITLE	DOC. NO.	POST. REF.	DEBIT	CREDIT	
1								1
2								2
3								3
4								4
5								5
6								6
7								7
8								8
9								9
10								10
11								11
12								12
13								13
14								14
15								15
16								16
17								17
18								18
19								19
20								20
21								21
22								22
23								23
24								24
25								25
26								26
27								27
28								28

3., 6.

ACCOUNT TITLE	DEBIT	CREDIT
Cash	42,489.25	
Petty Cash	200.00	
Accounts Receivable	16,418.50	
Allowance for Uncollectible Accounts		
Merchandise Inventory		
Supplies—Office		
Supplies—Store		
Prepaid Insurance		
Notes Receivable	3,200.00	
Interest Receivable		
Office Equipment	12,491.00	
Accumulated Depreciation—Office Equipment		
Store Equipment	62,194.00	
Accumulated Depreciation—Store Equipment		
Accounts Payable		4,981.26
Sales Tax Payable		2,109.05
Employee Income Tax Payable—Federal		720.00
Social Security Tax Payable		1,525.00
Medicare Tax Payable		356.82
Health Insurance Premiums Payable		346.92
Retirement Benefits Payable		350.60
Unemployment Tax Payable—Federal		224.00
Unemployment Tax Payable—State		111.18
Federal Income Tax Payable		
Dividends Payable		10,000.00
Capital Stock		20,000.00
Retained Earnings		52,826.35
Dividends	40,000.00	

(Note: Trial balance is continued on the next page.)

Name ____________ Date ________ Class ________

15-M MASTERY PROBLEM (continued)

ACCOUNT TITLE	DEBIT	CREDIT
Income Summary		
Sales		501,810.98
Sales Discount	2,148.52	
Sales Returns and Allowances	2,948.36	
Purchases	124,893.50	
Purchases Discount		2,489.14
Purchases Returns and Allowances		3,749.51
Advertising Expense	6,200.00	
Credit Card Fee Expense	6,148.25	
Depreciation Expense—Office Equipment		
Depreciation Expense—Store Equipment		
Insurance Expense		
Miscellaneous Expense	12,495.05	
Payroll Taxes Expense	16,218.18	
Rent Expense	24,800.00	
Salary Expense	138,945.50	
Supplies Expense—Office		
Supplies Expense—Store		
Uncollectible Accounts Expense		
Utilities Expense	9,482.25	
Federal Income Tax Expense		
Interest Income		

GENERAL LEDGER

2., 5.

ACCOUNT Allowance for Uncollectible Accounts — ACCOUNT NO. 1135

DATE		ITEM	POST. REF.	DEBIT	CREDIT	BALANCE DEBIT	BALANCE CREDIT
20-- Dec.	1	Balance	✔				25 60

ACCOUNT Merchandise Inventory — ACCOUNT NO. 1140

DATE		ITEM	POST. REF.	DEBIT	CREDIT	BALANCE DEBIT	BALANCE CREDIT
20-- Dec.	1	Balance	✔			51 843 50	

ACCOUNT Supplies—Office — ACCOUNT NO. 1145

DATE		ITEM	POST. REF.	DEBIT	CREDIT	BALANCE DEBIT	BALANCE CREDIT
20-- Dec.	1	Balance	✔			4 219 36	

ACCOUNT Supplies—Store — ACCOUNT NO. 1150

DATE		ITEM	POST. REF.	DEBIT	CREDIT	BALANCE DEBIT	BALANCE CREDIT
20-- Dec.	1	Balance	✔			5 148 19	

ACCOUNT Prepaid Insurance — ACCOUNT NO. 1160

DATE		ITEM	POST. REF.	DEBIT	CREDIT	BALANCE DEBIT	BALANCE CREDIT
20-- Dec.	1	Balance	✔			17 000 00	

ACCOUNT Interest Receivable — ACCOUNT NO. 1175

DATE		ITEM	POST. REF.	DEBIT	CREDIT	BALANCE DEBIT	BALANCE CREDIT

Name ______________________ Date ____________ Class ____________

15-M MASTERY PROBLEM (continued)

ACCOUNT Accumulated Depreciation—Office Equipment — ACCOUNT NO. 1210

DATE		ITEM	POST. REF.	DEBIT	CREDIT	BALANCE DEBIT	BALANCE CREDIT
20-- Dec.	1	Balance	✔				5 195 00

ACCOUNT Accumulated Depreciation—Store Equipment — ACCOUNT NO. 1220

DATE		ITEM	POST. REF.	DEBIT	CREDIT	BALANCE DEBIT	BALANCE CREDIT
20-- Dec.	1	Balance	✔				22 448 00

ACCOUNT Federal Income Tax Payable — ACCOUNT NO. 2170

DATE		ITEM	POST. REF.	DEBIT	CREDIT	BALANCE DEBIT	BALANCE CREDIT

ACCOUNT Income Summary — ACCOUNT NO. 3150

DATE		ITEM	POST. REF.	DEBIT	CREDIT	BALANCE DEBIT	BALANCE CREDIT

ACCOUNT Depreciation Expense—Office Equipment — ACCOUNT NO. 6120

DATE		ITEM	POST. REF.	DEBIT	CREDIT	BALANCE DEBIT	BALANCE CREDIT

ACCOUNT Depreciation Expense—Store Equipment — ACCOUNT NO. 6125

DATE		ITEM	POST. REF.	DEBIT	CREDIT	BALANCE DEBIT	BALANCE CREDIT

ACCOUNT Insurance Expense ACCOUNT NO. 6130

DATE		ITEM	POST. REF.	DEBIT	CREDIT	BALANCE DEBIT	BALANCE CREDIT

ACCOUNT Supplies Expense—Office ACCOUNT NO. 6155

DATE		ITEM	POST. REF.	DEBIT	CREDIT	BALANCE DEBIT	BALANCE CREDIT

ACCOUNT Supplies Expense—Store ACCOUNT NO. 6160

DATE		ITEM	POST. REF.	DEBIT	CREDIT	BALANCE DEBIT	BALANCE CREDIT

ACCOUNT Uncollectible Accounts Expense ACCOUNT NO. 6165

DATE		ITEM	POST. REF.	DEBIT	CREDIT	BALANCE DEBIT	BALANCE CREDIT

ACCOUNT Federal Income Tax Expense ACCOUNT NO. 6205

DATE		ITEM	POST. REF.	DEBIT	CREDIT	BALANCE DEBIT	BALANCE CREDIT
20-- Dec.	1	Balance	✔			30 0 0 0 00	

ACCOUNT Interest Income ACCOUNT NO. 7110

DATE		ITEM	POST. REF.	DEBIT	CREDIT	BALANCE DEBIT	BALANCE CREDIT
20-- Dec.	1	Balance	✔				2 1 4 00

Name ______________________ Date ____________ Class ____________

15-M MASTERY PROBLEM (concluded)

4.

Total of income statement credit accounts .... $ ________

Less total of income statement debit accounts
excluding federal income tax.. ________

Equals net income before federal income tax......................... $ ________

Net Income before Federal Income Tax	–	Of the Amount Over	=	Net Income Subject to Marginal Tax Rate	×	Marginal Tax Rate	=	Marginal Income Tax
$	–	$	=	$	×		=	$

Bracket Minimum Income Tax	+	Marginal Income Tax	=	Federal Income Tax
$	+	$	=	$

15-C CHALLENGE PROBLEM (LO2, 8), p. 467

Journalizing adjusting entries

1., 2., 3.

GENERAL JOURNAL

PAGE 16

	DATE		ACCOUNT TITLE	DOC. NO.	POST. REF.	DEBIT	CREDIT	
1								1
2								2
3								3
4								4
5								5
6								6
7								7
8								8
9								9
10								10
11								11
12								12
13								13
14								14
15								15
16								16
17								17
18								18
19								19
20								20
21								21
22								22
23								23
24								24
25								25
26								26
27								27
28								28

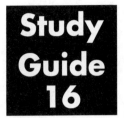

Study Guide 16

Name	Perfect Score	Your Score
Identifying Accounting Terms	11 Pts.	
Preparing Financial Statements for a Merchandising Business Organized as a Corporation	12 Pts.	
Analyzing Financial Statements for a Merchandising Business	30 Pts.	
Total	53 Pts.	

Part One—Identifying Accounting Terms

Directions: Select the one term in Column I that best fits each definition in Column II. Print the letter identifying your choice in the Answers column.

Column I	***Column II***	***Answers***
A. current liabilities	**1.** The revenue earned by a business from its normal business operations. (p. 475)	**1.** ________
B. cost of merchandise sold	**2.** The amount of sales, less sales discounts and sales returns and allowances. (p. 475)	**2.** ________
C. gross profit	**3.** The original price of all merchandise sold during a fiscal period. (p. 476)	**3.** ________
D. income from operations	**4.** The revenue remaining after cost of merchandise sold has been deducted. (p. 476)	**4.** ________
E. long-term liabilities	**5.** The expenses incurred by a business in its normal operations. (p. 478)	**5.** ________
F. net sales	**6.** The operating revenue remaining after the cost of merchandise sold and operating expenses have been deducted. (p. 478)	**6.** ________
G. operating expenses	**7.** A financial statement that shows changes in a corporation's ownership for a fiscal period. (p. 482)	**7.** ________
H. operating revenue	**8.** A value assigned to a share of stock and printed on the stock certificate. (p. 483)	**8.** ________
I. par value	**9.** Liabilities due within a short time, usually within a year. (p. 489)	**9.** ________
J. statement of stockholders' equity	**10.** Liabilities owed for more than a year. (p. 489)	**10.** ________
K. supporting schedule	**11.** A report prepared to give details about an item on a principal financial statement. (p. 492)	**11.** ________

Part Two—Preparing Financial Statements for a Merchandising Business Organized as a Corporation

Directions: Write a number from 1 to 12 to the left of each step to indicate the correct sequence of all the steps in the accounting cycle. (p. 504)

Answers

1. ______ An adjusted trial balance is prepared from the general ledger.

2. ______ A post-closing trial balance is prepared from the general ledger.

3. ______ Journal entries are posted to the accounts payable ledger, the accounts receivable ledger, and the general ledger.

4. ______ Closing entries are journalized.

5. ______ An unadjusted trial balance is prepared from the general ledger.

6. ______ Source documents are checked for accuracy, and transactions are analyzed into debit and credit parts.

7. ______ Adjusting entries are journalized.

8. ______ Financial statements are prepared from the adjusted trial balance.

9. ______ Schedules of accounts payable and accounts receivable are prepared from the subsidiary ledgers.

10. ______ Closing entries are posted to the general ledger.

11. ______ Transactions, from information on source documents, are recorded in journals.

12. ______ Adjusting entries are posted to the general ledger.

Name ______________________ Date __________ Class __________

Part Three—Analyzing Financial Statements for a Merchandising Business

Directions: Place a *T* for True or an *F* for False in the Answers column to show whether each of the following statements is true or false.

	Answers
1. Financial statements provide the primary source of information needed by owners and managers to make decisions on the future activity of a business. (p. 472)	**1.** ______
2. Reporting financial information the same way from one fiscal period to the next is an application of the accounting concept Adequate Disclosure. (p. 472)	**2.** ______
3. An income statement for a merchandising business has four main sections: operating revenue, cost of merchandise sold, operating expenses, and other revenue. (p. 473)	**3.** ______
4. The amount of sales, less sales discounts, returns, and allowances is called gross profit. (p. 475)	**4.** ______
5. Cost of merchandise sold is also known as cost of goods sold. (p. 476)	**5.** ______
6. Operating revenue less cost of merchandise sold equals net income. (p. 476)	**6.** ______
7. Calculating a ratio between gross profit and net sales enables management to compare its performance to prior fiscal periods. (p. 476)	**7.** ______
8. To calculate vertical analysis percentages on an income statement, each amount is divided by net sales. (p. 477)	**8.** ______
9. Interest earned on notes receivable is reported in the Operating Expenses section of an income statement. (p. 478)	**9.** ______
10. Total operating expenses on an income statement are deducted from gross profit to determine income from operations. (p. 478)	**10.** ______
11. Federal income tax expense is an example of an operating expense. (pp. 478–479)	**11.** ______
12. All the information required to prepare a statement of stockholders' equity is obtained from the income statement and the adjusted trial balance. (p. 482)	**12.** ______
13. A statement of stockholders' equity contains two major sections: (1) Capital Stock and (2) Retained Earnings. (p. 483)	**13.** ______
14. The beginning balance of the capital stock account is the amount of capital stock issued as of the beginning of the year. (p. 483)	**14.** ______
15. The amounts in the capital stock section of the statement of stockholders' equity are obtained from the general ledger account, Capital Stock. (p. 483)	**15.** ______
16. Net income is shown on the last line of a statement of stockholders' equity. (p. 484)	**16.** ______
17. The amount of dividends reported on a statement of stockholders' equity is obtained from the adjusted trial balance. (p. 484)	**17.** ______
18. Data needed to prepare the liabilities section of a balance sheet are obtained from an adjusted trial balance. (p. 486)	**18.** ______
19. The difference between an asset's account balance and its related contra account balance is known as its book value. (p. 487)	**19.** ______
20. A mortgage payable is an example of a current liability. (p. 489)	**20.** ______
21. The amount of dividends paid during the year is presented on the balance sheet. (p. 490)	**21.** ______
22. The amounts reported on the balance sheet in the stockholders' equity section are obtained directly from general ledger accounts. (p. 490)	**22.** ______
23. The amount owed to a certain vendor would appear on a supporting schedule. (p. 492)	**23.** ______

Answers

24. Amounts needed for the closing entries are obtained from the adjusted trial balance and from the statement of stockholders' equity. (p. 494) 24. _______

25. The Income Summary account has a normal credit balance. (p. 494) 25. _______

26. A closing entry that results in credit to Income Summary would close sales, contra purchase, and other revenue accounts. (p. 495) 26. _______

27. Closing a contra revenue account results in a credit to Income Summary. (p. 496) 27. _______

28. A corporation with net income would post a closing entry that credits Retained Earnings. (p. 498) 28. _______

29. The Dividends account is closed by recording a debit to Retained Earnings. (p. 498) 29. _______

30. In the accounting cycle, adjusting entries are posted to the general ledger prior to the preparation of the financial statements. (p. 504) 30. _______

Name ______________________ Date __________ Class __________

16-1 WORK TOGETHER, p. 481

Preparing an income statement for a merchandising business

Superior Corporation

Adjusted Trial Balance

December 31, 20--

ACCOUNT TITLE	DEBIT	CREDIT
Cash	43,355.47	
Petty Cash	200.00	
Accounts Receivable	16,305.45	
Allowance for Uncollectible Accounts		2,484.22
Merchandise Inventory	81,017.26	
Supplies—Office	777.65	
Supplies—Store	516.36	
Prepaid Insurance	2,800.00	
Notes Receivable	4,960.00	
Interest Receivable	95.00	
Office Equipment	19,916.14	
Accumulated Depreciation—Office Equipment		12,436.20
Store Equipment	47,318.49	
Accumulated Depreciation—Store Equipment		16,626.00
Accounts Payable		13,191.28
Sales Tax Payable		2,859.71
Employee Income Tax Payable		760.00
Social Security Tax Payable		1,618.45
Medicare Tax Payable		378.51
Health Insurance Premiums Payable		368.00
Retirement Benefits Payable		372.00
Unemployment Tax Payable—Federal		237.62
Unemployment Tax Payable—State		117.94
Federal Income Tax Payable		3,879.69
Dividends Payable		3,000.00
Capital Stock		82,500.00
Retained Earnings		15,283.40
Dividends	12,000.00	

(Note: Adjusted trial balance is continued on next page.)

Superior Corporation

Adjusted Trial Balance

December 31, 20--

ACCOUNT TITLE	DEBIT	CREDIT
Income Summary	5 7 7 1 89	
Sales		505 8 9 7 40
Sales Discount	1 3 1 8 55	
Sales Returns and Allowances	3 1 5 3 26	
Purchases	203 8 8 1 01	
Purchases Discount		7 3 7 71
Purchases Returns and Allowances		1 1 9 6 01
Advertising Expense	3 7 4 4 00	
Credit Card Fee Expense	5 4 7 3 76	
Depreciation Expense—Office Equipment	7 4 8 5 00	
Depreciation Expense—Store Equipment	9 8 3 0 00	
Insurance Expense	6 0 0 0 00	
Miscellaneous Expense	2 7 9 6 03	
Payroll Taxes Expense	14 3 7 5 91	
Rent Expense	6 7 2 0 00	
Salary Expense	131 9 7 8 76	
Supplies Expense—Office	2 8 6 0 89	
Supplies Expense—Store	3 5 2 3 33	
Uncollectible Accounts Expense	2 3 8 4 10	
Utilities Expense	3 9 7 2 34	
Federal Income Tax Expense	19 8 7 9 69	
Interest Income		4 6 6 20
Totals	664 4 1 0 34	664 4 1 0 34

Name ______________________ Date ______________ Class ______________

16-1 WORK TOGETHER (concluded)

1., 2.

					% OF NET SALES

16-1 ON YOUR OWN, p. 481

Preparing an income statement for a merchandising business

Eastern Imports

Adjusted Trial Balance

December 31, 20--

ACCOUNT TITLE	DEBIT	CREDIT
Cash	19,019 92	
Petty Cash	180 00	
Accounts Receivable	34,674 91	
Allowance for Uncollectible Accounts		2,650 00
Merchandise Inventory	122,461 80	
Supplies—Office	780 00	
Supplies—Store	1,323 00	
Prepaid Insurance	2,600 00	
Notes Receivable	4,464 00	
Interest Receivable	82 00	
Office Equipment	17,924 53	
Accumulated Depreciation—Office Equipment		11,941 08
Store Equipment	42,586 64	
Accumulated Depreciation—Store Equipment		15,946 40
Accounts Payable		14,872 15
Sales Tax Payable		2,573 74
Employee Income Tax Payable		684 00
Social Security Tax Payable		1,456 61
Medicare Tax Payable		340 66
Health Insurance Premiums Payable		331 20
Retirement Benefits Payable		334 80
Unemployment Tax Payable—Federal		213 86
Unemployment Tax Payable—State		106 15
Federal Income Tax Payable		1,617 90
Dividends Payable		2,700 00
Capital Stock		136,000 00
Retained Earnings		29,474 56
Dividends	24,000 00	

(Note: Adjusted trial balance is continued on next page.)

Name ______________________ Date ____________ Class ____________

16-1 ON YOUR OWN (continued)

Eastern Imports

Adjusted Trial Balance

December 31, 20--

ACCOUNT TITLE	DEBIT	CREDIT
Income Summary	5,648.44	
Sales		432,432.64
Sales Discount	1,186.70	
Sales Returns and Allowances	2,837.93	
Purchases	193,492.91	
Purchases Discount		663.94
Purchases Returns and Allowances		1,076.41
Advertising Expense	3,369.60	
Credit Card Fee Expense	4,926.38	
Depreciation Expense—Office Equipment	8,485.00	
Depreciation Expense—Store Equipment	8,830.00	
Insurance Expense	5,120.00	
Miscellaneous Expense	2,516.43	
Payroll Taxes Expense	12,938.32	
Rent Expense	6,048.00	
Salary Expense	109,485.25	
Supplies Expense—Office	2,494.69	
Supplies Expense—Store	2,512.72	
Uncollectible Accounts Expense	2,650.00	
Utilities Expense	3,575.11	
Federal Income Tax Expense	9,617.90	
Interest Income		416.08
Totals	655,832.18	655,832.18

16-1 ON YOUR OWN (concluded)

1., 2.

					% OF NET SALES

Name ______________________ Date ____________ Class ____________

16-2 WORK TOGETHER, p. 485

Preparing a statement of stockholders' equity

16-2 ON YOUR OWN, p. 485

Preparing a statement of stockholders' equity

Name ______________________ Date ____________ Class ____________

16-3 WORK TOGETHER, p. 493

Preparing a balance sheet for a corporation

16-3 ON YOUR OWN, p. 493

Preparing a balance sheet for a corporation

Name ______________________ Date __________ Class __________

16-4 WORK TOGETHER, p. 501

Journalizing closing entries

GENERAL JOURNAL PAGE

	DATE		ACCOUNT TITLE	DOC. NO.	POST. REF.	DEBIT	CREDIT	
1								1
2								2
3								3
4								4
5								5
6								6
7								7
8								8
9								9
10								10
11								11
12								12
13								13
14								14
15								15
16								16
17								17
18								18
19								19
20								20
21								21
22								22
23								23
24								24
25								25
26								26
27								27
28								28
29								29
30								30
31								31

16-4 ON YOUR OWN, p. 501

Journalizing closing entries

GENERAL JOURNAL PAGE

	DATE		ACCOUNT TITLE	DOC. NO.	POST. REF.	DEBIT	CREDIT	
1								1
2								2
3								3
4								4
5								5
6								6
7								7
8								8
9								9
10								10
11								11
12								12
13								13
14								14
15								15
16								16
17								17
18								18
19								19
20								20
21								21
22								22
23								23
24								24
25								25
26								26
27								27
28								28
29								29
30								30
31								31

Name ______________________ Date ____________ Class ____________

16-5 WORK TOGETHER, p. 505

Preparing a post-closing trial balance

ACCOUNT TITLE	DEBIT	CREDIT

16-5 ON YOUR OWN, p. 505

Preparing a post-closing trial balance

ACCOUNT TITLE	DEBIT	CREDIT

Name ____________ Date ________ Class ________

16-1 APPLICATION PROBLEM (LO1), p. 509

Preparing an income statement for a merchandising business

Top-Light Corporation

Adjusted Trial Balance

December 31, 20--

ACCOUNT TITLE	DEBIT	CREDIT
Cash	14 024 81	
Petty Cash	300 00	
Accounts Receivable	16 957 67	
Allowance for Uncollectible Accounts		2 107 00
Merchandise Inventory	88 142 54	
Supplies—Office	390 00	
Supplies—Store	750 00	
Prepaid Insurance	2 000 00	
Notes Receivable	6 110 00	
Interest Receivable	48 88	
Office Equipment	23 814 00	
Accumulated Depreciation—Office Equipment		18 609 25
Store Equipment	51 948 65	
Accumulated Depreciation—Store Equipment		23 507 84
Accounts Payable		13 718 93
Sales Tax Payable		2 574 10
Employee Income Tax Payable		790 00
Social Security Tax Payable		1 683 19
Medicare Tax Payable		393 65
Health Insurance Premiums Payable		380 00
Retirement Benefits Payable		420 00
Unemployment Tax Payable—Federal		247 13
Unemployment Tax Payable—State		122 66
Federal Income Tax Payable		907 37
Dividends Payable		4 600 00
Capital Stock		57 500 00
Retained Earnings		50 403 31

(Note: Adjusted trial balance is continued on next page.)

Top-Light Corporation

Adjusted Trial Balance

December 31, 20--

ACCOUNT TITLE	DEBIT	CREDIT
Dividends	17,200.00	
Income Summary	2,118.18	
Sales		557,900.50
Sales Discount	1,371.30	
Sales Returns and Allowances	3,279.39	
Purchases	260,036.25	
Purchases Discount		2,218.16
Purchases Returns and Allowances		3,119.45
Advertising Expense	18,411.32	
Credit Card Fee Expense	5,692.71	
Depreciation Expense—Office Equipment	5,460.00	
Depreciation Expense—Store Equipment	8,440.00	
Insurance Expense	12,000.00	
Miscellaneous Expense	4,159.31	
Payroll Taxes Expense	14,019.64	
Rent Expense	8,400.00	
Salary Expense	155,773.80	
Supplies Expense—Office	2,481.72	
Supplies Expense—Store	3,645.81	
Uncollectible Accounts Expense	1,494.12	
Utilities Expense	4,995.14	
Federal Income Tax Expense	7,907.37	
Interest Income		170.07
Totals	741,372.61	741,372.61

Name ______________________ Date ______________ Class ______________

16-1 APPLICATION PROBLEM (concluded)

1., 2.

					% OF NET SALES

16-2 APPLICATION PROBLEM (LO2), p. 509

Preparing a statement of stockholders' equity

Name ______________________ Date ____________ Class ____________

16-3 APPLICATION PROBLEM (LO3), p. 509

Preparing a balance sheet for a corporation

16-4 APPLICATION PROBLEM (LO4), p. 510

Journalizing closing entries

GENERAL JOURNAL PAGE

	DATE		ACCOUNT TITLE	DOC. NO.	POST. REF.	DEBIT	CREDIT	
1								1
2								2
3								3
4								4
5								5
6								6
7								7
8								8
9								9
10								10
11								11
12								12
13								13
14								14
15								15
16								16
17								17
18								18
19								19
20								20
21								21
22								22
23								23
24								24
25								25
26								26
27								27
28								28
29								29
30								30
31								31

Name ______________________ Date ____________ Class ____________

16-5 APPLICATION PROBLEM (LO5), p. 510

Preparing a post-closing trial balance

ACCOUNT TITLE	DEBIT	CREDIT

16-M MASTERY PROBLEM (LO1, 2, 3, 4), p. 511

Preparing financial statements and closing entries

Paulson Corporation

Adjusted Trial Balance

December 31, 20--

ACCOUNT TITLE	DEBIT	CREDIT
Cash	28,362.11	
Petty Cash	200.00	
Accounts Receivable	21,197.09	
Allowance for Uncollectible Accounts		2,514.26
Merchandise Inventory	107,177.46	
Supplies—Office	1,745.76	
Supplies—Store	1,728.27	
Prepaid Insurance	2,800.00	
Notes Receivable	8,900.00	
Interest Receivable	71.20	
Office Equipment	25,890.98	
Accumulated Depreciation—Office Equipment		23,921.56
Store Equipment	61,514.04	
Accumulated Depreciation—Store Equipment		28,664.80
Accounts Payable		17,148.66
Sales Tax Payable		3,217.62
Employee Income Tax Payable		988.00
Social Security Tax Payable		2,103.99
Medicare Tax Payable		492.06
Health Insurance Premiums Payable		478.40
Retirement Benefits Payable		483.60
Unemployment Tax Payable—Federal		308.91
Unemployment Tax Payable—State		153.32
Federal Income Tax Payable		1,519.82
Dividends Payable		5,000.00
Capital Stock		50,000.00
Retained Earnings		66,259.31

(Note: Adjusted trial balance is continued on next page.)

Name ______________________ Date ____________ Class ____________

16-M MASTERY PROBLEM (continued)

Paulson Corporation

Adjusted Trial Balance

December 31, 20--

ACCOUNT TITLE	DEBIT	CREDIT
Dividends	20,000.00	
Income Summary	5,648.44	
Sales		697,375.62
Sales Discount	1,714.12	
Sales Returns and Allowances	4,099.24	
Purchases	325,045.31	
Purchases Discount		1,959.02
Purchases Returns and Allowances		2,554.81
Advertising Expense	4,867.20	
Credit Card Fee Expense	7,115.89	
Depreciation Expense—Office Equipment	7,885.00	
Depreciation Expense—Store Equipment	9,430.00	
Insurance Expense	8,640.00	
Miscellaneous Expense	3,634.84	
Payroll Taxes Expense	18,688.68	
Rent Expense	8,736.00	
Salary Expense	184,770.26	
Supplies Expense—Office	2,984.34	
Supplies Expense—Store	3,523.33	
Uncollectible Accounts Expense	2,384.10	
Utilities Expense	5,164.04	
Federal Income Tax Expense	21,519.82	
Interest Income		293.76
Totals	905,437.52	905,437.52

16-M MASTERY PROBLEM (continued)

1., 2.

					% OF NET SALES

16-M MASTERY PROBLEM (continued)

3.

4.

Name ______________________ Date ____________ Class ____________

16-M MASTERY PROBLEM (concluded)

5.

GENERAL JOURNAL PAGE

	DATE		ACCOUNT TITLE	DOC. NO.	POST. REF.	DEBIT	CREDIT	
1								1
2								2
3								3
4								4
5								5
6								6
7								7
8								8
9								9
10								10
11								11
12								12
13								13
14								14
15								15
16								16
17								17
18								18
19								19
20								20
21								21
22								22
23								23
24								24
25								25
26								26
27								27
28								28
29								29
30								30
31								31

16-C CHALLENGE PROBLEM (LO1), p. 511

Preparing an income statement

KLT Corporation

Adjusted Trial Balance

December 31, 20--

ACCOUNT TITLE	DEBIT	CREDIT
Cash	54,194.34	
Accounts Receivable	20,381.81	
Allowance for Uncollectible Accounts		2,509.25
Merchandise Inventory	64,322.59	
Income Summary	2,642.37	
Domestic Sales		252,466.34
International Sales		325,436.34
Internet Sales		264,245.22
Sales Discount	5,214.32	
Sales Returns and Allowances	6,523.23	
Purchases	364,324.25	
Purchases Discount		6,542.16
Purchases Returns and Allowances		3,879.85
Advertising Expense	32,400.00	
Credit Card Fee Expense	7,534.23	
Depreciation Expense—Office Equipment	6,900.00	
Depreciation Expense—Store Equipment	12,500.00	
Insurance Expense	13,000.00	
Miscellaneous Expense	19,327.34	
Payroll Taxes Expense	36,230.85	
Rent Expense	24,000.00	
Salary Expense	262,542.36	
Supplies Expense	6,262.95	
Uncollectible Accounts Expense	5,390.65	
Utilities Expense	4,168.96	
Federal Income Tax Expense	6,560.99	
Interest Expense	433.96	
Interest Income		565.50
Totals	987,253.61	987,253.61

Name ______________________ Date ____________ Class ____________

16-C CHALLENGE PROBLEM (concluded)

1., 2.

					% OF NET SALES

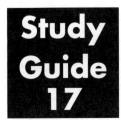

Study Guide 17

Name	Perfect Score	Your Score
Identifying Accounting Terms	20 Pts.	
Analyzing Financial Ratios	19 Pts.	
Calculating Financial Ratios	11 Pts.	
Total	50 Pts.	

Part One—Identifying Accounting Terms

Directions: Select the one term in Column I that best fits each definition in Column II. Print the letter identifying your choice in the Answers column.

Column I	Column II	Answers
A. benchmark	1. A ratio that measures the ability of a business to generate income. (p. 516)	1. ______
B. comparative financial statements	2. A standard used to compare financial performance. (p. 516)	2. ______
C. current ratio	3. Financial statements that provide information for multiple fiscal periods. (p. 517)	3. ______
D. debt ratio	4. An analysis of changes over time. (p. 517)	4. ______
E. dividend yield	5. Net income after federal income tax as a percent of net sales. (p. 517)	5. ______
F. earnings per share	6. Gross profit as a percent of net sales. (p. 518)	6. ______
G. gross margin	7. Income from operations as a percent of net sales. (p. 519)	7. ______
H. horizontal analysis	8. Total operating expenses as a percent of net sales. (p. 519)	8. ______
I. liquidity ratio	9. A ratio that measures the ability of a business to pay its long-term liabilities. (p. 526)	9. ______
J. market ratio	10. Total Liabilities divided by Total Assets. (p. 526)	10. ______
K. operating expense ratio	11. A comparison of one item on a financial statement with the same item on a previous period's financial statement. (p. 528)	11. ______
L. operating margin	12. Net income after federal income tax divided by the number of outstanding shares of stock. (p. 533)	12. ______
M. price-earnings ratio	13. A ratio that measures a corporation's financial performance in relation to the market value of its stock. (p. 534)	13. ______
N. profit margin	14. The relationship between dividends per share and market price per share. (p. 534)	14. ______
O. profitability ratio	15. The relationship between the market value per share and earnings per share of a stock. (p. 534)	15. ______
P. quick assets	16. A ratio that measures the ability of a business to pay its current financial obligations. (p. 535)	16. ______
Q. quick ratio	17. The amount of total current assets less total current liabilities. (p. 535)	17. ______
R. solvency ratio	18. A ratio that measures the relationship of current assets to current liabilities. (p. 535)	18. ______
S. trend analysis	19. Cash and other current assets that can be quickly converted into cash. (p. 535)	19. ______
T. working capital	20. A ratio that measures the relationship of quick assets to current liabilities. (p. 535)	20. ______

Part Two—Analyzing Financial Ratios

Directions: Place a *T* for True or an *F* for False in the Answers column to show whether each of the following statements is true or false.

	Answers
1. Vertical analysis ratios are an example of a profitability ratio. (p. 516)	**1.** ________
2. A benchmark ratio can be stated as a single value or a range of values. (p. 516)	**2.** ________
3. To perform vertical analysis on an income statement, each amount is divided by net sales. (p. 516)	**3.** ________
4. An increase in merchandise costs reduces the gross margin. (p. 518)	**4.** ________
5. Gross profit is also referred to as the rate of return on sales. (p. 518)	**5.** ________
6. The operating margin gives investors the best indication of how effectively a business is earning a profit from its normal business operations. (p. 519)	**6.** ________
7. Best Company's benchmark operating expense ratio is between 29.0% and 31.0%. A decline in its operating expense ratio from 34.5% to 33.6% is a favorable trend. (p. 519)	**7.** ________
8. Reducing the amount of operating expenses always has a positive impact on a business. (p. 520)	**8.** ________
9. A business should never make a business decision for the sole purpose of meeting a benchmark ratio. (p. 524)	**9.** ________
10. A vertical analysis ratio for accounts receivable above the target range may indicate that ThreeGreen is too restrictive in extending credit to its customers. (p. 524)	**10.** ________
11. Investors use the debt ratio to rate the ability of the business to pay its current and long-term liabilities. (p. 526)	**11.** ________
12. The debt ratio is an example of a solvency ratio. (p. 526)	**12.** ________
13. Best Company's target range for its debt ratio is 20.0% to 25.0%. The company's debt ratio decreased from 34.5% to 26.7%. This is an unfavorable trend. (p. 526)	**13.** ________
14. A horizontal analysis ratio is calculated by dividing the difference between the current and prior period amounts by the current period amount. (p. 528)	**14.** ________
15. EPS is the most widely recognized measure of a corporation's financial performance. (p. 533)	**15.** ________
16. A corporation's earnings per share can only be compared to the earnings per share of other corporations in the same industry. (p. 533)	**16.** ________
17. The dividend yield is an example of a market ratio. (p. 534)	**17.** ________
18. Investors are willing to pay a higher P/E ratio for income stocks than for growth stocks. (p. 534)	**18.** ________
19. The income statement is the primary source of data to calculate liquidity ratios. (p. 535)	**19.** ________

Name ______________________ Date ____________ Class ____________

Part Three—Calculating Financial Ratios

Directions: For each of the following items, select the choice that best completes the statement. Print the letter identifying your choice in the Answers column.

Selected financial information for Lambert Company is presented below.

Sales	$840,000.00
Cost of Merchandise Sold	$400,000.00
Total Operating Expenses	$360,000.00
Net Income after Federal Income Taxes	$68,000.00
Quick Assets	$38,000.00
Current Assets	$95,000.00
Total Assets	$175,000.00
Total Liabilities (all current)	$25,000.00
Dividends per Share	$3.00
Market Price	$60.00
Number of Shares Outstanding	10,000

Answers

1. The earnings per share is — 1. ______
(A) $3.00 (C) $6.80
(B) $14.70 (D) 8.1% (p. 533)

2. The debt ratio is — 2. ______
(A) 26.3% (C) 7.00
(B) 14.3% (D) 17.0% (p. 526)

3. The current ratio is — 3. ______
(A) $70,000.00 (C) 54.3%
(B) 0.74 (D) 3.80 (p. 535)

4. The dividend yield is — 4. ______
(A) 5.00% (C) 20.00%
(B) 0.03% (D) 10.00% (p. 534)

5. The gross margin is — 5. ______
(A) 42.9% (C) 52.4%
(B) 9.5% (D) 54.3% (p. 518)

6. The price-earnings ratio is — 6. ______
(A) 8.8 (C) 5.0%
(B) 17.6 (D) 11.3% (p. 534)

7. The operating margin is — 7. ______
(A) 19.0% (C) 54.3%
(B) 42.9% (D) 9.5% (p. 519)

8. The working capital is — 8. ______
(A) $95,000.00 (C) $120,000.00
(B) $70,000.00 (D) 26.3% (p. 535)

9. The operating expense ratio is — 9. ______
(A) 54.3% (C) 42.9%
(B) 47.6% (D) 9.5% (p. 519)

10. The gross profit margin is — 10. ______
(A) 52.4% (C) 47.6%
(B) 54.3% (D) 42.9% (p. 518)

11. The quick ratio is — 11. ______
(A) 0.4 (C) 0.2
(B) 1.5 (D) 2.5 (p. 535)

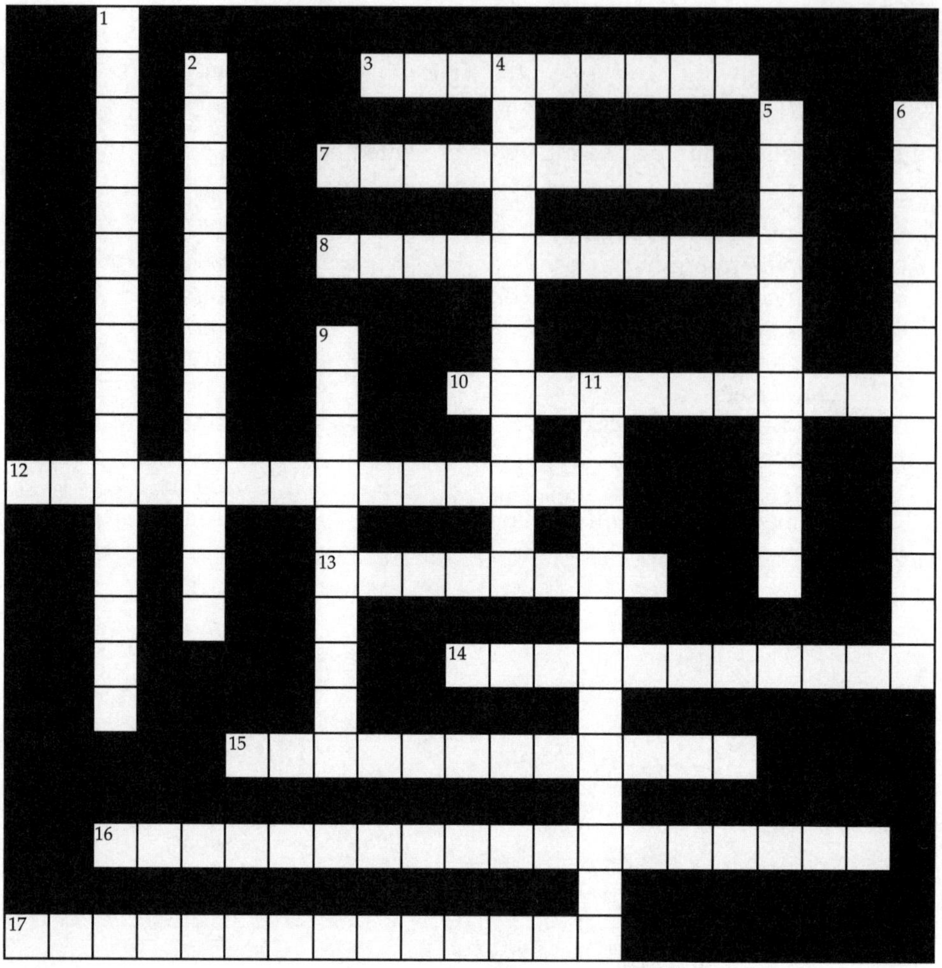

Across

3. A standard used to compare financial performance.
7. Total liabilities divided by total assets.
8. A ratio that measures a corporation's financial performance in relation to the market value of its stock.
10. Gross profit as a percent of net sales.
12. The amount of total current assets less total current liabilities.
13. The movement of funds from one qualified retirement plan to another.
14. Cash and other current assets that can be quickly converted into cash.
15. Net income after federal income tax as a percent of net sales.
16. A ratio that measures the ability of a business to generate income.
17. A ratio that measures the ability of a business to pay its current financial obligations.

Down

1. Net income after federal income tax divided by the number of outstanding shares of stock.
2. The relationship between dividends per share and market price per share.
4. A ratio that measures the relationship of current assets to current liabilities.
5. The amount of dividends divided by net income.
6. An analysis of changes over time.
9. A ratio that measures the relationship of quick assets to current liabilities.
11. A ratio that measures the ability of a business to pay its long-term liabilities.

Name ______________________ Date ______________ Class ______________

17-1 WORK TOGETHER, p. 521

Analyzing an income statement

1.

Tri-State Pipe

Comparative Income Statement

For Years Ended December 31, 20-- and 20--

	Current Year		Prior Year	
	Amount	Percent	Amount	Percent
Net Sales	659 470 53	100.0	642 189 81	100.0
Cost of Merchandise Sold	321 034 21		301 843 28	
Gross Profit	338 436 32		340 346 53	
Operating Expenses:				
Advertising Expense	24 981 05	3.8	23 149 84	3.6
Credit Card Fee Expense	6 977 95	1.1	6 819 25	1.1
Depreciation Expense—Office Equipment	7 850 00	1.2	7 650 00	1.2
Depreciation Expense—Store Equipment	6 490 00	1.0	6 080 00	0.9
Insurance Expense	8 400 00	1.3	8 200 00	1.3
Miscellaneous Expense	3 826 79	0.6	4 194 19	0.7
Payroll Taxes Expense	8 298 94	1.3	8 568 54	1.3
Rent Expense	8 447 55	1.3	8 400 00	1.3
Salary Expense	92 194 99		95 190 11	
Supplies Expense—Office	3 949 22	0.6	4 109 28	0.6
Supplies Expense—Store	4 989 92	0.8	4 219 10	0.7
Uncollectible Accounts Expense	16 487 08	2.5	12 197 16	1.9
Utilities Expense	5 269 69	0.8	4 910 82	0.8
Total Operating Expenses	198 163 18		193 688 29	
Income from Operations	140 273 14		146 658 24	
Other Revenue	598 78	0.1	449 14	0.1
Net Income before Federal Income Tax	140 871 92	21.4	147 107 38	22.9
Less Federal Income Tax Expense	38 190 05	5.8	40 621 88	6.3
Net Income after Federal Income Tax	102 681 87	15.6	106 485 50	16.6

2.

Ratio	Acceptable Range		Actual Ratio		Favorable Trend	Within Target Range
	Low	High	Current Year	Prior Year		
Gross margin	50.4%	52.0%				
Operating expenses	27.0%	29.0%				
Operating margin	21.4%	25.0%				

17-1 ON YOUR OWN, p. 521

Analyzing an income statement

1.

PBH Corporation

Comparative Income Statement

For Years Ended December 31, 20-- and 20--

	Current Year		Prior Year	
	Amount	Percent	Amount	Percent
Net Sales	747,923.57	100.0	694,841.18	100.0
Cost of Merchandise Sold	339,418.69		318,189.99	
Gross Profit	408,504.88		376,651.19	
Operating Expenses:				
Advertising Expense	9,655.70	1.3	11,084.92	1.6
Credit Card Fee Expense	7,467.60	1.0	5,914.81	0.9
Depreciation Expense—Office Equipment	4,550.00	0.6	4,250.00	0.6
Depreciation Expense—Store Equipment	6,830.00	0.9	6,710.00	1.0
Insurance Expense	13,126.68	1.8	13,014.92	1.9
Miscellaneous Expense	4,192.71	0.6	5,148.61	0.7
Payroll Taxes Expense	9,627.46	1.3	8,765.28	1.3
Rent Expense	8,447.55	1.1	7,848.00	1.1
Salary Expense	106,953.84		97,375.74	
Supplies Expense—Office	4,396.25	0.6	4,184.19	0.6
Supplies Expense—Store	5,353.08	0.7	5,019.71	0.7
Uncollectible Accounts Expense	8,042.78	1.1	7,319.36	1.1
Utilities Expense	9,823.69	1.3	9,220.08	1.3
Total Operating Expenses	198,467.34		185,855.62	
Income from Operations	210,037.54		190,795.57	
Other Revenue	475.33	0.1	662.08	0.1
Net Income before Federal Income Tax	210,512.87	28.1	191,457.65	27.6
Less Federal Income Tax Expense	65,350.02	8.7	57,918.48	8.3
Net Income after Federal Income Tax	145,162.85	19.4	133,539.17	19.2

2.

Ratio	Acceptable Range		Actual Ratio		Favorable Trend	Within Target Range
	Low	High	Current Year	Prior Year		
Gross margin	54.2%	54.9%				
Operating expenses	25.0%	26.0%				
Operating margin	28.2%	29.9%				

Name ______________________ Date ____________ Class ____________

17-2 WORK TOGETHER, p. 527

Analyzing a balance sheet

1.

Tri-State Pipe
Comparative Balance Sheet
December 31, 20-- and 20--

	Current Year		Prior Year	
	Amount	Percent	Amount	Percent
ASSETS				
Current Assets:				
Cash	27,413.71	12.7	25,238.46	14.0
Petty Cash	250.00	0.1	200.00	0.1
Accounts Receivable (net)	18,543.50		16,198.38	
Merchandise Inventory	105,111.94		99,194.10	
Supplies—Office	623.58	0.3	695.18	0.4
Supplies—Store	487.52	0.2	447.15	0.2
Prepaid Insurance	2,800.00	1.3	1,200.00	0.7
Notes Receivable	6,355.00	2.9	2,400.00	1.3
Interest Receivable	95.65	0.0	62.50	0.0
Total Current Assets	161,680.90		145,635.77	
Plant Assets:				
Office Equipment (net)	11,978.55	5.5	12,918.64	7.2
Store Equipment (net)	42,410.83	19.6	21,948.39	12.2
Total Plant Assets	54,389.38		34,867.03	
Total Assets	216,070.28	100.0	180,502.80	100.0
LIABILITIES				
Current Liabilities:				
Accounts Payable	16,633.44	7.7	11,889.95	6.6
Sales Tax Payable	3,589.68	1.7	3,281.18	1.8
Employee Income Tax Payable	988.00	0.5	926.00	0.5
Social Security Tax Payable	2,071.04	1.0	1,946.78	1.1
Medicare Tax Payable	484.36	0.2	455.30	0.3
Health Insurance Premiums Payable	463.00	0.2	435.00	0.2
Retirement Benefits Payable	465.00	0.2	437.00	0.2
Unemployment Tax Payable—Federal	304.06	0.1	285.82	0.2
Unemployment Tax Payable—State	150.92	0.1	141.86	0.1
Federal Income Tax Payable	3,683.00	1.7	6,148.00	3.4
Dividends Payable	20,000.00	9.3	10,000.00	5.5
Total Liabilities	48,832.50		35,946.89	
STOCKHOLDERS' EQUITY				
Capital Stock	25,000.00	11.6	25,000.00	13.9
Retained Earnings	142,237.78	65.8	119,555.91	66.2
Total Stockholders' Equity	167,237.78		144,555.91	
Total Liabilities and Stockholders' Equity	216,070.28	100.0	180,502.80	100.0

17-2 WORK TOGETHER (concluded)

2.

	Acceptable Range		Actual Ratio		Favorable Trend	Within Target Range
	Low	High	Current Year	Prior Year		
Accounts receivable	12.0%	14.0%				
Merchandise inventory	50.0%	55.0%				
Total current assets	73.0%	76.0%				
Total plant assets	24.0%	27.0%				
Total liabilities	20.0%	25.0%				
Total stockholders' equity	75.0%	80.0%				

Name ______________________ Date ____________ Class ____________

17-2 ON YOUR OWN, p. 527

Analyzing a balance sheet

1.

PBH Corporation

Comparative Balance Sheet

December 31, 20-- and 20--

	Current Year		Prior Year	
	Amount	Percent	Amount	Percent
ASSETS				
Current Assets:				
Cash	42,250.56	12.6	22,965.32	9.2
Petty Cash	500.00	0.1	500.00	0.2
Accounts Receivable (net)	24,918.33		22,918.35	
Merchandise Inventory	142,894.19		109,718.25	
Supplies—Office	624.00	0.2	258.00	0.1
Supplies—Store	995.00	0.3	1,095.00	0.4
Prepaid Insurance	3,400.00	1.0	3,200.00	1.3
Notes Receivable	10,950.00	3.3	6,498.00	2.6
Interest Receivable	109.50	0.0	88.25	0.0
Total Current Assets	226,641.58		167,241.17	
Plant Assets:				
Office Equipment (net)	44,918.10	13.4	36,991.18	14.8
Store Equipment (net)	62,988.14	18.8	45,194.99	18.1
Total Plant Assets	107,906.24		82,186.17	
Total Assets	334,547.82	100.0	249,427.34	100.0
LIABILITIES				
Current Liabilities:				
Accounts Payable	14,379.90	4.3	36,198.74	14.5
Sales Tax Payable	6,562.36	2.0	6,129.19	2.5
Employee Income Tax Payable	1,852.00	0.6	1,703.00	0.7
Social Security Tax Payable	3,893.56	1.2	3,582.07	1.4
Medicare Tax Payable	910.60	0.3	837.75	0.3
Health Insurance Premiums Payable	870.00	0.3	800.40	0.3
Retirement Benefits Payable	874.00	0.3	804.08	0.3
Unemployment Tax Payable—Federal	571.64	0.2	525.90	0.2
Unemployment Tax Payable—State	283.72	0.1	261.02	0.1
Federal Income Tax Payable	296.00	0.1	8,194.00	3.3
Dividends Payable	8,000.00	2.4	7,500.00	3.0
Total Liabilities	38,493.78		66,536.15	
STOCKHOLDERS' EQUITY				
Capital Stock	150,000.00	44.8	150,000.00	60.1
Retained Earnings	146,054.04	43.7	32,891.19	13.2
Total Stockholders' Equity	296,054.04		182,891.19	
Total Liabilities and Stockholders' Equity	334,547.82	100.0	249,427.34	100.0

17-2 ON YOUR OWN (concluded)

2.

	Acceptable Range		Actual Ratio		Favorable Trend	Within Target Range
	Low	High	Current Year	Prior Year		
Accounts receivable	12.0%	14.0%				
Merchandise inventory	40.0%	45.0%				
Total current assets	60.0%	68.0%				
Total plant assets	32.0%	40.0%				
Total liabilities	25.0%	30.0%				
Total stockholders' equity	70.0%	75.0%				

Name ______________________ Date ____________ Class ____________

17-3 WORK TOGETHER, p. 532

Analyzing financial statements using horizontal analysis

1.

Tri-State Pipe

Comparative Income Statement

For Years Ended December 31, 20-- and 20--

	Current Year	Prior Year	Increase (Decrease) Amount	Increase (Decrease) Percent
Net Sales	659,470.53	642,189.81		
Cost of Merchandise Sold	321,034.21	301,843.28		
Gross Profit	338,436.32	340,346.53		
Operating Expenses:				
Advertising Expense	24,981.05	23,149.84		
Credit Card Fee Expense	6,977.95	6,819.25	158.70	2.3
Depreciation Expense—Office Equipment	7,850.00	7,650.00	200.00	2.6
Depreciation Expense—Store Equipment	6,490.00	6,080.00	410.00	6.7
Insurance Expense	8,400.00	8,200.00	200.00	2.4
Miscellaneous Expense	3,826.79	4,194.19	(367.40)	(8.8)
Payroll Taxes Expense	8,298.94	8,568.54	(269.60)	(3.1)
Rent Expense	8,447.55	8,400.00	47.55	0.6
Salary Expense	92,194.99	95,190.11		
Supplies Expense—Office	3,949.22	4,109.28	(160.06)	(3.9)
Supplies Expense—Store	4,989.92	4,219.10	770.82	18.3
Uncollectible Accounts Expense	16,487.08	12,197.16		
Utilities Expense	5,269.69	4,910.82	358.87	7.3
Total Operating Expenses	198,163.18	193,688.29	4,474.89	2.3
Income from Operations	140,273.14	146,658.24		
Other Revenue	598.78	449.14	149.64	33.3
Net Income before Federal Income Tax	140,871.92	147,107.38	(6,235.46)	(4.2)
Less Federal Income Tax Expense	38,190.05	40,621.88	(2,431.83)	(6.0)
Net Income after Federal Income Tax	102,681.87	106,485.50	(3,803.63)	(3.6)

17-3 ON YOUR OWN, p. 532

Analyzing financial statements using horizontal analysis

1.

Tri-State Pipe

Comparative Balance Sheet

December 31, 20-- and 20--

	Current Year	Prior Year	Increase (Decrease) Amount	Increase (Decrease) Percent
ASSETS				
Current Assets:				
Cash	27,413.71	25,238.46	2,175.25	8.6
Petty Cash	250.00	200.00	50.00	25.0
Accounts Receivable (net)	18,543.50	16,198.38		
Merchandise Inventory	105,111.94	99,194.10		
Supplies—Office	623.58	695.18	(71.60)	(10.3)
Supplies—Store	487.52	447.15	40.37	9.0
Prepaid Insurance	2,800.00	1,200.00	1,600.00	133.3
Notes Receivable	6,355.00	2,400.00	3,955.00	164.8
Interest Receivable	95.65	62.50	33.15	53.0
Total Current Assets	161,680.90	145,635.77		
Plant Assets:				
Office Equipment (net)	11,978.55	12,918.64	(940.09)	(7.3)
Store Equipment (net)	42,410.83	21,948.39	20,462.44	93.2
Total Plant Assets	54,389.38	34,867.03		
Total Assets	216,070.28	180,502.80	35,567.48	19.7
LIABILITIES				
Current Liabilities:				
Accounts Payable	16,633.44	11,889.95	4,743.49	39.9
Sales Tax Payable	3,589.68	3,281.18	308.50	9.4
Employee Income Tax Payable	988.00	926.00	62.00	6.7
Social Security Tax Payable	2,071.04	1,946.78	124.26	6.4
Medicare Tax Payable	484.36	455.30	29.06	6.4
Health Insurance Premiums Payable	463.00	435.00	28.00	6.4
Retirement Benefits Payable	465.00	437.00	28.00	6.4
Unemployment Tax Payable—Federal	304.06	285.82	18.24	6.4
Unemployment Tax Payable—State	150.92	141.86	9.06	6.4
Federal Income Tax Payable	3,683.00	6,148.00	(2,465.00)	(40.1)
Dividends Payable	20,000.00	10,000.00	10,000.00	100.0
Total Liabilities	48,832.50	35,946.89		
STOCKHOLDERS' EQUITY				
Capital Stock	25,000.00	25,000.00	—	0.0
Retained Earnings	142,237.78	119,555.91	22,681.87	19.0
Total Stockholders' Equity	167,237.78	144,555.91		
Total Liabilities and Stockholders' Equity	216,070.28	180,502.80	35,567.48	19.7

Name _______________ Date _______ Class _______

17-4 WORK TOGETHER, p. 537

Analyzing financial statements using financial ratios

1., 2.

	Current Year	Prior Year	Increase over Prior Year (Yes or No)	Evaluation
Earnings per share		$3.26		
Dividend yield		6.63%		
Price-earnings ratio		9.5		

3., 4.

	Acceptable Range		Actual Ratio	Within Target Range
	Low	High		
Working capital	$150,000.00	$200,000.00		
Current ratio	1.50	2.00		
Quick ratio	1.00	1.50		

17-4 ON YOUR OWN, p. 537

Analyzing financial statements using financial ratios

1., 2.

	Current Year	Prior Year	Increase over Prior Year (Yes or No)	Evaluation
Earnings per share		$0.56		
Dividend yield		0.12%		
Price-earnings ratio		44.7		

3., 4.

	Acceptable Range		Actual Ratio	Within Target Range?
	Low	High		
Working capital	$1,200,000.00	$1,800,000.00		
Current ratio	1.30	1.70		
Quick ratio	1.00	1.40		

Name ________________ Date ________ Class ________

17-1 APPLICATION PROBLEM (LO1), p. 541

Analyzing an income statement

1.

TR's Quik Mart

Comparative Income Statement

For Years Ended December 31, 20-- and 20--

	Current Year Amount	Current Year Percent	Prior Year Amount	Prior Year Percent
Net Sales	979,292.15	100.0	951,848.08	100.0
Cost of Merchandise Sold	703,779.06		673,184.19	
Gross Profit	275,513.09		278,663.89	
Operating Expenses:				
Advertising Expense	3,101.00	0.3	15,481.18	1.6
Credit Card Fee Expense	14,914.28	1.5	13,498.09	1.4
Depreciation Expense—Office Equipment	3,418.00	0.3	2,180.00	0.2
Depreciation Expense—Store Equipment	4,198.00	0.4	3,220.00	0.3
Insurance Expense	6,200.00	0.6	6,000.00	0.6
Miscellaneous Expense	12,748.14	1.3	14,188.07	1.5
Payroll Taxes Expense	8,834.84	0.9	8,027.91	0.8
Rent Expense	18,000.00	1.8	18,000.00	1.9
Salary Expense	98,148.50		89,184.08	
Supplies Expense—Office	2,148.21	0.2	1,848.66	0.2
Supplies Expense—Store	9,418.19	1.0	10,198.17	1.1
Uncollectible Accounts Expense	1,480.00	0.2	914.00	0.1
Utilities Expense	6,848.89	0.7	6,871.09	0.7
Total Operating Expenses	189,458.05		189,611.25	
Income from Operations	86,055.04		89,052.64	
Other Revenue	92.00	0.0	22.50	0.0
Net Income before Federal Income Tax	86,147.04	8.8	89,075.14	9.4
Less Federal Income Tax Expense	17,539.99	1.8	18,527.90	1.9
Net Income after Federal Income Tax	68,607.05	7.0	70,547.24	7.4

2.

Ratio	Acceptable Range Low	Acceptable Range High	Actual Ratio Current Year	Actual Ratio Prior Year	Favorable Trend	Within Target Range
Gross margin	27.5%	28.0%				
Operating expenses	18.8%	19.5%				
Operating margin	8.0%	9.2%				

17-2 APPLICATION PROBLEM (LO2, 3), p. 541

Analyzing a balance sheet

1.

TR's Quick Mart

Comparative Balance Sheet

December 31, 20-- and 20--

	Current Year		Prior Year	
	Amount	Percent	Amount	Percent
ASSETS				
Current Assets:				
Cash	33,178.76	8.6	40,217.86	10.8
Petty Cash	300.00	0.1	300.00	0.1
Accounts Receivable (net)	7,992.17	2.1	6,489.38	1.7
Merchandise Inventory	248,911.08		231,944.19	
Supplies—Office	1,490.00	0.4	1,690.00	0.5
Supplies—Store	3,489.00	0.9	3,320.00	0.9
Prepaid Insurance	2,600.00	0.7	2,500.00	0.7
Notes Receivable	6,184.00	1.6	1,840.00	0.5
Interest Receivable	95.00	0.0	10.50	0.0
Total Current Assets	304,240.01		288,311.93	
Plant Assets:				
Office Equipment (net)	14,720.50	3.8	16,948.50	4.5
Store Equipment (net)	66,691.25	17.3	68,194.25	18.3
Total Plant Assets	81,411.75		85,142.75	
Total Assets	385,651.76	100.0	373,454.68	100.0
LIABILITIES				
Current Liabilities:				
Accounts Payable	32,178.04	8.3	15,918.91	4.3
Sales Tax Payable	4,194.24	1.1	4,098.99	1.1
Employee Income Tax Payable	1,020.00	0.3	999.00	0.3
Social Security Tax Payable	2,180.44	0.6	2,136.83	0.6
Medicare Tax Payable	509.95	0.1	499.74	0.1
Health Insurance Premiums Payable	488.00	0.1	478.24	0.1
Retirement Benefits Payable	474.00	0.1	464.52	0.1
Unemployment Tax Payable—Federal	320.13	0.1	313.72	0.1
Unemployment Tax Payable—State	158.89	0.0	155.71	0.0
Federal Income Tax Payable	4,980.00	1.3	1,848.00	0.5
Dividends Payable	20,000.00	5.2	16,000.00	4.3
Total Liabilities	66,503.69		42,913.66	
STOCKHOLDERS' EQUITY				
Capital Stock	200,000.00	51.9	200,000.00	53.6
Retained Earnings	119,148.07	30.9	130,541.02	35.0
Total Stockholders' Equity	319,148.07		330,541.02	
Total Liabilities and Stockholders' Equity	385,651.76	100.0	373,454.68	100.0

Name ______________________ Date ____________ Class ____________

17-2 APPLICATION PROBLEM (concluded)

2.

	Acceptable Range		Actual Ratio		Favorable Trend	Within Target Range
	Low	High	Current Year	Prior Year		
Merchandise inventory	65.0%	68.0%				
Total current assets	76.0%	78.0%				
Total plant assets	22.0%	24.0%				
Total liabilities	15.0%	20.0%				
Total stockholders' equity	80.0%	85.0%				

17-3 APPLICATION PROBLEM (LO4, 5), p. 541

Analyzing financial statements using horizontal analysis

1.

Vector Industries

Comparative Income Statement

For Years Ended December 31, 20-- and 20--

	Current Year	Prior Year	Increase (Decrease)	
			Amount	Percent
Net Sales	721,199.15	558,365.40		
Cost of Merchandise Sold	348,117.38	228,424.84		
Gross Profit	373,081.77	329,940.56		
Operating Expenses:				
Advertising Expense	25,002.23	24,719.24	282.99	1.1
Credit Card Fee Expense	7,247.31	5,607.40	1,639.91	29.2
Depreciation Expense—Office Equipment	8,030.00	7,850.00	180.00	2.3
Depreciation Expense—Store Equipment	6,920.00	6,750.00	170.00	2.5
Insurance Expense	8,868.04	8,129.78	738.26	9.1
Miscellaneous Expense	3,996.67	5,474.82		
Payroll Taxes Expense	15,214.27	15,418.58		
Rent Expense	24,000.00	24,000.00		
Salary Expense	169,019.10	166,138.42		
Supplies Expense—Office	4,245.08	3,517.48	727.60	20.7
Supplies Expense—Store	5,273.77	5,028.48	245.29	4.9
Uncollectible Accounts Expense	17,045.17	13,481.04	3,564.13	26.4
Utilities Expense	5,539.80	6,207.75	(667.95)	(10.8)
Total Operating Expenses	300,401.44	292,322.99	8,078.45	2.8
Income from Operations	72,680.33	37,617.57	35,062.76	93.2
Other Revenue	158.39	148.18	10.21	6.9
Net Income before Federal Income Tax	72,838.72	37,765.75		
Less Federal Income Tax Expense	13,209.68	5,664.86		
Net Income after Federal Income Tax	59,629.04	32,100.89		

Name ______________________ Date ______________ Class ______________

17-3 APPLICATION PROBLEM (concluded)

2.

Vector Industries

Comparative Balance Sheet

December 31, 20-- and 20--

	Current Year	Prior Year	Increase (Decrease)	
			Amount	Percent
ASSETS				
Current Assets:				
Cash	51,989.62	15,445.82	36,543.80	236.6
Petty Cash	500.00	300.00	200.00	66.7
Accounts Receivable (net)	16,489.18	13,198.18		
Merchandise Inventory	121,843.06	116,164.49		
Supplies—Office	521.00	552.00		
Supplies—Store	411.00	348.00	63.00	18.1
Prepaid Insurance	2,800.00	2,400.00	400.00	16.7
Notes Receivable	1,850.00	3,200.00	(1,350.00)	(42.2)
Interest Receivable	14.00	26.00	(12.00)	(46.2)
Total Current Assets	196,417.86	151,634.49	44,783.37	29.5
Plant Assets:				
Office Equipment (net)	24,918.18	21,894.18	3,024.00	13.8
Store Equipment (net)	32,194.48	36,914.13	(4,719.65)	
Total Plant Assets	57,112.66	58,808.31	(1,695.65)	(2.9)
Total Assets	253,530.52	210,442.80	43,087.72	20.5
LIABILITIES				
Current Liabilities:				
Accounts Payable	10,808.04	18,486.17		
Sales Tax Payable	4,030.07	3,249.25		
Employee Income Tax Payable	982.00	920.00		
Social Security Tax Payable	2,319.18	2,108.18	211.00	10.0
Medicare Tax Payable	489.27	444.75	44.52	10.0
Health Insurance Premiums Payable	466.00	424.00	42.00	9.9
Retirement Benefits Payable	418.00	380.00	38.00	10.0
Unemployment Tax Payable—Federal	282.57	256.86	25.71	10.0
Unemployment Tax Payable—State	140.25	127.49	12.76	10.0
Federal Income Tax Payable	6,148.00	228.00	5,920.00	2,596.5
Dividends Payable	4,000.00	4,000.00	—	0.0
Total Liabilities	30,083.38	30,624.70	(541.32)	(1.8)
STOCKHOLDERS' EQUITY				
Capital Stock	50,000.00	50,000.00	—	0.0
Retained Earnings	173,447.14	129,818.10	43,629.04	33.6
Total Stockholders' Equity	223,447.14	179,818.10	43,629.04	24.3
Total Liabilities and Stockholders' Equity	253,530.52	210,442.80	43,087.72	20.5

17-4 APPLICATION PROBLEM (LO6, 7, 8), p. 541

Analyzing financial statements using financial ratios

1., 2.

	Current Year	Prior Year	Increase over Prior Year (Yes or No)	Evaluation
Earnings per share		$3.29		
Dividend yield		5.87%		
Price-earnings ratio		12.4		

3., 4.

	Acceptable Range		Actual Ratio	Within Target Range
	Low	High		
Working capital	$900,000.00	$1,100,000.00		
Current ratio	1.40	1.60		
Quick ratio	1.00	1.30		

Name ______________________ Date ____________ Class ____________

17-M MASTERY PROBLEM (LO1, 2, 3, 4, 5, 6, 7, 8), p. 542

Analyzing financial statements

1.

Aqua Products, Inc.

Comparative Income Statement

For Years Ended December 31, 20-- and 20--

	Current Year Amount	Current Year Percent	Prior Year Amount	Prior Year Percent
Net Sales	838,941.16		774,827.66	
Cost of Merchandise Sold	391,491.71		366,608.74	
Gross Profit	447,449.45		408,218.92	
Operating Expenses:				
Depreciation Expense	24,600.00		22,560.00	
Office Expense	10,491.18		9,742.49	
Salaries and Payroll Tax Expense	204,184.58		192,919.43	
Store Expense	169,184.15		170,194.55	
Total Operating Expenses	408,459.91		395,416.47	
Income from Operations	38,989.54		12,802.45	
Other Revenue	642.00		228.00	
Net Income before Federal Income Tax	39,631.54		13,030.45	
Less Federal Income Tax Expense	5,944.73		1,954.57	
Net Income after Federal Income Tax	33,686.81		11,075.88	

Aqua Products, Inc.
Comparative Balance Sheet
December 31, 20-- and 20--

	Current Year Amount	Current Year Percent	Prior Year Amount	Prior Year Percent
ASSETS				
Current Assets:				
Cash	23,905.98		8,029.57	
Accounts Receivable (net)	18,142.15		17,915.63	
Merchandise Inventory	98,142.36		82,194.38	
Other Current Assets	9,148.25		8,143.37	
Total Current Assets	149,338.74		116,282.95	
Plant Assets:				
Office Equipment (net)	32,989.04		38,195.52	
Store Equipment (net)	35,184.47		40,914.83	
Total Plant Assets	68,173.51		79,110.35	
Total Assets	217,512.25		195,393.30	
LIABILITIES				
Current Liabilities:				
Accounts Payable	14,189.10		26,491.11	
Dividends Payable	2,000.00		1,800.00	
Other Current Liabilities	9,481.76		10,947.61	
Total Liabilities	25,670.86		39,238.72	
STOCKHOLDERS' EQUITY				
Capital Stock	100,000.00		90,000.00	
Retained Earnings	91,841.39		66,154.58	
Total Stockholders' Equity	191,841.39		156,154.58	
Total Liabilities and Stockholders' Equity	217,512.25		195,393.30	

Name ______________________ Date ____________ Class ____________

17-M MASTERY PROBLEM (continued)

2.

Aqua Products, Inc.

Comparative Income Statement

For Years Ended December 31, 20-- and 20--

	Current Year	Prior Year	Increase (Decrease) Amount	Increase (Decrease) Percent
Net Sales	838,941.16	774,827.66		
Cost of Merchandise Sold	391,491.71	366,608.74		
Gross Profit	447,449.45	408,218.92		
Operating Expenses:				
Depreciation Expense	24,600.00	22,560.00		
Office Expense	10,491.18	9,742.49		
Salaries and Payroll Taxes Expense	204,184.58	192,919.43		
Store Expense	169,184.15	170,194.55		
Total Operating Expenses	408,459.91	395,416.47		
Income from Operations	38,989.54	12,802.45		
Other Revenue	642.00	228.00		
Net Income before Federal Income Tax	39,631.54	13,030.45		
Less Federal Income Tax Expense	5,944.73	1,954.57		
Net Income after Federal Income Tax	33,686.81	11,075.88		

Aqua Products, Inc.

Comparative Balance Sheet

December 31, 20-- and 20--

	Current Year	Prior Year	Increase (Decrease) Amount	Increase (Decrease) Percent
ASSETS				
Current Assets:				
Cash	23,905.98	8,029.57		
Accounts Receivable (net)	18,142.15	17,915.63		
Merchandise Inventory	98,142.36	82,194.38		
Other Current Assets	9,148.25	8,143.37		
Total Current Assets	149,338.74	116,282.95		
Plant Assets:				
Office Equipment (net)	32,989.04	38,195.52		
Store Equipment (net)	35,184.47	40,914.83		
Total Plant Assets	68,173.51	79,110.35		
Total Assets	217,512.25	195,393.30		
LIABILITIES				
Current Liabilities:				
Accounts Payable	14,189.10	26,491.11		
Dividends Payable	2,000.00	1,800.00		
Other Current Liabilities	9,481.76	10,947.61		
Total Liabilities	25,670.86	39,238.72		
STOCKHOLDERS' EQUITY				
Capital Stock	100,000.00	90,000.00		
Retained Earnings	91,841.39	66,154.58		
Total Stockholders' Equity	191,841.39	156,154.58		
Total Liabilities and Stockholders' Equity	217,512.25	195,393.30		

Name ______________________ Date ____________ Class ____________

17-M MASTERY PROBLEM (concluded)

3.

Ratio	Acceptable Range		Actual Ratio		Favorable Trend	Within Target Range
	Low	High	Current Year	Prior Year		
Gross margin	53.0%	54.0%				
Total operating expenses	46.0%	48.0%				
Operating margin	5.0%	8.0%				
Merchandise inventory	40.0%	42.0%				
Total plant assets	30.0%	35.0%				
Total liabilities	12.0%	15.0%				

4.

	Current Year	Prior Year	Increase over Prior Year (Yes or No)	Evaluation
Earnings per share		$1.23		
Dividend yield		0.82%		
Price-earnings ratio		26.6		

5.

	Acceptable Range		Actual Ratio	Within Target Range
	Low	High		
Working capital	$125,000.00	$145,000.00		
Current ratio	4.50	5.00		
Quick ratio	1.00	2.00		

17-C CHALLENGE PROBLEM (LO1, 3, 8), p. 542

Analyzing industry standards

A. ____________________

B. ____________________

C. ____________________

D. ____________________

E. ____________________

Name ______________________ Date ____________ Class ____________

REINFORCEMENT ACTIVITY 2, Part B, p. 545

An Accounting Cycle for a Corporation: End-of-Fiscal-Period Work

11.

GENERAL JOURNAL PAGE 13

	DATE		ACCOUNT TITLE	DOC. NO.	POST. REF.	DEBIT	CREDIT	
1								1
2								2
3								3
4								4
5								5
6								6
7								7

12.

REINFORCEMENT ACTIVITY 2, Part B (continued)

13.

Gulf Uniform Supply, Inc.

Unadjusted Trial Balance

December 31, 20--

ACCOUNT TITLE	DEBIT	CREDIT
Cash		
Petty Cash		
Accounts Receivable		
Allowance for Uncollectible Accounts		
Merchandise Inventory		
Supplies—Office		
Supplies—Store		
Prepaid Insurance		
Notes Receivable		
Interest Receivable		
Office Equipment		
Accumulated Depreciation—Office Equipment		
Store Equipment		
Accumulated Depreciation—Store Equipment		
Accounts Payable		
Sales Tax Payable		
Employee Income Tax Payable		
Social Security Tax Payable		
Medicare Tax Payable		
Health Insurance Premiums Payable		
Retirement Benefits Payable		
Unemployment Tax Payable—Federal		
Unemployment Tax Payable—State		
Federal Income Tax Payable		
Dividends Payable		
Capital Stock		
Retained Earnings		

(Note: Unadjusted trial balance is continued on next page.)

Name ______________________ Date ____________ Class ____________

REINFORCEMENT ACTIVITY 2, Part B (continued)

Gulf Uniform Supply, Inc.

Unadjusted Trial Balance

December 31, 20--

ACCOUNT TITLE	DEBIT	CREDIT
Dividends		
Income Summary		
Sales		
Sales Discount		
Sales Returns and Allowances		
Purchases		
Purchases Discount		
Purchases Returns and Allowances		
Advertising Expense		
Cash Short and Over		
Credit Card Fee Expense		
Depreciation Expense—Office Equipment		
Depreciation Expense—Store Equipment		
Insurance Expense		
Miscellaneous Expense		
Payroll Taxes Expense		
Rent Expense		
Salary Expense		
Supplies Expense—Office		
Supplies Expense—Store		
Uncollectible Accounts Expense		
Utilities Expense		
Federal Income Tax Expense		
Interest Income		

REINFORCEMENT ACTIVITY 2, Part B (continued)

14.

Age Group	Amount	Percent	Uncollectible
Current	$13,232.18	2.0%	
1–30	811.50	4.5%	
31–60	1,470.75	10.0%	
61–90	5,824.25	30.0%	
Over 90	1,489.15	60.0%	
	$22,827.83	———	
Current Balance of Allowance for Uncollectible Accounts			
Estimated Addition to Allowance for Uncollectible Accounts			

14., 15., 16., 19.

GENERAL JOURNAL PAGE 14

	DATE		ACCOUNT TITLE	DOC. NO.	POST. REF.	DEBIT	CREDIT	
1								1
2								2
3								3
4								4
5								5
6								6
7								7
8								8
9								9
10								10
11								11
12								12
13								13
14								14
15								15
16								16
17								17
18								18
19								19

Name ______________________ Date ____________ Class ____________

REINFORCEMENT ACTIVITY 2, Part B (continued)

17., 20.

Gulf Uniform Supply, Inc.

Adjusted Trial Balance

December 31, 20--

ACCOUNT TITLE	DEBIT	CREDIT
Cash		
Petty Cash		
Accounts Receivable		
Allowance for Uncollectible Accounts		
Merchandise Inventory		
Supplies—Office		
Supplies—Store		
Prepaid Insurance		
Notes Receivable		
Interest Receivable		
Office Equipment		
Accumulated Depreciation—Office Equipment		
Store Equipment		
Accumulated Depreciation—Store Equipment		
Accounts Payable		
Sales Tax Payable		
Employee Income Tax Payable		
Social Security Tax Payable		
Medicare Tax Payable		
Health Insurance Premiums Payable		
Retirement Benefits Payable		
Unemployment Tax Payable—Federal		
Unemployment Tax Payable—State		
Federal Income Tax Payable		
Dividends Payable		
Capital Stock		
Retained Earnings		

(Note: Adjusted trial balance is continued on next page.)

Gulf Uniform Supply, Inc.

Adjusted Trial Balance

December 31, 20--

ACCOUNT TITLE	DEBIT	CREDIT
Dividends		
Income Summary		
Sales		
Sales Discount		
Sales Returns and Allowances		
Purchases		
Purchases Discount		
Purchases Returns and Allowances		
Advertising Expense		
Cash Short and Over		
Credit Card Fee Expense		
Depreciation Expense—Office Equipment		
Depreciation Expense—Store Equipment		
Insurance Expense		
Miscellaneous Expense		
Payroll Taxes Expense		
Rent Expense		
Salary Expense		
Supplies Expense—Office		
Supplies Expense—Store		
Uncollectible Accounts Expense		
Utilities Expense		
Federal Income Tax Expense		
Interest Income		

REINFORCEMENT ACTIVITY 2, Part B (continued)

18.

Total of income statement credit accounts................................ $ ________

Less total of income statement debit accounts

excluding federal income tax .... ________

Equals net income before federal income tax .... $ ________

Net Income before Federal Income Tax	–	Of the Amount Over	=	Net Income Subject to Marginal Tax Rate	×	Marginal Tax Rate	=	Marginal Income Tax
$	–	$	=	$	×		=	$

Bracket Minimum Income Tax	+	Marginal Income Tax	=	Federal Income Tax
$	+	$	=	$

REINFORCEMENT ACTIVITY 2, Part B (continued)

21.

					% OF NET SALES

Name ______________________ Date ______________ Class ______________

REINFORCEMENT ACTIVITY 2, Part B (continued)

22.

REINFORCEMENT ACTIVITY 2, Part B (continued)

23.

Name ______________________ Date ______________ Class ______________

REINFORCEMENT ACTIVITY 2, Part B (continued)

24.

GENERAL JOURNAL

PAGE 15

	DATE		ACCOUNT TITLE	DOC. NO.	POST. REF.	DEBIT	CREDIT	
1								1
2								2
3								3
4								4
5								5
6								6
7								7
8								8
9								9
10								10
11								11
12								12
13								13
14								14
15								15
16								16
17								17
18								18
19								19
20								20
21								21
22								22
23								23
24								24
25								25
26								26
27								27
28								28
29								29
30								30
31								31

REINFORCEMENT ACTIVITY 2, Part B (continued)

25.

Health Fashions, Inc.

Comparative Income Statement

For Years Ended December 31, 20-- and 20--

	Current Year		Prior Year	
	Amount	Percent	Amount	Percent
Net Sales	349 184 81		329 114 71	
Cost of Merchandise Sold	149 784 15		141 414 31	
Gross Profit	199 400 66		187 700 40	
Operating Expenses:				
Depreciation Expense	12 194 64		11 944 39	
Office Expense	12 491 22		10 914 72	
Salaries and Payroll Tax Expense	74 918 15		73 148 39	
Store Expense	39 481 19		37 494 08	
Total Operating Expenses	139 085 20		133 501 58	
Income from Operations	60 315 46		54 198 82	
Other Revenue	235 00		194 00	
Net Income before Federal Income Tax	60 550 46		54 392 82	
Less Federal Income Tax Expense	10 137 62		8 598 21	
Net Income after Federal Income Tax	50 412 84		45 794 61	

REINFORCEMENT ACTIVITY 2, Part B (continued)

Health Fashions, Inc.
Comparative Balance Sheet
December 31, 20-- and 20--

	Current Year Amount	Current Year Percent	Prior Year Amount	Prior Year Percent
ASSETS				
Current Assets:				
Cash	24,896.33		8,414.46	
Accounts Receivable (net)	25,195.49		16,484.39	
Merchandise Inventory	45,884.46		34,118.17	
Other Current Assets	17,948.28		16,481.27	
Total Current Assets	113,924.56		75,498.29	
Plant Assets:				
Office Equipment (net)	22,494.65		18,495.17	
Store Equipment (net)	25,948.69		24,914.71	
Total Plant Assets	48,443.34		43,409.88	
Total Assets	162,367.90		118,908.17	
LIABILITIES				
Current Liabilities:				
Accounts Payable	13,448.34		12,498.17	
Dividends Payable	2,000.00		2,000.00	
Other Current Liabilities	1,744.99		1,648.27	
Total Liabilities	17,193.33		16,146.44	
STOCKHOLDERS' EQUITY				
Capital Stock	50,000.00		50,000.00	
Retained Earnings	95,174.57		52,761.73	
Total Stockholders' Equity	145,174.57		102,761.73	
Total Liabilities and Stockholders' Equity	162,367.90		118,908.17	

26.

Health Fashions, Inc.

Comparative Income Statement

For Years Ended December 31, 20-- and 20--

	Current Year	Prior Year	Increase (Decrease) Amount	Increase (Decrease) Percent
Net Sales	349,184.81	329,114.71		
Cost of Merchandise Sold	149,784.15	141,414.31		
Gross Profit	199,400.66	187,700.40		
Operating Expenses:				
Depreciation Expense	12,194.64	11,944.39		
Office Expense	12,491.22	10,914.72		
Salaries and Payroll Tax Expense	74,918.15	73,148.39		
Store Expense	39,481.19	37,494.08		
Total Operating Expenses	139,085.20	133,501.58		
Income from Operations	60,315.46	54,198.82		
Other Revenue	235.00	194.00		
Net Income before Federal Income Tax	60,550.46	54,392.82		
Less Federal Income Tax Expense	10,137.62	8,598.21		
Net Income after Federal Income Tax	50,412.84	45,794.61		

Name ______ Date ______ Class ______

REINFORCEMENT ACTIVITY 2, Part B (continued)

Health Fashions, Inc.

Comparative Balance Sheet

December 31, 20-- and 20--

	Current Year	Prior Year	Increase (Decrease) Amount	Increase (Decrease) Percent
ASSETS				
Current Assets:				
Cash	24,896.33	8,414.46		
Accounts Receivable (net)	25,195.49	16,484.39		
Merchandise Inventory	45,884.46	34,118.17		
Other Current Assets	17,948.28	16,481.27		
Total Current Assets	113,924.56	75,498.29		
Plant Assets:				
Office Equipment (net)	22,494.65	18,495.17		
Store Equipment (net)	25,948.69	24,914.71		
Total Plant Assets	48,443.34	43,409.88		
Total Assets	162,367.90	118,908.17		
LIABILITIES				
Current Liabilities:				
Accounts Payable	13,448.34	12,498.17		
Dividends Payable	2,000.00	2,000.00		
Other Current Liabilities	1,744.99	1,648.27		
Total Liabilities	17,193.33	16,146.44		
STOCKHOLDERS' EQUITY				
Capital Stock	50,000.00	50,000.00		
Retained Earnings	95,174.57	52,761.73		
Total Stockholders' Equity	145,174.57	102,761.73		
Total Liabilities and Stockholders' Equity	162,367.90	118,908.17		

REINFORCEMENT ACTIVITY 2, Part B (concluded)

27.

Ratio	Acceptable Ranges for GUS		Actual Ratios for HFI		Favorable Trend	Within Target Range
	Low	High	Current Year	Prior Year		
Gross margin	57.0%	58.0%				
Total operating expenses	38.0%	40.0%				
Operating margin	17.0%	20.0%				
Merchandise inventory	26.0%	28.0%				
Total plant assets	25.0%	30.0%				
Total liabilities	12.0%	15.0%				

28.

	Current Year	Prior Year	Increase over Prior Year (Yes or No)	Evaluation
Earnings per share				
Dividend yield				
Price-earnings ratio				

29.

	Acceptable Ranges for GUS		Actual Ratios for HFI	Within Target Range
	Low	High		
Working capital	$75,000.00	$100,000.00		
Current ratio	5.00	7.00		
Quick ratio	2.00	4.00		